78270

ML
3551.5
.P58
2008

Phull, Hardeep.

Story behind the
protest song.

$65.00

DATE			

STORY BEHIND THE PROTEST SONG

STORY BEHIND THE PROTEST SONG

A Reference Guide to the 50 Songs That Changed the 20th Century

Hardeep Phull

GREENWOOD PRESS
Westport, Connecticut • London

Library of Congress Cataloging-in-Publication Data

Phull, Hardeep.
    Story behind the protest song : a reference guide to the 50 songs that changed the 20th century /
    Hardeep Phull.
        p. cm.
    Includes bibliographical references and index.
    ISBN 978-0-313-34141-0 (alk. paper)
    1. Protest songs—United States—20th century—History and criticism. 2. Folk songs, English—
United States—20th century—History and criticism. 3. Popular music—United States—20th
century—History and criticism. 4. Music—Political aspects—United States—History—20th century. 5.
Music—Social aspects—United States—History—20th century. I. Title.
ML3551.5.P58 2008
782.42'159—dc22   2008020719

British Library Cataloguing in Publication Data is available.

Library of Congress Catalog Card Number: 2008020719
ISBN: 978-0-313-34141-0

First published in 2008

Greenwood Press, 88 Post Road West, Westport, CT 06881
An imprint of Greenwood Publishing Group, Inc.
www.praeger.com

Printed in the United States of America

The paper used in this book complies with the
Permanent Paper Standard issued by the National
Information Standards Organization (Z39.48–1984).

10 9 8 7 6 5 4 3 2 1

This book is wholeheartedly dedicated to
The cities of Coventry, England, and New York City, U.S.A.
To R.E.M. for waking me up as a kid and, to this day, making sure
I never fall asleep.
And to Gillian A. Quilley because there are some teachers you don't forget
for all the right reasons.

CONTENTS

ACKNOWLEDGMENTS

No book of this scope is complete without a cast of support players. The input, assistance, and encouragement of the following people have helped me stave off insanity in the short term, and for that I am truly grateful.

Professionally, I would like to salute the following (listed in the order I can remember them). First, I thank all at Greenwood Press—especially Kristi Ward for her astounding levels of enthusiasm and Chris Smith for plucking me from relative obscurity and getting me involved in the first place. Also, thanks go to C. P. Baker, Alan Clayton, Bobbie Lane, and Ross Bennett at EMAP London, Phil Sutcliffe, and Elizabeth Goodman and Marc Spitz for providing me with some reassuring words at a point when I really needed them. A huge amount of appreciation is due Ben Myers, whom I have always considered to be one of my finest contemporaries in British music journalism. Despite only ever meeting once, I have always considered him a friend, too, and his invaluable help in the production of *Story Behind the Protest Song* has proven my suspicions.

I would also like to pay tribute to the writers who continue to inspire with their work and without whom, I would never have had the will or desire to do this, especially Barney Hoskyns, Michael Azerrad, Simon Reynolds, Ian MacDonald (R.I.P.), Jeff Chang, and the very great James Maycock whose *Mojo* piece on James Brown playing in Vietnam in 1968 is possibly the most thrilling single article ever written. I advise you to seek it out immediately. A more personal thanks also goes to David Fricke not only for the decades of flawless prose, but for the impromptu peptalks given in dark corners of various New York City venues. But the biggest tip of the hat has to go to Greil Marcus—a man whose writing constantly reminds me that I will never be anywhere near as good as he, but still pushes me to try anyway.

Personally, I would like to show my gratitude to the following: Colin Freeman, Simon Connolly, Hope Beach, Mark and Andrea Hamilton (for feeding me when I could not be bothered to feed myself), Jennifer Chochinov (for just being), and my dear old mum, Rani, for furnishing the early part of this project with endless cups of tea. Oh, yeah, she gave birth to me, too, . . . that was really nice of her.

My apologies go to anyone I may have forgotten. Please know that it (probably) was not intentional.

INTRODUCTION

It is an unpredictable treat that never fails to gladden the heart of any school kid: the sight of a Physical Education teacher drafted at the last minute to substitute for a sick teacher in another subject. Growing up as I did in England and attending a pretty tough high school, this usually meant that the normal lesson plan went out the window and the substitute teacher was there simply to make sure the classmates did not injure each other. On occasion, the substitute might try to keep the lesson somewhat vaguely near the actual subject—I remember one Physical Education teacher bravely trying to engage my English class in a group reading of a Shakespeare play, although at one point he looked up with a wry smile and freely admitted he could not understand a word. But one particular occasion sticks in my mind. It was a Humanities class where we normally studied the history of the troubles in Northern Ireland (actually a subject I really liked). The substitute teacher happened to be one of those stern Physical Education types that pretty much no one liked—we will call him Mr. "A" for the sake of his anonymity and my lack of a lawyer. The machinations of hundreds of years of Irish history were *way* too complicated for him to even begin to tackle, so he decreed that we could have a whole hour of "quiet reading." How is that for a blatantly obvious crowd control measure?

Still, I could not have been happier for in my bag that day, I happened to have a copy of the British music magazine *Q*. I was 15 at the time and fast beginning to descend into music-geek territory by reading music press meant for people twice my age, listening to the radio at any chance I could, and endlessly enthusing to my Oasis-obsessed peers about such bands as Weezer, Green Day, Radiohead, and R.E.M., which was on the cover of that latest edition of *Q*. About halfway through the "lesson," Mr. A was stalking through the class to make sure we were not reading anything unsuitable when he came across me reading said magazine and tersely remarked, "where's the educational value in that?" before adding a glare for good measure. To my eternal dismay, I did not have an answer and he told me to put it away. If only I had known then what I know now.

During my extensive and tiring research for this book, I was buoyed massively by reading about the legendary Pete Seeger—a true American hero if ever there was one. In particular, I was thrilled to learn that as a youngster, he got a job working for folk music archivist Alan Lomax and found himself learning about American history through the many field recordings to which he was exposed. That is *exactly* what made music so important for me. Sure, I love dancing, and singing, and playing air guitar, and doing all the other things that it is great for, but music actually fostered my love of history. I learned so much from the bands I loved. R.E.M. was, of course, crucial; without that group, I may never have learned the name of Joe McCarthy or found out about American military intervention in Central America during the 1980s. My obligatory period as a Bob Dylan obsessive taught me about the political and social shifts of the early 1960s. And listening to songs of Woody Guthrie brought home the struggles of the Great Depression during the 1930s in a way that was almost unbearably sad. Even today, the ability of music to teach me something new remains. Before writing this book, for example, I had only the vaguest idea about the effect of the 1970 Kent State shootings, but the power of Crosby, Stills, Nash & Young's "Ohio" changed all that, while my knowledge of Rastafarianism was nonexistent until researching the music and religion of Bob Marley. I cannot say that I entirely subscribe to Bruce Springsteen's declaration in the 1984 song "No Surrender" that he "learned more from a 3-minute record" than he ever learned at school, but I definitely learned a lot more from music than I ever did in any of Mr. A's classes, Physical Education or other.

In an ideal world, this alternative method of learning is what I would love to imagine *Story Behind the Protest Song* getting used for. Popular culture can provide such an effective insight into many other aspects of history, and, in that respect, this is a title that should hopefully appeal to young scholars as well as music enthusiasts of all ages. The objective of each song entry is not to provide a comprehensive biography of the artists or even to outline the precise details of the era/event/incident that inspired them—these are subjects that warrant further investigation by the reader. Instead, each entry is intended to give an overview of the song, what inspired the artist to write it, how it delivered its rancor, and what kind of legacy it has. One of my main aims in the selection of songs was to be as broad as possible with the artists and with the subject matter they addressed in the hope that this would help dispel the commonly held image of protest songs being almost exclusively about war and largely sung by flower-toting longhairs. It is an understandable perception given the immense cultural changes that occurred in the 1960s, but in the course of this book, you will find antireligion songs by immigrant laborers, antiracism songs by personally troubled jazz vocalists, antipolice songs by enraged rappers, even antiprotest songs by proud southern rock groups and a lot more in between. Of course, there are a lot of hippies voicing their discontent over Vietnam, too, but the scope of protest music reaches far beyond that as indicated by the full list of songs in the chronological and alphabetical appendixes.

It should also be remembered that 50 is a finite number, so there were many songs that had to be left out for that reason. Wherever possible, there are sidebars that give a brief description of songs related to the main entry, but there are many that could not be included in this way either. Although many artists and songs fell by the wayside, honorable mentions have to go to Country Joe & The Fish's "I-Feel-Like-I'm-Fixin'-to-Die Rag" (1967), Stevie Wonder's "You Haven't Done Nothin'" (1974), and indeed, the entire back catalog of British singer Billy Bragg, which could have easily provided the 50 songs in this book alone. Despite the 20th century time frame of the title, it would have been absurd for *Story Behind the Protest Song* to not at least touch on such recent political events as the war in Iraq that have seen protest music return to the mainstream with a vehemence not seen for decades; this topic is outlined in the epilogue. Indeed, it seems more than likely that future generations will use the work of such bands as Green Day and System of a Down to recall some of the big issues of the 21st century, just as we are now doing with the artists of the 20th century.

Finally, I think that it is somewhat inevitable that this book is likely to raise the age-old question, "Can music change the world?" I say "inevitable" because while I was working on this project, at least every third person I told about it presumed I was some kind of do-gooder who was determined in my belief that singing protest songs really loudly would help bring about some kind of revolution. Some would even wave a sarcastic fist in the air and shout "Fight the Power" as a mock rallying cry—at which point I would usually reply by saying that I just wanted a cup of tea and an early night, but promised to overthrow the government first thing in the morning. It is all in good fun, of course, but it is a great question—one that I have used myself many times in interviews with various bands to instigate what usually is a lengthy and entertaining debate. For the record, my opinion is thus. There is no doubt in my mind that music has the power to change your thinking and increase your knowledge—whether that means music can change the world depends on how much you consider yourself to be a part of it.

Hardeep Phull
Brooklyn, February 29, 2008

CHAPTER 1

``WE SHALL OVERCOME"

The development of "We Shall Overcome" has taken over a century so far and has seen it go from being a source of religious comfort in the early 1900s, to a song of the labor movement in the 1940s, to a civil rights anthem in the 1960s, and much else in the time since. More than anything, its long journey, numerous recordings, and countless reinterpretations show that "We Shall Overcome" can be applied to almost any situation of social or political conflict and, as such, is one of the main progenitors of modern protest music.

Having been adapted and altered from person to person as a traditional folk song across the United States throughout the first half of the 20th century, tracing the origins of "We Shall Overcome" with any kind of absolute authority is very difficult. If the truth be told, there is almost no way to definitively answer where it really came from, and it is highly unlikely that there ever will be; however, the broad consensus among music scholars and historians revolves primarily around the Reverend Charles Tindley. A Philadelphia preacher born of slave parents in 1851, Tindley also composed many original religious songs, one of which was called "I'll Overcome Some Day" and was first published in 1901. He based its lyrical determination on the Bible verse Galatians 6:9, which implores believers not to tire in their good deeds for they will eventually reap rewards. Although Tindley wrote his own melody for the song, it was gradually married to different tunes as it traveled—most notably that of an old slave spiritual "I'll Be All Right," which itself appeared to be indebted to the melody of a European hymn dated from the late 18th century called "O Sanctissima." It was this gradual combination of lyrics and melody that emerged during a more clearly documented event in 1945 when black workers at the American Tobacco factory in

Pete Seeger performing at the Highlander Folk School, Tennessee, in 1959. Both Seeger and the Highlander were instrumental in spreading the power of "We Shall Overcome" across the United States.
Courtesy AP Images/Tennessee State Archives.

Charleston, South Carolina, went on strike over pay. In doing so, they seeded the blossoming of "We Shall Overcome" into popular consciousness.

As the staff marched in protest, one member of the workforce named Lucille Simmons attempted to rally the spirits of those on the picket lines by singing "I Will Overcome"—a song she had heard in church that featured elements of both Tindley's composition and "I'll Be All Right." But rather than deliver it in the gospel style that she usually heard, Simmons used her immense vocal talent to sing it as a slow ballad with no rhythm (sometimes referred to as the "long meter style") as the workers were carrying placards and would not be able to clap in unison anyway. Most importantly, she reflected the hope and defiance of the group rather than the individual by changing the "I" in the song to "We," and, as the strike continued, several different verses were added with the specific cause of the workers in mind. By the end of the strike in 1946, the incident and indeed the song had instilled a new sense of social and political consciousness in African American workers in the area that was no small achievement in a time when lynchings were still a possibility for errant Negroes.

News of the tobacco factory strike circulated, and in 1947 two of the workers were invited to the Highlander Folk School in Monteagle, Tennessee, which was an integrated institution dedicated to helping the labor movement across the United States.

It was there that Zilphia Horton (a white woman and also wife of the School's co-founder Myles Horton) learned "We Will Overcome"[1] and began teaching it at workshops both at the Highlander as well as on her travels across the land. One of the most important people to pick up the song from her was folksinger Pete Seeger, who was also heavily involved in the labor movement. Aside from using his banjo as musical accompaniment and thereby adding a steady but slow rhythm, Seeger is also widely credited for changing "Will" to "Shall" under the reasoning that it was a word that sounded and could be enunciated better (although another Highlander cohort named Septima Clark reportedly preferred using "Shall," too). His addition of the "We'll walk hand in hand" verse circulated longer than most new lyrics thanks to its all-encompassing sentiment of unity, but Seeger's influence on "We Shall Overcome" was not simply artistic—he also helped to direct the song toward the developing civil rights movement where it would have a seismic impact on American culture as a whole.

While Seeger published a version of "We Shall Overcome" in a book of songs during 1952, one of his primary methods of exposing the song to other people was by performance—most notably among them was a young Martin Luther King Jr. While playing at the Highlander Folk School's 25th anniversary celebration in 1957, Seeger's rendition evidently stuck in the mind of the activist as his aides later recounted King humming the tune as they left the event. In the ensuing period, the song often featured a verse that promised to end the Jim Crow laws that enforced segregation across the South, but a particularly enduring lyrical addition would emerge in 1959 during a raid by local authorities on Highlander (which had changed the emphasis of its activities from the labor movement to civil rights). During the incident, an impromptu chorus of "We are not afraid" began and is usually thought to have been started by either Jamilia Jones or Mary Ethel Dosier—both of whom were teenage students at the school.

The most important and direct exposure that "We Shall Overcome" received to the civil rights movement came primarily through the efforts of Guy Carawan. Another politically minded music enthusiast, Carawan had learned the song in California from folksinger Frank Hamilton (who had learned it from Seeger) back in the early 1950s. By the end of the decade, Carawan had also ended up at Highlander as the director of music, replacing Zilphia Horton who died in 1956. During 1960, Carawan came across a number of student sit-ins and demonstrations against segregation across the South, and as these protests developed into the establishment of the Student Nonviolent Coordinating Committee (SNCC), he was on hand to teach them "We Shall Overcome" as a galvanizing cry. Carawan's sedate treatment of the song as a ballad, however, proved to be unpopular with the African American youths who injected instead a more spirited, soulful rhythm. As their protests rose rapidly in number and gained more national publicity (including television news bulletins), "We Shall Overcome" traveled farther and faster than ever before.

Observing how popular the song was becoming, Seeger's manager Harold Leventhal advised him that a copyright should be taken out on "We Shall Overcome" by people sympathetic to the movement rather than anyone simply looking to cash in on its usage. Seeger, Carawan, and Hamilton opted to take up the publishing, adding Horton's name as the fourth "songwriter" (Lucille Simmons was left off simply because no one could remember her name at the time), and it was also decided that the proceeds would be donated to the SNCC.[2] Had Leventhal not had that foresight, an unscrupulous carpetbagger may well have earned a small fortune off the movement because not only did "We Shall Overcome" almost instantly became the sound of civil rights in the early 1960s, it became its resounding motto, too. At every meeting, rally, or affiliated concert, a ritualistic joining of hands became the norm whenever it was sung, symbolizing a sense of cross-racial unity. The official poster that advertised the March on Washington in August 1963 came emblazoned with the words "We Shall Overcome," and, naturally, it turned out to be the anthem of the day with folksinger Joan Baez leading a recital that was earnestly backed by the thousands in attendance. Perhaps most poignantly, the song that so many people lived by also became one that some died by—not least Viola Liuzzo. In the many accounts of her death in March 1965, it is frequently reported that the white civil rights activist sang "We Shall Overcome" while driving in her car and being chased by another car driven by the white supremacists who would eventually shoot and kill her. That very same month, the song would appear to reach the peak of its social and political power in the United States when President Lyndon Baines Johnson addressed the nation over the need to push through the Voting Rights Bill and enfranchise a greater number of African Americans. During the famous speech, he used the phrase "we shall overcome" to underline his determination to see the country's race relations move forward, and it was enough to reduce Martin Luther King Jr. to tears as he watched on television.

However, the civil rights movement was about to shift toward more radical realms, and barely a year after Johnson's epochal words, the song was beginning to drop out of favor with activists. As King glumly noted in his biography, the traditional singing of "We Shall Overcome" was becoming muted especially during a verse referring to the unity of black and white people. When he sought to find out why at one march in Mississippi in 1966, one protestor replied flatly, "We don't sing those words anymore. In fact the whole song should be discarded. Not 'We Shall Overcome' but 'We Shall Overrun.' "[3] But just as some African Americans appeared to be giving up on it, "We Shall Overcome" appeared to gain a new lease on life in other lands, particularly in South Africa where the government policy of apartheid also enforced segregation. In 1965, the white antiapartheid activist John Harris was hanged for planting a bomb in Johannesburg and was heard singing the song on his way to the gallows, resulting in its suppression until 1989 when apartheid was officially ended.

But "We Shall Overcome" has been used as a sonic beacon of human resoluteness in many more corners of the world since America's civil rights movement fizzled out. The minority population of Catholics in Northern Ireland frequently used it as a rallying cry for civil rights throughout the worst of the country's political troubles in the 1970s. Protestors pushing for democracy were reported singing the song at Tiananmen Square in the Chinese capital of Beijing during 1989. Even student demonstrations in Indonesia in 1998 were sound tracked to renditions of "We Shall Overcome." Language is also no longer an issue as proved by the Indian translation, which has patriotic undertones and is often taught in schools. Although a core of verses expressing hope, fearlessness, and determination still remains at the heart of most versions thanks to the song's firm relationship with the era of civil rights, the addition of new, cause-specific lines continues—a trend that has inspired Seeger to refer to "We Shall Overcome"[4] as a "portfolio" song. It may have had extremely uncertain beginnings, but what is certain is that "We Shall Overcome" has become virtually universal in its reach and instantly recognizable in its sound.

Notable Recorded Versions

Joe Glazer and the Elm City Four (recorded as "We Will Overcome"), *Eight New Songs for Labor* (CIO, 1950).

Guy Carawan, the Montgomery Gospel Trio, and the Nashville Quartet, *We Shall Overcome: Songs of Freedom Riders and Sit-Ins* (Folkways, 1961).

Joan Baez, *Joan Baez in Concert Pt. 2* (Vanguard, 1963).

Pete Seeger (live), *We Shall Overcome: The Complete Carnegie Hall Concert* (Columbia, 1963)

Pete Seeger (solo), *Broadsides* (Folkways, 1964).

The Freedom Singers, *The Newport Folk Festival 1963: The Evening Concerts, Vol. 1* (Vanguard, 1964).

Mahalia Jackson, *Sings the Best-Loved Hymns of Dr. M. L. King* (Columbia, 1968).

Green on Red, *Gas Food Lodging* (Enigma, 1985).

Bruce Springsteen, *We Shall Overcome: The Seeger Sessions* (Sony/BMG, 2006).

Notes

1. Some stories claim that Horton learned the song while actually at the 1945 American Tobacco picket.

2. Since the SNCC's demise in the 1970s, proceeds go to the Highlander Research and Education Center, which uses the money to provide grants for community programs that further African American music in the South.

3. Quoted in Clayborne Carson, ed., *The Autobiography of Martin Luther King* (New York: Warner Books, 1998), 316.

4. Quoted by Dave Marsh in his notes to accompany the release of Bruce Springsteen, *We Shall Overcome: The Seeger Sessions,* Sony/BMG, 2006, retrievable at http://www.brucespringsteen.net/Seeger_Marsh_notes.pdf.

CHAPTER 2

THE BIRTH OF A NATION (1939-1964)

One of the greatest and most influential sources of protest music in the early part of the 1900s was the growing American labor movement. Although organizations designed to protect workers and improve conditions had been in place before the turn of the century, 1905 saw a more radical impetus develop with the founding of the Industrial Workers of the World (known colloquially as the Wobblies). They encouraged workers to unite as an entire class and move toward actually overthrowing their employers rather than simply demanding a fair day's wage, and songs were a crucial part of the group's weaponry. One of their most renowned composers was the Swedish immigrant Joe Hill, who contributed **"The Preacher and the Slave"** (1911) and many other songs to *Little Red Songbook*—an extremely popular compendium first published in 1909 and which continues to get reprinted to this day. Internal divisions reduced the political effectiveness of the Wobblies by the mid-1920s, but their technique of using songs as ways to vocalize their annoyance and issue rallying cries of unity lived on through the Great Depression of the 1930s. As many in America's workforce were forced to endure serious financial hardship, the country saw a swell of left-wing activism, and this climate turned out to be a huge influence on the likes of Pete Seeger and Woody Guthrie. Both folksingers took a special interest in playing for the recreational and political benefit of the country's most disenfranchised, but both saw it as an act of simple patriotism rather than as being an attempt to incite a class struggle. Even so, unionism and leftist thinking of all kinds underwent stern suppression during the late 1940s and 1950s as the cold war between the United States and the communist Soviet Union emerged. This state of affairs left the pair under heightened political suspicion, but Seeger could still be heard pledging allegiance to his fellow man on "**If I Had a Hammer**" (1949), while Guthrie stood resolutely by his notion that America had a duty to serve Americans and not just the other way around through "**This Land Is Your Land**" (1951).

As the anticommunist sentiment became less partisan by the start of the 1960s, the groundwork laid by Seeger and Guthrie began to produce a new generation of folksingers who strove to address modern ills with a youthful vigor—none of whom did it better or with more success than Bob Dylan. Spurred on by the legacy of Guthrie, the Jewish boy from Minnesota rose to fame after arriving in New York thanks to a penchant for topical songs. In particular, the seething "**Masters of War**" (1963) found Dylan cursing the industry of conflict that had built up during the cold war. Another prominent concern of these young and idealistic musicians was civil rights that had also started to dominate headlines across the country. Although musical expressions of African American discontent had been heard since the times of slavery, the first major recorded song to deal with such issues emerged in 1939 when jazz vocalist Billie Holiday released "**Strange Fruit**." Despite the fact that poet Abel Meeropol penned the song's lyrical reflections of lynchings in the South, her delivery of these brutal and shocking words was so emotive that many audiences were left literally stunned when they heard it. Other folk-blues artists of the era, such as Huddie Ledbetter (aka Lead Belly) and Josh White, frequently bemoaned the everyday difficulties of being black in their works, too.

But while Joan Baez, Phil Ochs, Tom Paxton, and a number of other white liberals in the early 1960s folk scene denounced discrimination and advocated racial equality in their songs, it would be two black artists who arguably produced the most memorable ruminations on the drive for civil rights. The March on Washington in 1963 saw the movement's figurehead Martin Luther King Jr. explain his vision of a desegregated America through his legendary "I have a dream" speech, but despite these determined words, not all Americans appeared to have the same hope for an interracial utopia. The same year, the assassination of activist Medgar Evers in Mississippi and the church bombings that left four young girls dead in Alabama rocked civil rights supporters. Both of these events prompted singer Nina Simone to compose an angry tirade called "**Mississippi Goddam**" (1964) by way of response in which she condemned not only those who instigated these atrocities, but also offered her frustration at the slow progress of the movement itself. In contrast, rhythm and blues (R&B) star Sam Cooke appeared to exhibit a sense of quiet stoicism by promising that perseverance would be rewarded in "**A Change Is Gonna Come**" (1964), but the song's weary feel suggested that he, too, had become disheartened by the everyday experiences of racism that African Americans had to endure. The Civil Rights Act of 1964 may have offered a theoretical solution by legally outlawing segregation, but as these tracks indicated, routine bigotry was proving to be much harder to eradicate.

Artist: NA

Song: "The Preacher and the Slave" (aka "Pie in the Sky")

Songwriter: Joe Hill

Album: NA

Label: NA

1911

Sections of the American workforce were beginning to make a concerted effort to produce better circumstances for themselves through unionism during the early 1900s, and members of the Industrial Workers of the World (IWW) were unique in their use of songs to help them achieve such goals. One of the most important members of the organization was a Swedish immigrant named Joe Hill who composed "The Preacher and the Slave" as a protest against the constrictive effects of religion on the country's workers. The song and Hill's much-debated execution helped create a huge part of American culture that still exists, but now extends far beyond the realms of the IWW.

The life of Joe Hill continues to be debated to this day, but despite exhaustive efforts, tracing the movements of an immigrant laborer who used at least three different names, covered the length and breadth of the United States during the early 1900s, and who has been repeatedly mythologized in song is an almost impossible task to do with absolute authority. However, the bulk of research by historians has created a broad outline of Hill's brief existence, which begins with his birth as Joel Emmanuel Hägglund in the town of Gävle, Sweden, in 1879. He was one of nine children in total, but only he and five siblings lived into adulthood. The Hägglunds were strictly religious Lutherans, and Joel, in particular, apparently attended Salvation Army meetings. He also showed a love of music from a very early age, but the innocence of his childhood was short-lived due to the death of his father following an injury sustained while working. The children were forced to find employment to support the family as a result, and Joel for his part worked in a rope factory before later becoming a fireman. By 1902, his mother had also died; with neither a maternal or paternal figure to hold them together, the family members went their separate ways with Joel deciding to move to the United States in search of a better opportunity.

Having suffered an economic slump during the last years of the 19th century, the United States was on a slow upturn as Hägglund arrived, but instead of recession, workers were now faced with the prospect of progressivism during the first decade of the 20th century. Endorsed by President Theodore Roosevelt, this term denoted a swing toward big business and advancing technology that slowly began to reduce the need for skilled labor and helped to foster a more radical lilt in sections of the workforce accordingly. The American Federation of Labor (AFL) had been in place since 1886; as one of the country's first major unions, it concerned itself with improving pay and conditions for workers in piecemeal and pragmatic measures. But the more radical Western Federation of Miners (WFM) and other similarly minded protagonists in the workforce gradually became disillusioned with this approach and established the Industrial Workers of the World or IWW in 1905 as an alternative to the AFL. Referred to by many as the Wobblies for short, the group was not content with just making life more bearable for the average laborer, but instead devised a manifesto that sought to galvanize the working class into a powerful force capable of overthrowing capitalism altogether. The influence of Marxist thinking was not difficult to spot, and the Wobblies enforced an all-inclusive policy on membership that welcomed women, minorities, and immigrants. They also eschewed the hierarchy of contracts and designated negotiators that most other unions employed in favor of effective striking and other methods of direct action. But perhaps their most enduring and culturally significant tactic was the use of songs and parodies as a way of communicating their grievances and buoying the spirits of their members. Eventually, they would be collated into a compendium called the *Little Red Songbook,* which was first published in 1909.

It was this combination of theory and method that attracted Hägglund to the organization. Since arriving in the United States, he had been known as Joseph Hillstrom and, more commonly, Joe Hill, as he traveled across the country finding jobs and organizing workers wherever he could until finally joining the Wobblies (according to most sources) around 1910 while employed on the docks in San Pedro, California. The musical interest and talent he had shown as a child inspired Hill to compose songs for the cause prolifically, and he appeared to be convinced of their power to spread the Wobbly word.

> A pamphlet, no matter how good, is never read more than once, but a song is learned by heart and repeated over and over; and I maintain that if a person can put a few cold, common sense facts into a song, and dress them up in a cloak of humor to take the dryness off of them, he will succeed in reaching a greater number of workers who are too unintelligent or too indifferent to read a pamphlet or an editorial on economic science.[1]

During his time with the group, Hill wrote over two dozen documented songs that warned against breaking strikes, conveyed antiwar sentiment, and even took on the evils of prostitution, but arguably the most famous and most influential was the very first one. Having observed how the Salvation Army piously preached to hard-up workers about the rewards that would await them after their difficult lives on earth came to an end, he responded by lampooning the organization he was allied to as a child in the shape of a song called "The Preacher and the Slave," which was intended to be sung to the tune of a jaunty Salvation Army hymn named "In the Sweet Bye and Bye."

In addition to the main critique of religious moralists, the five verses also feature further swipes at the Salvation Army's pandering for donations from those who have little to spare, and Hill makes little attempt to hide his distaste for scaremongers who promise hell to anyone who seeks to better his or her earthly situation. The promise of Jesus miraculously curing all sickness and disease is also rubbished, and a typical Wobbly call for working men to unite in the face of all kinds of oppression and to seek better circumstance is issued. The most crucial part of the song is its frequently repeated chorus that emphasizes the perceived ridiculousness of heavenly reward by creating—and dismissing—the image of workers enjoying "pie in the sky." Despite being impossible to prove beyond doubt, this now common phrase (used as an expression of absurdity) is frequently thought to have originated from "The Preacher and the Slave."

The song was first published in the third edition of the *Little Red Songbook* in 1911 and immediately became popular at Wobbly rallies. With this and the steady flow of compositions that succeeded it, Hill became the group's primary songwriter and continued with the method of applying his lyrics to popular tunes of the day. But his reputation in this respect would be eclipsed dramatically in January 1914 when Hill was arrested on a double murder charge following the killings of a grocery store owner and his son in Salt Lake City, Utah. They had been held up by two bandits wearing bandanas, one of whom had sustained a gunshot injury in the standoff. On the same night, Hill had arrived at a local physician's office with a gunshot wound, and this possible correlation initially led to the Wobbly being accused of the crime despite Hill claiming he had been shot by a friend who mistakenly believed Hill had insulted his wife. However, Hill refused to name his alibi for fear of harming the reputation of the woman—something that led to rumors that he had actually been in bed with the married woman and her husband had discovered them.

The trial was heavily publicized, and Hill's sentence invoked rage among Wobblies who argued that he was being framed by Utah authorities for his efforts in mobilizing the union movement. The perceived unfairness of the trial and its eventual verdict also brought much sympathy from much further afield; at one point, President Woodrow Wilson even wrote to the governor of Utah pleading that Hill's execution be reconsidered. The pleas made no difference, however, and Hill was sent to a firing squad in November 1915—almost two years from his initial arrest. In his final communiqués, he remained unflinchingly committed to the cause and famously decreed to his long-time Wobbly comrade Bill Haywood, "Don't waste any time mourning—organize!"[2] Hill's defiance to the very end was underlined by reports of him ordering his executors to fire himself.

Despite its unfortunate nature, the entire episode gave Hill's work as a Wobbly organizer and songwriter a national platform, while the grim conclusion ascribed him the status of martyr for the working class. The *Little Red Songbook* naturally carried numerous eulogies (and still does), but after a lull in Wobbly activity during the First World War effort, the legend of Joe Hill began to blossom fittingly through the medium of song—the most noted of which initially came in the form of the 1925 poem "I Dreamed I Saw Joe Hill Last Night" by Alfred Hayes. This was later set to music by the composer Earl Robinson and was subsequently popularized during the late 1930s by the singer Paul Robeson. During the same era, leftist thinking in general was on the increase as the Popular Front grew, and this also contributed to Hill's growing posthumous reputation. Folksingers such as Woody Guthrie and Pete Seeger cited him as an ideological and musical inspiration and "The Preacher and the Slave," in particular, sound tracked the birth of a new generation of trade unions such as the Congress of Industrial Organizations (CIO). Regardless of whether Hill genuinely invented it, the phrase "pie in the sky" certainly became embedded into American phraseology due to the song's repetition during this period, and it remains there to this day. Through the 1940s and 1950s, "The Preacher and the Slave" would also be recorded by many artists, including Seeger, Cisco Houston, and Joe Glazer. Following another lull brought about by the cold war witch-hunts, the folk revival of the early 1960s again signaled a renewal of interest in Hill's legacy with Phil Ochs, Joan Baez, and even Bob Dylan acknowledging him. His final wish was honored as it seems as though little time has been spent on mourning Hill if only because there was little need to; both he and his songs lived on, creating a musical lineage that continues to flourish almost a century after his death.

Artist: Billie Holiday

Song: "Strange Fruit"

Songwriter: Lewis Allan (aka Abel Meeropol)

Album: NA

Label: Commodore

1939

It was a white, Jewish schoolteacher from the Bronx who wrote one of the most powerful reflections of lynchings in the South, but it was the gripping performance of a black jazz singer that delivered it into the minds of most Americans. Inspired by some particularly gruesome images of dead bodies swinging from trees, Abel Meeropol's poem "Strange Fruit" was first published in 1937 and given musical treatments by various singers before Billie Holiday recorded a devastating and definitive version two years later. Not only did it help revolutionize the potential subject matter of popular songs, it provided the spark for decades of musical protests against racial injustice.

Billie Holiday.
Courtesy AP Images.

During the first quarter of the 1900s, lynchings still occurred with a reasonable frequency in the southern states of America. With the so-called "Jim Crow laws" enforcing segregation on the basis of race since the previous century, Negroes, and other minorities who transgressed these legislations, ran the risk of incurring the harshest of penalties. Despite being unspeakably brutal, lynchings were often communal affairs carried out in buoyant atmospheres with hundreds, even thousands of men, women, and children turning out to witness this form of mob justice. One such incident occurred in August 1930 in the town of Marion, located in the more northerly state of Indiana, where three young black men by the names of Abram Smith, Thomas Shipp, and James Cameron had been jailed, accused of robbery, rape, and murder. A small army of locals descended on the jail and attempted retribution themselves, forcing their way into the building, dragging the men out of their cells, and beating them viciously with one of the mob even thrusting a crowbar through Smith's chest. Cameron was spared after a member of the crowd absolved him of blame for the supposed crimes committed, but the other two were killed and then hung from a nearby tree. Smith and Shipp certainly made a gruesome exhibition, but judging from a famous and widely circulated picture of this lynching, the residents of Marion found the whole spectacle morbidly satisfying. Taken by photographer Lawrence Beitler, the image captures the two men's bloody and mutilated bodies swinging lifelessly from a large branch while people swarm around the tree. One man is prominently depicted looking straight at the camera while simultaneously pointing upward toward Smith and Shipp as something approaching pride radiates from his eyes.

The horrific picture was circulated across the country, and one of the many people to see it was Abel Meeropol—a Jewish schoolteacher living in the Bronx. Aside from teaching, Meeropol (an ardent communist) also wrote poetry and composed music; his disgust at seeing the corpses of Smith and Shipp inspired him to pen a stark rumination titled "Strange Fruit." The poem was initially published during early 1937 under the pseudonym of Lewis Allan (the names of his two stillborn children) in the union publication the *New York Teacher*. Meeropol also added some musical accompaniment, and the piece was quickly adopted by various performers operating in progressive political circles around the city. At the time, even in New York City, segregation was still enforced in almost all nightclubs and entertainment spots, but one exception was the Greenwich Village venue Café Society that attracted a suitably left-wing clientele. A year after "Strange Fruit" was first published, Meeropol approached owner Barney Josephson and presented the piece to him with the idea of having it performed at Café Society—but not just by anyone. After immediately flooring Josephson with the evocative nature of his poem, Meeropol suggested that it be presented for consideration to Billie Holiday (termed more affectionately by many as "Lady Day"), who had already made quite a name for herself in American vocal jazz despite her extremely humble and harsh beginnings.

Born Eleanora Fagan in Philadelphia during 1915, she had endured abandonment by her father, a poverty-stricken childhood, rape, prostitution, and even spells in reform school and jail before finding work singing in various Harlem nightclubs as a teenager. It was through this that talent scout John Hammond (who would later nurture the talent of a young Bob Dylan) came across Holiday in 1933 and convinced her to collaborate with Benny Goodman, an increasingly popular jazz musician of the era. The combination proved to be a success and spawned such hits as "What a Little Moonlight Can Do" and "I Wished on the Moon" in the mid-1930s before Holiday went on to work with the Count Basie Orchestra and Artie Shaw. But by the end of 1938, she had returned to a solo billing performing at—among other places—Café Society, and it was in these liberal surroundings and through Holiday's delicate yet emotive voice that Meeropol felt the message of "Strange Fruit" would be conveyed most effectively.

Holiday's initial reaction to the song is surrounded by contradictory viewpoints. In her autobiography *Lady Sings the Blues* (which was co-written by *New York Post* writer William Dufty and was widely discredited for its numerous passages of unreliable information), she claimed she had been keen to perform "Strange Fruit" from the very start. Meeropol, however, felt her first feelings were of discomfort sparked perhaps by a fear that the song's content may bring retaliation. Josephson was not even sure that Holiday actually understood the song's content at all. Nevertheless, Holiday agreed to perform it first at a party and then at Café Society during early 1939 where Josephson added a little theatrical direction to heighten the emotional power of Meeropol's imagery. He ordered all waiters and cashiers to stop serving while arranging for the room to be darkened save for a single spotlight to illuminate the singer's face. Furthermore, Josephson instructed Holiday to walk off stage immediately after the last note had been played and to not return under any circumstances for he was adamant that it would always be the finale of every performance. Even to an audience as open-minded as that found inside Café Society, the effect was still shocking with the first performances initially being met with stunned silence before the sound of a lone clapper initiated an applause that would gradually swell to uproarious levels.

Irrespective of what her initial opinion of "Strange Fruit" was, the intensity and pathos of Holiday's performances would frequently reduce audiences to tears and silence the rowdiest of club goers. Even though some reviews showed little regard for "Strange Fruit," it was only a matter of time before the song would be recorded for posterity, but Columbia (her label at the time) refused to release it feeling that the lyrics would alienate southern record buyers and the general lack of commercial appeal would render it a flop anyway. John Hammond was also not especially keen to record it, so Holiday instead convinced Milt Gabler of the independent label Commodore Records to allow her to record and release the song. Gabler wanted to capture the affecting nature of the live performance and so encouraged Holiday and her band to record it quickly. Indeed, a total of four hours is all it took and from that small timeframe emerged a disc that would revolutionize the social and political possibilities of music.

The sombre mood is established within seconds as "Strange Fruit" begins with what sounds like a gasp—a long, elongated trumpet motif is accompanied by rustling cymbals and a mournful droning, all of which create a dramatic atmosphere that then suddenly subsides to make way for some more contemplative piano chords. At over a minute long, it is an unusually long introduction, but one that is entirely necessary as a device to set the very specific tone. It is almost as though the first half of the introduction marks the hubbub and commotion of an actual lynching, while the second section denotes the beginnings of a sad reflection—an emotion that Holiday achieves very well through her opening lines in which she describes the victims as the bloodied produce of trees, swinging lifelessly in the southern wind. This immensely powerful imagery capitalizes on the arresting opening section making "Strange Fruit" impossible to ignore even at this early phase. Holiday does not employ hysteria or try to overemphasize anything at this stage—she simply lets the words do all the work while elegantly employing her eloquent voice to add color to the pictures that Meeropol creates. The second verse encapsulates the tragically deep contrasts of grotesquely deformed and horribly mutilated corpses being burned to a beautiful background of the South's open countryside, idyllic environments, and fresh, floral scents. The final verse communicates a hope that nature will purge these strange fruits, either through crows stealing them, the effect of the sun, wind, or rain serving to perish them, or merely just through the tree itself shedding them. An instant before the last line, all instruments drop out for just a second, reintroducing the dramatic feel from the start of the song and the previously resigned-sounding Holiday injects her voice with a sudden anguish as she laments, "here is a strange and bitter . . . crop." The final word, in particular, is exulted with a noticeable and extended level of force complete with the band uniting for one last flurry of sound —all of which is abruptly stopped to signal the song's end.

As expected, "Strange Fruit" had too much of a radical subject matter and melancholic tone to be a huge hit in popular music terms and unsurprisingly was rarely played by radio stations. But among the more intellectual audiences, it attracted huge praise and critical acclaim, particularly in the left-leaning press. Writing in what was then a comparatively liberal incarnation of the *New York Post,* Samuel Grafton heaped the kind of adulation on "Strange Fruit" that Holiday and particularly Meeropol would have no doubt been looking for, remarking that the record had the power to "make you blink and hold onto your chair. Even now as I think of it, the short hair on the back of my neck tightens and I want to hit somebody. And I think I know who."[3] Indeed, Grafton's viewpoint indicated that the song was forcing certain people to confront the inhumanity of their country to its own citizens. The simple fact that many still felt black people to be subhuman shows that "Strange Fruit" was years ahead of its time, thus helping to explain why it was that the antilynching sentiments resonated more with enlightened listeners.

Regardless of the song's seemingly esoteric appeal, Holiday's life and career quickly became intertwined with "Strange Fruit" with the singer beginning to peddle the erroneous story that it had been written especially for her. It remained the most frequently requested number and continued to draw extreme reactions from enraptured awe to outright hostility, and despite Meeropol's compositional efforts, the song's fans felt it belonged to Holiday in spirit. No one could sing it with the affecting grace and world-weary heart that she could, and, for a period, Holiday was known to be hostile to anyone else attempting to perform the piece—even going so far as to threaten the gospel and blues singer Josh White with a knife one night backstage at Café Society for daring to add his own interpretation. More tragically, the song's imagery of withered and lifeless black bodies seem to be embodied by Holiday herself in later years as frequent drug use, heavy drinking, and torrid, abusive relationships all took their toll on her physical appearance. Cirrhosis of the liver finally claimed her life in 1959, at which point Holiday had just a few hundred dollars to her name.

It is highly unlikely that "Strange Fruit" would have actually prevented any lynchings outright, but in 1939 it would have taken a lot more than just a song to bring a halt to this barbaric yet widely accepted form of southern justice. What was crucial about Meeropol's composition and Holiday's delivery is that it provided a realization of wrongdoing, an awakening to injustice, and an alert to inhumanity. In planting this seed of knowledge into the most fertile minds of the time, "Strange Fruit" would eventually grow into something that would create another epoch of American social evolution. As the founder of Atlantic Records and jazz aficionado Ahmet Ertegun explained, this was not just a record, it was "a declaration of war . . . the beginning of the civil rights movement."[4] While "Strange Fruit" has gradually found a place of high regard and social importance in American history, the decades since its release have not softened its emotional impact very much. Strange fruit may have stopped growing on southern trees now, but in this fleeting three-minute window of sound, Meeropol and Holiday still have the power to recreate the injustices of the early 1900s with a starkness that is haunting.

Artist: The Weavers

Song: "If I Had a Hammer" (aka "The Hammer Song")

Songwriters: Lee Hays and Pete Seeger

Album: NA

Label: Hootenanny[5]

1949

When Lee Hays and Pete Seeger composed "If I Had a Hammer" and released it as part of the Weavers, it was almost too controversial to mention in the United States. As the country descended into cold war with the Soviet Union during the late 1940s and 1950s, the song's defiant lyrical themes of human unity were at odds with the suspicious air of the era and were interpreted as left-wing language by anticommunist factions. But Seeger refused to let the song be silenced and made a point of singing it at his solo performances for years, no matter how sensitive the time or how threatening the circumstance. It was a persistence that paid off and with the additional aid of many cover versions by other artists, "If I Had a Hammer" is now firmly established as an American folk standard.

Despite having parents who both boasted years of classical training and experience, the young Pete Seeger had little interest in learning the technical aspects of music and chose instead to concentrate on its broader possibilities. Born in New York during 1919, Seeger's teenage years were greatly influenced by his father, Charles, who applied his musical ability to a strong personal commitment to the socialist cause that was growing steadily in the United States during the 1930s. This era of increased left-wing consciousness (often referred to as the Popular Front) rubbed off on Seeger and, like his father, he began to view music as being a part of social and political struggle rather than merely entertainment. Central to this ideal was the idea of evaluating music not by whether it was good, but whether it had any purpose. With the dawn of the Second World War in 1939, Seeger had a perfect chance to give purpose to his burgeoning interest in folk music and began singing peace songs and union songs with a briefly popular collective called the Almanac Singers, which featured Woody Guthrie as one of its core members. This pacifist streak in the group's music changed in 1941 as Germany invaded the Soviet Union (the world's only socialist country at the time), but even that shift in attitude could not hide its old left-wing sympathies that were now regarded with increasing suspicion in much of America. As a result, the group found itself being monitored by the Federal Bureau of Investigation (FBI), and it was an administrative shadow that would follow Seeger incessantly over the next few decades.

With the bombing of Pearl Harbor by the Japanese in 1941 and the beginning of an American war effort, the Almanac Singers soon disbanded and Seeger even served in the U.S Army. But upon returning to the United States following the end of the conflict, he found that leftists were no longer treated with suspicion but with outright contempt. Long-standing disagreements between the United States and the Soviet Union had come to a head as the two nations argued over the restructuring of Europe, and while Seeger's mission to give his music a purpose now propelled him into performing mainly union songs, this had also become a source of anticommunist fear. It was in this developing political tension and social distrust that a musical antidote called "If I Had a Hammer" first began to emerge. The words were written primarily by Seeger's old bandmate from the Almanac Singers, Lee Hays, who used his love of gospel music to inform the song's repetitious lyrical structure and optimistic feel. The first verse finds the narrator wishing for a hammer and imagines how it could be used to help protect, warn, and unify the land, but in the second and third verses, this galvanizing tool becomes a bell and then a song, respectively. The fourth and final verse brings all these symbols together as the narrator realizes that like everyone else, he actually does possess a "hammer of justice . . . a bell of freedom . . . a song about love" as basic human rights. In a time of complex and divisive political machinations, "If I Had a Hammer" used these deliberately simple but powerful symbols as a way of underlining an enduring spirit of egalitarianism and unity.

Seeger added a melody to the song, and it was first performed at a rally for imprisoned communist leaders in 1949. Although both he and Hays repeatedly denied that "If I Had a Hammer" was specifically pro-communism, it was clear that this clarion call was being issued from defiantly leftist ground. This sense of determination would be subject to an immediate and brutal test when Seeger played a civil rights benefit concert with the African American artist Paul Robeson at Peekskill, New York, in September 1949. The event had been scheduled to take place two weeks earlier, but was canceled when war veterans in the area rioted, incensed at exaggerated reports of Robeson's Soviet sympathies in the local press. After rescheduling the show, both Robeson and Seeger appeared as planned (Seeger sang the still relatively new "If I Had a Hammer"), but upon leaving the site, the thousands of concert goers were met with an ambush orchestrated partly by Ku Klux Klan members. Seeger's car was pelted with rocks, and his wife, Toshi, was forced into shielding their young children from flying glass; but to his horror, Seeger found that policemen refused to intervene. The incident was grim proof that the cold war had arrived, but even under this level of duress, Seeger retained his belief in the power and purpose of song, which he reinforced by daubing his banjo with the Guthrie-esque inscription "This machine surrounds hate and forces it to surrender."

Despite the attack, the reaction to "If I Had a Hammer" had been positive at Peekskill, and even though anything vaguely left-leaning was now equated as un-American and therefore dangerous, the track was recorded and boldly released as a single by the Weavers in 1949. They had formed late in the previous year with Seeger and Hays reestablishing their musical relationship from the Almanac Singers and enlisting Freddie Hellerman and female singer Ronnie Gilbert to complete the lineup. Together, the quartet took turns singing the first three verses, adding vibrant harmonies and a sense of aural unity, while Seeger's banjo work continued to underpin the entire song before all four members united to deliver the last verse as a rousing finale. Unsurprisingly, the release met with no commercial success but a great deal of controversy as "only 'Commies' used words like 'peace' and 'freedom' "[6] during the era. A further swing to the political right ensued during the early 1950s, particularly with Senator Joe McCarthy's attempts to publically purge America of communists through rigorous investigations and, when possible, prison sentences. This served only to make "If I Had a Hammer" an even greater taboo and, as the Weavers gained an unexpected level of success by concentrating on popular and much less fervently political material, they refrained from playing it. Despite that, the song's purpose was still paramount, and it took a firm hold in the world of hidden radicalism, installing itself almost as a torch song for those striving to stick to their contentious political views. Indeed, the folk music publication *Sing Out!* (first published in 1950) took its name from a line in the song, and co-founder Irwin Silber was one of the growing number of leftists who insisted that the lyrics be changed from promising a love between "my brothers" to the less chauvinistic "my brothers and sisters." After initially resisting, Hays capitulated, and the adapted version was taught and relayed between folksingers for the next few years.

The Weavers continued to enjoy radio play and even the odd TV appearance, but their apolitical public image was shattered in 1952 when an FBI informant named Harvey Matusow testified to the House Un-American Activities Committee (HUAC —an organization dedicated to identifying potentially dangerous left-wingers) that three of the group were active members of the Communist Party. Matusow had been an associate of the Weavers from the start and in years to come would admit to giving a false testimony under oath, but for now, the damage was done and the group became almost untouchable. Despite millions of record sales, promoters suddenly refused to book them, and they eventually split before the end of the year. Blacklisted politically and outcast socially, Seeger was forced to go without the huge platform he had with the Weavers and concentrated on playing schools, universities, and, of course, a number of low-key socialist gatherings both as a way of scratching out a living, but more importantly, to pass on the power of such songs as "If I Had a

Hammer." Like many true folksingers, Seeger felt audience participation was crucial, and he always encouraged crowds to sing along in the belief that this was the fundamental way for folk music to infiltrate America's consciousness. If reaping the instant rewards of a mainstream profile was no longer an option, Seeger was certainly prepared to sow the seeds of folk music at a grassroots level again.

By 1955, the witch-hunt for rogue communists in the United States showed no signs of abating, and despite Seeger's retreat to the underground following the Weavers' split, he was personally issued with a subpoena to testify about his work, beliefs, and life in front of the HUAC. Although the seriousness of such an appearance was not to be taken lightly, Seeger was well aware that many who had also been asked to appear simply pleaded the Fifth Amendment—the part of the Bill of Rights that meant Americans did not have to testify against themselves. But when Seeger made his appearance, he chose against the advice of his legal counsel to plead the First Amendment instead—a risky maneuver that relied on the constitutionally guaranteed right to free speech but which left him open to further litigation and even imprisonment. During the highly publicized hearing, it was not just his free speech that Seeger resolutely defended, but also his freedom of song. Under intense cross-examination, Seeger repeatedly suggested that he be allowed to perform in front of the committee members in the hope that it would help convert their suspicions into a better understanding of how his "songs seem to cut across and find perhaps a unifying thing, basic humanity."[7]

As the fallout from the hearing resulted in Seeger experiencing an even greater political and social isolation, it seemed fitting that he would begin one of the most prolific recording periods of his entire life, recording dozens of songs across a range of different records released mainly through the Folkways label, as well as briefly rejoining the Weavers who reunited in 1955. Among his solo work was a re-recording of "If I Had a Hammer," which was released in 1956 on the album *Love Songs for Friends and Foes*. Doing away with the grand sound of the Weavers' original, this version featured just Seeger and a banjo; despite the stripped down arrangement, Seeger's belief in the hammer of justice, the bell of freedom, and the song about love rang out as loud as ever through his bright vocal delivery. It was just as well because his experiences at the hands of HUAC seemed to indicate that these human rights now needed more defending than ever before.

In 1957, Seeger was finally indicted for contempt of Congress for his action in front of the HUAC, but his case did not go to trial until 1961. The interim period saw Seeger's popularity grow steadily, and the singer's unshakable faith in the power of music was made apparent yet again as he strode into the courtroom carrying a banjo and requested that the judge allow him to play a song. The judge flatly refused and sentenced him to a year in jail for his "crime," of which Seeger served just a few hours before getting out on bail pending an appeal. Even when the appeals court finally dismissed his case in 1962, Seeger voiced irritation when judges refused to clarify his right to sing and perform wherever he wanted. However, there was much consolation to be had in the knowledge that the grassroots performances during the 1950s were now beginning to produce a new generation of artists willing to perform Seeger's songs, too. A full-blown folk revival had begun to emerge in the early 1960s with

SPRINGSTEEN SINGS SEEGER

In 1998, Bruce Springsteen contributed a version of "We Shall Overcome" to the Pete Seeger tribute album *Where Have All the Flowers Gone?*, which also featured such artists as Billy Bragg, Ani DiFranco, and even actor Tim Robbins. The experience led to Springsteen developing a broader interest in Seeger's life and work before finally deciding in 2004 to record a whole album's worth of songs that the folk legend had made famous. However, the unreleased material from the recording sessions that produced "We Shall Overcome" was not quite enough to fill a full-length release, so Springsteen regrouped the same set of musicians at his farmhouse for two further sessions—both of which were deliberately unrehearsed. The album was finally released in 2006 as *We Shall Overcome: The Seeger Sessions* and featured versions of "Pay Me My Money Down," "Old Dan Tucker," "Froggie Went A-Courtin,'" and the 1998 interpretation of "We Shall Overcome." A version of "If I Had a Hammer" was also recorded, but Springsteen opted to leave it off the final release fearing that it would eclipse the other, less well-known songs. The collection received rapturous reviews for its playful, off-the-cuff spirit and went on to sell over 2 million copies, while Springsteen also took the band on tour to support the album, which again proved to be a huge success. This sudden patronage from one of the world's biggest rock stars caught Seeger (who was by now in his mid-80s) completely unaware, instantly reigniting a new wave of press interest in his legacy and burying the slightly embarrassed singer in an avalanche of fan mail.

Seeger being heralded as one of its forefathers and "If I Had a Hammer" naturally proving to be a staple of the scene. Just months after Seeger had been cleared by the appeals court, it was made into a Top 10 hit by the New York folk group Peter, Paul and Mary—the latter of whom had learned songs directly from Seeger as a girl growing up in Greenwich Village during the 1950s. Although Peter, Paul and Mary kept faithful to the modern lyrics (complete with the "brothers and sisters" line added after the Weavers recording), they altered the melody slightly and used just an acoustic guitar to supplement their vocal talents. Seeger freely admitted that he thought their tune was better than the one he wrote, but was delighted to find that both versions harmonized with each other perfectly—an accidental yet very apt reflection of the theme of unity presented in its lyrics.

After the years of suppression that Seeger endured, the hammer of justice had struck a victorious blow, the bell of freedom had sounded, and thanks to Peter, Paul and Mary, the song about love could finally be heard all over the land, but the message of "If I Had a Hammer" had even farther to travel. The song was swiftly adopted as a civil rights anthem after the trio performed it at the March on Washington in 1963, and a succession of further covers throughout the rest of the decade served only to further ingrain it into American life. Artists who reinterpreted it included Latin singer Trini Lopez (1963), Motown starlets Martha Reeves & the Vandellas (1963), R&B legend Sam Cooke (1964), and even actor Leonard Nimoy took a break from playing the character Spock on the *Star Trek* TV series to release his own unique version in 1968. Although a number of recorded covers still emerge regularly to this day, it is a song that survives predominantly as a folk standard rather than through continued recycling as a pop number. It is unlikely that many Americans under the age of 40 own a copy of "If I Had a Hammer" as performed by the

Weavers, Pete Seeger, or even Peter, Paul and Mary, but because of the song's position as a cornerstone of musical culture, the vast majority of those people will have heard it from parents, schools, or churches and will at least be able to sing you a line or two.

Artist: Woody Guthrie

Song: "This Land Is Your Land"

Songwriter: Woody Guthrie

Album: *American Work Songs—Songs to Grow On, Vol. 3*

Label: Folkways

1951

As he traveled around the United States during the 1930s, Woody Guthrie saw countless Americans being all but abandoned by their own country as the Great Depression took hold. Despite these hardships, the folk-singer found that many Americans were still willing to be swept up by the spirit of patriotism—something that was exemplified by the popularity of Kate Smith's "God Bless America" toward the end of the decade. But as the song's inescapable jingoism began to irritate him, Guthrie's response was to compose "This Land Is Your Land," which subtly challenged the traditional ideas of what it means to be an American and laid the foundation for decades of musical innovation, too. As a result, it now stands as one of the most culturally, politically, and socially important songs of all time.

The Wall Street crash of 1929 was a central trigger for the Great Depression that would be felt in the United States until well after the Second World War. But life for those living in rural parts of the country had been far from easy even before this cataclysmic financial event. The economic boom of the 1920s was in part bolstered by such emerging blue-collar cities as Detroit and Pittsburgh where car and steel production provided widespread employment and fostered a thriving consumer culture.

Woody Guthrie killing fascists with his guitar.
Courtesy of Michael Ochs Archives/Getty Images

This relative prosperity was not so clearly visible in the plains where farmers had already begun to overproduce. Crop surpluses were commonplace, and, subsequently, good quality yields could be sold only for next to nothing. When the crash finally struck, the blue-collar workforce was crippled and resulted in the cruel tragedy of farmers "producing food that starving city-dwellers could not afford to buy."[8]

Not long after Wall Street nose-dived, the Midwest suffered a prolonged and devastating drought that decimated the soil so badly that it created a new kind of weather—the "dust storms"—which would prove to be a literal killer blow for many of the area's farmers. The election of President Franklin D. Roosevelt in 1932 and subsequent "New Deal" reforms in 1933 offered some degree of hope; the Agricultural Adjustment Act, for example, was intended to encourage farmers to produce less by offering subsidies. But in practice, very few landowners received what they were entitled to for reducing the rate of cultivation and minimizing their possible profits. Burdened by both a surplus of crops that no one could afford to buy and farms that had lost the ability to grow anything more in the future, the farmers began a mass exodus to California in the hope of finding employment, opportunity, or as just an escape from the utter desolation they faced at home.

Among the hundreds of thousands of dust-bowl refugees was Woodrow "Woody" Wilson Guthrie. Born in 1912 in Okemah, Oklahoma, to musically knowledgeable parents who taught him many traditional folk songs, Guthrie grew up during an era in which the local discovery of oil transformed his home into a bustling boomtown and bestowed a reasonable amount of prosperity on the family. But once the excitement faded and the black gold ran out, Okemah was left to descend into an economic wilderness, forcing them to move. As the 1930s dawned and the recession began to bite, Guthrie had relocated to Pampa, Texas (another oil-boom town), but found himself unsettled in marriage, unsatisfied painting signs for a living, and keen to indulge his love of cross-country rambling. Although not necessarily in the same grave predicament as the farming communities that surrounded them, he and his wife, Mary, still lived in relative squalor. This was partly due to Guthrie's habit of giving away much of the money he earned to hobos and whoever else he felt needed it more than he did. Meanwhile, the great dust storms of 1935 decimated the area even further; by 1937, he decided to leave his young family behind and head out west, too.

Guthrie's journey across the American landscape truly brought home the hardship suffered by his fellow "Okies" (a derogatory term used to describe people from Oklahoma) as he rode with them in freight trains and boxcars, all of them in search of something other than a face full of dirt. Upon arriving in California, the migrants found the promise of gainful employment to be merely a limited number of poorly paid jobs mainly picking fruit or cotton and were often treated with open resentment and hostility by locals. Authorities were even known to erect barricades on the state line and around certain areas of Los Angeles in a bid to keep them at bay. It was during this period that he would write and perform the likes of "So Long, It's Been Good to Know You," "Dust Pneumonia Blues," "Washington Talkin' Blues," and "Do Re Mi"— songs that documented the hard traveling experiences of migrants and were laced with the bitterness of being made to feel like an outcast in your own country. John Steinbeck would famously capture this humanitarian disaster in his 1939 novel *The Grapes of Wrath*, but Guthrie was already doing something very similar in his songs.

Guthrie's musical talent quickly earned him a radio show on the Los Angeles station KFVD during which he and his partner Maxine Crissman (or "Lefty Lou") would perform hillbilly standards and new compositions. As the West Coast had swollen with hundreds of thousands of Okies, there was an obvious audience for Guthrie and Crissman. Subsequently, the pair received huge amounts of fan mail from migrants delighted to be given such evocative reminders of home. He also established connections with the Communist Party USA and played a number of left-wing rallies and trade-union benefits, often aided by a guitar with the words "This Machine Kills Fascists" daubed on the body. But crucially, he stopped short of becoming a full-fledged member of this or any other leftist political organization—a smart move in the long run after the 1939 Non-Aggression Pact between the Soviet Union and Nazi Germany damaged the credibility of the socialist cause.

In any case, his reputation as an emerging American folk hero was already spreading fast and after returning briefly to Pampa, Guthrie's hobo spirit took him onward to New York in 1940. By this time, the patriotic fervor of the song "God Bless America" was sweeping the country. Performed by Kate Smith but written by Irving Berlin during the First World War, it was played incessantly on the radio following its first broadcast on Armistice Day, 1938. The song enjoyed a huge swell in popularity as the Second World War began, and there was even a campaign to have it installed as the new national anthem. Irritated by the jingoistic undertones and musical grandiosity he saw in "God Bless America," Guthrie wrote down the lyrics of a response called "God Blessed America," which he began to perform soon afterward but did not release as a recording until 1951—by which time it carried the title of "This Land Is Your Land."

Compared to the song that so riled Guthrie, the recorded version of "This Land Is Your Land" is the embodiment of simplicity. It features just a guitar, a rudimentary chord sequence, the simplest rhymes, and a memorable meter—the classic components of folk music. The composition's melody also has a strong resemblance to that of a previous song—in this case, "When the World's On Fire," which was first released in 1930 by country group the Carter Family. In each of the six verses, Guthrie appears to use his rambling experience to proudly herald America's natural beauty by filling almost every line with idyllic visions of forests, seas, golden valleys, stretching skies, sparkling deserts, and waving fields. Even the dust clouds that destroyed the lives of so many Okies are strangely romanticized. But whereas Smith promised to support and protect her homeland in "God Bless America," Guthrie inverts that sentiment and pledges the power of America to its people by stating, "this land was made for you and me" at the end of every verse. In a time in which so many people had been neglected, ignored, and failed by the country that they were supposed to serve, "This Land Is Your Land" seemed to be subtly suggesting that America should be serving them, too.

The recorded version was eventually issued via the Folkways compilation *American Work Songs—Songs to Grow On, Vol. 3*. However, it surprised many who had become familiar with the song through radio broadcasts or in-person performances because it omitted two verses (which had been written by Guthrie on the original manuscript dated February 23, 1940, when it still had the title "God Blessed America"). The lyrics in question were arguably the most crucial for they seemed fueled by more overt socialist leanings and contrasted the patriotism of "God Bless America" more decisively, whereas the recorded version was clearly tamer in political terms. The first missing verse describes the vision of a large wall and a private-property sign that stands guard and wards off intruders. Criticizing the idea of ownership in the land of the free, Guthrie had written that the blank side of the sign represents a truer vision of the rights of Americans—specifically, the right to go wherever they please without fear of persecution. It was a notion that could not have failed to be inspired in some part at least by the experience of witnessing hoards of migrant midwesterners being prevented from entering Los Angeles a few years earlier. Moreover, it seems highly plausible that time spent in the company of left-wing factions toward the end of the 1930s had left him with a working knowledge of these kind of Marxist ideas at the very least. The missing second verse also has similar themes, recalling the sight of hungry people huddled outside a relief office with a sadness and stunted indignation at how these Americans are treated by their countrymen.

In 1945, a handwritten songbook called *Ten Songs* was also issued and contained four more missing lines in which the idea of walking, being, and living entirely free of obstruction is further underlined. But the verses on the original 1940 manuscript remain the most debated omissions from the 1951 recorded release. The manuscript itself remains in the possession of Nora Guthrie (one of Guthrie's children from the marriage to his second wife, Marjorie), and she has reasoned that the more partisan lyrics were removed partly to avoid Folkways being placed on a damaging political blacklist of left-wing sympathizers. The dawn of the 1950s saw the United States descend into the beginnings of the cold war with the Soviet Union, and communism in virtually all its forms was quickly earmarked as a decidedly un-American pastime. "This is the early '50s and McCarthy's out there,"[9] she remembered in 2000, referring to Senator Joe McCarthy who made it his own personal mission to rid America of a perceived threat of clandestine communists during the era. "It was considered dangerous in many ways to record this kind of material. If my dad had done the recording I don't think it would have meant anything to him . . . he was quite used to living without and having nights in prison!"[10]

The differing versions of "This Land Is Your Land" produced a split legacy, but each side still made a huge impact on popular and political culture during the following decades. Due to its more moderate content and subsequent scope for a broader interpretation, the recorded version would become wholeheartedly adopted by Middle Americans who seemed blissfully unaware of Guthrie's original inspiration and political sympathies. It was sung in schools, quickly came to represent patriotism in the postwar years, and was again put forward as another alternative (if not a replacement) for "The Star-Spangled Banner." The irony was distressing for the singer who had written the song as a rebuke of "God Bless America" and its nauseating nationalism, but perhaps even more galling were the uses of "This Land Is Your Land" in advertising campaigns for United Airlines and the Ford Motor Company. The royalty payments for these and numerous cover versions certainly proved to be a great help to Guthrie's family as his health deteriorated due to Huntington's chorea toward the end of the 1950s and the beginning of the 1960s. However, many of his avid devotees raged at the continual confusion. The eminent 1960s folksinger Phil Ochs composed his 1964 song "Bound for Glory" (named after Guthrie's autobiography) on this subject and complained that "one of the sad aspects of the growing fame of Guthrie and his songs is the lack of understanding by some and the prostitution by others."[11]

The more radical side to the song's legacy was made possible by the folk movement's operation below political radar during the 1950s. Many of its more resolute exponents, such as Pete Seeger, Ramblin' Jack Elliot, and even the young Bob Dylan, kept the original version of "This Land Is Your Land" (and its more stringent connotations) alive through the oral tradition. Even Guthrie himself made efforts to preserve the song's core statements by making a point of teaching his son Arlo (Nora's brother) the complete version before the crippling effects of Huntington's completely robbed him of the ability to play guitar.[12] By the start of the 1960s, these torchbearers emerged from the wilderness and helped head up a groundswell of activity that constituted a comprehensive folk revival across America. This was the new generation of politically and socially conscious youth who would instigate a tumultuous decade of progressively minded activism. Guthrie would be heralded as their central inspiration, and "This Land Is Your Land" would be viewed as his most important work.

> Without question he was the folk pioneer; not merely the composer and populariser of "songs for working people" but also the inspiration for the late '50s early '60s post-McCarthy wave of protest singers who fuelled the Civil Rights, Pacifist and Ban The Bomb bandwagons ... "Woody's Children" they were called.[13]

Guthrie would pass away at the age of 55 in October 1967—a time in which the threads of his artistic lineage were virtually omnipresent and beginning to embed themselves into the fabric of American society where they now seem destined to remain indefinitely.

Artist: Bob Dylan
Song: "Masters of War"
Songwriter: Bob Dylan
Album: *The Freewheelin' Bob Dylan*
Label: Columbia Records
1963

As the United States and the Soviet Union amassed huge stockpiles of nuclear weaponry during the 1950s, the concept of the cold war as business become a dangerous reality. Even more frightening was the very real possibility that the two superpowers would one day use their arsenals on each other—a catastrophe that almost came to pass during the Cuban Missile Crisis of 1962. It was this sense of callous profiteering that Bob Dylan angrily addressed in "Masters of War," which was one of the many topical songs that cemented the idea of the young folksinger as a poster boy for protest music during the early 1960s. However, the song's widespread adoption as an all-purpose antiwar anthem in the years since has gradually obscured Dylan's original target of scorn.

Bob Dylan in 1963. He was rarely at a loss for words except when playing the harmonica.
Courtesy AP Images.

After becoming the first president to be constitutionally forced out of office following two terms at the White House, President Dwight D. Eisenhower made his farewell address to the nation on January 17, 1961, and left an eerie warning for the American people. The 1950s had seen a steady buildup in the cold war standoff, reflected domestically in the increased amount of funding being ploughed into research and testing of nuclear weapons. While the United States still boasted a monopoly in that area, it was becoming clear that the Soviet Union was also engaged in the perturbing buildup of stockpiles, and efforts to put an end to this potentially catastrophic political contest had all proved to be in vain. Subsequently, Eisenhower issued a warning that while the United States must be in possession of a large and instantly accessible body of weaponry to both deter and fight aggressors, there was now a fully fledged arms industry surrounding national security. The outgoing president also made worrying indications that this symbiotic relationship between industry and security may move power away from central government by gifting military influence to third parties interested not so much in the protection of the country but in private profiteering. In his speech, Eisenhower referred to this new phenomenon of postwar politics as the "military-industrial complex"; in an already tense era, this strangely chilling phrase offered little reassurance.

During that exact same month, a 19-year-old would-be folksinger named Robert Allen Zimmerman traveled to New York City with the immediate goal of visiting his hero Woody Guthrie. Zimmerman had grown up mainly in the town of Hibbing, Minnesota, and was known by the teachers and students at his high school to be a devotee of the blues, R&B, and early rock 'n' roll. But after enrolling at the University of Minnesota in Minneapolis in 1959, he developed an avid interest in folk music. It was at that point that he also took to introducing himself as Bob Dylan, and after rapidly fashioning a Guthrie-indebted, faux-hobo image to go with this new alias, he began playing bars and coffeehouses in the bohemian Dinkytown district of the city. He soon outgrew its possibilities, however, and gave up college for that fabled pilgrimage to New York where there was not only a booming folk scene, but where Guthrie was now sadly ailing in a hospital under the effects of the degenerative neurological disease Huntington's chorea.

Despite Guthrie's ill health and Dylan's tireless playing around the downtown folk circuit, the two were still able to strike up a relationship with the young singer even performing for his mentor on a one-to-one basis during visits. Before long, *New York Times* music critic Robert Shelton wrote Dylan up with a pivotal review of one of his live performances, raving at his distinctive musical style and unusual phrasing ability. A record deal with Columbia Records duly followed; for his first self-titled release in 1962, Dylan offered up an album mainly comprised of covers and reinterpretations of traditional songs—as was the norm for the folk fraternity at the time. Not only did Dylan's Guthrie fixation inform the roguish cover image and the adopted Okie lilt of his delivery, it was referred to explicitly in the only two tracks penned by Dylan himself. First, "Talkin' New York" made good use of the talking blues style popularized by Guthrie and even made direct reference to his lyrics of "Pretty Boy Floyd." However, the most famous homage came in the shape of "Song to Woody"—a touching tribute addressed to his subject with the greatest of respect and affection.

The album made little commercial impact and as the young singer began working toward a second album, a number of executives had identified Dylan as an expendable part of the label. In relation to this lack of sales clout, Dylan did not appear to be doing himself any favors by single-mindedly pursing the intention of writing more of his own material rather than recycling standards. Additionally, his lack of lyric-writing practice meant that the process of creating songs for a second album would last the best part of a year, but as 1962 wore on, both domestic and world events would provide Dylan with much inspiration. Like most of the left-leaning folk in Greenwich Village, he took a growing interest in the civil rights movement that was growing at a steady pace. Dylan also made note of the post-McCarthy scaremongering of conservative such groups as The John Birch Society that were at times obsessively keen to root out communists thought to be infiltrating American life.[14] But what transpired in October 1962 proved to be a huge turning point not just for Dylan, but for political history as a whole.

Having overseen a bungled 1961 attempt to overthrow Cuban leader Fidel Castro and his newly established socialist republic, Eisenhower's successor John F. Kennedy now faced sobering evidence that the country—located less than 100 miles south of Florida—was allowing the Soviet Union to build nuclear missile bases on its territory. A reconnaissance plane had taken pictures confirming the presence of weaponry, and Kennedy was advised by some military officials to launch a full-scale attack immediately. The ramifications of such a measure would have quickly spilled across mainland Europe and essentially begun a nuclear war across the globe. Mercifully, the president chose to instigate the less severe tactic of a naval blockade preventing any more arms shipments arriving on the island and informed the nation of the situation—dubbed by most as the Cuban Missile Crisis—in a televised address. During a critical four-day period between October 24 and 28, 1962, a long-winded exchange of communiqués between Kennedy and Soviet premier Nikita Khrushchev took place during which the level of U.S. military readiness was raised to DEFCON (defense condition) 2 (one level away from the authorized use of nuclear weapons) for the only time in history. Meanwhile, Castro felt that a U.S. invasion was imminent and implored the Union of Soviet Socialist Republics (USSR) to launch a preemptive attack. War seemed inevitable, but Khrushchev and Kennedy managed to settle on a secret deal. The agreement specified that the USSR would dismantle its Cuban bases under the assurance that there would be no American invasion of Cuba itself and that U.S. arms located in Turkey would also be decommissioned. Worldwide obliteration had been avoided by the narrowest of margins.

The fear of such a catastrophic event did not dissipate from the public sphere following the Cuban Missile Crisis. Political tensions remained and despite the fact that Kennedy and Khrushchev established an emergency telephone to make critical negotiations easier, there was no indication that such a device would never be needed. It was in this tense atmosphere that Dylan's second album, *The Freewheelin' Bob Dylan,* arrived in May 1963, and many of its songs seemed to connect closely with the sense of dread and paranoia lingering around the world. "Talkin' World War III Blues" gave him a chance to showcase a bleak sense of humor in his vision of a world after a nuclear holocaust, while the landmark composition "A Hard Rain's A-Gonna Fall" almost single-handedly justified his decision to write original material thanks to its apocalyptic torrent of beautiful, yet harrowing imagery. But of all the album's 13 tracks, none proved to be as startling in its suggestion or as raging in its tone as "Masters of War."

The song had taken shape as Dylan visited England toward the end of 1962. He had adapted the melody from an old English folk song called "Nottamun Town" as arranged by folksinger Jean Ritchie, who subsequently sought official credit for "Masters of War" but eventually settled out of court. The lyrics that Dylan wrote for it, however, were very much his own with the central theme revolving around naked outpourings of rage and repugnance capped with a near frightening final wish for retribution. Strumming out a simmering minor-chord motif on his guitar that seldom changes and nails a markedly grim mood to the song, Dylan begins the onslaught of finger-pointing within seconds of the first note, and there is no respite until the very last chord. Initially, "Masters of War" conveys a sense of awareness addressed to the shadowy figures that construct and orchestrate operations of war from a safe distance. These characters are swiftly dismissed as worthless cowards who generate battles for others as though they were playing a game yet are the first to remove themselves from the theater of conflict. Gradually, the tone becomes darker and the criticisms become more damning. The narrator likens the promise of easy victory to the biblical betrayal by Judas in the Old Testament, while the notion that this practice is as transparently filthy as drain water again alludes to the sentiment that not everyone is being fooled.

By the midpoint of "Masters of War," the cumulative sense of fury makes for an uncomfortable listen as the avalanche of scathing words continues. More exasperation at ill-gotten privilege and protection is voiced before a particularly pointed verse histrionically suggests that unborn children are being risked—all of which culminates in the misanthropic assessment that these people are not worth the blood in their bodies. After envisioning that his own detractors might reject this display of youthful naivety and petulance, the narrator then brings back more biblical parallels by adding that even Jesus could not forgive such callousness and that monetary gain will never compensate for a lack of soul and the eternal damnation it will bring. But by far the most horrifying verse comes at the song's end and begins with an infamously brutal expression of hate aimed squarely at a master of war.

> I hope that you die, and your death will come soon.

The narrator goes on to add a personal desire to oversee a funeral wake right up until a body is committed to the earth before a final guitar flourish (which sounds like a creepy death knell in this context) concludes the song and brings about a silence that feels pregnant with shock.

DYLAN'S "PROTEST" YEARS: *THE FREEWHEELIN' BOB DYLAN* (1963)

Aside from "Masters of War," Bob Dylan's second album featured a number of other tracks that were inspired by topical events and helped to cement the idea that he was an archetypal protest singer.

"Blowin' in the Wind"

A mass of philosophical questions laced with allusions to social and political ills of the era, the opening track of *The Freewheelin' Bob Dylan* still remains an enduring torch song. It is all the more impressive considering Dylan's frequent claim that it was written in 10 minutes.

"Oxford Town"

This track is a quiet rumination on the problems encountered by James Meredith, a black student who was physically prevented on numerous occasions from entering the University of Mississippi in Oxford during 1962. His eventual enrollment led to extensive rioting in the town.

"A Hard Rain's A-Gonna Fall"

Arguably Dylan's first great song; a vision of the roundly feared (if not roundly expected) nuclear holocaust that frequently manages to be terrifying, captivating, and thought-provoking in one breath.

"Talkin' World War III Blues"

Dylan gets witty in this darkly satirical depiction of life after the bomb drops in which he envisions how one of the few things to survive the nuclear holocaust is a faintly absurd fear of communism.

DYLAN'S "PROTEST" YEARS: *THE TIMES THEY ARE A-CHANGIN'* (1964)

Preoccupied with social, cultural, and racial issues of the day, this album clearly captures Dylan at his most conscientious. But the persistent typecasting of him as a protest singer inspired Dylan to move away from such subject matter very quickly—not least with the deliberately titled *Another Side of Bob Dylan,* which also emerged in 1964.

"The Times They Are A-Changin'"

This anthemic call for awareness contributed hugely to Dylan becoming a voice for the younger side of the generation gap developing during the mid-1960s although, Dylan almost immediately attempted to distance himself from this perceived alignment.

"With God on Our Side"

This was one of Dylan's cleverest songs during this period, commenting on the role of religion in war and the irony of two sides being propelled into battle by the same belief that God is sanctifying their cause.

"Only a Pawn in Their Game"

Inspired by the murder of activist Medgar Evers in 1963, Dylan offers another astute interpretation of a modern problem—this time arguing that the institutionally ingrained dictum of white superiority is responsible for hostility toward the civil rights movement (see the entry on Nina Simone for additional information).

"The Lonesome Death of Hattie Carroll"

This is based on a true incident in which a black barmaid was racially abused and assaulted by a wealthy farmer named William Zantzinger in 1963. In spite of Carroll's subsequent death, the assailant was given what appeared to be a surprisingly lenient six-month sentence, resulting in this mournful Dylan composition.

That a singer aligned with a musical scene known for generally liberal politics and a similarly benevolent social standpoint could suddenly vocalize this kind of extreme hate was staggering at the time and still feels incongruous to this day. In the sleeve notes to the album, Dylan exhibited a hint of embarrassment at "Masters of War" and seemed to suggest that while the naked emotions of anger were unusually coarse, the song was nevertheless a valid moment of spleen venting given the desperation in the air. "I've never really written anything like that before,"[15] he is quoted as saying by writer Nat Hentoff. "I don't sing songs which hope people will die, but I couldn't help it in this one. The song is a sort of striking out, a reaction to the last straw, a feeling of what can you do?"[16] Hentoff himself goes on to add that catharsis is the ultimate goal and that it voiced the frustration of those who could not understand how increasing the potential for oblivion (that is, increasing levels of weaponry) moved the world closer to peace. That was a paradox eerily reflected in the way "Masters of War" desperately wished death on those who vicariously cause it.

There was no way that such a potent statement could fail to go unnoticed, and "Masters of War" (and indeed Dylan himself) immediately became intrinsically linked to the protest movement. With the subsequent escalation of the Vietnam conflict eclipsing cold war issues during the second half of the decade, the song became even further imbedded into the counterculture and its criticism of government foreign policy. But this adoption may have inadvertently moved "Masters of War" away from its original intentions. The masters of the title are envisioned as faceless figures, but the many monetary references subtly suggest that politicians who direct warfare are not the song's primary aim. Instead, Dylan's lyrics indict those privately motivated to *heighten* a dispute like the cold war by personal financial gain—the very same business and industry factions that Eisenhower warned of in his farewell speech in 1961. As Dylan himself noted 40 years later, there were no criticisms of the act of war itself but of those who deviously exacerbate it —a fact that was contrary to mass interpretation.

> Unfortunately, people have been led down the wrong path by quasi-intellectuals who never really get the cultural spirit in the air when these songs are performed . . . ["Masters of War"] is supposed to be a pacifistic song against war. It's not an antiwar song. It's speaking against what Eisenhower was calling a military industrial complex as he was making his exit from the presidency. That spirit was in the air, and I picked it up.[17]

Whatever the song's finer points, "Masters of War" was ascribed an antiwar piety that would saddle Dylan with the label of being a protest singer (see the sidebars) despite the fact that he would drop the song from his repertoire barely a year later and by 1965 would stun his folk contemporaries by going electric.

There have, however, been many relevant points in history at which Dylan has seen fit to revisit the song. During the mid-1980s when cold war paranoia hit one last peak under the presidency of Ronald Reagan, "Masters of War" seemed pertinent enough to add to the set list of many live shows. Under the shadow of an Allied invasion of Iraq in 1991, the song was again revitalized most notably during the 1991 Grammy Awards where Dylan was being presented with a lifetime achievement award. The controversy surrounding the second Iraq war has inevitably brought about yet another lease on life for "Masters of War" in Dylan's live show, but this modern era of conflict has also produced the most infamous cover of the song. Despite being reinterpreted by everyone from Odetta to Pearl Jam over the years, it was a high school punk band from Boulder, Colorado, called the Coalition of the Willing, that unexpectedly attracted the most media coverage during 2004. While the group was preparing to perform its version at a talent show, a fellow student reported that the bandmates had changed the lyrics of the song to include a death threat aimed at President George W. Bush. After the rumor circulated around town, the Secret Service was eventually called in and briefly questioned teachers before deciding that no threat was being posed, although the intervention still made national news.

A final factor that seems to keep "Masters of War" at a remarkably high profile is the polarizing debate that continues to surround the song among Dylanologists for what is admirably honest for one critic may well be nauseatingly simplistic for another. British music magazine *Mojo,* for example, listed the song as No. 1 in its list of the 100 best protest songs during 2004 while putting it at No. 16 in an identically sized list of greatest Bob Dylan songs the following year. In contrast, the noted writer Greil Marcus (author of a number of esteemed books and essays on Dylan) mused in response to this lofty award that "Masters of War" was too "sententious, too self-righteous— stilted, as if it was less a matter of someone writing a protest song than the protest song as such spontaneously generating its own copy, or its own cartoon."[18] After all these years, "Masters of War" continues to be just as contentious as war itself.

Artist: Nina Simone
Song: "Mississippi Goddam"
Songwriter: Nina Simone
Album: *Nine Simone in Concert*
Label: Philips Records
1964

As the civil rights movement began to grow during the early 1960s, Nina Simone became one of the many artists to reflect black America's push for equality in her work. But while the 1963 shooting of prominent activist Medgar Evers in Mississippi and the bombing of a church in Alabama proved to be great setbacks for the cause, they would also provide Simone with the inspiration for "Mississippi Goddam." It become one of the jazz singer's most famous songs and helped to mark the point at which the movement's hopeful spirit began changing into naked indignation.

She may not have realized it at the time, but the young Nina Simone made her first protest against racial discrimination over a decade before the civil rights movement

Nina Simone in concert.
Courtesy of Photofest.

began. Born Eunice Kathleen Waymon in 1933 in Tryon, North Carolina, she had shown a natural gift for the piano while still a toddler, and her devoutly Methodist mother encouraged her to play in church whenever possible. Local residents—both black and white—soon learned of this prodigious talent and sought to nurture it by setting up a fund to provide the child with further lessons. By the time Waymon was 10, her ability had become remarkably advanced, and she was ready for her public debut—a piano recital for many of her benefactors. As she prepared to start, an anonymous white couple exercised what was then its state-supported right and ordered Waymon's parents out of their front-row seats simply because they were black. Enraged at the sight, the young girl adamantly refused to play unless they were reseated at their original places. That harsh reality of segregation undoubtedly damaged her innocence, but as Waymon would later reflect, the experience helped her become a little more hardened to the world as well as heightening the sense of her own ethnicity.

Her ambition to be a classical pianist would continue to drive Waymon onward, but a few years later she was again held back by the apparent disadvantage of her race. She attended New York's Julliard School of Music at the age of 17 with the intention of enrolling at the prestigious Curtis Institute in nearby Philadelphia a year later, but was rejected after taking the entrance exam. For years after, Waymon would claim that her musical credentials were well beyond the minimal requirements for admission at the Curtis Institute and her rejection was based simply on the grounds of color. With the money gifted by her hometown sponsors now drying up, she was forced to add her own source of income to balance out the costs of further education. It was that necessity that led Waymon to Atlantic City in 1954, where an owner of a local club explained that a paid performance would require her to sing popular songs of the day rather than simply play instrumental pieces on the piano. Worried that a step into this slightly less high-brow realm of public performance would be frowned upon by her religious mother, Waymon attempted to cover her tracks by adopting the stage name Nina Simone—Nina being the Spanish word for "little girl" (and a term of endearment used by her Hispanic boyfriend) and Simone as a reference to French actress Simone Signoret. It did not take very long before this newly christened act began to develop a loyal following thanks to her effortless molding of classical techniques with jazz, blues, and gospel elements, which would quickly become her signature sound. Over the next few years, music-industry interest began to build until Simone signed with a New York jazz label, Bethlehem Records, which issued her first album, *Little Girl Blue,* in 1958. Although it spawned her biggest U.S. hit, "I Loves You Porgy" (from the Gershwin opera *Porgy and Bess*), Simone felt that the label was doing too little to promote her work, so she resigned from Colpix Records the following year.

Meanwhile, the sporadic disquiet over civil rights at the end of the 1950s began to develop into a more sustained movement at the start of the 1960s, and, simultaneously, many black artists of the time were beginning to address the problems of racial disparity in their work. The groundswell of activism coupled with Simone befriending such politically inspired black writers as Langston Hughes and Lorraine Hansberry

FURTHER ELEGIES TO MEDGAR EVERS

Among other songs to lament his death, Medgar Evers was mourned by Phil Ochs in "Too Many Martyrs" (included on his 1964 album *All the News that's Fit to Sing*), but it was his folk-singing compatriot Bob Dylan who produced the most famous rumination on the civil rights activist's killing. In the track "Only a Pawn in Their Game," Dylan avoids dwelling on the obvious tragedy of his death and instead elects to examine the psyche of the actual assailant and highlights the kind of social conditioning that drives a man to such an extreme. In doing so, Dylan argues that people such as Evers's assassin are not directly to blame for their actions as they have been led to believe that white people are superior and therefore feel racially motivated crimes are justifiable. With this threat of violence and marginalization constantly surrounding black Americans, white politicians and law enforcers strengthen their power merely by applying racial indoctrination to more compliant areas of the public. Dylan's song presented a complicated but clever argument that forced listeners to take a broader view on the increasing problems of southern life. The most famous performance of "Only a Pawn in Their Game" came during the March on Washington in August 1963 when Dylan played a version of the song just minutes after Martin Luther King Jr. had delivered his epochal "I have a dream" speech at the same podium in front of the Lincoln Memorial.

(whose 1959 play *A Raisin in the Sun* and its grim depiction of poverty particularly hit a nerve) motivated the singer to further develop her own sense of conscience. The 1962 album *Nina at the Village Gate* hinted at her first steps away from popular themes, most notably with the song "Brown Baby"—a dignified hymn of higher social aspirations for the new generation of black children. However, the tumultuous events of 1963 proved to be a turning point for Simone and the movement in general. While the March on Washington in August helped to galvanize protestors and sympathizers, major incidents of violence provided setbacks both before and afterward. In June, the prominent campaigner Medgar Evers was killed just outside his home in Jackson, Mississippi, by Byron De La Beckwith, a local member of the Ku Klux Klan who was not jailed for his murder until 1994 because the all-white juries at his two initial trials failed to reach a verdict. After returning from the army in World War II, Evers eventually became involved in the burgeoning quest for civil rights and became the first Mississippi field officer for the National Association for the Advancement of Colored People (NAACP) in 1954. During subsequent years, he held instrumental roles in the desegregation of the state's university, encouraged boycotts against white merchants who discriminated against black customers, and campaigned to scrap the Jim Crow laws that dictated that black people were to live separately yet equally from white people, but instead resulted in open marginalization. His very public efforts in these fields left him vulnerable to attack from local conservatives, and following several unsuccessful attempts on his life (including one attempt to run him over just days earlier), De La Beckwith shot Evers in the back from the cover of nearby bushes. Three months later in Birmingham, Alabama, a Sunday morning church service was bombed, claiming the lives of four girls—none of whom were more than 14 years old. Again, members of the Ku Klux Klan were suspected of carrying out the attack in the hope of scaring civil rights protestors into retreat. Like the Medgar

Evers case, initial trials concluded without conviction, but in 1977, Robert E. Chambliss was sentenced to life in prison after it was revealed that the FBI had previously withheld evidence implicating him in the church bombing. Two of Chambliss's accomplices—Thomas E. Blanton Jr. and Bobby Frank Cherry—were also convicted in 2001 and 2002, respectively.

Even before these two tragic events, the nonviolent impetus behind much civil rights activism had begun to show signs of erosion. Martin Luther King Jr. had hinted at his growing frustration in "Letter from a Birmingham Jail," an open address to his followers that was written after his arrest at a protest in April 1963. The slaying of Evers was for many further justification of a more direct course of action, but, naturally, the deaths of those four innocent girls provoked the most amount of public outrage. Two more black teenagers were also killed during the violent retaliation following the bombing. Barely able to contain her own fury, Nina Simone opted not to take it to the streets but to channel her frustration into song and on the very same day as the church bombing, she composed a ranting, raging, and relentless set of lyrics called "Mississippi Goddam." Although she quickly began to play the song live, the first recorded version did not appear until 1964 when *Nina Simone in Concert* was released—her first album after leaving Colpix and signing to the Philips Records

FURTHER ELEGIES TO THE ALABAMA CHURCH BOMBING

The church bombing in Alabama that claimed the lives of four girls in September 1963 produced a significant artistic outcry beyond "Mississippi Goddam." Jazz musician John Coltrane recording the instrumental "Alabama" as a tribute to the victims, but it was a folk artist (and close friend of Dylan) who recorded the most noted response. Joan Baez recorded "Birmingham Sunday" for her album *Joan Baez/5* in 1964—the lyrics of which were actually written by her brother-in-law and fellow protest singer Richard Farina. Starkly recorded and dominated mainly by Baez's immensely powerful voice, the song acts as a harrowing commentary of the day's events, even going so far as mentioning each victim of the attack by name. Interestingly, the liner notes for *Joan Baez/5* were written by Langston Hughes—the playwright who had partly inspired Nina Simone's more socially conscious material in the early 1960s. The church bombing incident provided the subject for Spike Lee's 1997 documentary *4 Little Girls,* which used Baez's song during the opening sequence. The feature went on to receive an Academy Award nomination and helped to bring home the horror of the atrocity in Birmingham for a new generation to understand.

label. A largely immaculate document of Simone's singing prowess and playing ability recorded at Carnegie Hall during March and April 1964, the album also denoted a lyrical watershed in regard to the political flavor now characterizing the subject matter of her songs. The track "Old Jim Crow," in particular, clearly alludes to the need for revoking the segregation laws through a narrative that personifies the legislation as an old man outstaying his welcome. However, it is the album finale, "Mississippi Goddam," that holds the greatest social gravitas—so much so that the mainly white audience that Simone was playing to was audibly shocked by her uncomfortable directness.

Just the unholy cursing of the title and the way that she introduces the song is provocative; as the incongruously jaunty rhythm begins, she is heard insisting in no uncertain terms that the vitriol about to be unleashed is entirely sincere—to which the crowd responds with a seemingly nervous laughter. Simone's strangely buoyant delivery and the bright, big-band beat that anchors the entire song are both juxtaposed with the lyrics from the very first verse in which the narrator vents frustration at recent events in Tennessee (in which racial flash points were also becoming increasingly commonplace), Alabama (where the church bombing took place), and the eponymous Mississippi (where Evers was murdered and unrest was a regular occurrence). Making a wry and indeed accurate prediction of the number of plays, productions, and films that would document the era, as well as the unusually lighthearted musical tone, Simone quickly ad-libs her view of "Mississippi Goddam" as a show tune for an as-yet-unwritten work. The song then goes on to describe the constant sense of dread and pressure omnipresent in southern states, even going so far as to question the value of prayer—an idea bordering on the outrageous for both blacks and whites in this uniformly Bible-abiding part of North America.

The high point of the narrator's fury, however, lies in the second half where centuries of institutionalized oppression are taken to task and the entire country is viciously denounced as being untrustworthy—a notion that would become the foundation of the entire counterculture during the remainder of the decade. The narrator is clearly heard to reject the idea of gradual racial reforms, stating that centuries of marginalization (referred to in song through examples of enforced menial labor) require an immediate redress and that black people need to make themselves heard in that respect. It is a sentiment that also reflects how Martin Luther King Jr.'s advocacy of nonviolent struggle was now beginning to move into the Black Power realm of direct action. As the anger begins to overflow, Simone offers another ad-lib to the by-now-silent audience remarking that they probably thought her emotional sincerity was merely a joke. But if there were any lingering doubt as to her naked outrage, the song's final verses underline it with an almost brutal bluntness. With resentment infiltrating Simone's voice, the narrator rejects the idea of gentrification as being a rouse to keep black people under control while the notion that civil rights was a communist plot (even after the end of McCarthyism, any kind of seditious activity was still viewed suspiciously by anti-leftists) is also hatefully rebuffed as symptomatic of a nation filled with falsehood. Instead, the intention is simply stated as "equality for my sister, my brother, my people and me" while the chilling alternative offered for those who do not pursue this aim is a worthless, futile, insect-like death. After one final call-and-response sequence warning of the danger inherent at a piecemeal march toward reform and another plea for equality, a concluding flourish again laments Mississippi and Alabama before the song halts abruptly to an enthusiastic—but still slightly startled—round of applause.

The track's content and semiprofane title ensured that "Mississippi Goddam" was never likely to secure any kind of mainstream exposure for Simone, but that was never the point. The acts of terrorism and violence that occurred in 1963 seeded an increasing fervor for action among black people, and this song "was the first to unearth the sense of impatient indignation now permeating the optimism of the civil rights movement."[19] For Simone herself, this unearthing grew into a huge body of protest that would last until the end of the 1960s and see her occupying a role as a central artistic figurehead for black America. It was a role that she took very seriously, playing countless benefits, appearing at numerous protest marches, and backing the teachings and political thoughts of such prominent activists as Malcolm X. Simone also claimed that the FBI was monitoring her movements during this era due to the size of her profile and level of influence among black Americans. Aside from showing an increasing penchant for appearing on stage in traditional African regalia, Simone's recorded output continued to emphasize her strong allegiance to the cause. Subsequently released songs such as "Four Women," "Turning Point," a cover of Billie Holiday's "Strange Fruit," the Langston Hughes–penned "Backlash Blues," and a rendition of the self-explanatory "I Wish I Knew How It Would Feel to Be Free" (originally by jazz pianist Billy Taylor) all dealt with racial issues in differing contexts and all became immediately popular with those involved in the civil rights movement. In 1970, Simone released the song "To Be Young, Gifted and Black" in memory of her old friend Lorraine Hansberry and one of her unfinished plays. That song was covered by Aretha Franklin two years later under the shortened title "Young, Gifted and Black" and subsequently grew to be a black anthem of the 1970s. It was an extensive legacy of protest that grew directly out of "Mississippi Goddam" and its deeply riled attitude.

However, like many others involved in civil rights, Simone felt a sense of weariness setting in toward the end of the 1960s. With the assassinations of Malcolm X and Martin Luther King Jr. robbing the movement of two if its most important leaders, activists such as Black Panther Party founders Bobby Seale and Huey P. Newton languishing in prison, and other nonviolent strategists such as Stokely Carmichael now in exile abroad, the last years of the decade saw levels of pro-black activity floundering. That subdued state of affairs saddened the singer immensely, and in 1970, she turned her back on the United States deciding instead to live in Barbados, Liberia, Switzerland, and Holland before finally settling in France in 1992. Over the years, a sense of embitterment had taken hold of Simone and she deeply regretted her many years of activism during the 1960s, not only for what she felt were their ultimate failings in social and political spheres, but for tarnishing her subsequent career as well. "Maybe it helped black people, but it hurt me. That's why I'm not making the money I should be right now,"[20] she reasoned in one interview, while in another she remembered, "I was labeled a protest singer. Record companies either thought I'd be trouble or that nobody would be interested in me singing love songs. It was a stigma I couldn't get away from."[21] Her financial insecurity was also compounded by a series of ill-advised business deals during Simone's early career that excluded her from substantial subsequent payments—particularly when the song "My Baby Just Cares for Me" was used in a Chanel No. 5 commercial in the United Kingdom during 1987, becoming a hit single in the process—but that did not dilute her regret for the time invested in furthering civil rights. Simone died in April 2003 with her dislike of America still very much in place. Touring the country irritated her and over the years Simone saw little progression from the land she once accused of being full of lies and oppression. "I call it the United Snakes of

America . . . they [the American government] want to keep their black people in slavery forever."[22]

Artist: Sam Cooke
Song: "A Change Is Gonna Come"
Songwriter: Sam Cooke
Album: *Ain't That Good News*
Label: RCA Victor
1964

After limited success on the gospel circuit, Sam Cooke became a mainstream star by using his immense vocal talents to perform lightweight and immediately accessible pop music in the late 1950s and early 1960s. However, it was a period that coincided with the gradual emergence of the civil rights movement, and the singer became well acquainted with the unfairness of segregation while on tour. After finally realizing that social sea change was extending to music and experiencing one-too-many incidents of racism himself, Cooke released the unusually earnest "A Change Is Gonna Come" and gave African Americans a source of aural hope that would last well beyond his premature death in 1964.

A typically dapper looking Sam Cooke posing for another flawless publicity shot.
Courtesy AP Images.

The young Sam Cook always knew he was going to be a singer and was never embarrassed to say as much. Born in 1931 in Clarksdale, Mississippi, the first seeds of his huge self-belief were planted at an extremely early age when as a toddler, he developed a habit of collecting popsicle sticks, placing them into the ground in the back yard, and singing at them. Whenever questioned about this unusual behavior, he replied simply that the sticks represented people and he was practicing for his future career. Due to the his father's decision to relocate, Cook did most of his growing up in Chicago and took the first steps toward this long-term ambition by performing with members of his family in a gospel group, then joining a local quartet called the Teenage Highway QCs before finally being invited to be a part of the well-established Soul Stirrers—all by the time he was 20. As the group toured, its godly material did nothing to obscure the fact that the devilishly good-looking Cook had plenty of female admirers, and the Soul Stirrers used it to their advantage. But Cook's ambition even was greater than that and he finally made a tentative move into more secular realms by issuing his first pop tracks in 1956 under the pseudonym of Dale Cook so as to not offend his gospel fan base. However, he quickly reverted back to his real first name and added an extra "e" to his surname, feeling that it gave an added touch of showbiz class to his image, as well as giving the superstitious singer comfort in the knowledge that there were now an even number of letters in his name overall. It certainly did not appear to do any harm because by the following year, Cooke was at No. 1 in the Billboard chart with the R&B-flavored single "You Send Me," proving emphatically that his decision to enter the mainstream had been a worthwhile gamble and that his childhood conviction was well-founded.

Cooke's arresting vocal croon and unapologetic attempts to write simple, catchy material that fans would enjoy singing along to helped ensure continued commercial appeal while the lyrical themes of such singles as "Only Sixteen" (1959) and "Wonderful World" (1960) hit a nerve with the teenage crowd that had begun to emerge as a crucial new demographic of record buyers. But behind this popular sensibility and cross-racial reach, Cooke's African American consciousness was developing in conjunction with the civil rights movement that had surfaced across the southern states toward the end of the 1950s and the start of the 1960s. The initial impetus was mainly geared toward challenging segregation between blacks and whites in schools, restaurants, facilities, transportation, and many other areas of everyday life through peaceful sit-ins and protests. These were the kind of racial divisions that Cooke came across frequently while performing in the South as concert crowds were also subject to similar laws. However, the singer was able to assist the movement by using his profile to flatly insist that his audience be desegregated, and it was not unknown for Cooke to cancel a performance altogether were these demands not met. Additionally, he provided a model of black self-betterment and financial autonomy by establishing his own label in the shape of SAR Records in 1959—a rarity for any African American. But in some cases, Cooke's fame and fortune were still overruled by the color of his skin; his growing annoyance for this prejudice was evident in a syndicated article written during 1960 in which he ruefully recalled having to miss a singing engagement in Georgia because no white cab driver would take him to the venue, while also spelling out his distaste for people "of any color, religion or nationality who have lacked courage to stand up and be counted."[23]

The pop hits and chart successes would continue over the next few years, but in 1963 Cooke experienced a chain of events that would alter his character and inspire a shift away from the lighthearted nature of the vast majority of his back catalog. The tragic death of his son Vincent had a profound effect on the singer, but by this point, a huge surge in civil rights activity was becoming inescapable. Cooke still came face-to-face with many more peaceful sit-ins and demonstrations across the South, but the push for equality now had a national profile thanks to such events as the March on Washington where Martin Luther King Jr. gave his "I have a dream" speech as millions watched on television. Furthermore, Cooke had become friendly with more radical exponents of the movement, such as Malcolm X and even boxer Cassius Clay, who both presented him with ideas of black empowerment through Islamic teachings. Ever mindful of popularity, Cooke also noticed how this sociopolitical struggle was emerging in music, especially with Bob Dylan's track "Blowin' in the Wind," which had been covered by folk trio Peter, Paul and Mary and made into a No. 2 hit single that same year. While the song did not make specific references to civil rights, the spirit of human struggle that Dylan poignantly addressed could easily be applied to the movement. Indeed, Cooke could scarcely believe that it had been a white man who had managed to capture the feelings of black Americans so effectively and saw it as a challenge for his own songwriting skills.

The progression toward racial integration was now unmistakable in American life, but it was by no means unopposed; this grim reality was illustrated for Cooke in October 1963 as his latest tour took him to the town of Shreveport, Louisiana. Having prebooked rooms at a Holiday Inn with no problems, the singer and his entourage arrived only to be refused entry and subsequently arrested for trying to check into a whites-only hotel. It was a sobering reminder that for every March on Washington, every Malcolm X, and every Bob Dylan, there were still disheartening setbacks like this one with which to deal. Coverage of the incident in the press suddenly made Cooke look like a civil rights crusader, but his greatest contribution to the cause would materialize just weeks later. Inspired directly by events in Shreveport, he returned to the studio in December and recorded a surprisingly mournful new song called "A Change Is Gonna Come," which first earned a release in 1964 as an album track on *Ain't That Good News*.

A swell of grandiose strings colored by a distant horn sound combine to set a distinctly melancholic mood to the track from the very start, before Cooke's voice surges through the mix with all the power of a gospel sermon, delivering the first lines that recall a humble birth in a tent by an unnamed river (although Cooke's own arrival into the world was not quite so destitute, the Sunflower River is a genuine landmark in the locale of Clarksdale). As a slow, almost exhausted sounding rhythm is established, the river is then used as a metaphor for a life spent on the run, but despite the overbearing sadness, the narrator is quick to reassure the listener that a change of some kind is due. After lamenting the hardship of living, the fear of dying, and the doubt over what lies beyond the grave, the second verse also ends by offering that same promise. A more prominent horn part is audible in the next verse, and it underscores the narrator's description of going downtown to see a movie only to be scared away by sinister threats—something that Cooke would have undoubtedly seen happening for real during the height of segregation. But another, more brutal encapsulation of this adversarial atmosphere follows in the dramatic middle section when a simple request for help is rebutted with what seems to be outright violence. Despite such deflating experiences and the doubt over how long they can be endured, the fourth and final verse sees a wholehearted reaffirmation of faith in a forthcoming change and concludes the song with a subtly optimistic tone. While "A Change Is Gonna Come" is clearly sung from the perspective of someone under a great and sustained amount of duress, these are exactly the same factors that provide the narrator with the unwavering belief that something better has to lie ahead. There is nothing precise about this promise, nor is there any kind of time scale, it is just a convincing provision of hope for the future for those struggling to find any in the past or present.

Ain't That Good News sold solidly thanks to its usual preponderance of slick pop songs, but "A Change Is Gonna Come" clearly stood out as a powerful centerpiece both literally and artistically. As he made his usual round of television appearances in the first quarter of 1964 to promote the album, Cooke appeared on *American Bandstand* and fielded questions from presenter Dick Clark who asked him what the secret to his ongoing success was. In reply, Cooke chose to single out his knack for observation and argued that "if you observe what's going on—try to figure out how people are thinking and determine the times of your day—I think you can always write something that people understand."[24] It was this sense of empathy that made "A Change Is Gonna Come" more emotionally effective than anything else the singer had yet released, and in these tumultuous times, a close association between the song and the civil rights movement naturally followed. During July, Cooke even donated the song to a compilation album dedicated to Martin Luther King Jr. and designed to raise funds for the Southern Christian Leadership Conference (SCLC), which continued to play a pivotal role in the attempt to create racial equality across America. That very same month, a long-awaited change of the kind described in the song did indeed come to pass as the Civil Rights Act was signed by President Lyndon Baines Johnson, and public segregation was officially banned. But before the year was out, the weary aura of "A Change Is Gonna Come" would be given an eerie new significance when news broke of Cooke being shot dead in a cheap motel in Los Angeles in December. The tawdry circumstances of his killing remain debated to this day, but his friends and associates still can not help but wonder if Cooke somehow saw the song as an omen, particularly Bobby Womack,[25] who recalled him somberly saying "it sounds like somebody died"[26] at an early playback.

Cooke may have been gone, but his success continued without a moment's pause. Just days after his death, the song "Shake" was released and backed with an edited version of "A Change Is Gonna Come," which omitted the movie theater verse in the hope that a shorter, radio-friendly running time would ensure exposure. That factor, combined with the inevitable glut of posthumous publicity, helped the single reach No. 7 in early 1965, but as the civil rights movement continued to establish a greater sense of social parity for black people during the rest of the decade, "A Change Is Gonna Come" remained an anthem and was passionately reinterpreted by the likes of Otis Redding (1966) and Aretha Franklin (1967). But it did not serve just as a stirring call of encouragement; it also had the ability to be a source of comfort when the cause suffered the kind of setbacks that Cooke himself had experienced in Shreveport. Perhaps the most poignant and most documented example of this occurred in 1968 when Rosa Parks mourned the death of Martin Luther King Jr. by tearfully listening to Cooke's version over and over again. Parks, who had long been considered the mother of civil rights for refusing to give up her bus seat for a white passenger in 1955, explained that the song and Cooke's velvet voice acted as "medicine for the soul."[27] By achieving such a huge and sustained emotional impact, it is hardly surprising that "A Change Is Gonna Come" was regarded as one of the greatest songs of the civil rights era, but it also lives on in the modern age through the stream of cover versions that continue to surface year after year and (according to Allmusic) now number well over 100 in total. While Cooke did a commendable job of observing the thoughts and feelings of people in his day, the human struggle against doubt, fear, and adversity is something that evidently never gets old.

Notes

1. Quoted in Gibbs M. Smith, *Joe Hill* (Salt Lake City, UT: Peregrine, 1984), 19.

2. Ibid., 172.

3. Quoted in David Margolick, *Strange Fruit: The Biography of a Song* (New York: Ecco Press/HarperCollins, 2001), 53.

4. Ibid., 5.

5. Hootenanny is the label credited for releasing the song by Seeger biographer David Dunaway, but many discographies list the label to be Charter.

6. Pete Seeger, quoted in David Dunaway, *How Can I Keep From Singing: Pete Seeger* (Cambridge, MA: DaCapo Press, 1990), 157.

7. Ibid., 177.

8. Anthony J. Badger, *The New Deal: The Depression Years, 1933–1940* (London: Macmillan, 1989), 15.

9. Quoted in *All Things Considered,* NPR Radio Broadcast, first aired July 3, 2000 (streamed at www.npr.org/programs/specials/vote/list100.html#T).

10. Ibid.

11. Quoted in *All the News That's Fit to Sing,* album sleeve notes, Elektra Records, 1964.

12. A 1944 recording of Woody Guthrie himself singing a version of "This Land Is Your Land" complete with the missing "private property" verse was eventually discovered by an archivist and released during 1997 on *This Land Is Your Land: The Asch Recordings, Vol. 1.*

13. Len Brown, "Woody Guthrie: Glory Days," *Record Hunter,* January 1991.

14. Dylan's song "Talkin' John Birch Paranoid Blues" was inspired by this. Although it was performed regularly live, Dylan was prevented from playing it on *The Ed Sullivan Show*

in May 1963 and walked off in protest. The song was subsequently left off *The Freewheelin' Bob Dylan* at the 11th hour.

15. Quoted in *The Freewheelin' Bob Dylan,* sleeve notes, Columbia Records, 1963.

16. Ibid.

17. Quoted in Edna Gunderson, "Dylan Is Positively on Top of His Game," *USA Today,* September 10, 2001.

18. Greil Marcus, "Stories of a Bad Song," *The Threepenny Review,* Winter 2006.

19. James Maycock, "The Music and Politics of Nina Simone," *Independent* (London), November 10, 1999.

20. Quoted in Gavin Martin, "Nina Simone: Diary of a Princess Noir," *NME,* February 4, 1984.

21. Quoted in Lloyd Bradley, "Nina Simone: Here Comes Trouble," *Q,* November 1991.

22. Quoted in Precious Williams, "Nina Simone," *The Big Issue,* December 1998.

23. Quoted in Daniel Wolff, with S. R. Crain, Clifton White, and G. David Tenenbaum, *You Send Me: The Life and Times of Sam Cooke* (New York: Quill, 1995), 215.

24. Ibid., 298.

25. Womack was a member of the SAR Records group the Valentinos and would cause scandal by turning up to Cooke's funeral dressed in his old clothes before marrying his widow, Barbara, just months later.

26. Quoted in Peter Guralnick, *Dream Boogie: The Triumph of Sam Cooke* (New York: Back Bay, 2005), 549.

27. Ibid., 651.

CHAPTER 3

EVERYBODY LOOK WHAT'S GOING DOWN (1965–1968)

Although he was billed as the Sunday night headliner, Bob Dylan's electric set at the Newport (Rhode Island) Folk Festival in July 1965 lasted for just three songs, but the booing he received for this raucous performance would continue well into the following year. The socially and politically conscious spirit of albums like *The Freewheelin' Bob Dylan* (1963) and *The Times They Are A-Changin'* (1964) had defined him as the archetypal protest singer and had built Dylan a huge fan base—many of whom were subsequently incensed at his decision to plug in and pursue what folk purists felt to be the trivial, lowbrow sound of rock 'n' roll. However, these negative reactions served only to strengthen Dylan's resolve, and his response was simply just to play louder or even goad his hecklers from the stage. In a particularly memorable and well-documented exchange during a show in London during 1966, Dylan responded to fans screaming for his older work by dryly assuring them that "these are all protest songs."[1]

While the world lost its most prominent exponent of this genre, Dylan's legacy was clear to see as the idea of communicating a message through music had now become virtually omnipresent. Folk music had gone from having a cultish appeal concentrated mainly around America's youthful intelligentsia in the early 1960s to being a mainstream phenomenon with many variants, all of which had the potential to be profitable as well as conscientious. Nowhere was this put into practice better than Barry McGuire's shamelessly Dylan-esque attempt to survey the world's social and political problems in the single **"Eve of Destruction"** (1965). Meanwhile, the hippy movement was also experiencing a peak of exposure, but instead of articulating the problems within existing American culture, the self-contained communities in San Francisco and Los Angeles made their protests by striving to realize an entirely new culture that existed separately. Instead of division, they offered unity. Instead of societal control, they promoted individual expression. Instead of hate, there was love. By the mid-1960s, these attitudes had helped to give rise to such bands as the Byrds, the Doors, and Love that helped popularize the sound of folk rock and psychedelia. Although there was no shortage of youngsters willing to buy into this vision of a hippy utopia, there were also many who treated the culture with violent contempt—a fact that was profoundly noted by Buffalo Springfield in its 1967 single "**For What It's Worth**," which documented the face-off between longhairs and police on Los Angeles' Sunset Strip during 1966.

It was no accident that this groundswell of people speaking and/or opting out came at a time when the country went through massive upheaval both home and abroad. The struggle for civil rights was a subject that still surfaced in music regularly, but the most prominent concern was the U.S. presence in Vietnam, which was now growing into a major issue having gone largely unnoticed by most Americans during the first half of the decade. The year 1965, in particular, proved to be a huge turning point with the commencement of a three-year bombing campaign named Operation Rolling Thunder and an overall escalation of the ground campaign against North Vietnamese insurgents. These events dominated headlines, but with TV now a part of the vast majority of U.S. households, the plight of many thousands of troops from both sides was something that could now be seen as well as read—a gruesome new spin on entertainment touched on by the Doors in "**The Unknown Soldier**" (1968). As the conflict deepened, the images would get only more disturbing, and the graphic visual illustration of what new enlistees would face in this distant country helped foster a resistance to recruitment. If that was not enough, the string of American wars through history—as catalogued by folksinger Phil Ochs in "**I Ain't Marching Anymore**" (1965)—also gave perspective soldiers much to consider. Any healthy American of service age and not in further education could potentially be sent to the front line, and it was a shadow that began to loom large over the country's youth during the mid-1960s. But even that supposedly egalitarian selection process would begin to attract criticism for its ability to be manipulated by the wealthy, the educated, and the privileged, not to mention the absurdly bureaucratic nature of the screening process as satirized by folksinger Arlo Guthrie in "**Alice's Restaurant Massacree**" (1967). Dylan may have given up on protest songs, but there were plenty of artists following in his footsteps and a number of pressing issues to sing about.

Artist: Phil Ochs

Song: "I Ain't Marching Anymore"

Songwriter: Phil Ochs

Album: *I Ain't Marching Anymore*

Label: Elektra Records

1965

Phil Ochs's knowledge of world politics was so immense and sophisticated that he was expressing concern over the situation in Vietnam before many in America had even heard of the country. But as U.S. involvement increased, the topically inspired folksinger looked back on centuries of conflict and bloodshed as a way of justifying the pacifist spirit in "I Ain't Marching Anymore." Not only did it become one of Ochs's most famous songs, it would also accompany the burning of many draft cards during the second half of the 1960s.

It took Phil Ochs a little time to find his political muse, but once he did, it rapidly came to define his life. From the time of his birth in 1940 in Texas, Ochs's largely apolitical family moved frequently, but despite his early musical promise with the clarinet and his love for rock 'n' roll, there was no indication that he might make it a career, much less become a righteously minded folksinger. His early years at The Ohio State University, however, proved to be a huge turning point. While on a short trip to Florida in 1959, he was arrested and imprisoned for a period of 15 days on a charge of vagrancy, during which he experienced an epiphany of sorts and decided to pursue a career in journalism. Upon returning to college, he worked toward this new goal relentlessly by writing for the student paper; his burgeoning left-wing sympathies and views, however, were quickly putting him out of step with the publication's more mainstream politics. Aided by the input and recommendations of his roommate Jim Glover (who would later comprise half of the folk duo Jim and Jean), Ochs began to internalize the works of Karl Marx and Friedrich Engels. He also declared an open admiration of Fidel Castro in the wake of the 1959 Cuban revolution—a risky move considering the enduring memory of communist witch-hunts during the early 1950s. Furthermore, Glover also taught him how to play the guitar and introduced him to the most pivotal names in American folk, such as Pete Seeger, the Weavers, and, of course, Woody Guthrie. Not only did Ochs subsequently translate these new sources of inspiration into print via his own separate student publication called *The Word*, he also protested at the university's stipulation that male students participate in the Reserve Officer Training Corps. At one point, he even teamed up with Glover to form a singing duo that for a short time went under the name of the Singing Socialists.

As the 1960s dawned, Glover traveled to New York City to pursue his interest in folk music. Initially, Ochs stayed on at the university to continue his journalistic ambitions, but dropped out just short of graduation after being passed over for the role of editor at the main student newspaper. By this time, Ochs had begun to use the musical education he received from Glover to compose his own songs, and by 1962 he, too, found himself in New York City as the folk boom gripped downtown Manhattan. The norm for singers at the time was not to compose original material but to reinterpret old standards, so Ochs again found himself at odds with the larger community. Nevertheless, he still played the circuit gamely and almost immediately ran into a rising star called Bob Dylan. The two developed a mutual admiration for each other and helped to move the folk scene beyond the realms of mere repetition by indulging their desires to perform self-penned songs. Dylan's first self-titled album had been released that same year and had been comprised almost entirely of covers, but *The Freewheelin' Bob Dylan* (1963) and *The Times They Are A-Changin'* (1964) both dramatically proved his stature as a lyricist.

Ochs was just as prolific in terms of writing, but did not get a chance to release his own album until 1964 when *All the News That's Fit to Sing* emerged on Elektra Records. Instilling him firmly as a topically inspired writer and living up to Ochs's self-styled image of the singing journalist, the album addressed many of the day's political and social issues with a witty, thought-provoking directness. As indicated by the title, Ochs frequently made the claim that his songs were seeded from news stories and current affairs articles he had read in *Newsweek*—something that seemed all the more feasible upon closer lyrical examination. But while the more prevalent concerns of America's politically active youth revolved around the cold war and the civil rights movement (both of which were covered on the album), Ochs also included a lament on American intervention in Vietnam. At that point, U.S. military personnel were deployed in a mainly advisory role with the intention of aiding President Ngo Dinh Diem in his battle with the communists of the North Vietnamese army. Although Diem had been killed in November 1963 (just days before John F. Kennedy was assassinated) and his corrupt regime had been removed in the process, Ochs's song "Talking Vietnam" used the popular talking blues style to critique the arrogance of training Vietnamese troops to fight the American way for American values. He also made an eerie prediction of the atrocities that would occur and took a swipe at Diem's nepotistic rule for good measure.

In pinpointing this growing problem, Ochs was ahead of many of his contemporaries, particularly as Vietnam's internal strife was still below the radar of the wider American populace and occupied more of a secondary position in mass media. But outside of more enlightened folk circles, the album made little impact although Ochs's desire to be commercially successful did receive an unexpected boost in the shape of Joan Baez who had a hit by covering his unreleased song "There but for Fortune" the same year. He also had public endorsement from Dylan, who famously commented in a letter to folk magazine *Broadside* that Ochs's improvement as a songwriter was difficult to emulate even for him. With Ochs's profile unexpectedly raised via his contemporaries, he released the second album *I Ain't Marching Anymore* in the summer of 1965. It instantly revealed itself as a more refined, arresting, and indignant collection than its predecessor and demonstrated how accurate Dylan had been with his assessment of Ochs's artistic progress. By now, the Americanization of the Vietnam conflict was well under way; U.S. troops had been deployed into a ground war during March 1965, while the devastating campaign of aerial bombing called Operation Rolling Thunder (which would last until 1968) had also begun. Conscription drives were now on the agenda at home and resistance was inevitable, but at this early stage there were few who would articulate it as well as Ochs on the album's title track. Although "I Ain't Marching Anymore" does not actually mention Vietnam by name, the association is obvious—especially given the time of its composition and release. Sung flawlessly, presented with a proud melody, and delivered in a resolute tone of defiance, the song had an unmistakable integrity while still managing to be every bit as patriotic as any expression of jingoism.

The clarion call begins with a distinctive, rolling guitar riff, nimbly picked out by Ochs and imbedded with strange, stately quality that is itself almost worth a salute. The militaristic lilt is apt as it quickly becomes apparent that Ochs is remembering America's great battles from the perspective of an American soldier—of *every* American soldier. The opening lines recall the Battle of New Orleans, the final major battle of the War of 1812 (1812–1815), that was fought against the British—a key event in the development of what was then still a young nation. But the sense of pride in victory is misleading for at the end of this (and every) verse comes the soldier's refusal to repeat his service and subject himself to the horrors of war again. The song then continues to catalog America's victorious campaigns and equates them more with atrocity than dignity. The defeat at Little Big Horn (1876) at the hands of a coalition of Native Americans is referred to in the second verse as the narrator again deplores the human cost of this monumental moment. A third verse references both the American-Mexican War (1846–1848) in which California was gained—or stolen as the song declares—as well as the abominable sight of countrymen killing each other in the American Civil War (1861–1865).

The fourth verse continues the chronology by encompassing American clashes with the German Empire in World War I, the sheer breadth of which meant that many thought it would be the war that would end all wars. But after an unparalleled number of deaths across the European continent, the narrator acknowledges with frustration that he is now wanted again. Next is the brutal annihilation of Hiroshima and Nagasaki from American atomic bombs in 1945 that effectively ensured Japan's surrender, but the victory is viewed as hollow in the light of two entire cities reduced to ash. Finally, America's continued face-off with Cuba is denounced—first through the sight of labor unions bemoaning the dismantling of U.S. missile bases following the Cuban Missile Crisis of 1962 (a move intended as a peaceful measure to reduce the possibility of nuclear obliteration). Additionally, the narrator also makes a sneering reference to the famously corrupt American company United Fruit that was already known for its exploitative trading tactics in Central America and was now demanding compensation after being removed from its holdings in Cuba by Fidel Castro during the revolution of 1959. The narrator's final sentiment is to state that whether his standpoint is regarded as peace, treason, love, or reason, his days of compliance are gone before adamantly reiterating one last time that he will march no more.

Despite the nature of its composition, "I Ain't Marching Anymore" is not just a list of America's most savage conflicts. One of the central tragic ironies of war is encapsulated poignantly in the song's chorus (sung after the second and fourth verses) in which the narrator remarks how it is always the older generation that is responsible for commencing conflicts, and yet it is the young who are sacrificed. He then weighs up the country's gains and asks the rhetorical question that would haunt America for the duration of the Vietnam conflict—"is it worth it all?" With so many celebrated historical events taken to task in the song as well as the fact that in rejecting conscription, the song's narrator was essentially committing a crime, Ochs knew that it was unlikely to be given much media exposure. It was something that he acknowledged with a bullish attitude through his own printed annotations within the album.

> This [song] borders between pacifism and treason, combining the best qualities of both. The fact that you won't be hearing this song over the radio is more than enough justification for the writing of it.[2]

Echoing his politically ostracized days at the university when the censorship of his views at the student paper made him only more determined to put them across in his own, alternate publication, Ochs was now using his role as a singing journalist to put an alternative view of warfare across to the music fans who needed to hear it. The record label did manage to convince Ochs to record a radio-friendly electric version of the song for release in the United Kingdom during 1965 (no doubt hoping to emulate the success of Dylan who had left the folk fraternity for rock stardom), but the move reaped little commercial reward. It was, however, adopted by early antiwar protestors as an anthem of dissent not long after the album's release, and as the rate of troop deployment increased over the next few years, so did the incidents of young men burning draft cards while singing "I Ain't Marching Anymore" to underline their protests. According to Elektra founder Jac Holzman (who would later go on to sign Love, the Doors, and the Stooges), the reason for its popularity in such circles was deceptively easy to identify—"It was easy to remember, it was catchy, and it was singable. All of those are good things."[3] For all of Ochs's musical craft, carefully constructed prose, and faultless historical knowledge, the song also had a simplicity that was arguably its greatest advantage.

Ochs continued to struggle in his attempts to be a mainstream name, but he retained a loyal fan base and remained active in political circles—particularly the anti-Vietnam faction that continued to regard "I Ain't Marching Anymore" as one of its musical staples during the rest of the 1960s. However, the song would also play a central role in an event that would signal a downturn in Ochs's fortunes. In the years after the song first emerged, he had helped to establish the Youth International Party (known as the Yippies), which became famous for advancing its radical viewpoints by using pranks and theatrical methods. The Yippies had a strong presence at the Democratic Party Convention held in Chicago during August 1968, which turned out to be an event besieged by all kinds of countercultural demonstrations. Ochs was asked to appear by the Yippies and specifically to play "I Ain't Marching Anymore" to which a protestor responded by scaling one of the park's flagpoles and attempting to pull down an American flag. With tensions already at breaking point, the police violently dealt with the offender and widespread clashes ensued.

To his horror and disillusion, Ochs found that this kind of activism (or even sympathy for it) was no longer a mainstream concern and that "most of the whole world didn't care [about events in Chicago] and among those who did, many felt the cops hadn't gone far enough."[4] At the trial that followed in 1969, "I Ain't Marching Anymore" was mentioned by name when a prosecutor requested that Ochs play it in court. Although the performance was blocked by the judge, he did play it to assembled media outside and the CBS network proceeded to air the footage on an evening news bulletin. The whole episode forced Ochs to rethink his entire political standpoint, the way in which he conveyed it in his music, and his long-held idea that a well-crafted song could change people's attitudes. It was a shift in thought that was symbolically represented on the cover of his sixth album *Rehearsals for Retirement,* which featured a vision of the singer's gravestone with his place and date of death being Chicago, 1968. Following the rethink, Ochs attempted to communicate his politics back to the American everyman by trying to combine the cultural allure of Elvis Presley with the revolutionary determination of Che Guevara within his own image. But as time went by, it was a vision that seemed implausible due to his

PHIL OCHS SINGS THE NEWS

Ochs once defined the protest song as being "a song that's so specific that you cannot mistake it for bull—"[5] and throughout the album *I Ain't Marching Anymore,* he took aim at a number of unmistakably specific targets. These are five of the most notable.

"That's What I Want to Hear"

Despite Ochs's well-established leanings toward the Left, this was a song that brought criticism from the same factions for a narrative that implores a destitute man to not merely beg for change, but to make a concerted effort to change his situation.

"The Iron Lady"

This song is a solemn condemnation of the death sentence as administered through the archaic method of the electric chair (aka the Iron Lady). Ochs also takes issue with the inequalities of the justice system through his notion that the wealthy are afforded special treatment, observing that "a rich man never died upon on the chair."

"Links on the Chain"

Ochs criticizes the self-defeating exclusivity of labor unions and, in particular, the commonplace refusal to admit black workers despite both races ultimately being united in the ongoing struggle to preserve employment.

"Talking Birmingham Jam"

In 1965, Birmingham, Alabama, remained a hotbed of racial tension and even with the advances made through the civil rights movement, unofficial segregation was still a part of everyday life. Not only does the song bitterly criticize this, the narrator also recognizes the hostility toward his own white-liberal views, all via Ochs's typically funny style of talking blues.

"Here's to the State of Mississippi"

The album's closing track is a scathing attack on virtually every part of Mississippi life—complacent schooling, murderous policemen, oppressive religion, racially biased justice, and statewide narrow-mindedness. Though clearly in the same vein as Nina Simone's "Mississippi Goddamn," Ochs's composition is much broader and more comprehensive in its critique, even going so far as to ask the state to "find yourself another country to be part of."

dwindling creativity and the less-than-favorable feedback from fans and critics. Furthermore, his personal life was deteriorating by the start of the 1970s due to mental problems exacerbated by an absense of the commercial success he still craved. Finally, in April 1976—one year from celebrating the end of the Vietnam War by performing with Dylan, Baez, and many other contemporaries in New York's Central Park—the 35-year-old Ochs hanged himself at his sister's home in New York.

Of all of the songs he recorded during his life, "I Ain't Marching Anymore" remains one of the most enduring for the way it unifies every conflict—no matter how just or worthy it may be deemed—by pointing out the inequalities, futilities, and barbarities that remain inherent in all of them. It also proves Ochs to be right in his rejection of the theory that folksingers should refrain from using current political events as inspirations, lest their work become dated. Not only is the song's sentiment universal, the chronology of "I Ain't Marching Anymore" means it is open to reinterpretations and the addition of extra verses that might encapsulate further American conflicts—a fact that aligns the song to the classic folk tradition. Indeed, it may well be argued that if Ochs had still been alive to witness the military interventions in Central America during the 1980s or the invasions of Iraq, the song may have been at least two verses longer by now. Or maybe a modern folk enthusiast has already made such extensions in a version that remains unrecorded and played only for a small audience of friends. As it is, "I Ain't Marching No More" remains the quintessential protest song of both the immortal American soldier and of pacifist/treasonous Americans everywhere.

Artist: Barry McGuire
Song: "Eve of Destruction"
Songwriter: P. F. Sloan
Album: *Eve of Destruction*
Label: Dunhill Records
1965

After enjoying success with the New Christy Minstrels in previous years, Barry McGuire had become all but a has-been on the West Coast music scene by 1965. But a number of fortuitous events led the singer into a recording session in which he laid down a demo version of a P. F. Sloan song called "Eve of Destruction." Clearly indebted to Bob Dylan's sense of social consciousness, its folky survey of war, racial tension, and injustice made for a starkly unoptimistic outlook on American life, but still struck enough of a chord to win instant radio play. Gradually, the hastily released single rose up to reach the No. 1 spot and helped to establish the idea of protest music as a mainstream idiom, although some were angered by the seemingly unpatriotic spirit while others simply found McGuire's histrionics a little too much to take entirely seriously.

During the 30 years that preceded the recording of "Eve of Destruction," Barry McGuire had already acquainted himself with the many faces of fortune. Although he had been born in Oklahoma in 1935, McGuire's parents quickly divorced, and he moved to California with his mother where she would remarry. McGuire's youth was largely nomadic, dictated by the construction jobs taken on by his stepfather, and even in his early adulthood, this rootless existence continued. McGuire served briefly in the U.S. Navy despite being underage and then drifted from job to job with no real long-term purpose in mind. The beginnings of the folk boom in California led him to buy a guitar mainly for his own personal amusement, but a botched date in 1960 began a bemusing chain of events that would see McGuire establish a solid reputation as a folksinger on the local circuit. Having mistakenly arrived an hour late to meet his lady friend, McGuire was under the impression he had been stood up and subsequently retired to his uncle's bar in Santa Monica to drown his sorrows. While there, the bartender coerced him into playing an impromptu gig that was witnessed by enough people to help circulate McGuire's talent through word of mouth around the area, eventually leading him to collaborate with friend and fellow singer-songwriter Barry Kane. After initially operating as a duo, they went on to join a fledgling folk group called the New Christy Minstrels in 1962 and enjoyed a fair amount of mainstream success almost immediately with their self-titled debut album. By the following year, the band's McGuire-penned "Green, Green" landed the Minstrels their biggest hit single, peaking at No. 14 on the Billboard Chart.

If McGuire's gradual ascent through the music world stemmed from a happy accident, his descent was certainly more self-inflicted and much more abrupt in comparison. As the musical progressions of Bob Dylan and the Beatles began to permeate through America during 1964, the New Christy Minstrels appeared to be getting left behind. McGuire himself also began to feel frustrated both at the lack of any social substance in the material they continued to produce and the fact that the group was traded between managers (or "owners") almost as property. By early 1965, McGuire left the New Christy Minstrels under a cloud with one of the band's managers promising to see to it that McGuire would never again record or release any music in the area. This acrimonious departure did indeed result in him being blackballed by many in the city's music industry. Despite the years of success he had enjoyed with his main band and the small collection of solo work he had released, McGuire quickly wound up broke nonetheless. On one occasion, the singer found himself walking in Los Angeles with barely five dollars in his pocket while two different songs by the New Christy Minstrels simultaneously blared out of a record store and a car stereo.

Fortune would, however, return to deal the singer a more favorable hand later in the year when he was invited by his old friends Roger McGuinn and former New Christy Minstrel Gene Clark to attend a performance by a band they had recently formed called the Byrds. While gleefully dancing to their style of psychedelic folk-rock, McGuire was beckoned to a table by a voice who turned out to be Lou Adler—a famed record producer known for his work with soul legend Sam Cooke and surf-duo Jan & Dean. At Adler's table sat one Bob Dylan (whose song "Mr. Tambourine Man" was being covered by the Byrds for their first single) and a young songwriter named P. F. Sloan. After establishing that McGuire was not currently in a recording contract, Adler invited him to hear some of Sloan's newest compositions at his office. McGuire agreed but did not follow up on the offer, and Adler chased him down by calling a few days later and sending a car to where McGuire was staying, bringing him directly to the office. It was there that McGuire first heard "Eve of Destruction"—a song rejected by the Byrds and one of a handful recently written by Sloan that were clearly influenced by the sound and conscience of Dylan's latest work. The concerns of Sloan's lyrics also seemed to echo those of McGuire who was hungry for more than the lightweight output issued by the New Christy Minstrels.

Although it was given less regard than some of Sloan's other numbers, it was nonetheless slated to be the last of four songs to be recorded at a subsequent studio session scheduled for mid-July 1965—but only if there was time.

On the day of recording, there were only 30 minutes remaining from a three-hour time slot when McGuire and the rest of the studio musicians decided to tackle "Eve of Destruction." A rough, one-take version was rattled off and committed to tape, but the intention had been to return to the studio and improve it at a later date. However, yet another lucky string of events began a few days later when local record promoter Ernie Farrell visited Adler to see if there were any new songs he could hear. Apparently without Adler's knowledge, he had come into possession of McGuire's latest cuts, including "Eve of Destruction" (which at that point was slated to be a B-side) and had taken them to a birthday party being held for the daughter of the program director at KWFD—a leading LA radio station. It was there that Farrell decided to gage the reaction to this selection of unknown music, and the track that elicited the most partisan response was the clumsy, unpolished rendition of "Eve of Destruction." After word got back to Adler about the positive response and that KWFD was willing to play the song, he speedily mixed it, overdubbed some backing vocals, and sent out a pressing. McGuire himself was out of contact during this quick turnaround and so the record was issued with the same rough vocal take he had intended to redo. Much to his enduring amusement, there is even an audible groan of frustration leading into an awkwardly delivered line (around the 1.49 point in the track), which McGuire recalls being caused by his inability to read the song's lyrics and momentarily losing his place on the wrinkled paper on which they were written. Even so, barely a week after the initial recording session, "Eve of Destruction" was already gaining popularity at a remarkable rate.

The track itself commences with an eerie drum sound that reverberates with a sinister, almost deathly echo before a comparatively lighter acoustic guitar sound drifts into earshot. As soon as McGuire somberly begins the first lines with his ragged, rasping voice, it becomes clear from the audible contrast between the two plains that the words are taking precedence over the music. The opening verse appears to address the burgeoning war in Vietnam, which was only just starting to become a concern by the summer of 1965. But rather than lament for too long on the well-established horrors of war, the narrator chooses instead to make the striking point that many of the same people who are selected to fight this latest American war are still not eligible to participate in the country's democracy. The age of conscription at the time was 18, but in the vast majority of U.S. states, the minimum voting age was 21. That inequality is followed by the observation that those who claim not to believe in war can still be found brandishing weapons—a probable reference to the constitutional right to bear arms. Finally in this verse, the narrator delivers a contradictory image of the sacred Jordan River being awash with bodies as a result of the religious conflict long imbedded in the Middle East. With that, a gentle drum beat kicks in and the first chorus begins with the narrator expressing the complacent views of someone who refuses to believe that the world is in danger of annihilation despite the evidence presented to the contrary. And so the pattern continues over the remainder of the song: the narrator catalogs the problems plaguing the world, and a listener appears to disregard their importance.

The second verse begs further attention mainly by citing the threat of nuclear oblivion, which had not been entirely removed in the wake of the 1963 Cuban Missile Crisis. Preceded by a short, melancholic harmonica fill, the third verse is dominated by some tenuous rhyming, but also by a sense of personal frustration aimed at both a public inability and a lack of governmental inclination to rectify some obvious societal wrongs. Specifically mentioned is the continuing specter of racism and segregation that the civil rights movement had been able to alter only in small increments with its peaceful protests. It is not so much a failure on the movement's part necessarily, but just another reflection of an overall lack of basic human respect—so much so that the narrator appears on the verge of resignation and certainly seems stumped for any solutions of his own. Another brief but slightly more melodic harmonica interlude heralds the final set of lyrics that begin with a comparison between the demonized communist stronghold of China and the town of Selma, Alabama, where a civil rights demonstration for voting rights had been held in March 1965. The participants were brutally countered by state troopers and local law enforcement while footage of the injured led to the incident being dubbed "Bloody Sunday" in the media. This is followed by a subtle critique of the space race and its frivolous, short-term explorations that do nothing to solve the ongoing problems on Earth, while the pride of serving America in war is then equated with the comparative sense of embarrassment associated with dying for America in war. Finally, the narrator brings home a final hypocrisy of hatred on an everyday level between neighbors who then revel in their own sense of religious piety. An especially forlorn rendition of the chorus concludes the song's lyrics and one more final flourish of harmonica brings "Eve of Destruction" to a cheerless end.

The speedy release and initial airplay ensured that "Eve of Destruction" had a swell of support almost immediately after it was first issued. But patronage from media soon dried up as many radio stations were reticent about the song's controversial lyrical standpoint, its perceived anti-American feeling, and an unmistakably desolate tone that most programmers wanted to avoid. Indeed, McGuire soon found himself to be the subject of hate mail from members of the public who took offense to his apparent lack of patriotism. As a result, it took two months of gradual exposure to build "Eve of Destruction" up to a peak of popularity, but it finally reached No. 1 on the chart in September 1965. As much ill feeling as there was toward it, the song had evidently connected with a huge number of Americans who saw the same omnipresent hypocrisy and sensed a similar feeling of impending apocalypse.

The success of "Eve of Destruction" was due in no small part to the simplistic manner in which its concerns were presented. On a purely musical level, it was aided by a catchy melody married to the most rudimentary of chord sequences that even the most incompetent of guitarists would have no trouble picking up. Additionally, it had a lyrical clarity that had hitherto been seldom employed by the more famous exponents of the genre. Whereas the socially conscious members of the folk fraternity were inclined to lace their work with ironic narratives, satirical observations, and a

THE SPOKESMEN—"THE DAWN OF CORRECTION"

Just months after "Eve of Destruction" claimed the No. 1 spot, a song called "The Dawn of Correction" by a group called the Spokesmen emerged as a direct response to Barry McGuire's hit. The band was a trio from Philadelphia comprising Johnny Madara, Ray Gilmore, and Dave White—the latter of whom had been part of the fleetingly successful vocal group Danny & the Juniors. Borrowing the slow tempo, folk-friendly melody, and incessant rhyming of "Eve of Destruction," the Spokesmen put an unusually positive spin on world events as a way of retorting to McGuire's unrepentant scenarios of doom. Whereas "Eve of Destruction" focused on the negative perceptions of communism and a lack of domestic suffrage, "The Dawn of Correction" replied by suggesting that the Western world needed to keep freedom intact from the Red threat and that voting rights would be unnecessary in a future utopia. McGuire's fear of nuclear war is also rubbished with the assurance that no one would dare to implement such measures of obliteration and that the weaponry is there only to offer an ultimately idle threat. The lack of overall social effect through protests and demonstrations bemoaned in the original is also rebuffed with the Spokesmen pointing out the fortune of living in a country that allows freedom of expression (thereby administering another dig at communism). Finally, an overall celebration of human progress is offered through mentions of medical advances, increased food and farming supplies, and even the movement away from imperialism. Like "Eve of Destruction," it is a deliberately simple song almost to the point of naivety, but which nonetheless demonstrated the fact that acoustic guitars did not always go hand-in-hand with left-wing politics.

scholarly air of intelligence to which not everyone could relate, McGuire's song merely offered an impassioned, uncomplicated, and unpretentious diagnosis of the world's ills. To have such a foreboding song rubbing shoulders with what was still a chart largely dominated by upbeat pop appeared to be testament to its straightforward style. As McGuire himself put it, "Eve of Destruction" was

> nothing more than a societal mirror, reflecting back … Political hypocrisy, Industrial hypocrisy, Social hypocrisy, Spiritual hypocrisy. The song offers no answers, it just asks the questions and hopefully the listener will wake up and look around.[6]

Aside from garnering a swift response in the shape of "The Dawn of Correction" by the Spokesmen (see the sidebar), "Eve of Destruction" also proved for the first time that socially mindful songs could unarguably be mainstream successes. As the 1960s wore on, it would be proven time and time again. McGuire's fortune, however, took another turnabout when he passed up the opportunity to release a song called "California Dreamin'" as a follow-up single, gifting it back to its composers John and Michelle Phillips, who would release the single as part of the Mamas and Papas. Despite continuing to record and perform up to the present day, McGuire never again reached the success of "Eve of Destruction," leading him to be regarded as something of a one-hit-wonder. Sloan meanwhile also became best known for the song and even rewrote the song for McGuire in 1990, but this more environmentally concerned version received little fanfare and even Sloan subsequently admitted that his revision attempts were ill-advised. There can be no doubt that the years have left "Eve of Destruction" with a split legacy. While many celebrate the song for still being relevant by managing to tap into the unsettlingly similar issues of modern society, its slipshod recording, McGuire's lack of vocal finesse, and the overly earnest tone have resulted in it being derided just as frequently. In their unambiguously titled book *The 50 Worst Rock 'n' Roll Records of All Time*, writers Jimmy Guterman and Owen O'Donnell critique the song for its lifeless sound, silly rhyming, and argue that in his tone, McGuire is "not angry; he's just petulant."[7] They also list the song as No. 1 in a Top 10 list of Worst Dylanesque Songwriting Ripoffs although "The Dawn of Correction" is listed as what must presumably be a very close No. 2. If nothing else, its immovable status as a No. 1 single ensures that "Eve of Destruction" remains a comprehensive representation of the fears and frustrations pervading the popular mind-set at the time even if some listeners feel its power has been tarnished in the years since.

Artist: Buffalo Springfield
Song: "For What It's Worth"
Songwriter: Stephen Stills
Album: *Buffalo Springfield*
Label: Atlantic Records
1967

As the clientele on LA's Sunset Strip began to change from preppy to hippy during the 1960s, the methods of policing used by local authorities appeared to increase in severity. Such measures created a tension that erupted into disorder in November 1966, and while Buffalo Springfield released "For What It's Worth" as a way of capturing the unjust treatment dished out during this specific incident, it was a song that lived on as an anthem of countercultural resistance for the rest of the decade.

Buffalo Springfield in 1967. The group's live lineup changed frequently; this TV performance features (L–R) Dewey Martin, Richie Furay, Stephen Stills, Jim Fielder, and Neil Young.
Courtesy of Photofest.

For those who had the means, Los Angeles' Sunset Strip was the place to be during the first half of the 1900s. The reputation it gained as a playground for the rich and famous stemmed particularly from the 1920s and the days of prohibition when the area became a haven for many so-called "speakeasies" that sold alcohol illegally to select groups of customers. Once prohibition ended in 1933, these establishments quickly developed into fully operational nightclubs that already boasted a wealthy clientele and no longer needed to be run secretively. Such clubs as Ciro's and the world famous Trocadero subsequently boomed and attracted the financial elite of California—especially the first generation of major Hollywood actors who were regularly spotted living it up on the Strip. Even when the movie stars slowly left in the 1950s to pursue their personal pleasures in other parts of LA, the Sunset Strip remained an area synonymous with upmarket entertainment that attracted a crowd of the "crew-cut-and-varsity-sweater variety."[8] By the 1960s things were clearly beginning to change. All over the city, a new crop of bands and new musicians were emerging, and as they did, the new genres of folk-rock and psychedelia slowly entered the public's imagination. By 1966, the Byrds and the Mamas and Papas had already enjoyed big hits and national exposure, Love was gaining praise if not huge sales for its early material, and around the Venice Beach area, a band called the Doors was also germinating. It was also during this time that the streets of LA (quite literally) gave rise to a quintet calling itself Buffalo Springfield.

A number of seemingly serendipitous events led to the band's actual formation—the first of which occurred miles away from LA in Fort William, Canada, where in 1965, the paths of aspiring musicians Neil Young and Stephen Stills first crossed. Young was playing in a local band called the Squires, while Stills was touring with his own outfit the Company. The two immediately found that not only did they bond personally, they also complemented each other's creativity remarkably well. However, it was a brief encounter, and shortly after the tour, the Company disbanded with Stills moving to California in the hope of finding more musical opportunity. Young meanwhile returned to his native Toronto in 1966 and joined the Mynah Birds who at that point also featured future funk-pioneer Rick James in the lineup. The band promptly signed a deal with Motown Records before events took a bizarre turn with the discovery that James was, in fact, absent without leave from the U.S. Navy. He was jailed, the record contract was canceled, and the advance was stolen by the group's manager.

Deflated though he was, Young still wanted to play music, so, along with his friend and Mynah Birds bassist Bruce Palmer, he decided to make the journey down to LA in the hope of tracking down Stills. It proved to be a nearly impossible task to accomplish in the vast sprawl of the city, and the two felt they might be better off investigating the burgeoning San Francisco music scene that they had heard about. On their way out of the city, Young and Palmer got caught up in a traffic jam that was also holding Stills and his musical compatriot Richie Furay hostage. It was Stills who spotted Young's distinctive hearse and Ontario licence plates; after much yelling and gesticulating, the two cars pulled over. The quartet subsequently recruited drummer

Dewey Martin, and just days after forming Buffalo Springfield, the group was already lining up gigs.

Like many LA bands of the time, Buffalo Springfield scored its first shows in the gradually changing environment of the Sunset Strip where the glitz and glamour were being challenged by a string of new rock clubs and concert venues, such as the Whiskey a Go Go, the Roxy, and the London Fog—all of which were ideal places for local talent to cut their teeth. Indeed, it was during a seven-week stint as the house band at the Whiskey during the early summer of 1966 that Buffalo Springfield earned itself a huge amount of acclaim and the bandmates' musical chemistry was solidified. It was not long after this legendary residency that the band signed a deal with Atlantic Records. With his part of the advance, Young replaced the infamous hearse that had been so crucial in bringing the band together with a Corvette. Young was driving in this car one day in July 1966 when he spotted a friend being harassed by police over a minor offense on the Sunset Strip. Upon stopping to help, the officers swiftly began inflicting their overzealous enforcement of the law on Young himself, taking exception to his long hair and scruffy appearance and promptly dragging him to a nearby police station where things took an even more unpleasant turn.

> They [the police] were running a make on me, whatever. [This] guy walks by and calls me a filthy animal, this cop. He had on these big horn-rimmed glasses and a brush cut. I told him he looked like some kind of . . . insect, a grasshopper. He came in the cell and beat the s— out of me.[9]

Young's run-in was symptomatic of growing tensions on the Sunset Strip over the summer. Clearly perturbed by the change in the area's nightlife and the shift from primarily clean-cut patrons to younger music fans with longer hair and a tendency to smoke marijuana, police concern was remarkably high especially given that antisocial or even violent behavior was still rare in the mid-1960s. Nevertheless, preemptive action was soon taken when a 10 P.M. curfew for those under 18 years of age was passed and a popular bar called Pandora's Box was also earmarked for closure by authorities who felt it to be the hub of delinquent behavior in the area. Both measures were met with dismay, and the weeks of ill feeling led to a flash point on November 12, 1966, when approximately 300 arrests were made during one night of rioting in the neighborhood. The evening had again started off with peaceful intentions, but the estimated crowd of around 1,000 people demonstrating against the curfew and the bar's closure again accused the police of using unnecessarily heavy-handed tactics in a bid to control proceedings. As outraged as the local youths were, it was an incident that had been waiting to happen for some time.

During these days of disquiet, Buffalo Springfield was in San Francisco playing a handful of shows and soaking up the city's musical creativity by spending time with some of the more interesting local acts—particularly the newly formed psychedelic outfit Moby Grape. Since getting signed to Atlantic Records, Buffalo Springfield had not experienced the best of times with Young's health suffering due to his recently diagnosed epilepsy. The unpredictable side effects of his medication only exacerbated the friction that was already developing among the bandmates. Musically at least, the time spent in San Francisco reinvigorated them to some extent and upon learning about the events on the Sunset Strip, Stills was inspired to write a song about it and the mood that dominated the area in the period immediately after. Titled "For What It's Worth" and influenced sonically by their contact with Moby Grape, the song was speedily recorded in December, earning its first radio play just days later. Although the band was not overly enthusiastic about the composition, it gave Buffalo Springfield its first and only Top 10 hit in March 1967.

Despite being offset by a simple structure and a short, catchy chorus, "For What It's Worth" is a decidedly tense two-and-a-half minutes of music, but all the more arresting for it. Young rings out the two mournful notes on his guitar and gives the track its famous riff while Stills delivers his lyrics with a weary soulfulness at an almost wake-like pace. The uncertainty and danger of the riots is encapsulated in the first two verses alone in which Stills presents the threat of an armed man looming with a menacing intent over young people trying to make their voices heard. None of the exact places or names were ever mentioned, but the third verse features references that appear to relate specifically to the incident on the Sunset Strip. Aside from mentioning the number of people widely estimated to be in attendance on the night of the riot, the nonviolent nature of the initial demonstration is also alluded to by Stills who explains that the protesters were merely expressing their solidarity by singing and holding up signs. The arrests and incidents of violence brought the evening to an unpleasant conclusion, and the song itself reflects that by touching on the levels of police paranoia that meant that those who dissented (or even showed the potential for it) would pay the price. The miscarriage of justice might be obvious, but the song addresses it not with anger or even defiance, but rather a prevailing sense of melancholia.

The source of inspiration for Stills in writing "For What It's Worth" had been established and documented at the time of release and to this day, all surviving members of Buffalo Springfield refer back directly to the simmering tensions on the Sunset Strip during 1966 whenever they are asked about the origins of the song. Even with that knowledge in mind, the song enjoyed an extended half-life thanks to it being adopted as one of the torch songs of the entire decade. With the Vietnam War and the counterculture movement escalating at similar speeds, "For What It's Worth" began to take on new significance as the events on the Sunset Strip were quickly relegated to a relatively minor status thanks to a more virulent sense of youthful anger reaching across the nation. This broader application of the song's themes stems from Stills's vision of clear battle lines getting marked out—an image that could also reflect a unified generation making its political voice heard instead of just a small group of LA music fans complaining about their favorite bar being closed down. What had started off as a document of small-scale unrest would quickly become a national anthem for fighting the good fight and a plea for awareness of the changing social landscape—something that is communicated succinctly in the chorus.

> Stop, hey, what's that sound?
> Everybody look what's going down.

Even today, "For What It's Worth," and indeed its central couplet, has become integral to the memory of an entire era—particularly the unrest and uncertainty sparked by the Vietnam conflict. This association has been further ingrained by the song's iconic use in such notable films as *Born on the Fourth of July* (1989) (the biographic account of Vietnam War veteran-turned-anti-war-protester Ron Kovic) and *Forrest Gump* (1994) (the movie's main character serves on the front line in Vietnam). Inevitably, the notion that the song was specifically inspired by the war remains very much intact even though the original source of inspiration clearly lays elsewhere. However, it has proven to be a misunderstanding that has enabled "For What It's Worth" to occupy a more prominent position in rock history than it otherwise may have.

Artist: Arlo Guthrie

Song: "Alice's Restaurant Massacree"

Songwriter: Arlo Guthrie

Album: *Alice's Restaurant*

Label: Reprise Records

1967

His father, Woody, had long been established as a major part of American music history, but rather than being intimidated by this, Arlo Guthrie continued the family's huge cultural significance by adding his own contribution. As anti-Vietnam protests were becoming increasingly earnest, he emerged with "Alice's Restaurant Massacree"—an almost jovial tale that exposed the absurdities of conscription and damned the war effort with mirth rather than malevolence. Through this epic track, Guthrie made a unique mark on the folk tradition that continues to be clearly visible to this day.

From the very beginning, Arlo Guthrie always had a lot to live up to. Born in 1947 as the second child of Marjorie Mazia and American folk hero Woody Guthrie, he had been schooled in the importance of music early on. While still a child, his father made a point of teaching him "This Land Is Your Land" with its all-important "missing" verse (see "This Land Is Your Land" discussed in Chapter 2) so that the song's core ideals would not be forgotten. But over time, it became apparent that there were many more people striving to keep that message intact. Arlo's adolescence coincided with a period in which his father's musical exploits during the Depression were far from becoming faded historical relics, but in fact were being used as building blocks for a new epoch in American culture. The communist witch-hunts of the 1950s had forced the folk-music movement (of which Woody was one of the originators) underground to some extent due to its well-established links with the Left. But after a decade of underappreciation, if not outright suppression, the dawn of the 1960s heralded a new generation of conscientious youngsters toting acoustic guitars and antiestablishment rhetoric. Naturally, Woody Guthrie was idolized across the entire demographic, and, as he slowly succumbed to Huntington's disease during the last years of his life, he was paid numerous visits by aspiring folksingers—including a young Bob Dylan. Some wanted to speak to him, some wanted to sing to him, some just wanted to stare at him, but whatever the interaction that took place, the now teenage Arlo grew to be very aware of the high esteem in which his father was held. It may have been this weighty legacy that fostered Arlo's initial ambition not to follow in these patriarchal footsteps but to instead become a forest ranger.

Nevertheless, as the folk-music scene in New York boomed during the early 1960s, Guthrie the younger played and frequented many of the city's hippest acoustic venues hoping to find his own, unique artistic territory. But it was an incident that occurred on Thanksgiving Day, 1965, that would lead to Guthrie receiving more accolades for one composition than he had for all of his previous performances put together, and it would instantaneously cement his position as a central exponent of the genre, too. Recorded live and included as the only song on the entire first side of his 1967 debut album *Alice's Restaurant,* the track "Alice's Restaurant Massacree" recounts the events of that day and its subsequent ramifications over an extended talking-blues monologue—a style popularized greatly by Arlo's father. A light-hearted 16-bar guitar motif and a gentle beat played out with brushes provide a necessarily simple arrangement for a song dominated by Guthrie's amusing-yet-pertinent narrative that adroitly critiques cultural prejudice and societal ineptitude.

He opens with a knowingly riddled introduction that attempts to clarify the song's title before delivering a jaunty rendition of the now iconic chorus and its child-like melody. The real story then begins to unfold as Guthrie recalls the day in question —November 28, 1965—when he and his friend[10] had decided to visit their friends Alice and Ray Brock in their deconsecrated church.[11] As a measure of appreciation for their hosts' hospitality, the pair offered to help clear the Brock's garbage and Guthrie explains how they filled up their van and headed to the local dump only to find it closed. While trying to find somewhere else to empty their van, they happened across another collection of garbage and decide to add theirs to it under the rationale that one pile is better than two.

Guthrie and his companion return to the church for dinner but receive a phone call the next morning from a police officer, referred to in the song as Obie,[12] who inquires about the garbage and the fact that an envelope with the name Brock had been found in the pile. Guthrie owns up and offers to clean up the mess, but upon arriving at the police station is arrested. Quipping to Obie about the difficulties of cleaning up with handcuffs on, the unamused officer drives them to the supposed scene of the crime and then documents the evidence with an unusual thoroughness. All of this is referred to with comic severity by Guthrie as he delivers his narrative, raising his voice to lampoon the sense of gravity with which his misdemeanor is being treated. Both Guthrie and his friend are stripped of their belongings right down to their belts (just in case either should feel so much guilt at their offense that they might contemplate suicide) and are thrown into a cell until Alice bails them both out. After enjoying another Thanksgiving dinner at the church, they are then summoned to appear in court the next morning and are faced with the absurd sight of a visually impaired judge using a dog to survey the mass of police evidence accrued—much to the frustration of Obie whose fastidious work is clearly going to waste. The blind justice connotations are obvious as the judge hands out a $25 fine as punishment for both Guthrie and his friend (making the $50 sum mentioned in the song), as well as ordering them both to clean up the garbage. It is hard to miss the sense of absurdity not only in the story itself, but also in Guthrie's exaggerated descriptions and vocal tones during this opening episode. But the sense of ridiculousness heightens as the narrative then skips to an encounter with the U.S. Army's conscription department.

As the Vietnam conflict rolled on during the mid-1960s, the demand for able-bodied young men to serve in the armed forces grew in tandem, but many would try to avoid combat by using their knowledge of conscription criteria. There were many possible routes to exemption; the pursuit of further education offered many an alternative to front-line life, while some even migrated to Canada knowing that the country's refusal to support the war would give them a safe haven. Feigning homosexuality, physical illness, and mental instability were also popular tactics, and it is the latter of these that Guthrie employs in the song. After an undisclosed period of time has passed since his encounter with officer Obie, he begins to recount arriving at the army induction center in New York for his evaluation. The physical inspections appear to be satisfactory despite Guthrie mentioning that he had deliberately gotten drunk the night before in an amusing aside. His real master plan, however, appears to be an elaborate façade of insanity, designed to convince one of the resident psychologists that he should be exempted from serving. The manic outburst of crazed blood lust and suppressed violence that follows is a high point of hilarity in the song. His desire for guts, veins, and gore elicits clearly audible belly laughs from the audience—particularly as Guthrie's voice reaches an unnaturally high pitch while screaming "KILL, KILL." The rouse to avoid being drafted does not work as a delighted sergeant (apparently impressed by the youngster's enthusiasm for slaughter) approves him for conscription, and Guthrie is sent for a final round of physical tests.

Finally, he arrives at the last hurdle for admission and the repeating guitar motif drops out of the song for extra dramatic effect as another army official asks if Guthrie had ever been arrested. In response, he tells the story of Thanksgiving Day, 1965, which he has playfully renamed "Alice's Restaurant Massacree" as a way of satirizing the perceived seriousness of his actions. But before Guthrie can even finish, the guitar drops out again and the equally crucial question of whether he had to appear in court is asked. He then responds with his recollections of the blind judge and masses of evidence before being told to sit on a bench marked "Group W" where he finds himself among hardened criminals. After succeeding in his attempts at assimilation with the convicts, Guthrie is then faced with more pointless bureaucracy as the sergeant orders him and his new friends to fill out more paperwork explaining the background to their convictions. Finally, a shred of indignation arises in the narration as Guthrie finds one of the officials has inquired about his state of rehabilitation on the back of one of the forms in the hope that an otherwise ideal candidate could still be admitted to service. At that moment, the central paradox of modern day warfare is revealed—much to the narrator's disgust who castigates the sergeant for attempting to ascertain whether the morality of a litterbug is suited to the activities of killing, burning, and destroying.

That dissent is enough to confirm Guthrie's final classification as being unfit for service but not only that, his attitude earns him a rebuke from the official and the

ALICE'S RESTAURANT, THE FILM

Such was the detail and effectiveness of Guthrie's narrative in the song that two years later in 1969, it provided the backbone for a full-length feature film carrying the slightly shortened titled *Alice's Restaurant*. Directed by Arthur Penn (whose previous work was the landmark outlaw picture *Bonnie and Clyde*) and boasting a poster that recomposed the original album art, the film starred Guthrie as himself and depicted an elaborated version of the song's events. The film won several accolades, including an Oscar nomination for Best Director, and featured a host of cameo appearances, including folk legend Pete Seeger and the real Officer William Obanhein—both of whom play themselves. Alice Brock also makes several appearances in the film bearing her name as a prominent extra in a wedding sequence and a dinner scene.

promise that his fingerprints would now be kept on record. With the narrative now completed, Guthrie issues a call for resistance using the song as a unifying symbol. The chain of events relayed in the narrative has accidentally provided the narrator with a way to avoid contributing to an unwanted war and the adoption of the song as a term of nonconformity is encouraged. Guthrie's humorous but thought-provoking notion is that if one person might face an army psychologist and recite the song's opaque chorus hook-line—"You can get anything you want, at Alice's restaurant"—then that person might avoid conscription on the grounds of mental instability. Two people singing it might lead them both to be assumed as homosexual, 3 people might constitute an organization, but 50 people might be classed as a counterculture movement. In the hope of creating such a thing, Guthrie instigates two final rounds of unified singing—the first of which proves to be sluggish. He then insists on more passion and conviction explaining that those qualities would help put an end to war before leading a more spirited rendition and after 18 minutes, "Alice's Restaurant Massacree" is finally over.

Guthrie had always claimed that aside from employing a small element of artistic license, all the events detailed in the song were based on true-to-life experiences that happened over the course of a year after Thanksgiving, 1965. In relation to the littering offense, this has certainly been proven—indeed, officer Obie became a minor celebrity in the wake of the song's release and remained a cult figure in Massachusetts history until his death in 1994. Guthrie's military rejection because of his convict status, however, is brought into question in Laura Lee's book *Arlo, Alice, & Anglicans: The Lives of a New England Church,* in which it is claimed that he was in actual fact classified as "1A" (denoting full eligibility) and that it was only luck in avoiding random selection that saved him.[13] But irrespective of its possibly fictional content, "Alice's Restaurant Massacree" is nonetheless a satire-driven protest against inefficiency, double standards, and prejudice running through America's authoritarian bodies.

Despite its gargantuan running time, Guthrie ensures that his audience is kept interested by delivering the monologue with a warmth and wit that does not demand attention, but wins it. The overzealous maintaining of order is made to look idiotic and arguably fosters an extra spirit of resilience—as persecution often does. But in the context of the Vietnam conflict (which had worsened markedly by the time the song was released in 1967) and the increasingly angry rejections being vocalized in popular culture, "Alice's Restaurant Massacree" manages to provide a rare and skillfully handled comic antidote laced with the tragic irony of how stupidity at home was fueling stupidity abroad. Its intelligence did not fall on deaf ears either, as the entire 18-minute version quickly became a favorite among college and counterculture media, while the album's sales were propelled by the lead track, helping it reach the Top 20 on the Billboard chart.

"Alice's Restaurant Massacree" has undoubtedly endured the test of time to become part of American folklore irrespective of the song's specific settings. It is still played by many radio stations with an almost ceremonial regularity on Thanksgiving with Guthrie himself stating that he feels it to be closer to the tradition of the holiday rather than the Vietnam War. In 1995, he also marked the 30th anniversary of his environmental error by re-recording the album in its entirety, including an extended version of "Alice's Restaurant Massacree," which clocks in at 22 minutes. But thanks to some all-too-obvious parallels between foreign policy in the late 1960s and the early 21st century, "Alice's Restaurant Massacree" still has a continuingly relevant sense of political satire. Preparing for another tour and the 40th anniversary of the song's release, Guthrie explained his decision to reinclude it in his set by pointing to the ongoing conflict in Iraq and noting how "these times are looking eerily familiar. Right now, you never know where the next group of soldiers are going to come from. So the song has some legs."[14]

Artist: The Doors

Song: "The Unknown Soldier"

Songwriters: John Densmore, Robby Krieger, Ray Manzarek, and Jim Morrison

Album: *Waiting for the Sun*

Label: Elektra Records

1968

The abundance of anti-Vietnam sentiment in American pop during the late 1960s meant that even Jim Morrison's bandmates in the Doors wondered whether his lyrics for "The Unknown Soldier" were worth using. But the singer added a slightly different spin to the standard musical protests about war by subtly critiquing television's role in relaying images of the lives and deaths of unidentified troops as ghoulish, mealtime entertainment.

Military life was something that Jim Morrison developed an aversion to at a very young age. Born in 1943 in Florida as the eldest of three children, his formative years were greatly affected by the unpredictable naval career of his father, George Stephen Morrison. Aside from having to spend significant periods away from his family, Morrison's father would also be forced to uproot them whenever he was given a new posting, all of which prevented the two from enjoying anything like a close relationship. By the time Morrison had reached college, the antiauthoritarian streak in him had developed to the point that he decided to enroll at the University of California, Los Angeles to study film apparently without his parents' knowledge or permission. Despite maintaining contact through occasional letters, it would be the last time he would see either of them face to face. After arriving in California, it was not

The Doors (L–R): John Densmore, Robby Krieger, Ray Manzarek, and Jim Morrison.
Courtesy AP Images.

long before Morrison took to telling new friends that he had no family and that his parents were dead.

As he settled in Los Angeles during the mid-1960s, anti-Vietnam feeling had not become widespread, but Morrison already knew he wanted no part in the campaign partly from his unhappy experiences of the armed forces as a child. He successfully avoided the draft by deliberately failing the army physical, and, as a result, Morrison could continue singing with a fledgling band he had formed with fellow film student Ray Manzarek (keyboards, vocals), Robby Krieger (guitar), and John Densmore (drums). The bandmates called themselves the Doors as a reference to the 1954 Aldous Huxley book *The Doors of Perception*—a document of the author's experiences on the hallucinogenic drug mescaline. It was an apt choice given Morrison's lyrical mantras and the quartet's psychedelic slant on rock 'n' roll, but the Doors could also write radio-friendly pop songs when so inclined. These two sides to the band's repertoire were slowly perfected during 1966 when the Doors performed extended residencies at the London Fog and the Whisky a Go Go—two prime venues for LA bands hoping to get noticed in the industry. Despite getting fired from the latter club for performing a taboo-breaking oedipal sequence in a song called ''The End,'' the group still managed to land a deal with Elektra Records and released a self-titled debut album in the first weeks of 1967.

The Doors would quickly develop into a huge success helped greatly by the single ''Light My Fire,'' which hit No. 1 in the summer and proved the group's credentials as a mainstream proposition, as well as having more than enough musical adventure to impress critics. Morrison's captivating presence as the Doors' front man also secured them plenty of attention on both fronts; poetic, intelligent, enigmatic, unpredictable, and undeniably good-looking all at once, he was becoming a genuine rock icon. By the second half of the year, the band had already released a second album titled *Strange Days* and the commercial achievements continued to come, but a bloody backdrop to the Doors' apolitical hits was provided by the worsening conflict in Vietnam. As the band gradually became a household name, the details of America's campaign in the Far East also reached a similar height of familiarity thanks to regular television coverage. Though still a relative luxury in the immediate postwar period, television sets had rapidly become a part of the vast majority of households, meaning that by 1967, around 50 million people watched nightly news bulletins—90 percent of which were devoted to coverage of events in Vietnam.[15] As the war intensified, news networks had taken up permanent positions in Vietnam with journalists regularly using one-on-one interviews with American soldiers to gain an insight into the war effort. With the journalists in among the worsening chaos, the news reportage was going to get only more graphic, and with so many viewers now tuning in to watch these updates, an acute awareness of the horrors of conflict began to infiltrate everyday American life.

As the Doors continued their touring duties in 1967, the images being transmitted back to the United States inspired Morrison to write a new set of lyrics that he called "The Unknown Soldier," which he then presented to the band. Aside from making an obvious nod to the Tomb of the Unknowns in Arlington National Cemetery in Virginia (a monument that memorializes unidentified American soldiers who died in battle), the song also appeared to lament a new breed of unknown soldiers who were appearing on television daily and yet still remained ultimately anonymous to most viewers. Assuming that the singer was attempting to make a political statement on the war, Manzarek initially queried the composition and, pointing to the growing amount of pop music that seemed to address the conflict, argued that the world did not need another song about Vietnam. Although clearly taking a cue from current events, Morrison assured the keyboardist that it was intended to be a reflection of war in general, so the band began to work on the composition while still on the road. By the start of 1968, the Doors returned to the studio to work on a third album; despite being put through over 100 tortuous takes by perfectionist producer Paul A. Rothchild, "The Unknown Soldier" was one of the first songs that the group completed.

The opening of "The Unknown Soldier" sounds almost like a prayer as the narrator solemnly envisions an end to the war while being accompanied by Manzarek's ghostly keyboard. A drum beat kick-starts the song's first verse, which describes an almost literal consumption of war in the modern age by referencing breakfast news bulletins being fed to children, exposing them to gruesome images of anonymous soldiers perishing in warfare. The chorus sees Manzarek begin to play a dizzying and strangely unsettling motif as the eerie declaration is made that the end has come for the unknown soldier before the song's unusual middle section commences. The only musical sound in this part is that of Densmore's militaristic, marching-band rhythm while Morrison apes the shouts of a drill sergeant in the distance. Densmore then begins to play a drum roll that gets gradually louder, building up a breathless sense of tension before it suddenly stops and a single gunshot chillingly echoes out across the track. The moment of melodrama passes and the narrator returns with the same solemn air of the intro, but this time he is heard requesting that a grave be made for the unknown soldier. A repeat of the first verse then follows, but Morrison delivers the same observations of television violence with a new sense of rage that transforms his voice from its previously soulful croon to a direct and powerful rasp. The final segment is almost buoyant in its declaration that "war is over," but it is difficult to miss the tragic irony how the unknown soldier heard being shot just seconds ago was relieved of his duty not through peace, but through death. Morrison continues to ad lib shrieks of joy as Krieger adds a chaotic solo while the sound of cheering crowds (and even a celebratory bell on the album version) can be heard as the song gradually fades out into a deliberately incongruous victory parade.

It may have been an unrealistic ambition for such a somber track that featured a 30-second execution sequence in the middle, but "The Unknown Soldier" was initially touted as another chart success for the Doors upon its release in March 1968. But given the growing sensitivity over the Vietnam conflict coupled with the song's downbeat content, its relatively lowly peak of No. 39 (the lowest chart position achieved by any of the band's singles up to that date) was probably to have been expected. However, as the Doors' first reference to the political world, "The Unknown Soldier," was evidently too important to simply be forgotten—irrespective of the song's lack of commercial appeal. As an additional promotional effort, Manzarek and Morrison also put together a short film to accompany the song, which was still an extremely rare sight in this pre-MTV era. In the footage, Morrison is seen surrounded by his bandmates while being tied to a huge post on a beach. Once the gunshot in the song's middle section rings out, the singer's body reacts violently as fake blood streams from his mouth and symbolically drips over an array of flowers. A stream of horrific images from the Vietnam conflict (not dissimilar to the kind being shown on television news bulletins) flash past in unison with the last verse before a montage of victory celebrations from World War II add a bittersweet end to this proto-music video. Its potentially controversial content meant that the film's audience was also limited and did little to boost the single's profile, but Manzarek and Morrison were clearly ahead of their time by attempting to compliment "The Unknown Soldier" with an equally provocative set of visuals.

Later in 1968, the group would eventually release its third album, *Waiting for the Sun*, which featured a slightly tweaked version of "The Unknown Soldier"; as the Doors continued to tour, the song would take on an elaborate theatrical element, becoming a central part of their set. During Densmore's drum roll (which would sometimes be augmented by an air-raid siren), Manzarek would often rise from his keyboards and march across the stage while Krieger would stop playing and instead, point his guitar toward Morrison as though it were a rifle until a simulated gunshot sound sent the front man crashing dramatically to the ground. Although "The Unknown Soldier" had received mixed reviews from critics for its recorded version, this incredibly tense highlight of the Doors live experience also helped to establish the song as being one of the more important in the band's canon, regardless of its initial failure as a single. With the fighting in the Far East escalating rapidly through 1968 and the graveness of the situation being relayed by news crews with just as much speed, the powerful sight of the Doors performing "The Unknown Soldier" retained a great deal of poignancy long after it flopped as a single.

The classic lineup of the Doors would remain intact only until 1971 when Morrison passed away in mysterious circumstances shortly after relocating to Paris, France, but "The Unknown Soldier" remained the band's most obvious political statement. For most casual fans (especially those who have become converted after the Vietnam War), the song has become a minor point of interest behind the band's bigger chart hits, not to mention the enduring legend of Morrison himself whose hedonistic life has become the very definition of rock mythology. However, the song's insight into the role of television in purveying images of warfare arguably make for one of the group's more enduring and relevant works, especially in light of how inescapable the medium is today. The development of the 24-hour news cycle has meant that coverage of modern wars is usually constant and even broadcast live rather than just being restricted to edited bulletins broadcast periodically at peak viewing times. As long as television or visual mediums of any kind remain part of the reportage process, the unknown soldiers of conflict will never be very difficult to spot.

Notes

1. Quoted in *No Direction Home,* Martin Scorsese, Director, Paramount Pictures, 2005.

2. Quoted in *I Ain't Marching Anymore* album sleeve notes, Elektra Records, 1965.

3. Quoted in *I Ain't Marching Anymore* (reissue) album sleeve notes, Collectors' Choice Music, 2005.

4. Phil Mershon, *Perfect Sound Forever,* September 2001, www.furious.com/perfect/philochs.html.

5. Quoted in *The Broadside Tapes1* album sleeve notes, Folkways, 1980.

6. Barry McGuire, blog entry, October 10, 2005, www.xanga.com/barrymcguire/364332725/item.html.

7. Jimmy Guterman and Owen O'Donnell, *The Worst Rock n' Roll Records of All Time* (New York: Citadel, 1991), 54.

8. Barney Hoskins, "Boulevard of Broken Dreams: A Trip Down the Sunset Strip," *Mojo,* January 1994.

9. Quoted in Jimmy McDonough, *Shakey: Neil Young's Biography* (London: Vintage, 2003), 174.

10. Guthrie's friend was 19-year-old Richard J. Robbins.

11. The Brocks lived in Great Barrington, Massachusetts, and were known locally as being an artistically minded couple who would offer a commune-like refuge to young people trying to escape mainstream society or just traveling through the area.

12. Obie was actually William J. Obanhein, a police officer from the nearby town of Stockbridge who was well regarded locally, but was also known to harbor a dislike for the Brocks' open-house policy with hippies and nonconformists.

13. Laura Lee, *Arlo, Alice, & Anglicans: The Lives of a New England Church* (Lee, MA: Berkshire House, 2000).

14. Quoted in Charles Bermant, "Arlo Guthrie: 'Alice' Is Back on the Menu," *What's Up,* March 23, 2007.

15. Figures from David E. Bonior, Steven M. Champlin, and Timothy S. Kolly, *The Vietnam Veteran: A History of Neglect* (New York: Praeger, 1984), 4.

CHAPTER 4

WHERE HAVE ALL THE FLOWERS GONE? (1968–1970)

Just 12 months after the United States had been enjoying the warmth and solidarity offered by the Summer of Love, a far more confrontational air seemed to be floating across the country during much of 1968. The first half of the year had already seen brutal blows to the spirit of political progressivism through the assassinations of Robert F. Kennedy and Martin Luther King Jr., but the crackdown on protestors at the Democratic Convention in Chicago during August marked a major turning point for grassroots activism, too. The event was earmarked as a potential platform for any-one with even the slightest interest in countercultural activity to voice social and political grievances. But in their response, authorities made no distinction between who was dissenting and who was merely listening as they "savagely attacked hippies, yippies, New Leftists, revolutionaries, dissident Democrats, newsmen, photographers, passersby, clergymen and at least one cripple."[1] It was a sign that youthful rebellion of all kinds was now being seen as a scourge on society, and it was with this knowledge that Richard M. Nixon shaped his presidential election campaign, promising the silent majority of older middle-class citizens that this kind of antisocial behavior would be forcibly tackled.

This hard swing toward antidisestablishmentarianism showed that the battle lines of America's cultural civil war were now drawn even more clearly over the generation gap. Some of the lessons that the youth of America would be taught by their elders in this polarized and adversarial atmosphere turned out to be shockingly harsh, particularly in the case of the student protestors killed at Kent State University during 1970—an incident lamented by Crosby, Stills, Nash & Young in "**Ohio**." But the sense of us against them was not entirely universal. The countercultural movement itself was coming under scrutiny from the kind of artists who might have added valuable and powerful voices. The Beatles were arguably the biggest band in the world during the late 1960s and boasted a young fan base that hung on their every note and examined their every word. So the sound of John Lennon (one of the band's central songwriters) distancing himself from the increasingly violent and disruptive nature of radicalism around the world through "**Revolution**" and "**Revolution 1**" in 1968 could not fail to generate controversy. Meanwhile, the Stooges brand of feral and frequently confrontational rock 'n' roll was developing in and around the political hotbed of Detroit, Michigan. But despite their radical surroundings, the quartet's members swiftly decided that they wanted no part of revolution, counterrevolution, violence, or even peace and indulged their unlikely boredom with the era by writing such songs as "**1969**" (1969).

These worsening domestic hostilities were constantly fueled by America's foreign policy, which was dominated by a still escalating campaign in Vietnam. During 1968, Vietnamese insurgents launched the Tet Offensive—an unprecedented series of fierce attacks that indicated that the United States was locked in a war that would not be won with the ease or speed that was first predicted. While Nixon promised peace with honor and an increasing Vietnamization of the war would be a priority of his first term as president, the U.S. invasion of Cambodia in 1970 seemed to contradict that aim and only increased public resentment at the conflict. With the establishment of the draft lottery, thousands more randomly selected young men were now in line to serve in the war, and this only added to the sense of frustration. The discontent could be heard in Creedence Clearwater Revival's "**Fortunate Son**" (1969) and even penetrated Motown's defiantly pop aesthetic with the markedly more serious "**War**" (1970) as performed by Edwin Starr. The former riled at the social bias inherent in the selection of new recruits, while the latter angrily pointed out the grim physical and mental effects those recruits were doomed to suffer.

Factionalism was also ravaging the civil rights movement during the last years of the 1960s, especially as the death of civil rights leader Martin Luther King Jr. in 1968 robbed African Americans of a prominent figurehead. Although James Brown affirmed black pride emphatically with "**Say It Loud—I'm Black and I'm Proud**" (1968), self-worth was not enough for some, and a new rhetoric of Black Power began to emerge into the national consciousness. Instead of working with white people to achieve interracial harmony through legislative reform, many radical organizations such as the Black Panthers and the Nation of Islam promoted the idea of Black Nationalism, which rejected integration and emphasized the development of a specific and self-sufficient African American identity that could exist separately from the rest of the country. As well as creating a rift between radical and moderate African Americans, these attitudes also served to heighten social fears and suspicions between black and white people—a scenario captured by Sly & the Family Stone in "**Don't Call Me Nigger, Whitey**" (1969), which did away with the idealism of integration and instead, pessimistically envisioned a permanent deadlock in race relations. It was just another symptom of how the push for unity had been rapidly displaced by division in almost every aspect of American life, and popular music was mirroring the change notably.

Artist: The Beatles

Song: "Revolution"/"Revolution 1"

Songwriters: John Lennon and Paul McCartney

Album: "Hey Jude" single B-side ("Revolution")/ *The Beatles* (aka *The White Album*) ("Revolution 1")

Label: Apple Records

1968

By 1968, the Beatles had established themselves as not just a band but a cultural force. As antiestablishment fervor in the West built to a crescendo around the quartet, John Lennon offered his viewpoint on the spirit of the era through "Revolution" and "Revolution 1." It was not the opinion that many expected, however, as the song spoke out against aimless civil disorder being used as a way of forcing political change. Despite the controversy surrounding Lennon's antiradical stance, it would not be long before countercultural factions splintered, giving a significant amount of credence to his criticisms.

Between the start of 1967 and the end of 1968, a shift in countercultural impetus was clearly visible across the entire Western world: apprehension appeared to be overtaking euphoria, hope was being succeeded by anger, and where there was once abundant talk of love there appeared an increasing nihilism. Whereas 1967 contained the so-called

The Beatles pictured in 1968 (L–R): Paul McCartney, John Lennon, Ringo Starr, and George Harrison.
Courtesy AP Images.

Summer of Love, the following year's warmer months were characterized by some severely heated tempers. Across the United States, the wave of anti-Vietnam sentiment surged following the Tet Offensive initiated against allied forces in January 1968, which dragged the United States into a deepening battle and demonstrated that the war would not be won as easily as first thought. Domestic anger over the conflict not only intensified, but began to echo around other parts of the world, too, most dramatically during March when an estimated 80,000 descended on the U.S. Embassy in London to add their disapproval, resulting in major clashes between protestors and police.

In mainland Europe, there were additional reasons for agitation. Since the middle of the decade, the student movement in Germany had already been actively rebelling—often violently—against the authoritarianism of government and voicing an open distrust of members of the country's older generation, accusing them of being legacies of the Third Reich. Such outspokenness led to the students frequently being vilified in the mainstream press, and events came to a head in May when thousands of young people protested against the passing of legislation allowing the government to restrict freedom of communication and enforcing national service during periods of emergency. During the same period across the western border in France, more students drew battle lines between themselves and perceived figures of oppression. An initial wave of student strikes grew to incorporate a broader national strike carried out by the majority of the economically disenfranchised workforce, leaving the nation largely immobilized. Heavy-handed attempts to deal with discontent led to a month of persistent rioting that came close to removing the government of President Charles de Gaulle altogether. The insurgencies in France and Germany, in particular, seemed to denote a new school of radical left-wing thought, sometimes referred to as the New Left. Judging by the employment of similar imagery and symbolism, this new political movement in Europe was partly rooted in Mao Zedong's brutal attempts as Chinese head of state to rid the land of bourgeoisie factions through the Cultural Revolution initiated in 1966.

The emphasis may have broadly gone from personal liberation to social and political activism, but the specific objectives of events in Germany and France during May 1968 were blurry. Aims and alternatives appeared to be without definition, while methods to actually achieve them were increasingly obscured by violence that symbolized much but fell way short of the idea of "revolution." In a climate dominated by the idea of direct action but lacking in salient ideas, many may have been forgiven for holding the view that "extremists [had] hijacked the hopeful energy of the Sixties, turning it into a rolling riot."[2] In certain realms of popular music, that sense of growing unrest provided some artists with an added political fervor that mirrored the times —the Rolling Stones, for example, released their raucous "Street Fighting Man" single after singer Mick Jagger witnessed the anti-Vietnam protest at the U.S. Embassy in London firsthand. But despite being the group with arguably the most influence on young people at the time, the Beatles appeared distinctly reluctant to involve themselves in the worldwide turmoil.

In 1963, the Beatles had rocketed to prominence in British pop culture following the release of their first album *Please Please Me*. Armed with a slew of instantaneous songs, an iconic style, and a witty charisma that owed a lot to their hometown of

Liverpool, the Beatles impressed critics and charmed fans across the country almost immediately. By the following year, they had managed to transfer that power across the Atlantic Ocean into the United States, and the term Beatlemania was coined by the press to describe the rabid reaction that John Lennon (vocals, guitar), Paul McCartney (vocals, bass), George Harrison (vocals, guitar), and Ringo Starr (drums) all received on a regular basis. But in subsequent years, the Beatles emphatically disproved the perception of being another teeny-bop fad and proceeded to release a string of sonically adventurous albums that embraced new studio techniques, foreign musical cultures, and even mind-altering drugs. In particular, the 1967 albums *Sgt. Pepper's Lonely Hearts Club Band* and the film soundtrack *Magical Mystery Tour* both indicated the band's psychedelic leanings and aligned it with the burgeoning hippy movement. However, after a spell in India away from the allure of hard narcotics at the start of 1968, the band returned to England in the spring with Lennon becoming especially wary of this new wave of radicalism sweeping across the West. It was this growing suspicion that prompted the band into taking a step back from the cruder factions of the counterculture.

As the turmoil unfolded in France and Germany during May, the Beatles were already well under way recording a new album; by the end of the month, Lennon had penned a set of lyrics encapsulating his observations on recent events. Married to a plodding, almost lackadaisical blues signature punctuated by some feisty electric guitar riffs, the song "Revolution 1" voiced a tentative critique aimed at would-be subversives. Lennon captured his relaxed delivery by famously recording the vocals lying down in the studio and, as a result, achieves a verbal parity with the track's laid-back musical tempo. Addressing his intended audience individually, the narrator begins each verse by explaining that he, too, wishes to change the world but takes issue with the rebel's choice of methodology in reaching the same goal. Throughout the course of the song, overt hatred, willful destruction, and the modern idolization of Chairman Mao are all brought into question. A greater sense of open-mindedness is encouraged while the provision of a genuine solution to the world's problems is welcomed—albeit very dryly and in the full knowledge that there is not one. Due to Lennon's own political indecision—as exemplified through the much debated "you can count me out, in" line—the overall spirit of the song seems to stop short of outright rejection, but it is clear that a sense of being disillusioned with disillusion is being conveyed through what is another classic Beatles melody. In stark contrast, the band also added an unplanned free-form coda to the song with Lennon substituting his calm vocals for feral screams and shouts. An array of extra overdubs was also added to this section as well as being further embellished by the input of Lennon's new partner and avant-garde artist Yoko Ono, thus creating the fabled sonic collage "Revolution 9." This companion track obviously documented the Beatles in their most experimental mode to date, and, initially at least, Lennon justified this unfathomable eight-minute interlude as being an aural representation of the May 1968 riots, although in later years, it was a claim from which he distanced himself.

Although both tracks would appear later in the year as part of the Beatles' eponymous double-release (predominately referred to as *The White Album* in reference to the featureless cover), Lennon became frustrated when the rest of the bandmates disagreed with his idea to release "Revolution 1" as a single, feeling it to be too slow. Subsequently, Lennon returned to the song in July and led his colleagues into recording a more powerful, more decisive, and, of course, a noticeably faster sequel entitled "Revolution." The argument over which of the two versions had the upper hand musically may have been entirely down to the personal taste of the listener, but this later re-recording was certainly the definitive version in terms of Lennon voicing his distrust of left-wing radicalism. Dominated by fuzzy guitars being pinned down by a surprisingly sturdy beat provided by Starr, "Revolution" is characterized by a purposeful energy and a more decisive lyrical sentiment. When responding to the idea of destruction, "Revolution 1" offers a noncommittal "out, in" hinting at a sense of hesitancy from the narrator, but in the new version, the same dilemma is greeted with a firm "out." The vocal (recorded by Lennon standing up this time) also has a jeering quality in its tone, helping to subtly critique the counterculture for its confused aims and unproductive methods. The narrator is clearly not presenting any kind of alternative approach for would-be insurgents, and so each verse ends with a whimsically upbeat section in which the narrator offers an apolitical assurance that things will be "alright."

It was this later version that the world got to hear first when it was issued as a B-side to the "Hey Jude" single in August 1968. The prospect of any new Beatles material was always eagerly awaited and backed with plenty of critical approval, so it was no surprise to see the single hit No. 1 in both the United States and the United Kingdom. Yet the way in which the band appeared to be mocking parts of its audience on "Revolution" riled many fans as McCartney, in particular, had feared. Because of the song's dismissive attitude toward using Chairman Mao as an inspiration, the New Left regarded "Revolution" with contempt, feeling that Lennon's wealth and fame had made it easier for him to recoil from the political influence he had the potential to wield. The fact that so many of his contemporaries, such as the Rolling Stones, were now using the platform they had to communicate messages of solidarity and social action isolated Lennon even further. Incensed by his apparent lack of conviction, the jazz singer and ardent civil rights activist Nina Simone even went so far as to write a direct rebuttal (included on her 1969 album *To Love Somebody*) that not only bore the same title, but was even divided into separate parts just like the Beatles' composition.

Although "Revolution" appeared to fly in the face of youth politics at the time, its protest against protest was not rooted in any kind of burgeoning neoconservatism on Lennon's part. Instead it reflected his growing commitment to achieving new states of harmony through a consistently positive and peaceful attitude rather than sporadic acts of anger and anarchism. Following the release of both "Revolution" and "Revolution 1," it was a standpoint that Lennon had to reiterate time and time again.

> I can't understand how highly-educated people, middle-class mainly, are so unaware as to think the game is really down to street fighting . . . I've said this a million times, all revolutions produce status quo or imitation, you know, like Russia and France and Britain, we've all had our revolutions and where is it? It is exactly the same, because the people's minds are the same . . . So if someone could show me one that

has worked then it might turn me a bit. I'd say, "All right, that's the way to do it", then turn the place upside down. But there isn't one.[3]

Both he and Ono made a point of distancing themselves from the front lines of confrontation, most notably through their two week-long "Bed-Ins" for peace in Amsterdam and Montreal during 1969. Intended as nonviolent protests against war and the promotion of social change, John and Yoko invited the world's press to their hotel rooms in the hope of publicizing their pleas. It was during the latter of the two week-long events that Lennon recorded the antiwar anthem "Give Peace a Chance"—later released as a single under the guise of the Plastic Ono Band.

The legacy of both versions of "Revolution" stems not so much from the musical finesse of the song, but the attitude that informs it. For Lennon to take issue with the instigators of revolt at a time when the counterculture consensus seemed overwhelmingly in favor of righteously aggressive behavior was certainly going against the tide—not to mention against some of the band's fans. But before long, many extremist tactics were indeed found to be wanting. The student uprisings in Germany and France during the summer of 1968 had been quelled well before either version of "Revolution" had even been released, and while events in Europe had been the primary inspiration for Lennon, the track's air of suspicion toward violence under the guise of revolution would also be proven right in the United States particularly when widespread rioting at the Democratic Convention in Chicago during August left the American counterculture struggling for credibility. Not only did these efforts from the New Left run aground at the time, "Tiananmen Square, the ignominious collapse of Soviet communism and the fact that most of his radical persecutors of 1968–70 now work in advertising have belatedly served to confirm [Lennon's] original instincts."[4] In that sense, Lennon may have been justified in critiquing the methods and motivations of the more extreme left-wingers operating at the heart of Western unrest. But that did not necessarily make "Revolution" a sacred text either, for the song's overly hopeful belief that everything would be "alright" one way or another did not ring even remotely true. His critics may have ended up in advertising, but ironically "Revolution" was not far behind. In 1987 (seven years after Lennon's murder in New York City), the song was used to soundtrack a television commercial commissioned by Nike with the proceeds being scooped up by Michael Jackson who by that time had purchased all publishing rights to the Beatles' back catalog.

Artist: James Brown

Song: "Say It Loud—I'm Black and I'm Proud"

Songwriters: James Brown and Alfred Ellis

Album: *Say It Loud—I'm Black and I'm Proud*

Label: King Records

1968

James Brown had a profile that surpassed any other black artist during the 1960s, but following the assassination of Martin Luther King Jr. in 1968, the singer's ability to calm the rage of black America made it clear that he wielded a power beyond the music world, too. With "Say It Loud—I'm Black and I'm Proud," Brown used his all-encompassing influence to deliver one of the ultimate expressions of racial pride. Not only did it help unite his fellow African Americans at the time of release, it still remains a clarion call for empowerment to this day.

James Brown in concert. Toward the end of the 1960s, he became the most important black man in America, both onstage and off.
Courtesy of Photofest.

In many ways, the unparalleled artistic success of James Brown as a black American man throughout the 1950s and 1960s made him a part of the civil rights movement just by default. For those left disenfranchised on the grounds of race, Brown represented a vision of possibility and empowerment particularly in light of his extremely destitute beginnings. Born into abject poverty in North Carolina in May 1933, the boy who would come to be known as the "Godfather of Soul" learned his first musical lessons inside a brothel run by his aunt. As a child, Brown would turn his hand to almost anything in an attempt to earn money, including dancing, washing cars, shining shoes, and even picking cotton, but these honest pursuits eventually gave way to riskier methods of procurement during later years. At the age of 16, he was sentenced to be imprisoned for almost as many years as he had lived for the crime of armed robbery, but an early release was granted, and in 1953, Brown set about using his liberty more productively. Initially, boxing and baseball provided him with potential careers, but an injury led to music becoming the most prominent factor in Brown's life, and in the shape of local gospel bandleader Bobby Byrd, he found a perfect mentor. Brown took up a place in Byrd's band the Gospel Starlighters, but due to Brown's increasing influence, the two gradually drifted toward a more forthright and populist R&B sound culminating in the release of the hugely successful debut single "Please, Please,

Please" in 1956. By that time, Brown had become the focal point, so the band was now billed as James Brown and the Famous Flames.

It would be another three years before the band would score another hit with "Try Me," but Brown developed something approaching a musical Midas touch afterward, and his scintillating live show quickly became a must-see. Filled with eye-watering leg splits, lightning-fast dance steps, and the now infamous signature scream, it solidified his reputation as a premier performer of the time. By 1963, the early fame that Brown experienced in the South had spread across the entire nation thanks to the spectacular success of the *Live at the Apollo* album, which would eventually hit No. 2 on the American Billboard chart. It was the moment that signified Brown transcending the lines of social race segregation and becoming a black icon both recognized and admired by many white Americans.

During the same year, Martin Luther King Jr. was also making a similar journey into these previously uncharted territories of black heroism. King had been a central figure in the civil rights movement from its very beginning most famously when he led the Montgomery Bus Boycott following the arrest of Rosa Parks in 1955 for refusing to give up her seat for a white passenger. King went on to be instrumental in setting up the Southern Christian Leadership Conference organization that promoted nonviolent measures of civil disobedience in the attempt to achieve the ultimate goal of race reforms and social equality. Although the movement gathered momentum throughout subsequent years, it was not until the March on Washington for Jobs and Freedom in August 1963 that the cause for civil rights gained a genuine national platform. Boosted by the attendance of around a quarter of a million protestors and the added attraction of such celebrities as Bob Dylan, Sidney Poitier, and Marlon Brando all lending their personal support, King delivered the legendary "I have a dream" speech in front of the Lincoln Memorial. His words were also beamed into the nation's homes via television and radio. Less than a year later, King looked on as President Lyndon Baines Johnson signed the Civil Rights Act of 1964 into existence and discrimination on the basis of race was finally made illegal under American law.

The everyday battle for equality still needed to be fought and while King continued to galvanize African Americans in a political sphere with his stately persona and inspiring rhetoric, Brown did the same on cultural and social plains with his continued musical innovations and an incomparable superstar status. The incredible position of influence held by both men in the black community was virtually unsurpassed and would be demonstrated as such through the dramatic chain of events that ran through 1968—beginning with King's assassination at a motel in Memphis on April 4. The following night, Brown had a performance scheduled to take place in Boston, but the wave of rioting and race violence that had spread across many major American cities in the wake of King's shooting placed the show under the threat. At the 11th hour, the city's mayor elected not only to go ahead with the gig, but also to broadcast it live on television under the knowledge that black Americans could not resist watching a James Brown concert. During the typically frenzied show, Brown made several between-song calls for calm, and the drastically reduced incidents of disorder reported throughout the city that night suggested that a huge number of the members of the audience were answering his pleas. The next night, Brown continued to preach for peace over the radio in Washington, D.C., and once again, the worst-case scenarios were averted.

A few weeks later when the disruption had finally waned, Brown accepted an invitation to a state dinner at the White House where President Johnson offered his personal thanks for helping quell the rioting, but domestic dissent among the black population was not the only problem that the government faced. In Vietnam, the sizable proportion of African American troops making up the ever-increasing U.S. presence had long complained of marginalization even though military service supposedly offered a more egalitarian life. Having witnessed the James Brown–effect at home, Johnson approved a plan to have the Godfather of Soul play a week-long tour of the region in June, knowing that such an appearance would help boost the morale of black soldiers and would certainly be gratefully received by a number of white troops, too. Brown's unprecedented popularity was reflected in the need to play anything up to three shows a day, all of which were performed before darkness and, therefore, during the most intense periods of heat. The final show took place in front of a crowd that Brown's bassist Tim Drummond estimated to be around the 40,000 mark—a sight that he likened to "the Hollywood Bowl."[5]

It was clear during this mountainous peak in his popularity that while Brown essentially remained a singer, he was revered as something much greater. Now that King had been slain, African Americans looked to him more than ever for entertainment, for inspiration, and for a message. The avoidance of overtly political language within his musical output had helped Brown curate the large white audience that was vital for a pop artist to succeed, but in this period of intense doubt, disharmony, and upheaval, it was time to give his brothers and sisters something unambiguous under which to unite. Just weeks after returning from Vietnam, Brown sat in a Los Angeles hotel room in the middle of the night watching another dispiriting TV report on the latest incidents of black crime reported in the local area. After voicing an annoyance to his manager, Charles Bobbit, Brown scrawled the lyrics to a new song called "Say It Loud—I'm Black and I'm Proud" on two napkins in a period of barely half an hour. He then impatiently summoned the by-now-slumbering Bobbit to book a studio for the band to record the new track and demanded that he also find a group of school children to assist with vocals. Despite the ungodly hour at which it was conceived, "Say It Loud—I'm Black and I'm Proud" emerged as a strutting yet highly dignified song of self-assertion that helped to reestablish black America's ultimate goal of equality.

Naturally, the firm sociopolitical standpoint was underlined with the kind of rhythmic flair that all of James Brown's fans had long enjoyed. The song's tone is celebratory from the onset thanks to drummer Clyde Stubblefield's tight funk beat and a selection of trumpets that are heard throughout playing motifs that beam with an almost regal pride. As with so much of Brown's finest work, "Say It Loud—I'm Black and I'm Proud" was made to be danced to, but his more cautious and restrained vocal (the infamous JB scream is deliberately held back for the duration) denotes the more serious message contained within. The fact that each verse is delivered as though Brown is making a speech is significant for he is clearly issuing a direct address for each listener to understand and internalize. But despite the song's racially specific title, Brown endeavors to make his concerns palatable for everyone during each verse—regardless of ethnicity.

The opening lines dismiss hearsay about black people becoming malicious or having aspirations beyond their social status before explaining that these are merely perceived transgressions in the fight for equality that, of course, should be a right, not a dream. Following on from this point, Brown voices frustration at centuries of subjugation and continually having to work for the other people before stating the black population's intent to become self-reliant like all humans. The potential consequences of attempting to reach these levels of independence are worth paying as Brown defiantly and repeatedly states that black people would rather "die on their feet" than live on their knees. However, the most popular and memorable aspect of "Say It Loud—I'm Black and I'm Proud" remains its infectiously simple and yet gloriously inspiring chorus that was ironically recorded with a group of mainly white and Asian children from suburban Los Angeles.

In September 1968, the single gained a release in the form of "Say It Loud—I'm Black and I'm Proud (pt 1)" (the full version would be released in 1969 on the album of the same name), but even this edited-for-radio version soon became recognized as an "anthem of self-worth"[6] for black America. Despite Brown's fear that it would alienate his white audience, the song's moderate levels of protestation appeared to tap into a far-reaching sense of injustice and it climbed to No. 1 on the R&B charts and No. 10 on the mainstream charts—a placing he would not surpass until 1985. As the 1960s drew to a close, the civil rights movement was beginning to splinter into many different factions varying from those who remained loyal to Martin Luther King Jr.'s pledge of nonviolent protest to more militant factions, such as the Black Panthers. But this was a piece of music from which all black people could derive a sense of unity and in doing so "helped the movement reach critical mass."[7] James Brown's ability to galvanize an entire race with his art was something that no political leader could match at the time, and it was not lost on the American media. *Look* magazine—a popular lifestyle publication of the era—ran a picture of Brown on the cover early in 1969 and asked the question "Is This the Most Important Black Man in America?"[8] The events of the previous 12 months indicated strongly that he certainly was.

The importance of Brown himself had long since been reduced to a level of firm and unwavering respect in the years before his death in 2006, but "Say It Loud—I'm Black and I'm Proud" continues to be regarded with an altogether greater reverence. Critically, it is firmly installed as a musical marvel not least through *Rolling Stone* magazine's 2004 list of the 500 Greatest Rock 'n' Roll Songs of All Time in which it appeared at No. 305. But perhaps more impressive was the way it changed America's racial vocabulary by differentiating the word "black" from lesser terms of reference.

A colored is a very frightened-to-death Afro-American. A negro is one that makes it in the system, and he wants to be white. A nigger, he's loud and boisterous, wants to be seen. Nobody likes a nigger. A black man has pride. He wants to build, he wants to make his race mean something. Wants to have a culture and art forms. And he's not prejudiced. I am a black American man.[9]

The very title itself has passed into African American phraseology and continues to be a firm assertion of pride over prejudice that generation after generation of black people will continue to reference long into the future. In that sense, the long-term impact of "Say It Loud—I'm Black and I'm Proud" is difficult to calculate due to a continual accumulation, but it already stands alone through its slick, stylish, and succinct representation of an entire race of people.

Artist: Sly & the Family Stone

Song: "Don't Call Me Nigger, Whitey"

Songwriter: Sylvester Stewart

Album: *Stand!*

Label: Epic Records

1969

When they first came to prominence in the late 1960s, Sly & the Family Stone were a glorious vision of human unity, both in their combination of white/black/male/female band members, as well as their ability to weave the optimistic spirit of the era into their music. But despite their multigenre and multiracial appeal, the group could see the dream of integration fading in a country that was becoming more divided by the day. It was a breakdown of race relations the bandmates documented in "Don't Call Me Nigger, Whitey," but with the glum knowledge that even they could probably do nothing about it.

If there was one band in the 1960s that seemed to represent the potential of music to racially unify America, it had to be Sly & the Family Stone. The group's first lineup came together in San Francisco during 1966 and revolved firmly around front man Sylvester Stewart, who was already a virtual music industry veteran despite barely being in his mid-20s. Stewart had begun performing as an infant alongside three of his siblings as part of a gospel singing group called the Stewart Four before moving on to a doo-wop outfit called the Viscaynes and even releasing some of his own solo work by the start of the 1960s. As the decade wore on, Stewart found himself at the center of San Francisco's blooming psychedelic rock scene thanks partly to landing the job of in-house producer for the Autumn Records label. At the same time, he expanded his tastes even further through a DJ slot at a radio station in nearby Oakland where he would indiscriminately play anything from the Beatles to James Brown. Stewart's broad musical schooling and his exposure to all kinds of ethnicities fueled a desire to form an interracial, intergender, intergenre band that would incorporate rock, soul, funk, R&B, and the many other things he had seen and heard. As a result, Stewart took the stage name of Sly Stone and initially enlisted his brother Freddie on guitar (his sister Rosemary would later join as vocalist), bassist Larry Graham, drummer Gregg Errico, saxophonist Jerry Martini, and trumpeter Cynthia Robison to form Sly & the Family Stone. With the Civil Rights Bill of 1964 only two years old by the time they started playing their first gigs, Sly & the Family Stone were still a radical sight in the world of pop music regardless of their harmonious moniker. But that deliberately integrated lineup coupled with the group's multifaceted sound suddenly made it look as though anything was possible both socially and artistically.

Even with its startlingly original tinges of psychedelic soul, Sly & the Family Stone's first album, *A Whole New Thing* (1967), turned out to be a flop, and the record label Epic advised Sly Stone to simplify his material a little in the hope of making it appeal

Sly & the Family Stone as pictured on the cover of *Rolling Stone*, 1970. Clockwise from top, Larry Graham, Freddie Stone, Gregg Errico, Sly Stone, Rose Stone, Cynthia Robinson, and Jerry Martini.
Courtesy of Photofest.

to the ever-powerful radio programmers. This advice paid off almost instantly when the group returned in early 1968 with the unrelentingly upbeat stomp of "Dance to the Music," which became the group's first Top 10 single in both the United States and the United Kingdom. However, the change in fortune was short-lived and the group's subsequent albums *Dance to the Music* and *Life* (both released in 1968) failed to capitalize on this first glimpse of commercial success. Once again, Sly Stone refocused his efforts and drilled his band sternly while staying mindful of what music fans of the day were responding to. During recording sessions for the fourth album, he would even take early versions of the songs to a nearby disco in San Francisco, observe crowd reactions, and then return to the studio to make adjustments accordingly. It was a technique that paid off handsomely when Sly & the Family Stone released "Everyday

People" in March 1969—a feel-good anthem of equality, humanism, and musical togetherness that seemed to reflect the utopian spirit for which the group stood. This would be reinforced briefly when Sly & the Family Stone stole the show at the Woodstock Festival in 1969 with a dazzling late night set that once again gave credence to the idea of music contributing to a greater interracial unity.

"Everyday People" was followed by the release of *Stand!* (1969), which also won the adoration of critics and fans thanks mainly to the continued sense of harmony that such songs as "I Want to Take You Higher," "You Can Make It If You Try," and "Stand!" all seemed to exude. But hidden away among that musical euphoria was a rogue track called "Don't Call Me Nigger, Whitey" (not released as a single) that may have appeared to fit in with the era's righteous and progressive spirit on the surface, but actually hinted at its slow unraveling. It was not a process that was especially difficult to spot in everyday life either, for the hopeful atmosphere that surrounded the signing of the Civil Rights Bill of 1964 was dissipating fast. The death of Martin Luther King Jr. in 1968 had left the nonviolent arm of the civil rights movement in disarray and sparked nationwide race riots in just about every major city. Meanwhile, the more militant Black Power advocates seemed to be pushing in the direction of African American separatism instead of a racially integrated United States. Partly as a result of this standpoint, such groups as the Black Panthers (formed in Oakland, just a few miles away from Sly & the Family Stone's San Franciscan base) found their activities rigorously countered by American authorities with such prominent members as Huey P. Newton and Bobby Seale being imprisoned in 1968 and 1969, respectively. In light of such growing racial distrust blighting the cause for social reform in America, the three days of peace and music at Woodstock seemed even more fleeting than they sounded.

It is this receding level of effectiveness in creating unity that "Don't Call Me Nigger, Whitey" reflects ominously in the song's lyrics, structure, and composition. There is no time wasted in getting to the issue; the song begins with a panicky two-note keyboard melody and what sounds like a psychedelic wah-wah guitar riff[10] before the chorus finds the bandmates singing the title phrase in an annoyed unison. But rather than merely being a rebuttal of abuse from the perspective of a black person, a white narrator is then heard angrily inverting the racial slurs into the response "don't call me whitey, nigger." It is a menacing face-off between two unpleasant characters, backed by some aptly foreboding fills from the horn section, but Rose Stone then interjects with a third perspective—that of the worried onlooker. She despairingly recounts hearing such arguments repeated across the country, but for all the bluster neither side is helping to advance racial integration in the slightest. After a repetition of the intro, the chorus makes a swift return as the two protagonists trade slurs again. The tense deadlock, however, remains firmly in place, and the band ambles into an extended instrumental section laced with more bluesy wah-wah sounds. After a minute and a half, the two voices return for yet another exchange, but again, the argument is circular and without conclusion. The switch between instrumental and chorus continues until the final section in which the whole song quickens and picks up a chaotic edge. But even after that, there is still no resolution either to the song or to the quarrel within it and "Don't Call Me Nigger, Whitey" stumbles to an anticlimactic end—a disappointingly apt metaphor for the movement toward integration itself.

Ultimately, this is a track that goes nowhere, but that is entirely the point. The repetitious lyrics portray the growing polarization of the U.S. population, and the circular nature of the song's musical construction points to the impending racial stalemate across the country. And who better to voice his observation of this scenario than Sly Stone? He was, after all, an artist who had purposefully placed himself between white and black culture in one of the country's more progressive cities, helping to incorporate them both into the broad scope and forward-thinking music of his band. If the sentiment of "Don't Call Me Nigger, Whitey" was what he saw developing from the supposedly integrated vantage point of San Francisco, then multicultural unity in the rest of America obviously had some way to go. But among the sanguine flow of *Stand!*, this was a subtlety that was almost too well disguised for anyone to pick up on. The album sold steadily, eventually shifting over 2 million copies and peaking at No. 13 in the U.S. album charts, but there were few people buying it to reflect on the hints that "Don't Call Me Nigger, Whitey" was dropping. Nevertheless, it was undoubtedly the point at which Sly & the Family Stone "dispense with good vibes and tell it like it is"[11] whether anyone wanted to hear it or not.

As the 1960s turned to the 1970s, it was becoming clear that the racial stalemate was solidifying. The Black Power movement splintered badly partly due to its inability to replace such leaders as Newton and Seale, while racial tension still manifested itself in continued flash points, such as the killing of two black youths at Jackson State, Mississippi, in 1970 following a civil rights demonstration. The era of progressivism appeared to be giving way to decadence and a stagnant division, and nowhere was this more apparent than in Sly & the Family Stone themselves. The group retreated to a giant house in Bel Air during 1970 and 1971 with the intention of recording a fifth album, but the sessions dragged on endlessly as the bandmates became embroiled in cocaine with Sly Stone in particular ending up almost incapacitated through his personal predilection for PCP (phencyclidine). The interracial unity of the band also began to show wear in this environment with members of the Black Panthers trying to convince Stone to get rid of the band's white contingent of Martini, Errico, and manager David Kapralik. By the time the album *There's a Riot Goin' On* did appear in 1971, the band's dynamic had dwindled to the point where Graham and Sly Stone suspected each of being involved in a plot to kill the other. Moreover, the album's muddy and sinister sound reflected the social and political apathy that had infiltrated American life. One of the only musical links between the darkness of *There's a Riot Goin' On* and the comparative light of *Stand!* was clearly "Don't Call Me Nigger, Whitey," and in retrospect, the song's hopelessness seemed to make so much more sense.

During Sly Stone's moments of clarity, he would release both solo work and albums with various incarnations of the Family during the 1970s before eventually becoming a recluse. But the legacy they left during the peak of their powers in the late 1960s is twofold and, bizarrely, almost entirely opposite. On the one hand, the vision of the bandmates in their most radical and upbeat songs (as captured on the more buoyant parts of *Stand!*) leaves an enduring image of a new phase of racial unity being ushered in. In contrast, the far less optimistic "Don't Call Me Nigger, Whitey" captures a protest at how divided black and white people had become by the end of the decade and sheds an unkind light on American race relations in the time since, too. In 1980, massive race riots in Miami left three dead following the acquittal of four police officers who were accused of the manslaughter of a black motorcyclist. In 1992, 55 people were killed in Los Angeles after the similar acquittal of officers accused of beating black motorist Rodney King. As recently as 2001, the city of Cincinnati suffered widespread rioting and a high-profile business boycott following the shooting of a black teenager by police. Given these reoccurring flash points and ongoing racial distrust, the developing impasse that Sly & the Family Stone captured in 1969 with "Don't Call Me Nigger, Whitey" still appears to be in place. It is also hardly a surprise to see that the track now rates as one of the band's most critically celebrated works thanks to an absence of "the self-satisfied righteousness that makes a fair amount of sixties music difficult to listen to today."[12]

Artist: The Stooges

Song: "1969"

Songwriters: James Osterberg, Scott Asheton, Ron Asheton, and Dave Alexander

Album: *The Stooges*

Label: Elektra Records

1969

Toward the late 1960s, America seemed to be at war with its own youth. A generation gap had clearly opened up with the increasingly radical counterculture on one side and a more conservative political administration on the other, but despite this polarization, the Stooges had no care for either camp. As the country descended into violence and disorder, the continually bored Detroit bandmates offered "1969" as a disengaged shrug of protest at everything around them—including themselves.

The so-called Summer of Love seemed to miss Detroit. As America came to grips with the idea that drug experimentation, sexual freedom, and progressive social thinking would help create a nationwide hippy utopia akin to that being established in San Francisco during 1967, the motor capital of the world was noticeably bereft of such harmony. Racked with segregation, economic decline, and resentment at what was perceived to be racist policing, the city exploded into violence during July. The central incident that triggered rioting occurred when an after-hours club located in a black neighborhood was raided by officers who attempted to arrest everyone present. Enraged at the sight, a group of onlookers began smashing the windows of a nearby clothing store, sparking a wave of violence that lasted for five days, required the deployment of 8,000 National Guardsmen, and cost 43 lives. It was certainly a far removed sight from the dictums of peace and love.

Musically, the Detroit scene was also an antidote to much of the material emerging from the West Coast. Aside from the Motown label, which was at the time reaching a clear peak of its hit-producing powers, one of the most highly regarded rock bands in

The Stooges looking bored as usual, 1969. (L–R): Scott Asheton, Ron Asheton, Dave Alexander, and Iggy Pop.
Courtesy of Photofest.

the area was a rambunctious rock 'n' roll outfit named the MC5 (an abbreviation for the Motor City 5). At the time of these disturbances, the group was already a highly regarded local band known for its exhilarating live shows and radical political convictions, which were partly fostered by the ongoing tensions in Detroit. As the MC5 gradually built a national profile to the point of signing a record deal with Elektra Records in 1968, the five-piece band developed a deliberately inflammatory edge to its image and aligned itself to subversive left-wing causes under the direction of its manager—the poet and well-known activist John Sinclair. Later that same year, Sinclair (along with his wife, Leni, and Lawrence Plamondon) would establish the White Panther Party, an organization with a political manifesto and 10-point program designed to emulate the goals of the Black Panther Party, which had taken the civil rights movement into more radical realms since beginning operations in 1966. One of the many things advocated by the White Panther Party was the rioting of 1967, which it argued was justified action under such social duress.

Despite their kinship with Sinclair and the MC5, their similarly dismissive attitude toward the hippy movement, and a close proximity to Detroit's civic disquiet both before and after July 1967, the Stooges somehow picked up virtually none of that insurrectionary edge. Although actually based in the nearby town of Ann Arbor, the city of Detroit was very much a second home and played a vital part in their rise. The band had been formed around James Osterberg, who had previously spent time drumming in a local garage-rock band called the Iguanas, from which he also acquired his nickname of "Iggy" (later extrapolating the name to become Iggy Pop). After they split, his love of the blues led Iggy to form the Stooges alongside brothers Ron and Scott Asheton (guitar and drums, respectively) while enlisting their friend Dave Alexander to play bass. The quartet was initially billed as the Psychedelic Stooges for its first show in October 1967 (supporting the MC5 in Detroit), but soon shortened its name to the Stooges and developed a primitive, stripped-down rock sound. Meanwhile, Iggy quickly became notorious for his maniacal on-stage performance, which could feature anything from insane acts of self-mutilation to downright illegal exhibitions of his genitalia.

Although the Stooges were hated by many audiences, the MC5 remained huge patrons and regarded them as a baby-brother band. When Danny Fields from Elektra Records came to Detroit to sign MC5 in 1968, the bandmates immediately recommended the Stooges to him, and he was suitably impressed to offer the boys from Ann Arbor a deal, too. As they moved toward releasing a debut album, the turmoil that ravaged Detroit had seemingly spread across the United States. The specter of race rioting continued to grow—escalating massively in the immediate wake of the assassination of Martin Luther King Jr. in April 1968. Gay rights were becoming an issue, particularly after the Stonewall riots during June 1969, which occurred during another clubfooted police raid of a bar in New York City. However, the most pressing issue was the country's anti-Vietnam sentiment that was manifesting itself in increasingly violent clashes. The disquiet reported at Columbia University in April 1968 and at Harvard University in April 1969 was typical of this, but such incidents were spreading across broader public spheres, too. One of the most notorious occurred at the Democratic Convention in Chicago during August 1968, which was besieged by protestors with all kinds of grievances—not least the MC5 that fired up the crowd with a typically raucous performance.

But despite—or perhaps because of—the prominence of these liberal and left-wing issues in the media and the increasingly disruptive manner in which they were being addressed, mainstream politics were simultaneously experiencing a swing to the Right. For all its apparent progressivism and position as the countercultural center of the United States, California was actually under the conservative governorship of Ronald Reagan. His election in 1967 had been due in no small part to a promise to crack down on dissension and amorality in the youth culture across the state.

Furthermore, Richard Nixon returned from the political wilderness to win the 1968 presidential election partly by focusing his efforts on the conservative electorate that frowned on these frequent incidents of disobedience—the "silent majority" as they would be termed. The generation gap was clear, the rift in ideologies was obvious, and the battle lines had been drawn.

It was not that the Stooges were oblivious to such an apocalyptic atmosphere; it was simply that they were largely unmoved by it. They lived anarchic private lives that are now famed for their levels of debauchery, drug-fueled indulgence, and sexual abandon; despite that, the Stooges still managed to represent a state of terminal boredom and apolitical idleness in an era in which youthful agitation was almost inescapable. In a time when us versus them appeared to sum up so many conflicts, these four men were in neither camp. Even when it came to band business, they were so unmotivated that a large proportion of their self-titled debut released in August 1969 (and produced by ex-Velvet Underground viola player John Cale) was made up of songs that had been written ad hoc. "They were such lazy bums ... they wouldn't make an effort to be articulate or decent to people,"[13] recalled Iggy of his bandmates in 1988. That general disconnection with society and lack of inclination to do virtually *anything* was voiced best in the album's opening track "1969," which stood as a complaint of boredom delivered not with rage but an insouciant shrug and an almost moronically simple vocabulary—factors that made it all the more authentic.

A lackadaisical drum intro starts the track with Ron Asheton adding a swirling wah-wah guitar sound over the top. The band then illustrated a rudimentary take on the Bo Diddley beat (a distinctive rhythm created by the blues legend), which pervades through the rest of the song. The opening lines salute 1969, which was already proving to be a momentous year by the time the album was released, but instead of acknowledging any of the cultural, political, and social upheavals taking place across the United States, what follows is the indifferent assessment that it is simply another year of meaningless existence and tedium. There seems to be no sense of the bandmates creating any excitement for themselves either. The second verse merely relays the passing of time through the fact that the narrator experienced precious little fun from being 21 years old (traditionally a time of carefree celebration) and greets the prospect of being 22 with the less-than-enthusiastic cry of "oh my and a boo-hoo."

Another repetition of the first verse follows, and barely halfway through the song's four-minute running time, "1969" does away with lyrics in favor of an extended guitar solo, interspersed with more short refrains heralding this turning point in American history with a sullen attitude. Only in the final yell does Iggy inject his vocal with an audible energy and anguish, but it is clearly a fleeting emotion. The song seems to accept this state of suspension with an undercurrent of pleasure, which, as writer (and future Patti Smith guitarist) Lenny Kaye pointed out in his review of the album, hinted that the Stooges actually "enjoy their rootlessness, almost sinking gratefully into the mud surrounding them, embracing the inevitable decadence to follow."[14] Whether balking or basking in that boredom, "1969" had no care for anything that involved effort or engagement. At a time of such widespread agitation, this was quite a unique statement of separation.

Naturally, the album was met with critical dismissal and commercial failure, and the subsequent release of "1969" as the flipside of the "I Wanna Be Your Dog" single did little to change that. The same lack of interest would follow for the Stooges groundbreaking 1970 album *Funhouse;* after an extended hiatus, they reconvened (partly through encouragement from David Bowie) with an altered lineup as Iggy and the Stooges for *Raw Power* in 1973. But by that time, Iggy, in particular, was addled with heroin addiction, and by 1975 he checked himself into a psychiatric institute. Although not quite as spectacular in comparison to the singer's mental breakdown, the counterculture's descent into decadence became evident as philanthropic aims began to dissipate under internal flaws and external suppression. The hippy dream was found to be wanting before 1969 was over, especially in light of the chaos that ensued at the giant Rolling Stones' gig at Altamont Speedway, California, where numerous outbreaks of violence seemed to prove the idea of an alternative utopia being ultimately unrealistic. Nixon meanwhile honed in on his conservative supporters by identifying them as the silent majority who quietly approved of hard-line suppression tactics against reckless troublemakers rebelling against authority.

But the importance of "1969" and indeed the Stooges' autonomy from all that surrounded them would become apparent when the first waves of punk rock began to develop on both sides of the Atlantic during the mid-1970s. Such bands as the Ramones idolized the Stooges, but the British contingent, in particular, was much more forceful in its vocalization of boredom and dissatisfaction with the hierarchy of the world around it (see the Sex Pistols for one example). In seeding this vociferous musical rejection of established pop culture and societal norms, the Stooges were without doubt years ahead of their time whether they cared or not.

Artist: Creedence Clearwater Revival

Song: "Fortunate Son"

Songwriter: John Fogerty

Album: *Willy and the Poor Boys*

Label: Fantasy Records

1969

As the Vietnam War raged in the late 1960s and more U.S. citizens continued to be called into the army, Creedence Clearwater Revival singer John Fogerty ruefully observed how the privileged and politically connected few could avoid serving their country abroad, while the majority of American youngsters had no choice. It was a feeling of injustice that he put succinctly into "Fortunate Son," which became a classic track of the era and continues to cause embarrassment for those who seemed to have dodged the draft through unfair means.

There was nothing fortunate about how Creedence Clearwater Revival became one of the most successful American bands of the late 1960s; it took almost 10 years, two name changes, and a slew of unnoticed recordings before the quartet would even register on the country's musical radar. The core members of Doug Clifford (drums), Stu Cook (piano), John Fogerty (guitar/vocals), and his older brother Tom Fogerty (guitar/vocals) originally gravitated together in 1959 when most of the band was still attending high school in El Cerrito, California. Appearing initially as Tom Fogerty

Creedence Clearwater Revival (L–R): Stu Cook, Tom Fogerty, Doug Clifford, and John Fogerty.
Courtesy of Photofest.

and the Blue Velvets, the quartet played regularly around the Bay Area before adopting the preposterous moniker of the Golliwogs (lifted from the racially insensitive child's rag doll) in 1964. Despite having a less than appealing name and enjoying minimal exposure, the band did maintain a prolific recording rate for the next two years until being put on ice when Clifford and the younger Fogerty were selected for the Vietnam draft. The conflict had yet to escalate to the level that would create widespread derision toward the end of the decade, but the threat of conscription was still a very real one for young American men. For his part, John Fogerty was able to avoid front-line combat and instead spent a six-month period in the Army Reserve Unit serving in domestic forts for the duration. By the time the relieved singer returned to the band, he had taken over the main song-writing duties from Tom, Cook had switched from piano to bass, and the band was mercifully renamed Creedence Clearwater Revival.

It was then that the years of effort and hard work began to pay off dramatically for the foursome. Their decidedly R&B influences, roots-rock sound, and Fogerty's soulful vocal rasps all led to the misconception that Creedence Clearwater Revival (frequently referred to as CCR or just Creedence for short) hailed from the South. It was also a musical combination that put the band out of sync with the emerging psychedelic scene blossoming around it in San Francisco. Despite that, success befell CCR immediately with the release of its debut single "Susie Q"—a Dale Hawkins cover—which reached No. 11 on the U.S. chart after being released in September

1968. From that point on, Creedence issued a string of stone-cold American rock classics, including the incessantly covered "Proud Mary," the swamp-rock defining "Green River," and the forbidding portents of "Bad Moon Rising"—the latter of which seemed to tie in with the increasingly untenable American involvement in Vietnam. By the time the song reached No. 2 in the summer of 1969, the number of U.S. troops serving in the region had sailed past half a million, and the social patterns of conscriptions were becoming clearly visible.

One of the most popular ways of avoiding the draft had been to enroll in college as it offered exemption, but this tactic often caused a feeling of injustice among members of the working class who were invariably unable to afford further education. Furthermore, the privileged few who had family connections in politically influential circles could also attain sanctuary from conflict. But, it was John Fogerty's observation of this bias in current affairs of the time that riled him more than anything. The marriage of President Nixon's daughter Julie to Dwight David Eisenhower II (former President Dwight David Eisenhower's grandson) in New York in December 1968 had been a suitably lavish affair preceded by bridal showers and shopping sprees and rounded off with a "tea-dance reception in the Grand Ballroom of The Plaza."[15] It was all a far cry from the jungle warfare being experienced thousands of miles away by half a million of their fellow Americans, and Fogerty was less than pleased at the sense of disparity.

> You just had the feeling that none of these people were going to be involved with the war . . . You got the impression that these people got preferential treatment and the whole idea of being born wealthy or being born powerful seemed to be coming to the fore in the late-sixties' confrontation of cultures. I was 23 years old, I think. I was mad at the specter of the ordinary kid who had to serve in an army in a war that he was very much against. Yet the sons of the well-to-do and the powerful didn't have to worry about those things. They were fortunate.[16]

Fueled by this rage, which had also been influenced by his own stint in the service, Fogerty documented his view in a composition called "Fortunate Son," written in just 20 minutes and originally appearing as the flip side of the band's "Down on the Corner" single that was released in September 1969. Commencing with Clifford's firm beat and one of the most instantly recognizable guitar riffs in the entire Creedence catalog, "Fortunate Son" immediately establishes a purposeful pace. The striking tones of Fogerty's voice then pierce through the mix as he begins to deliver the first verse, commenting on the dichotomy of the most prominent flag-wavers who advocate patriotism from an elevated level of authority and importance, but then rely on subordinates in their command to put themselves in the line of fire. It is an obvious allegory of not just modern army life or the unfairness of the Vietnam draft, but arguably the entire history of American warfare. Acknowledging that he is not one of the lucky ones blessed with financial power or political connections, Fogerty bellows out the song's anthemic chorus and central sentiment for the first time, but before it even has time to register with the listener, the song is already striding forward.

Barely taking a breath, the singer launches into an attack on the self-servers who attempt to preserve their wealth from those who may scrutinize it—in this case the tax man. Again, the chorus hammers home a feeling of frustration that these are the privileges bestowed on the few "millionaires' sons" before Fogerty's verbal onslaught is briefly interrupted by the instrumental middle eight complete with another skeletal, yet effective, riff. A final blast of bitterness again takes aim at the escalations of war ordered by those who are always a safe distance away from battle, and the chorus is repeated in raucous fashion until the song fades out. "Fortunate Son" is a perfect example of Creedence Clearwater Revival's ability to write direct and powerful music; in the period of less than 150 seconds, the bandmates have made a serious point, presented it emphatically within the context of an instantly memorable song, and disappeared as quickly as they emerged. With a formula like that, it hardly seems surprising that they were so popular with mainstream media and that "Fortunate Son" joined CCR's list of hits by reaching No. 14 on the U.S. chart.

In such a climate of vehement and, in many cases, violent rejection of America's establishment figures and institutions, it was somewhat inevitable that "Fortunate Son" would become part of that fraternity. As the song peaked in popularity toward the end of 1969, it seemed to be given an added sense of relevance with President Nixon's implementation of a draft lottery to select conscripts supposedly at random. The method involved placing 366 capsules into a jar (one representing every day of the year) and drawing them out one by one. The men of service age born on the day represented by the first capsule to be pulled out (in this case it proved to be September 14) were called to enlist first, while those in the last (June 8) were least likely to be used by the army. Although proposed as fair in theory, it proved to be haphazard in practice if only for the fact that studies of the draw suggested that the capsules were not mixed well enough. Ultimately, it was a process that served only to heighten the continuing sense of resentment and injustice around the draft and the war itself.

But true to the bandmates' lack of musical commonalities with those around them, "Fortunate Son" was not quite the counterculture torch song that many thought it was. Although it shared some of the same views as the band's antiestablishment counterparts, Fogerty's point was rooted more in working-class rage rather than a new generation of radical youth. Thus, it was not so much a political protest as a proletarian one, representing those who still felt an allegiance to their country but were not blinded enough to ignore social bias or to go unquestioningly along with the way America's elected leaders were conducting the war effort. In a time when so many embroiled in the Vietnam question appeared to be either conservative patriots or un-American rebels, "Fortunate Son" spoke to those who were neither, and yet both at the same time.

Creedence would eventually split up almost as fast as it came to prominence. Disputes between the Fogerty brothers led to Tom leaving the band in 1971, placing the first major nail in its coffin. Shortly afterward, John Fogerty insisted that Clifford and Cook share the song-writing burden with him much to the overall detriment of the 1972 album *Mardi Gras*, which suffered critically and commercially. By the following year, the band had broken up, but its five years of existence had left an indelible mark on American rock that remains visible today thanks in no small way to "Fortunate Son." It continues to be a song closely linked to the era's revolts, but the slight sense of misinterpretation has not been helped by some more incongruous uses propagated by Saul Zaentz—the owner of CCR's record label Fantasy who had also retained the lucrative publishing rights from the band's heyday. Most notable of these odd appearances was its employment in a Wrangler jeans advertisement in 2002, which enraged Fogerty for cheapening the message of the song.

Another curious legacy of "Fortunate Son" is how the unnamed targets of its lyrics came to be publicly exposed on the highest political stages in later years. During his ascent to the White House, Bill Clinton was repeatedly accused of seeking preferential treatment from the Arkansas Reserve Officer Training Corps (ROTC) in 1969 so as to shirk full conscription. Meanwhile, the tenure of his successor George W. Bush has been constantly saddled with questions over his suspiciously speedy entry into the National Guard in 1968. Attempting to join this reserve branch of the army was another popular choice with those wanting to avoid combat, and it has been frequently suggested that Bush's admission was aided by the political influence of his father who was already a congressman by that point. Draft dodgers were given an official pardon by President Jimmy Carter in 1977, but the insinuation alone can still be discrediting, especially for such high-ranking figures as Bush and Clinton. Whatever the truth is behind their respective cases, it is highly unlikely that they are the only fortunate sons of the late 1960s to have become embarrassed fathers of the early 21st century.

Artist: **Edwin Starr**

Song: **"War"**

Songwriters: **Barrett Strong and Norman Whitfield**

Album: ***War & Peace***

Label: **Motown Records**

1970

The Motown label had enjoyed numerous chart hits throughout the 1960s thanks to a formulaic system of producing strictly apolitical, feel good pop music that was rarely tampered with. Even with the Vietnam conflict reaching a peak of unpopularity in the United States, owner Berry Gordy Jr. still remained unconvinced about the more serious tone of "War" and feared it might flop. But thanks to Edwin Starr's vocal performance and the simplicity of its antiwar sentiment, the single added to Motown's tally of No. 1 hits and has since become a cross-generational protest anthem.

It was purported to be the Sound of Young America in advertising campaigns, and by the end of the 1960s Motown Records had dozens of billboard chart hits to prove it. Based in Detroit, Michigan—a city with a proud motoring heritage—the label replicated Ford Motor Company's plant production line ethic, but with pop music instead of automobiles. At the helm of the company was Berry Gordy Jr., a veteran of the Korean War who had subsequently returned to the United States and enjoyed some minor success as a songwriter mainly for soul star Jackie Wilson. Eyeing the more lucrative end of the music business, Gordy initially set up Tamla Records in 1959 and then added Motown to his miniempire in 1960, employing the production line ethic he had observed firsthand during a period of employment at the Ford factory.

The two imprints quickly converged, creating the fabled hit factory that would shoot such names as Smokey Robinson & the Miracles, Diana Ross & the Supremes, Martha Reeves & the Vandellas, and Marvin Gaye to national stardom over the next few years. Motown's unashamedly commercial intentions meant that Gordy ran the label with a strictness that mirrored his own upbringing. Artists were groomed and styled to be presentable to a multiracial market, while the music itself was geared explicitly toward accessibility. If anything seemed to be at odds with achieving this mass appeal, Gordy would ruthlessly exercise his power of veto on any proposed release.

As the decade wore on and the sociopolitical turmoil of the Vietnam conflict began to infiltrate popular culture, Gordy was resistant to allowing Motown's artists to become a prominent part of the same trend for fear of jeopardizing commercial interests. But by 1970, he was forced into making a concession to Marvin Gaye who was adamant that his somber composition "What's Going On" be released as a single (see chapter 5 for more on Marvin Gaye). After initially refusing, Gordy relented on account of Gaye's catalog of commercial success and immense artistic pedigree, but the Temptations were allowed no such leeway. Another of Motown's heaviest hitters, the Temptations, had released an album called *Psychedelic Soul* that same year that hid a brooding track, penned by the label's established song-writing team of Barrett Strong and Norman Whitfield called "War." Public feedback on the album had included a noticeable trend of younger listeners singling out the song for praise and requesting its release as a single.

Although "War" did not mention Vietnam directly, its firm sense of anger and bitterness no doubt echoed the emotions of so many young Americans in regard to the conflict. Despite President Nixon's policy of gradual U.S. withdrawal and the subsequent Vietnamization of the war (referred to as the "Nixon Doctrine"), there was still no sense of the conflict being at an end especially with the hugely unpopular draft lottery now forcing more unwilling conscripts into service. Additionally, knowledge of atrocities carried out by U.S. forces, such as the My Lai massacre of 1968 (in which hundreds of villagers were raped, mutilated, and murdered), had begun to emerge, ingraining antiwar sentiment further into the public consciousness. Violent campus-based opposition, in particular, was becoming extremely widespread, but in this respect Gordy still seemed reluctant to reflect the voice of young America in the way his label so famously claimed. Risking the Temptations' lucrative career by issuing such a controversial single proved to be too much of gamble for the Motown boss, but before long he was able to fashion an alternative.

One of the artists bringing up the rear on Motown's roster was Edwin Starr. Born Charles Edwin Hatcher in 1942, Starr returned in 1962 from two years of military service to enjoy only piecemeal success in the music industry thanks to his position in R&B pianist Bill Doggett's band. Frustrated at the lack of personal opportunity being offered to him, he quit in 1965 and signed to another Detroit label, Ric-Tic Records, where he scored a handful of hits before the label was incorporated into Motown after Gordy bought it out. Although he had experienced a lofty position in the pecking order of Ric-Tic, Starr immediately faded into the background among the superstars of Motown and noted how the company functioned under a clear hierarchy—"the

Supremes were royalty and I was carrying the buckets."[17] A Top 10 hit with the track "25 Miles" in 1969 did little to win favor with Gordy, and Starr remained firmly on the periphery—it was for exactly that reason that "War" was given to Starr to re-record as a single. If it flopped with Starr at the helm, Motown would stand to lose a bit-part player who was really with the label only by default. For Gordy, this made much more sense than potentially damaging the big earning credentials of the Temptations, but to maximize its potential as a hit, Whitfield revised his production work on the original. It helped transform the song's sullen, moody spirit and distant military marching calls into a bombastic body of funk-tinged sound, punctuated with huge horn stabs and a multitude of backing singers who all reinforced the lyrical sentiment with gusto. Starr meanwhile added a succession of his own vocal ad libs and James Brown–inspired grunts to underline a sense of frustration. Suddenly, the dignified Temptations track used as virtually a filler on their latest album now resembled a Technicolor statement of universal anguish.

The new version may not have fit Motown's apolitical standpoint too comfortably, but the onslaught of sound certainly reflected the label's aural signature much more closely. Opening with the same ominous drum roll retained from the first version, "War" literally explodes into the instantly memorable chorus that did so much to popularize the song. Whereas many other artists had addressed the same subject in years gone by using satire, pointing out social injustices, and shaming political hypocrisies, this track implements the most basic of human emotions, not least with the narrator's central question and answer—"War! huh, yeah. What is it good for? Absolutely nothing!" A sophisticated rhetoric it certainly is not, but the sheer forcefulness of Starr's vocal performance is more than enough to make an obvious point sound like a revelation. The subsequent sets of lyrics (interspersed with repetitions of the chorus) are similarly simplistic in thought, but devastatingly powerful in execution.

The destruction of innocent lives and the sight of tearful mothers are promised in the first verse, while the second outlines war as being a universal enemy but especially unsettling for the younger generation. It is, after all, this group of people that is not only enlisted to lead the front lines but that will also resist this selection with the greatest ferocity (the draft lottery of 1969 and the increased level of rebellion witnessed across U.S. universities in 1970 were clearly visible testaments to this idea). The obvious statements continue with a lament on how conflict leaves young men embittered and handicapped, while a marginally more sophisticated observation notes how war is allied only to the undertaker and is essentially an insult to the brief gift of life. The final verse issues the by-now-familiar call of peace, but also questions the idea of war being necessary to preserve freedom—a valid query especially in Vietnam, where the cost of helping to defend a foreign country from left-wing rebels was already proving to be greater than any American war where domestic interests appeared to be under threat. As the final repeat of the chorus begins, an eerie rhythm of marching soldiers punctuates the mix until the song fades out, replicating the militaristic tone of the opening drum roll.

The uncomplicated yet emphatic approach worked in a way that could give Gordy no cause for complaint as "War" hit the No. 1 spot on the Billboard Chart in the summer of 1970. Although he remained some way off being regarded as Motown royalty, Starr also earned more kudos for his vocal talent as a result of the success, but the label's continuing belief in creating hits through creative repetition and capitalizing on what was popular led to the release of "Stop the War Now" later in the year. Clearly an inferior derivative of its predecessor (see the sidebar), the track failed to have anything like the impact of "War" and the rallying effect it had on Starr's career was soon lost. Frustrated at Motown's formulaic approach, the singer left the label in 1975, but continued as a popular fixture on the live circuit, particularly in the United Kingdom where he would eventually settle. Despite his continued output, "War" remained the song he was most associated with, and it received numerous revisits from other artists. Among the most famous of these was one by British synth-pop act Frankie Goes to Hollywood that included an elongated version of "War" on its hugely successful debut album *Welcome to the Pleasuredome* in 1984, using the background of the cold war to emphasize the song's contemporary relevance.

However, it was the regular cover by Bruce Springsteen and the E Street Band during their 1985 world tour that would revitalize the song dramatically. A live album entitled *Live/1975–1985* was released in 1986 and compiled some of the group's most notable performances in the 10-year time frame. The version of "War" (recorded in September 1985 in Los Angeles) featured on the album was subsequently released as a Christmas single the same year and duly hit the Top 10. Springsteen had been inspired to sing "War" as a show of disapproval at American intervention in the Central American countries of El Salvador and Nicaragua during the first half of the 1980s. For many opponents, both of these campaigns had some worrying echoes

"STOP THE WAR NOW"

Released shortly after "War" and projected to repeat its runaway success, "Stop the War Now" (1970) proved to have only a fraction of the impact despite the similar sentiment and the nearly identical way in which it was delivered. As with its forerunner, "Stop the War Now" establishes a militaristic feel by beginning with a bomb falling to produce an echoing explosion. The arrangement is also very familiar with the song being built around a stuttering yet anthemic chorus and the sound of Starr replicating his grunts and ad libs to the point of being virtual carbon copies. His vocal performance is arguably slightly better than the one captured in "War" due to the verses in "Stop the War Now" being much denser and requiring a faster relay. The themes also touch on some slightly more precise idioms of war. For instance, the narrator comments on how refusal to fight might lead to an unjust criminal prosecution, while also adding a more specific insight into the futility of war by arguing that "a few measly pennies...a medal, a grave and a doggone cross" are hardly sufficient to compensate the mother of a slain soldier. Whereas the overall object of "War" is explaining the destructive nature of conflict in simplistic terms, "Stop the War Now"—by virtue of its title at the very least—is more precise in its aim and more demanding in its nature. Again, Vietnam is not mentioned by name, but the connotations are beyond obvious given the huge profile of the conflict at the time of the track's release. Whether superior or not, Starr made it well known in the years after the song's release that he never liked it, admitting that it was too derivative of "War" and that he was at the mercy of Motown in its desire for success through repetition.

of Vietnam thanks to their anticommunist motivations. The video for the release also underlined the similarities by beginning with a scene in which a father and a son quietly watch reports of escalating U.S. troop numbers in Vietnam on their home TV. The video then cuts to harrowing file footage of the war itself before fading into Springsteen's own on-stage recollections of the conflict as a teenager growing up in the 1960s. The singer then makes a dedication to young people in the crowd while offering the sinister warning that "in 1985, blind faith in your leaders or anything will get you killed."[18] The performance of "War" that follows is nothing less than stupendous (if Starr's version was Technicolor, then the E Street Band converted the song into widescreen). As a final portent, the video's last shot returns to the opening setting, but reveals that the father is now solemnly watching the TV alone. Springsteen would also duet with Starr for a performance of the song live in England in 1999.

In his final years, Starr had begun to think of his biggest hit in different terms to those that had been ascribed to it, frequently stretching the song's lyrical interpretations by explaining that it "was not about the Vietnam War. It was about any kind of war. It can be the war you have in your neighbourhood trying to survive. It can be about the war you have in your job or the problems you have because of your colour."[19] But despite this viewpoint, few people could be convinced that it was anything but a definitive antiwar song. Indeed, a particularly sad irony that surrounded Starr's death in April 2003 was that "War" was being made relevant again due to the U.S.–led invasion of Iraq, which had begun just days before. It was a rumination that peppered many of his obituaries, but the song certainly did not die with him. As recently as 2007, a British-based organization called Stop the War Coalition lampooned former Prime Minister Tony Blair (who supported the invasion and approved the dispatch of British troops) by releasing yet another cover of "War" under the guise of Ugly Rumours. The "band" featured a grinning Blair look-alike for a singer and also named itself after the outfit that the real Tony Blair had been a part of during his time at university.

Artist: Crosby, Stills, Nash & Young

Song: "Ohio"

Songwriter: Neil Young

Album: Single only, but later included on Neil Young's compilation *Decade* (1977)

Label: Atlantic Records

1970

Upset by the U.S. government's continuing policy of aggression in Vietnam, thousands of students at Kent State voiced their disapproval through a wave of protests across the university during May 1970. However, one particular flash point resulted in the deaths of four students that were graphically documented by press photographers on campus. One such image moved Neil Young into responding with "Ohio"—a song released under the guise of Crosby, Stills, Nash & Young and which captured the simmering rage inspired by the tragedy.

Having vowed to end the Vietnam conflict upon entering the White House in early 1969, President Richard Nixon addressed the nation on April 30, 1970, with a new strategy that he believed would help him keep that promise. The plan concerned

Vietnam's supposedly neutral neighbor Cambodia whose border had long been used by the rebel North Vietnamese army as a sanctuary to avoid attack and regroup away from allied forces. The intended neutralization of these areas would adversely affect their resistance and move the United States closer to some kind of closure in what had been one of the country's largest political issues for more than half a decade. Despite Nixon's assurances to the contrary, the feeling among the antiwar faction was that this was a needless escalation of an already unfounded conflict and thereby made a mockery of his pledge to bring troops home. Worse still was the realization that these measures were not merely proposals for discussion, but were already being put into practice. The movement toward Cambodia had already begun before Nixon made the country aware of the plan, further riling his opponents who had steadily been growing in number during his short period in office—especially around the nation's many universities. During his address that evening, the president would make a tragically ironic and uncannily portentous reference to these places of higher learning.

> My fellow Americans, we live in an age of anarchy, both abroad and at home. We see mindless attacks on all the great institutions which have been created by free civilizations in the last 500 years. Even here in the United States, great universities are being systematically destroyed.[20]

Little did Nixon know that with every word, he was making his own unwitting contribution to that very same destruction.

The president's address gave the fire of campus dissent an added fuel, and within hours, reports of protests, disturbances, and even violence had increased markedly. A particularly fertile area for such activities around this time was Kent State University in Ohio, and the politically minded students in attendance wasted no time in showing their disgust at this new military offensive. The very next day on May 1, a group made the gesture of burying a copy of the U.S. Constitution to symbolize its death through Nixon's decision to push ahead with the bombing campaign without congressional support. On May 2, proceedings escalated from a relatively peaceful realm into a much more disorderly chain of events culminating in arsonists setting fire to the campus ROTC building in which military coaching was offered to the next generation of soldiers. Fire crews had their hoses slashed, while police retaliated by using tear gas after being pelted by rocks. On the morning of May 3, the Republican governor of Ohio, James A. Rhodes, fiercely criticized protesters in a strongly worded and inflammatory speech, labeling them enemies of the state while vowing to eradicate the insurgency. Later the same day, a curfew was put into effect, but when groups of dissenters violated it, further clashes ensued, tear gas was deployed by the National Guard, and there were even reports of students being bayoneted.

This tumultuous 72-hour period proved only to be a precursor to a much more horrific clash that left the youth of America with an open wound for the rest of the decade. At around noon on Monday, May 4, a crowd of around 1,500–2,000 students gathered at the university's victory bell with the intention of commencing a pre-planned protest. Although many in the crowd were merely onlookers, the

Guardsmen, nevertheless, felt compelled to attempt dispersal with the aid of tear gas, but the measure had only a limited effect. In the confusion that followed, a 13-second blast of indiscriminate firing emanated from where the Guardsmen had positioned themselves on top of a hill, overlooking a parking lot many meters away. The unexplained burst of bullets resulted in nine wounded and four deaths. Even more tragically, some protestors had become mixed in with other students who had no interest in the demonstrations, and, as a result, two of the fatally wounded students were merely bystanders walking to their next classes.

The day marked a turning point for both the government and its opponents. With support for the Vietnam conflict dwindling, the pointless deaths of four more young people on American soil appeared to be an act of self-destruction. Unsurprisingly, Nixon would later declare the fallout from the shootings to be the worst moments of his presidency. But for those aligned with the countercultural movement, too, the incidents on May 4 heralded another nail in the coffin of the hippy generation and its utopian fantasies. In the shadow of Kent State, the concepts of peace, love, and harmony seemed extremely unrealistic. Division and danger permeated through American life more than ever, and here was the horrific evidence that seemed to prove it. A firsthand witness to the shootings was Gerald Casale—future guitarist with the now legendary Ohioan post-punk band Devo—who (along with singer Mark Mothersbaugh) was enrolled at the university at the time. Casale knew two of the slain students and noted that the entire unsavory episode "pretty much knocked any hippie I had left in me right out of me that day."[21]

The incident made headlines around the world, and one of the most harrowing images featured a deeply distressed young girl called Mary Ann Vecchio kneeling over the prone and presumably dead body of her friend Jeffrey Miller—one of the four students who was fatally shot. Taken by a photojournalism scholar named John Filo (who would win a Pulitzer Prize for his effort the following year), the image was syndicated through countless publications. Another equally harrowing still from the aftermath of the Kent State shootings was featured in the May 15, 1970, edition of *Life* magazine—a copy of which found its way into the hands of Neil Young. A veteran of the 1960s music scene, Young had emerged from the ashes of Buffalo Springfield to go solo in 1968. He also added his talent and surname to the trio of Crosby, Stills & Nash in time for the release of *Déjà Vu* in March 1970—their first album as a quartet. Each member had previously been successful as part of another band; David Crosby with the Byrds, Graham Nash with British outfit the Hollies, while Stephen Stills had previously collaborated with Young in the aforementioned Buffalo Springfield. It was because of this strong rock 'n' roll pedigree that Crosby, Stills, Nash & Young (CSN&Y) were regarded as one of the so-called "supergroups" of the era, and that reputation earned them instant commercial success and critical kudos. But a sense of political conscience remained in all four members of the group, and it was a suitably outraged Crosby who handed Young the issue of *Life* shortly after it arrived on newsstands. A similarly riled Young responded to the sad stimulus almost instantly by writing a brand new song as his bandmate looked on in amazement. Realizing that Young had plucked something magical virtually out of thin air, Crosby's own reaction was just as swift as he called Nash, imploring him to book a studio immediately. It was there that "Ohio" was captured just as quickly as it had been composed.

The sense of anger that prevailed in so many minds following the events of May 4 is summated unnervingly well by the brooding riff picked out during the intro of "Ohio." As the slow but sturdy beat emanates from behind the drums, it is almost as though an aural protest march has begun. To that end, Young wastes no time in addressing the targets of his rage—namely the trigger-happy officers of the National Guard and President Nixon who is mentioned by name in the first line (a critique that would get the song blacklisted by many AM radio stations). The second set of lyrics finds Young alternating between the perspectives of the Kent dissenters who feel aggrieved at the harsh treatment they are receiving and the more conservative elements of the country who felt that members of the counterculture should have been dealt with much sooner—and with a similar amount of force. Finally, a rhetorical and ultimately simple question reduces the distance between the victims and the onlooking world as Young asks all listeners to imagine the horror they might feel had one of the victims been someone they had known, just as Vecchio had known Miller. Barely a minute into the whole song, all 10 lines have been revealed, but in that extremely short space of time "Young captured the fear, frustration and anger felt by youth across the country, and set it to a lumbering D-modal death march that hammered home the dread."[22] After a repetition of these lyrics, "Ohio" reaches a clear peak of fury as the cry of "four dead in Ohio" rings out with a nightmarish intensity, repeated again and again while the drum beat suddenly quickens. During the song's fade-out, Crosby allows his own emotion to boil over as he adds his own indignant ad libs, asking "how many more?" during the last seconds. As widely reported by those in the studio at the time of recording (not least Young himself who attests to it in the sleeve notes of his greatest-hits package *Decade*), Crosby's outpouring of energy coupled with the track's overall power led to him spontaneously bursting into tears after the take was completed.

With the Kent State shootings still creating much debate, "Ohio" was given a speedy release in June 1970, complete with the reprinting of an excerpt from the first amendment—guaranteeing free speech, freedom to assemble, and freedom to express grievances—as its cover. If the lyrics were not a clear enough indictment of the campus killings then, this precisely chosen sleeve image with all its unfortunate ironies surely was. Continuing the theme of the release, the B-side featured another speedily recorded song cut at the same session entitled "Find the Cost of Freedom," which paid tribute to dead American soldiers in Vietnam and was penned this time by Stills. As President Nixon instigated the Commission on Campus Unrest in June 1970 (a direct result of the Kent State shootings and the national student strike that followed) the single hit a peak of No. 14 on the U.S. charts despite being banned from many radio playlists. It was clear that "Ohio" had struck a strong chord among the nation's youth. The song unquestionably provided a starkly definitive pop-culture document of both a crucial event in American history and the backlash that resulted—a factor that no doubt explains why Young continues to cite "Ohio" as being his finest contribution to CSN&Y. Given that Stills and Young had already produced the counterculture anthem "For What It's Worth" during their time in Buffalo Spring-field (see the entry "For What It's Worth"), it also underlined their reputation as spokesmen for a generation—although it was a label they would recoil from constantly. Ever since its release, "Ohio" has been intrinsically associated with the events of May 4, 1970, standing as the definitive aural representation of that tragic day; as recently as 1997, Crosby, Stills & Nash played the song (without Young) during the annual memorial at Kent State. As the years progress, this link is unlikely to weaken.

Notes

1. "Dementia in the Second City," *Time*, September 6, 1968.

2. Ian MacDonald, *Revolution in the Head* (London: Pimlico, 2005), 26.

3. Quoted in "My Blue Period: John Lennon," *Mojo*, November 1995.

4. MacDonald, *Revolution in the Head*, 296.

5. Quoted in James Maycock, "Death or Glory: James Brown in Vietnam," *Mojo*, July 2003.

6. Simon Witter, "James Brown," *Sky*, September 1990.

7. Gerri Hirshey, "Funk's Founding Father (1933–2006)," *Rolling Stone*, January 25, 2007.

8. *Look*, February 18, 1969.

9. Quoted in Hirshey, "Funk's Founding Father (1933–2006)."

10. This effect was actually created by Stone placing a microphone inside his mouth according to Barney Hoskyns's sleeve notes to the 2007 Epic/Legacy reissue of *Stand!*

11. Barney Hoskyns, *Stand!*, album sleeve notes, Epic/Legacy, 2007.

12. Craig Werner, *Music, Race and the Soul of America* (Ann Arbor: University of Michigan Press, 2006), 104.

13. Quoted in Mat Snow, "Iggy Pop: The Madcap Laughs Again," *Q*, September 1988.

14. Lenny Kaye, "The Stooges: The Stooges (Elektra)," *Fusion*, September 1969.

15. "David and Julie," *Time*, December 20, 1968.

16. Quoted in Craig Werner, *Up Around the Bend: The Oral History of Creedence Clearwater Revival* (New York: Spike, 1998), 123.

17. Quoted in Pierre Perrone, "How We Met: Mary Wilson & Edwin Starr," *Independent* (London), April 2, 2000.

18. Quoted in Bruce Springsteen & the E Street Band, "War" music video, Arthur Rostato, Director, Columbia Records, 1986.

19. Quoted in Spencer Leigh, "Obituary: Edwin Starr," *Independent* (London), April 4, 2003.

20. Richard Nixon, TV and Radio Broadcast, April 30, 1970.

21. Quoted on www.songfacts.com/detail.php?id=1124

22. Jimmy McDonough, *Shakey* (London: Vintage, 2003), 346.

CHAPTER 5

THINGS AIN'T WHAT THEY USED TO BE (1970–1974)

Hope and optimism were not especially easy to come by as the 1970s dawned in the United States. The progressive political dream that had been sparked by President John F. Kennedy and carried on by President Lyndon Johnson during the 1960s had begun to fizzle out when Republican President Richard Nixon arrived in the White House following his 1968 election victory, inspiring a swing toward conservatism in the process. The already decaying idea of hippy-led cultural unity was well and truly destroyed by the Tate-LaBianca killings of 1969, which were orchestrated by Charles Manson—a former hippy himself. But perhaps the most deflating sight for most Americans was the continuing deadlock in Vietnam. Troop numbers were peaking, peace negotiations were failing, and Nixon's promise to end the war with his election campaign pledge of "peace with honor" seemed a long way from being fulfilled. Although domestic protests continued, dissenters could be forgiven for thinking that they were being ignored with Vice President Spiro Agnew lambasting youthful unrest as being the product of "overprivileged, under-disciplined, irresponsible children of the blasé well-to-do permissivists"[1] while even Nixon weighed in from the highest level of government by angrily opining that they were merely "bums blowing up . . . campuses."[2] This darker atmosphere inevitably seeped into pop culture with greater frequency as such bands as Black Sabbath voiced their anger most notably with the loud, doom-laden "**War Pigs**" (1970), while Marvin Gaye's frustration was there for all to hear in "**What's Going On**"—his groundbreaking hit for Motown in 1971.

Even though the Vietnam conflict continued to dominate in political and social spheres, themes of protest in music were now splintering into many different directions and many different genres. The Black Power rhetoric issued by a number of radical groups such as the Black Panthers convinced a number of African Americans that parity with whites was not good enough and that they should strive for complete autonomy instead. This mooted revolution in the way black people lived was something that had a profound effect on New York poet Gil Scott-Heron and in "**The Revolution Will Not Be Televised**" (1971), he urged his fellow African Americans not to get distracted in the pursuit of this goal by the numbing effects of media. Ironically, it was television and radio that played a crucial role in exposing the country to Helen Reddy's statement of feminine strength in her single "**I Am Woman**" (1972), which would go on to essentially soundtrack the women's rights movement. Reggae superstars the Wailers stood up for the much-maligned (and outside of Jamaica, largely unknown) religion of Rastafarianism via their rousing track "**Get Up, Stand Up**" (1973). And despite being a performer who appeared to have a lot in common with the old guard of folksingers, Joni Mitchell brought the relatively new concerns of environmentalism to the world's music fans through the light-hearted "**Big Yellow Taxi**" (1970).

But perhaps the biggest sign that the style of musical indignation and finger-pointing prevalent in the 1960s was on the wane came in the exchanges between Neil Young and Lynyrd Skynyrd. Young's status as one of rock's liberal figureheads had been earned through his efforts in Buffalo Springfield and Crosby, Stills, Nash & Young, so it was with a typical righteousness that he took issue with backwoods racism across the old confederacy in "**Southern Man**"—taken from the 1970 album *After the Gold Rush*. As proud residents of Florida, Lynyrd Skynyrd refused to let Young's generalizations pass without some kind of a response, and the subsequent rebuttal of "**Sweet Home Alabama**" quickly became the unofficial anthem of the South. It was a particularly telling indication of how the realm of protest music was now beginning to include more than just folksingers, hippies, and countercultural rebels.

Artist: Joni Mitchell
Song: "Big Yellow Taxi"
Songwriter: Joni Mitchell
Album: *Ladies of the Canyon*
Label: Reprise Records
1970

Despite becoming a serious scientific cause for concern in the early 1960s, the cause of environmentalism did not emerge in popular culture until the start of the 1970s when folksinger Joni Mitchell released "Big Yellow Taxi." The song introduced a new subject matter for pop lyricism, and because of its catchy melody, playful spirit, and child-like imagery, it has become firmly established as a modern folk staple that continually gets reinterpreted across America.

Beneath the well-documented insistence that civil rights must be implemented and the inescapable anger directed at the Vietnam conflict, the American counterculture also harbored a growing interest in the need for environmental preservation during the 1960s. It was a subject that attracted far less media attention than the violent clashes over domestic racism and misguided foreign wars, but given the scientific evidence

Joni Mitchell—the so-called "hippy Queen" of the late 1960s and early 1970s.
Courtesy AP Images.

being used by supporters of this new strain of progressive culture, the green cause appeared to be open to far less debate. The most pivotal theory to emerge during the decade came in 1962 when American biologist Rachel Carson published the hugely influential *Silent Spring*. This book offered a startling critique of the use of pesticides and linked the chemical DDT (Dichloro-Diphenyl-Trichloroethane) to detrimental effects on wildlife—especially birds, hence the title alludes to a lack of birdsong in the spring months. Despite attracting controversy among sceptical scientists, Carson's theory helped to kick-start a broader awareness of changing environments; across the United States, it was something that could be observed with worrying regularity. Post-war affluence had seen the number of cars on the road skyrocket and the smoggy by-products could be felt in the country's bigger cities, while the effects of industry on the landscape could not be more graphically illustrated than by the Cuyahoga River in Ohio. Surrounded by paper plants and steel mills that were allowed to dump waste in the 100-mile stretch of water, the Cuyahoga had become so polluted that it would actually burst into flames at certain junctures—a sight famously depicted in *Time* magazine in 1969. All these factors led to the organization of the first annual Earth Day in April 1970 by Senator Gaylord Nelson who aimed to mobilize America into greater environmental awareness via grassroots protests and demonstrations.

It was around the same time of the first Earth Day that singer Joni Mitchell was reaching an early peak in her fame. Born Joan Anderson in 1943 in Alberta, Canada, she had shown a childhood interest in drawing, but had transferred that talent into music as a teenager and initially bought herself a baritone ukulele simply because it was cheaper than a guitar. Her college years saw Anderson give more guitar-based solo performances, and following a hasty marriage to fellow folksinger Chuck Mitchell, they moved to Detroit in the mid-1960s where the couple would often play as a duo. Although the marriage would end in failure, Joni kept her married name and moved to New York in 1967 with the aim of breaking into the still vibrant folk scene around Manhattan. It was during this period that she would meet ex-Byrds guitarist David Crosby who was immediately taken by Mitchell's resplendent voice, her vast array of tunings, and unusual guitar chords, all of which combined to give her songs a remarkably lush sound. After convincing her to move to Los Angeles (LA), Crosby would famously show off his discovery to the rock star community that had settled in the city's Laurel Canyon area, and, as a result, Mitchell's reputation spread around the higher reaches of the music industry. A deal with Reprise Records would soon result, and she released her Crosby-produced self-titled debut (also known as *Song to a Seagull*) in 1968 and followed it a year later with *Clouds*. The first album made little commercial impact and the second fared only a little better, but acclaim still found Mitchell through other artists covering her work, not least Judy Collins whose version of *Clouds* track "Both Sides Now" made the Top 10 in 1968.

Aside from the odd reference to Vietnam, social commentary was never really a part of Mitchell's work and despite professing to a personal dislike of LA's car-polluted air, there were certainly no green themes to her often confessional early lyrics. But as the new movement toward environmental action began to gain more speed toward the end of the 1960s, the singer would unwittingly make her own contribution during her first visit to Hawaii. After arriving at night, Mitchell woke the next morning and went to the window to take her first daylight views of what she presumed would be the Pacific island's magnificent coastal scenery. "I threw back the curtains and saw these beautiful green mountains in the distance. Then, I looked down and there was a parking lot as far as the eye could see, and it broke my heart . . . this blight on paradise."[3] As was her artistic disposition at the time, she channeled her personal feelings into a new set of lyrics for a song that would be called "Big Yellow Taxi." The public first heard it as part of the *Ladies of the Canyon* album that emerged in April 1970, but the song would also earn a single release shortly after.

Mitchell's strange guitar chords provide the main musical backdrop to the entirety of "Big Yellow Taxi," which is characterized by a strangely cheerful spirit—an odd contrast to the sense of loss contained within the lyrics. The first lines recall the singer's horror at seeing Hawaii's picture-perfect landscape invaded by gray concrete and then goes on to reference a pink hotel (widely acknowledged to be the Pink Palace on Waikiki Beach) and its various man-made attractions. The song's famous chorus follows with Mitchell lamenting the sad transformation, but realizing that a real appreciation of something occurs only after it disappears. A repeat of the main hook line "they paved paradise, and put up a parking lot" rounds off the sentiment, this time with the addition of some instantly memorable harmonies. The second verse expands on the absurdity of nature being contained and controlled by explaining how trees are now being presented for people to view at a price within the confines of a museum. Just as the first verse was inspired by Pink Palace, this section is based on the Honolulu Botanical Gardens and Mitchell's bemusement at the admission fees. A repetition of the chorus follows before the third verse issues a plea to farmers to stop using DDT as the narrator gladly offers to put up with imperfections on her apples in return for the safety of wildlife. As "Big Yellow Taxi" hits a peak of environmental concern, Mitchell adds a twist in the final verse where she addresses the death of a relationship through an image of the eponymous big yellow taxi carrying a loved one away (debate still rages over whether the "old man" mentioned is a boyfriend, father, or other). However, the central message is obviously the same—"look after what's yours, you don't know what you've got 'til it's gone."[4] A final set of chorus run-throughs takes the song to its conclusion, which is playfully signposted by Mitchell's laughter after delivering the last line in a voice both an octave higher and an octave lower than normal.

Released in the summer of 1970 (and backed with Mitchell's original version of "Woodstock," which Crosby, Stills, Nash & Young had covered and made into a hit earlier in the year), the track was highly successful in the United Kingdom and climbed to No. 11 on the chart—a peak yet to be surpassed. The U.S. single initially fared less well although a re-released live version managed a more respectable No. 24 in 1975. Nevertheless, "Big Yellow Taxi" marked the start of Mitchell's stardom, and both *Ladies of the Canyon* and the 1971 album *Blue* helped to establish the singer's credentials as a performer in her own right, rather than just a talented songwriter whose work was better realized by others. As well as expanding her audience into mainstream, the song simultaneously helped to heighten her association with the counterculture thanks to its environmental concern—a factor that would further engrain Mitchell's media image as a hippy queen much to her irritation. It may have had too much of a wry, satirical spirit to take entirely seriously (certainly in comparison to Marvin Gaye's 1971 track "Mercy Mercy Me (The Ecology)"—see the sidebar), but chronologically, "Big Yellow Taxi" clearly was "the first certifiably eco-friendly pop song."[5] Additionally, it predated the founding of such organizations as the U.S. Environmental Protection Agency, which would be established later in 1970, and Greenpeace, which would not begin operations until 1971. Although various campaigns to outlaw DDT were already under way at the time of the song's release, even that would remain in legal use until 1972—a full decade after *Silent Spring* was published. It might have only been brief, but there definitely was a period of time in which "Big Yellow Taxi" stood alone in voicing a protest at environmental change, and, as a result, it seems understandable that green-minded members of the public would have looked to Mitchell as a leader of some kind.

Hearing ecological concerns voiced through pop music would become an extremely familiar sound in subsequent years, particularly as knowledge of the potentially disastrous results of the Greenhouse effect became widespread throughout the 1980s. Especially active in raising awareness of this threat was R.E.M. who covered such topics as acid rain in "Fall on Me" and the aforementioned pollution of the Cuyahoga River in

MARVIN GAYE—"MERCY MERCY ME (THE ECOLOGY)"

Emerging almost exactly a year after "Big Yellow Taxi" in 1971, Marvin Gaye's "Mercy Mercy Me (The Ecology)" proved to be a much more sobering take on the changing environment than Joni Mitchell's relatively light-hearted effort. It was the second single to be lifted from Gaye's album *What's Going On*—a conceptual work designed to reflect the myriad of social and political problems that the singer felt were affecting the world at the time of release (see the entry on "What's Going On" in this chapter for more information). The track itself is a slow and soulful mourning of nature and laments the manner in which air has been polluted, fish have been poisoned, and waters have been defiled. There appears to be little in the way of hope that things can be reversed or even any kind of plea to change human practices as the narrator merely offers quiet exasperation at the sight of the planet being damaged. Despite the downbeat tempo and the grim subject matter, "Mercy Mercy Me (The Ecology)" turned out to be a huge hit, reaching No. 4 in the United States and fueling the continued success of *What's Going On,* which stayed on the charts for over a year after its release. It continues to be held in the very highest esteem by critics for its progressive social thinking, as demonstrated best by this track that (like "Big Yellow Taxi") predated public unease over the environment by many years.

"Cuyahoga" (both tracks were included on its 1986 album *Lifes Rich Pageant*). The quartet also issued frequent public statements on the issue and colluded closely with Greenpeace, allowing the organization to distribute literature to fans at its gigs, as well as playing benefit shows. But the legacy of "Big Yellow Taxi" is not merely limited to musicians and bands adding environmental slants to their songs, but actually extends into being a much broader cultural touchstone. For example, in several 1991 interviews, Mitchell told of her delight over the song's use in teaching schoolchildren about ecology after a third-grade teacher wrote to the singer explaining that every year, she would ask each of her students to illustrate a line from the song.

The cross-generational appeal to the song has also extended to the many reinterpretations and updates, all of which have made "Big Yellow Taxi" one of the most discernible modern examples of folk music. The cover versions have been countless and include Bob Dylan's 1973 take, Amy Grant's 1995 hit, and as recently as 2003, a revisit by Counting Crows featuring Vanessa Carlton, which again put the track on the charts on both sides of the Atlantic. Its influence has also reached a number of other genres as best exemplified by Janet Jackson's "Got 'til It's Gone"—a soulful hip-hop track released in 1997 that was built around a sample of "Big Yellow Taxi" and turned out to be yet another worldwide success. Perhaps most significant, however, is Mitchell's own re-recording of the song for her 2007 album *Shine.* In an era that had seen environmentalism become one of the most pressing social and political issues (the multicontinental Live Earth gig had been held just weeks before *Shine*'s release), it was hardly a big surprise to see the singer addressing the subject again on a number of newer songs. However, it was the jerky, jazzy, and mildly chaotic version of "Big Yellow Taxi" included on the album that attracted the most attention and was greeted by one reviewer as exhibiting an "I-told-you-so smugness."[6] But given that the original subject of her concern in the song had now developed into something that influences government policy all over the world, Mitchell's perceived egotism was probably justified.

Artist: Black Sabbath

Song: "War Pigs"

Songwriters: Tony Iommi, Ozzy Osbourne, Geezer Butler, and Bill Ward

Album: *Paranoid*

Label: Vertigo (United Kingdom)/ Warners Bros. (United States)

1970/1971

Black Sabbath's early sound reflected both the harshness of the group's hometown and an interest in the dark arts, but it was something that also proved apt once the band-mates decided to turn their lyrical attention to the injustices and evils of conflict. With "War Pigs," the English outfit tapped into the hopelessness of Vietnam, but also set a precedent for the downbeat mood descending on Western pop culture in the wake of the failed hippy dream. Thanks to songs like this, bands playing heavy metal would now have as much association with youthful disaffection as any acoustic guitar-toting folksinger—if not more.

As Black Sabbath front man John "Ozzy" Osbourne so emphatically explained, growing up in the florally decorated optimism of California during the 1960s contrasted dramatically with the teenage experience he and his bandmates had in central England.

> When I started with Sabbath, the music scene was soul, blues, pop, psychedelic and the flower power movement. Now us guys, living in the . . . dregs of Aston in Birmingham, no money, no shoes on your feet and we're hearing on the radio, "If you go to San Francisco/Be sure to wear some flowers in your hair," and we're thinking, "What the fuck's that all about?"[7]

It was little wonder that Osbourne (vocals), Terence "Geezer" Butler (bass), Tony Iommi (guitar), and Bill Ward (drums) struggled to identify with whimsical Scott McKenzie songs about gentle people and sun-soaked love-ins when they were constantly surrounded by the gray, unforgiving, working-class sprawl of England's second city. Dominated by decaying industry and the kind of intimidating postwar architecture shared by so many large cities north of the capital, Birmingham was not a place that communicated hope in any overt way. The quartet had few career prospects outside of factory labor (Osbourne may have had even less given his burglary convictions), so music would prove to be the only remotely plausible alternative.

As they moved toward making their hard-edged blues band Earth a serious project in 1969, it was the city that would again provide them with further inspiration. Spying that a cinema across the road from their rehearsal space was showing a horror film, Iommi pondered the oddity of people paying to see a film that would scare them and posited the idea that the band should try to make a musical equivalent. From that, they not only wrote a song called "Black Sabbath" (sharing its title with a Boris Karloff hammer-horror production from 1963), but also adopted the ominous title as their new band name, too. The occult-inspired self-titled debut album that would follow a year later was naturally a flower-free affair and was sonically characterized by

The members of Black Sabbath at their holiest (L–R): Geezer Butler, Bill Ward, Ozzy Osbourne, and Tony Iommi.
Courtesy of Photofest.

Iommi's doom-laden guitar that represented the grim atmosphere of their environment with a strange aptness. This aural signature (which in later years would be further ingrained by Iommi and Butler detuning their strings) gradually cemented Black Sabbath's status as a pioneer of a new genre dubbed "heavy metal."

While flower power meant nothing to Black Sabbath from the start, by 1970 it had begun to look distinctly outdated to the rest of the world, too. The Summer of Love in 1967 had been followed by a prolonged winter of discontent exemplified by a violent radicalization of the American counterculture. The peaceful civil rights move-ment had transformed into the Black Power movement complete with its advocacy of equality by any means necessary. But even that had begun to stutter badly after such prominent leaders as Huey P. Newton and Bobby Seale were imprisoned in the late 1960s. The notion that hippy-advocated values of mind expansion, optimism, and an all-encompassing love would provide the cornerstones of the next cultural and political epoch had also unraveled during 1969. This was due in no small way to chaos at the Woodstock Festival, the outright anarchy at the Rolling Stones' free show at Altamont Speedway, and perhaps most disturbingly, the vicious slayings instigated by former Haight-Ashbury district dweller Charles Manson.

After forming his own secluded "family" commune comprised mainly of drifting girls, Manson's psychotic mind began to foresee a race war—something that he also felt was being predicted in The Beatles' self-titled 1968 release (also known as *The White Album*). He felt the conflict would eventually destroy America, but Manson attempted to speed up its development by orchestrating the notorious killing spree at the Los Angeles homes of supermarket executive Leno LaBianca and of Sharon Tate, who was the wife of film director Roman Polanski and was heavily pregnant at the time. It was a sinisterly destructive end to a decade that had promised much peace-ful reparation, and the fact that this incident of orgiastic violence had stemmed from a cult with clear countercultural roots made a mockery of the notion that flower power would win the day. With optimism slowly turning to dread, such bands as Black Sab-bath seemed to naturally mirror the shift in mood across the world with their loud and foreboding sounds. The genre of heavy metal that they so typified began to thrive in this time of uneasiness, for if "flower-power music could not cure society's ills, then at least the louder rock could drown them out."[8]

As Osbourne and his compatriots began to write material for a second album, their rapidly deepening association with the occult quickly drew annoyance from band ranks. Although Butler was known to have a solid interest in the subject, neither he nor anyone else in Black Sabbath felt it should define the group. As chief lyricist as well as bass player, Butler revised a song called "Walpurgis"[9] (named after Walpurgisnacht —a noted date in the calendar of occultists) that had first been included in the group's live set back in the days of Earth. Filled with satanic imagery of marauding witches, bloody anointing rituals, and other "evil doings," it was exactly the kind of thing from which the bandmates were now aiming to distance themselves. Subsequently, during the summer of 1970, the song gradually morphed into a seething damnation of con-flict entitled "War Pigs," which the band was also keen to use as a title for its upcoming album, only for its record label to request that the title be changed. Such a contentious phrase would have been understandably problematic in the United States where politi-cal and social clashes over Vietnam were increasingly common. But events in the war had now become a worldwide issue that stretched even to the mind-sets of working-class men in central England, such as the members of Black Sabbath.

Despite President Nixon's promise of troop withdrawal shortly after acceding to the White House in 1969, it was announced in April 1970 that U.S. forces would now try to eliminate communist bases and supply lines in the previously neutral land of Cambodia. Outrage at this apparent escalation resulted in a wave of protests, culminating most notoriously in the shooting of four Kent State University students in Ohio (see Chapter 4 for more on Crosby, Stills, Nash & Young), which sent shock waves around the globe. Aside from this deadly level of tension, the term "pig" was also being scrutinized further after the Manson Family killings in light of the fact that the assailants had written the same word—or variants of it—in the victims' own blood at the scene of the crimes. The band capitulated in the knowledge that an album called "War Pigs" could potentially give it a commercial black eye and changed the title to *Paranoid*. But the song "War Pigs" remained, towering over the rest of the album from its position of opening track; while it contained no outright reference to Vietnam, it was not difficult to see the song's contemporary poignancy.

From Iommi's titanic first chord and the intro's menacing snarl, the tone of "War Pigs" is markedly downbeat and exacerbated by the haunting air raid siren that was a familiar sound for anyone who could remember the two world wars. Osbourne sings the opening set of lyrics in among a syncopated, stop-start arrangement and heralds the pagan-like gathering of generals, orchestrating a war effort like witches and sorcerers (evidently, the occult references from "Walpurgis" were not all purged). With the war machine in motion, more grim images of burning bodies and brainwashed minds are delivered before an interlude in which Iommi fires off a blast of power chords, while Ward responds with some chaotic drum fills. The chugging second verse has a more constant tempo that underpins the narrator's more direct—and in the history of Vietnam protest, extremely familiar—lambaste of politicians who instigate war but remove themselves from the front line, sending the poor and powerless to do battle instead. An eerie vision of biblical retribution follows with the assurance that unfavorable judgment awaits those who sacrifice others for their own means and pleasure. Iommi again leaps into action with a darkly dazzling solo before the stop-start rhythm of the first verse is reprised with the promised day of judgment apparently at hand. The war pigs of the title are pictured on their knees in the sight of God, repenting for their wrong doings as the war machine burns. But the last lines reveal Satan looking on with amusement, seemingly in the knowledge that the evil he endorses will one day return—such is the repetitious nature of war in mankind's history. Another furious interchange between Ward and Iommi ensues before the track stretches out into an extended instrumental that carried the title of "Luke's Wall" (a name comprised from two roadies working for the band at the time) and which speeds up into a freakish blur in the final seconds of the track.

Although not released as a single, the gravity of "War Pigs" was inescapable, and it would became an instant staple for the band. Obviously, it was a song that symbolically lamented world events, but it did so from a new perspective. There is no flower-power pacifism, no liberal pleas for humanity, not even any hard-left wing shouts of righteous rage. Instead, it is characterized by an overwhelming feeling of dread that simultaneously feels enthralling—not unlike a horror film, which was exactly what Iommi suggested they aim for when becoming Black Sabbath. As the possibilities of the 1960s developed into the pitfalls of the 1970s, this was one of the songs that provided a soundtrack to that depressive shift in mood. Coupled with the rest of the extremely strong cuts on the album (still regarded almost unanimously as their finest work), *Paranoid* hit No. 1 on the U.K. album chart after its release in September 1970 and peaked at No. 12 across the Atlantic Ocean following a delayed U.S. release in early 1971. This latter success helped to popularize the band across the country thanks to a particularly receptive audience of blue-collar Americans who seemed to connect with the feel of Black Sabbath and its metal-minded peers. The heartland of both America and England had been unmoved by the countercultural fervor that had occurred in the more gentrified areas of each country. As a result, such critics as Barney Hoskyns theorized that it was only in places like Birmingham "where the meadow meets the factory and the cows drink industrial sewage . . . and in the American Midwest, that heavy metal really makes sense."[10]

The landscape of protest was changing rapidly at the very moment "War Pigs" was released, and it was clearly of a very different spirit from so many previous musical dissents against war. However, its aural potency and the nonspecific slant of the lyrics have allowed the song to remain a celebrated piece well beyond that cultural turning point at the end of the 1960s. This continual relevance seemed to surge during the Iraq War as administered by President George W. Bush. In acknowledging this recent campaign, such bands as the Dresden Dolls, Hayseed Dixie, and Cake have all covered the song either on record or on stage, while Oklahoman outfit the Flaming Lips made the song a prominent part of its live set for much of its 2006 world tour. For better or for worse, it would seem that the sense of hope that Scott McKenzie embodied during "San Francisco (Be Sure to Wear Flowers in Your Hair)" died relatively quickly, whereas after all these years, the feeling of hopelessness that "War Pigs" represented appears to be alive and well.

Artist: Marvin Gaye

Song: "What's Going On"

Songwriters: Al Cleveland, Marvin Gaye, and Renaldo Benson

Album: *What's Going On*

Label: Motown

1971

Years of cultural, social, and political turmoil toward the end of the 1960s convinced Motown star Marvin Gaye of the need to move away from the pop material that had made him a star and concentrate on something more appropriate for the times. Despite the protests he encountered from label boss Berry Gordy, Gaye used the traumatic events in his personal life and a sense of disillusionment with the wider world to create "What's Going On." It remains not just a classic example of protest music, but one of the most celebrated singles of all time.

Before he had written his most famous album *What's Going On*, Marvin Gaye was already a legend in the music world, but it was a status that had been hard earned. Born in Washington, D.C., in 1939, Marvin Pentz Gay Jr. was subject to physical abuse from an early age by his father—a fundamentalist minister of the Apostolic Church, a strict disciplinarian, and, somewhat bizarrely, a secret cross-dresser. All of this fostered a lifelong acrimony between the two. Thanks mainly to the huge amount

Marvin Gaye.
Courtesy of Photofest.

of time spent in church, young Marvin quickly developed his vocal talents in the choir and soon distinguished himself as a drummer and organist. While his father insisted that these gifts be used in religious worship only, Gay Jr. began to embark on more secular routes during his teenage years. After a short spell in the air force in 1957, he joined a doo-wop group called the Marquees, which briefly boasted the pioneering bluesman Bo Diddley as its producer.

The quartet experienced little in the way of success, but when singer Harvey Fuqua saw the bandmates perform live, he was impressed enough to invite them to join his group, the Moonglows. It was an offer that the Marquees duly accepted, and Fuqua proceeded to further this new band's prospects by moving to Detroit, Michigan, in the hope of releasing something on a new label called Motown that had been set up by local entrepreneur Berry Gordy. This plan came to nothing, although Gay later signed with Motown in 1960, initially as a session musician and occasional songwriter. The role subsequently allowed him to contribute drums to such legendary hits as the Marvelettes' "Please Mr. Postman" (1961) and was also credited as co-writer of Martha Reeves & the Vandellas' "Dancing in the Street" (1964). However, Gordy envisioned more than just a behind-the-scenes role for him and commissioned Gay to record as a solo vocalist in 1961. At this time Gay added an "e" to the end of his name both as a way of escaping the inevitable homosexual taunts and to emulate one of his musical heroes, the legendary soul singer Sam Cooke, who also added the extra letter early in his career.

The sedate jazz ballads that made up most of Gaye's earliest output failed to connect with a mainstream audience, and Gordy soon began to coax him into recording material closer to Motown's house style of R&B that was quickly becoming popular across the country. His stubborn nature prompted Gaye to resist at first, but the pressure applied by his Motown executives proved to be enough to change his mind. In the summer of 1962, the not-coincidentally titled "Stubborn Kind of Fellow" earned Gaye his first hit. Gordy was vindicated, and many more solo successes followed. But it was the duets with some of Motown's finest female singers that elevated his career to stardom. In 1964, he recorded material with both Mary Wells and Kim Weston, but it was the formidable partnership forged with Tammi Terrell during 1967 that produced the most memorable and most successful singles. However, during a concert in October of that same year, Terrell began to exhibit the first signs of what was a malignant brain tumor when she collapsed into Gaye's arms while performing on stage. Even as her collaborations with Gaye continued to scale the charts over the next few years, Terrell's health would gradually deteriorate until she died in March 1970, at the age of 24.

Terrell's death deeply affected Gaye, who was already reeling from the failure of his first marriage to Gordy's sister, Anna, as well as the depressive side effects of his growing drug use. At the height of his own personal success, Gaye opted to seclude himself from the music world by refusing to perform live and trying to set up an alternative career for himself as a professional football player, although a tryout with the Detroit Lions came to nothing. His disillusion stemmed not just from the music business, but also from the social and economic problems being experienced across the United States. What was particularly close to home for Gaye was the ongoing Vietnam War. His younger brother, Frankie, was in Vietnam and frequently sent letters to the family during his period of service there. He was one of the many to return home following President Nixon's employment of the so-called Nixon Doctrine in 1969, which was one of the first attempts at reducing American personnel and influence in the conflict. With events in Vietnam escalating throughout the 1960s and no apparent end in sight, domestic disapproval of the war continued to become more vociferous, and Nixon appeared to be failing in his promise to find "Peace with Honor." The difficult experience that Frankie had not only in helping the war effort, but also in returning and readjusting to life in a newly fragmented American society scarred by self-inflicted wounds inspired his brother to write a set of solemn and introspective reflections that were given the ominous title of "What's Going On."

Recorded in June 1970 with some of Motown's finest resident musicians, Gaye fully intended to set the song apart from the signature pop sound that had characterized the label and made him a star the decade before. In an attempt to underline that he was turning his back on success and frivolity in favor of something more important, "What's Going On" begins with the sound of a party in full swing that quickly gives way to a slow, soulful introduction that cushions Gaye's smooth vocal delivery. It is a mood that rarely alters despite the frustration and disillusionment that inspires the song. Gaye also seems to expend a proportionally small amount of energy in achieving optimum emotional impact even during the famously poignant chorus. The omission of a question mark from the title is not accidental because this is not a song of anger or questioning; it is an honest portrayal of the world at its most brutal and worrying.

From the onset, it is a sad picture that Gaye paints with allusions to people mourning their loved ones, personal and political conflicts of all kinds spiraling out of control, and the sight of protests against violence being countered with yet more violence. The subsequent plea "to bring some understanding here today" is a simplistic one that nevertheless addresses the broad absence of solidarity and how effective a measure of compassion might be in helping to alleviate so many modern ills. Understandably, given some of the narrator's references to "brother" (in the context of one black man addressing another) as well as Gaye's own ethnicity, the song is regarded as a specific call for African American solidarity in the face of continued racial marginalization. Gaye refuted this common perception explaining that, "the only ethnicity . . . about 'What's Going On' is the fact that its author is black. I don't think the social content or the musical content is ethnic at all . . . [it] can apply to anybody, any race, any creed."[11]

The somber mood and epic musicality certainly marked "What's Going On" as being a step into uncharted territory for Motown, and it was exactly that which prompted a very unenthusiastic response from Berry Gordy (who was initially presented with a slightly rougher version of the song without the party intro). Wary of the song's serious content, he felt that it was not commercial enough for his audience and refused to issue it as a single, fearing a spectacular flop. This embargo infuriated Gaye greatly. But because of the singer's immense status and newfound autonomy, Gordy relented after his star performer threatened to cease all recordings for the label unless "What's Going On" was given a full release. This was an ironic turn of events given that at the start of his career, it was Gaye who was being cajoled into the musical directions that Gordy wanted. Nevertheless, it was Gaye who was emphatically vindicated this time around. Released in early 1971 (some sources say January, some say February), the single rapidly climbed to No. 2 on the mainstream chart and No. 1 on the R&B chart, and it would eventually sell 2½ million copies.

Not only had "What's Going On" lived up to Motown's "hit factory" reputation, it had strengthened that reputation, and, never being the kind of man to let pride get in the way of sales, Gordy promptly commissioned Gaye to record a whole album's worth of material that continued in the same socially conscientious and musically sophisticated mold. Only too pleased to oblige, Gaye reentered the studio and in just 10 days captured eight more songs that collectively formed an overview of the nation's problems as seen through the eyes of an everyday man. Fittingly, "What's Going On" was the album's first track as well as the title. In just about every aspect, it was a body of work that revolutionized the soul genre. The concept binding the album together was an entirely original idea, the recording techniques used in the studio were highly advanced (particularly Gaye's "multitracking" method of singing the lead and backing vocals himself), and the lyrical concerns again continued to break new ground. The song "What's Going On" acts as an obvious starting point, and from there Gaye addresses such specific problems as poverty in "Inner City Blues (Make We Wanna Holler)," the increasingly common problem of drug addiction in "Flyin' High (In the Friendly Sky)," and the relatively new worry over environmental decay in "Mercy Mercy Me (The Ecology)." Essentially, the album touched on everything that was wrong with the United States, and both the critical and the commercial response were notably positive if not euphoric. Released in June 1971, the album peaked at No. 4 and spawned another two Top 10 hits, leaving few in doubt that Gaye had scaled new heights and broadened the boundaries of popular music.

It may say as much about the flaws of humanity as it does about the vastness of Gaye's talent, but the themes of disquiet explored in *What's Going On* have rarely seemed outdated; as a result, adulation for both album and single has stayed at a consistently eulogistic level in the decades since it was recorded. In 1982 (just two years before Gaye's murder at the hands of Marvin Gay Sr.), the conservative politics of Ronald Reagan's first presidential term were beginning to take hold, and Gaye for one noticed with some dismay how similar kinds of social upheaval seemed just as entrenched into the fabric of society as they had been some 10 years earlier. "I'm even more appalled now than when I recorded 'What's Going On'; things have gotten worse and they'll continue to get worse."[12] In the time since, it is hard to pinpoint a period in world history where one of the album's concerns has not seemed applicable and that, in turn, has solidified "What's Going On" as a timeless piece of work. American singer Cyndi Lauper recorded her own version in 1986, which also became a huge hit, and in 2001 the song was covered again by a vast array of modern stars including Bono from U2, Michael Stipe from R.E.M., Britney Spears, P. Diddy, and Nas, as well as Marvin's daughter Mona on an AIDS-awareness charity single. As recently as 2004, *Rolling Stone* magazine voted Gaye's original single as the fourth best of all time, while *What's Going On* came in at No. 6 as part of an identical poll conducted with albums the year before. As long as division and disharmony manifest themselves in any significant way, "What's Going On" will always be a legitimate statement.

Artist: Gil Scott-Heron

Song: "The Revolution Will Not Be Televised"

Songwriter: Gil Scott-Heron

Album: *Small Talk at 125th and Lenox* (first version)/*Pieces of a Man* (main version)

Label: Flying Dutchman Records

1970/1971

As the civil rights movement developed a more radical element in the late 1960s, the idea of African Americans uniting to force a racial revolution was something that was given much credence by such people as Gil Scott-Heron. However, he felt that the demotivating effects of television provided a major obstacle and through "The Revolution Will Not Be Televised," the New York poet warned the black populace against its nullifying effects. The revolution never really materialized, but the cultural and political legacy of Scott-Heron's most famous piece is still evident in a great deal of black music to this day.

As a youngster growing up in Tennessee during the early 1960s, Gil Scott-Heron could claim to be among the first African Americans to notice the positive effects that the civil rights movement was having on the country. Born in 1949 to a librarian mother and a soccer-playing father, Scott-Heron spent much of his childhood in the South under the care of his grandmother and began to show a flair for creative writing at a very early age. As he hit his teenage years, the movement to end everyday segregation was beginning to produce results not least in Scott-Heron's historically white school, where he was one of the first black students to attend and enjoyed "smaller classes, better equipment, more books in the library, better circumstances"[13] as a result. It was this springboard that helped his talent develop further, and after relocating to New York, he continued to excel as a writer of poetry and fiction before eventually enrolling at Lincoln University in Pennsylvania. Scott-Heron's choice to attend the traditionally African American school had been made partly because it was also the alma mater of his major influence Langston Hughes—the black poet and playwright whose work had often been laced with political themes relating to the need for civil rights in the United States.

By the time Scott-Heron had arrived at Lincoln, the landscape of black politics had changed drastically since the early 1960s when he had been a schoolboy in Tennessee. The era of sit-ins, boycotts, and peaceful demonstrations had passed, and while many African Americans were beginning to question the nonviolent approach to reform, some even felt that the aim of civil rights was dated in itself. The idea of merely existing on the same terms as white people did not go quite far enough and as the 1960s wore on, exponents of the more radical "Black Power" ideology sought to create a new sense of empowerment for African Americans that involved racial pride, autonomy, and even separatism. Under the leadership of Elijah Muhammad, such organizations as Nation of Islam used a version of the Muslim religion to motivate black people toward self-betterment, but often at the expense of unity with other races. Meanwhile the Black Panther Party formed in Oakland, California, in 1966 as a militant group with the intention of leading its followers into an armed struggle against police, government, and any other instrument of oppression being used on black American society. Its manifesto consisted of a 10-point program that demanded land, bread, housing, education, clothing, justice, and peace not for Americans in general, but specifically for the black populace.

It was a school of thought that would soon begin to infiltrate broader culture, particularly music, thanks to the works of jazz singer Nina Simone and spoken word performers the Last Poets—both of whom were big influences on Scott-Heron's political mind. But Black Power would also make headlines around the world, most notoriously during the Mexico City Olympics of 1968 when American athletes Tommie Smith and John Carlos marked their 200m-medal ceremony by giving Black Power salutes from the podium. As former *Rolling Stone* writer David Dalton remembers, incidents like these produced a peak in the fervor around the movement toward the end of the 1960s and suggested that a genuine revolution might well be imminent.

> I remember going up on the roof of the building I lived in on 31st Street in New York in late '69 and looking uptown and thinking, it's only a matter of time before someone blows up the Empire State Building, before someone becomes enraged enough to torch the Stock Exchange, to demolish all the sweat shops, topple the corporate glass mausoleums, in five or ten years, Manhattan will be a ruin . . . New York City will revert to the state it was in before the white man came and messed it up.[14]

Such an atmosphere could not fail to have an impact on Scott-Heron's university life, but despite concentrating on writing initially, he turned his focus to music and performance due to his observation that people were no longer reading novels as widely. An added concern for the young artist was the effect of television in nullifying the revolutionary potential of the wider black population—a fear that could be statistically supported at the very least. In the immediate postwar years, television was still a relatively new medium and remained a luxury item for affluent Americans to enjoy. But the general prosperity of the late 1950s and 1960s coupled with developing technology in the field, such as color pictures and remote controls, led to a surge in numbers. In 1950, only 9 percent of households had a TV set, whereas by 1970, that number had risen to over 95 percent.[15]

This was a statistic that Scott-Heron addressed in a piece called "The Revolution Will Not Be Televised," which was featured on his debut recording *Small Talk at 125th and Lenox* (released in 1970, the same year as his first novel *The Vulture*). Deliberately given only minimal accompaniment on the entire album by congas, bongos, and some of his own piano work, the collection of performances showcased Heron's commanding oratory power and a sociopolitical mind-set that was very much in tune with the spirit of Black Power. In the album's sleeve notes, Scott-Heron attested to this fact by proudly declaring that he was "a Black man dedicated to expression; expression of the joy and pride of Blackness."[16] Compared to the scant instrumentation of *Small Talk at 125th and Lenox,* the follow-up *Pieces of a Man* showcased a fuller sound created by Scott-Heron's collaboration with Brian Jackson—a fellow Lincoln student who had stumbled into one of Heron's poetry recitals in 1969. The two had originally harbored the idea of writing music and words for other, established acts to perform, but decided to do it themselves after coming to the conclusion that there were few acts suitable to convincingly carry off their politically minded polemics. Whether or not that was the case, the pair combined to create a musically revamped and definitive version of "The Revolution Will Not Be Televised" as the opening track on *Pieces of a Man*.

Only a year separated the two recordings of "The Revolution Will Not Be Televised," but the difference is palpable. Scott-Heron's diction and directness are both notably sharper on the later version of the track, helped no doubt by his regular performance of the piece in concert. His vocals also benefit greatly from the smooth drum beat, the funky bass line, and the swirling flute part that create a business-like groove, but stops well short of intruding on the song's message. It is a constant sound throughout, replacing the simplistic pitter-patter of congas and bongos on the early version with a more dynamic edge. The lyrics, however, are unchanged and communicate the same scathing and frequently witty critique of black complacency in a language that TV watchers can understand. As he directly addresses the listener on a one-to-one basis, Scott-Heron sounds as though he is almost giving a motivational speech in time to the music and begins to rhythmically list (and subtly lambaste) all the activities that can no longer be an option for those wanting to trigger, partake, or even see a black revolution. Consuming drugs and drinking alcohol in front of the TV are the first things to be rubbished, but the sideswipes are then quickly directed not just at the indulgence of viewers, but at the pointless stream of images on TV itself. The monologue references sponsorship messages by Xerox, as well as imagined footage of such people as then President Richard Nixon, Vice President Spiro Agnew, and Attorney General John Mitchell—all were political figures for whom Scott-Heron repeatedly voiced an open distrust. Film stars Steve McQueen and Natalie Wood are cast aside in the same breath as cartoon characters and advertising slogans for toothpaste as Scott-Heron continues to pick apart the disposable elements of popular culture with a growing irritation that is audible in his voice.

"The Revolution Will Not Be Televised" then directs its attention to news bulletins, remarking that any revolutionary incidents will not feature footage of petty looting and police brutality against black people, all conveniently documented by major television networks. Scott-Heron also takes issue with the black political figures—specifically the antimilitant reformists Whitney Young and Roy Wilkins, denouncing them as ineffective media poseurs for their more moderate approaches to black inequality. Soaps and sitcoms are next to be dismissed as the lyrics curse over *The Beverly Hillbillies, Green Acres,* and *Search for Tomorrow,* while imagining a time in which "Black people will be in the street looking for a brighter day," thus making these popular shows suddenly irrelevant. Television's creation of celebrity culture and the constant airtime given to safe, family-orientated, and of course, white performers such as Tom Jones, Johnny Cash, and Glen Campbell, are all scrutinized. In one last volley of dialogue, Scott-Heron satirizes another stream of advertising slogans for everything from mouthwash to moonshine before referencing a phrase used in a Hertz car rental commercial to declare that the revolution will put politicized black people into a metaphorical driver's seat. After one final and insistent set of title repetitions, the final sentiment reminds the listener that this will be a strictly one-time event with no repeats, marking a turning point in history. Judging by the momentous and urgent way in which Scott-Heron regards it in the song, the revolution is not to be missed at any cost—least of all the fear of not seeing your favorite TV show.

Despite the all-round superiority of this second version of "The Revolution Will Not Be Televised," its appearance in 1971 coincided with noticeable regression of the Black Power movement. The sense of imminent revolution that Scott-Heron and his similarly minded compatriots may have felt toward the end of the 1960s was now beginning to fade as such prominent Black Panthers as Huey P. Newton and Bobby Seale were imprisoned and the movement splintered into a myriad of different factions. These ranged from moderate civil rights activists looking to force reform through legislation, such as Young and Wilkins, to the extreme radicals who pushed the notion of black supremacy. One especially grizzly example of the latter occurred between 1972 and 1974 in San Francisco when a splinter group of the Nation of Islam carried out a spate of murders specifically on white people. "The Revolution Will Not Be Televised" could not claim to have had galvanized enough black people to take to the streets and look for a brighter day, but it was certainly not forgotten either. Although not exclusively intended for black people, *Pieces of a Man* naturally lacked any crossover appeal and met with no palatable chart success. But critically, Scott-Heron would quickly be established as one of the most important political artists in the American underground not just for the virulent monologues like the "The Revolution Will Not Be Televised," but also the more soulful and traditionally song-based material that he and Jackson created together. By 1975, Scott-Heron signed a record deal with the Arista Records label, enjoying greater worldwide exposure as a result (a number of albums would even be co-billed with Jackson), but his preoccupation with political and social issues continued. In the subsequent years, he would tackle such subjects as the apartheid regime in South Africa, the potentially disastrous effects of nuclear energy, and make a number of critiques of Ronald Reagan's administrations in the 1980s.

Although he would create a body of highly regarded work, Scott-Heron was rarely able to deny that "The Revolution Will Not Be Televised" was the song that unequivocally defined his career; over time, this would become more and more evident, especially as hip-hop began to develop a broad commercial profile during the 1980s. Not only was the blossoming of this new genre traced back to Scott-Heron's proto-rapping by critics and fans almost immediately, virtually every political hip-hop artist to this day continues to cite him as being one of the most important, cross-generational musical communicators of Black Power ideology. Central to this legacy was "The Revolution Will Not Be Televised," which has been referenced by Public Enemy, Common, KRS-One, and most famously by the Disposable Heroes of Hiphoprisy in their 1992 single "Television, the Drug of the Nation" (see the sidebar). The Black Power revolution itself did not occur in the way in which Gil Scott-Heron may have envisaged, but his most famous piece certainly helped to pass on the hope that something similar may yet be possible to a new era of musical and political radicals.

DISPOSABLE HEROES OF HIPHOPRISY—"TELEVISION, THE DRUG OF THE NATION"

Formed in 1991 out of the ashes of thrash-punk outfit the Beatnigs, San Franciscan group the Disposable Heroes of Hiphoprisy were heralded for their ardently politicized material and dense hip-hop sound. Front man Michael Franti also boasted a commanding vocal style that had clearly been informed by Gil Scott-Heron, and that parallel was most apparent when the group released its first single "Television, the Drug of the Nation" in 1992. The track features one of Franti's most damning monologues, married to a hectic and forbidding mesh of samples (many of which are lifted from actual programming). In contrast to "The Revolution Will Not Be Televised," which railed against the negative effect TV was having on black people, the Disposable Heroes of Hiphoprisy attacked the medium (now hugely expanded and virtually omnipresent in Western life) for its anesthetization of the entire American populace. Inspired partly by the stream of images he saw being transmitted by 24-hour news channels during the first Iraq War of 1991, Franti repeatedly slams television's simplification of political issues and the subsequent perpetuation of American ignorance. Although not a mainstream hit, the critical success of the single and the group's first (and only) album *Hypocrisy Is the Greatest Luxury* (1992) briefly helped to establish the Disposable Heroes of Hiphoprisy as fervently political firebrands. This reputation also won them praise and attention from other groups, most notably U2, which selected the Disposable Heroes of Hiphoprisy to support it on its gargantuan ZOO TV concerts in 1992—an apt choice given that this tour was intended to be the Irish band's own elaborate satire of television culture.

Artist: Helen Reddy

Song: "I Am Woman"

Songwriters: Helen Reddy and Ray Burton

Album: *I Am Woman*

Label: Capitol Records

1972

Australian singer Helen Reddy had long felt that pop music did not offer women enough positive messages, and, in some cases, she argued that it was actually reinforcing negative gender roles. In response, she co-wrote "I Am Woman" as an attempt to bring a sense of empowerment to the world's female population, and its huge success signified a clear peak in the women's liberation movement of the early 1970s.

As a young child growing up in Australia, Helen Reddy's first pangs of feminism materialized before she could even articulate them. She was born in 1941 in Melbourne, Australia, to parents who regularly performed on the vaudeville circuit; by the time Reddy was four years old, she would make her own stage debut by singing alongside both her mother and her father at a variety show in Perth, Australia. The experience was tainted, however, when the child witnessed a comedy sequence during another part of the same show that featured a woman in a bathing suit posing for an artist. The joke revolved around the model asking to see his painting only to find that the canvas was still blank, and the "artist" was merely a lecherous old man. Despite being a fairly standard sketch during the time, Reddy would later remember feeling deeply upset but only realized why in hindsight. "Now of course, I see what offended me was a woman being exploited by a man. It was my first consciousness-raising experience and the beginning of my feminism, although it would be decades before I would learn that so many other women shared my views."[17]

As she grew up, Reddy continued to perform in nightclubs and even made occasional TV appearances that brought a moderate amount of exposure, but her long-term aim was always to build a much larger profile. The first steps toward this goal were taken when she won a talent contest in 1966, giving her the opportunity to move to the United States and audition for a contract with Mercury Records. Upon arriving in New York City, Reddy was told that the label had already rejected her on the strength of a previous recording. As a result, she found herself struggling to support her young daughter on the meager singing work she was given or could find. One of the few figures of support she could look to during this time proved to be fellow expatriate Lillian Roxon, an eminent journalist who had already earned a reputation for her writings on women's issues. Aside from providing Reddy with a reassuring Australian accent in the unfamiliar environment of the Big Apple, Roxon also offered her an insight into the blossoming second wave of feminist thinking. Almost half a century after the first wave (which was typified by various movements to achieve female suffrage), this new era had been inspired greatly by the publishing of *The Feminist Mystique* in 1963. In the book, author Betty Friedan drew partly on her own experiences as a housewife to explain how the family unit had eroded female identity in the postwar period. It was a theory that sparked a new push toward equality, helping to establish such groups as the National Organization for Women (NOW), which was co-founded in 1966 by Friedan in the hope of eliminating sexual discrimination in all aspects of American life. To her delight, Reddy found that many of the thoughts she held privately since her first childhood encounter with sexism were now being echoed by other women.

By 1968, Reddy had moved to Los Angeles; while Roxon kept her updated on the latest feminist developments, the singer continued in her quest to find a label willing to take her. After years of rejections, she finally received an offer to record a single with Capitol Records in 1970 and the resulting "I Don't Know How to Love Him" (a cover of the track from the newly released rock opera *Jesus Christ Superstar*) became a surprise hit the following year. That success was enough to convince the label to release a full-length album while strongly recommending that Reddy provide more popular cover versions, but she had also been working on original compositions that reflected her personal state of mind. Despite the growing prominence of women's issues in the media, Reddy remained dismayed that there was no one in the pop world speaking the language of feminism, and, even worse, found that certain songs, such as country singer Sandy Posey's 1966 hit "Born a Woman," actually reinforced subordinate female roles. Finally, Reddy came to the realization that if this trend were to be reversed, "I would have to write what needed to be said myself."[18] She subsequently enlisted Ray Burton (a guitarist with Australian band the Executives based in LA at the time) to help create musical accompaniment for her lyrics; together the pair came up with "I Am Woman"—a proud vocalization of femininity derived partly from Reddy's own experiences, which provided an uplifting addition to her debut album *I Don't Know How to Love Him* (1971). The song became a favorite in her live performances and was later selected to appear on the soundtrack of the Hollywood comedy *Stand Up and Be Counted* (1972). On the off chance that the film would be a hit, Capitol decided to release an extended and re-recorded version of "I Am Woman" as a single with Reddy adding an extra verse to the original, thus helping it to reach the three-minute duration preferred by radio programmers.

Beginning with a bright slide-guitar part and an equally upbeat flute melody, the intro to "I Am Woman" sets a gentle but very optimistic tone, and Reddy's vocals continue in this vein as she starts the first verse by simply stating "I am woman, hear me roar." This direct expression of empowerment ultimately became synonymous with the song in general, but the following lines add to the sense of resoluteness by pointing out the growing numbers of women who feel similarly motivated to achieve a stronger female identity. A rejection of ignorance is also issued alongside a determined protest against gender repression of all kinds, although the song stops short of using partisan language to specifically identify men as being solely responsible for this subversion. Key to "I Am Woman" is the chorus, which seems to blossom with musical color thanks to the addition of a string section and a set of background vocalists. This vibrant arrangement is mirrored lyrically as the narrator proudly describes a sense of wisdom derived from pain and compromise. But the trade-off has evidently been worth it because she completes the chorus by sagely declaring that these sacrifices have also made her into the robust, unflappable, and dignified woman she now is.

The second verse has a sense of even greater gravitas attached to it thanks to the inclusion of brass instruments—particularly a trombone part that accompanies the narrator's promise that any attempts to hold her down will only make her stronger and more resolute in the progression toward emancipation. The chorus then returns with an even higher level of bombast before moving into a third and final verse that Reddy added for the single release. Here, a sense of solidarity is communicated, and, despite the lessons learned and inroads made in the past, she admits that there is still a long way to go until this expression of womanhood is fully understood by her brothers. Again, the tone remains conciliatory rather than adversarial, for the aim of the song is clearly not to foster a gender war, but to raise awareness of the need for equality. An emphatic final run-through of the chorus is followed by a lively coda that is filled with Reddy's ad libs, vocal harmonies, horn fills, and a general exuberance that encapsulated the optimistic mood of so many women at the time. Like some of the most effective songwriters, Reddy tells the story of one person, but take one step back and it could do the same for an infinite number of others. More than any other aspect of the song, it is this lyrical potency that gives "I Am Woman" such an anthemic feel.

While this new version captured "I Am Woman" in its definitive form, the tie-in movie *Stand Up and Be Counted* sank without trace, airplay remained elusive, and the song made little chart impact when it first emerged in mid-1972. Reddy's promotional campaigns were by now being masterminded by her husband and manager Jeff Wald, who engineered a slew of TV appearances over the next few months to make up for the film's flop and lack of radio exposure. Gradually, the positive feedback from these performances translated into an increasing number of requests from the public for "I Am Woman" to be played on radio stations, and this groundswell of support coincided almost perfectly with a peak in the feminist movement. The early 1970s had seen a number of crucial developments in women's liberation, especially through the publication of Germaine Greer's massively influential book *The Female Eunuch* (1970), which used some shockingly direct language to dissect the sexual repression of women. *Ms.* also arrived on newsstands for the first time in 1971 and the magazine would rapidly become a major monthly platform for feminist concerns. It was not just a theoretical progression, but a practical one, too, as demonstrated through legislation such as the Equal Rights Amendment in 1972, which proposed that the constitution be changed to guarantee equal rights irrespective of gender. In the same year, a fierce debate surrounded the legalization of abortion, which would finally be pushed through by a Supreme Court Ruling in early 1973—another victory for many women who demanded the right to control their reproductive systems.

With this increasing female influence in social and political spheres, it was hardly surprising to see women across the country respond to the aural encouragement of "I Am Woman" once it began to appear in mainstream media. The song tapped into the spirit of the time and as 1972 drew to a close, the single had risen from obscurity to finally reach No. 1 in the United States in December during the same week that Reddy would give birth to her second child. An album of the same name was also concurrently issued; although few critics raved over its commercial pop sound, *I Am Woman* also enjoyed strong sales and helped to establish Reddy as the high-profile singer she had always intended to be. In 1973, her success would continue with more chart hits as well as the run of *The Helen Reddy Show*—a prime-time variety hour on

NBC, which briefly installed her as one of the most prominent female TV personalities in the United States. But it was her appearance at the Grammys in the same year that succinctly summed up her role in the changing attitudes of the time. After being presented with the award for Best Female Pop Vocal for "I Am Woman," Reddy took to the stage and in her acceptance speech, famously proceeded to thank God "because she makes everything possible."[19]

Reddy would have a string of hits throughout the 1970s, but none of them came near to eclipsing the stature of "I Am Woman"; as women's liberation gained momentum, the song became an automatic first choice to represent the cause both officially and unofficially. Having been one of the main sources for Reddy's feminist awakening, *The Feminine Mystique* author Betty Friedan saw that the members of NOW were being galvanized by the single. At the closing of a group convention in 1973, Friedan noted with delight how "women got out of their seats and started dancing around the hotel ballroom and joining hands in a circle that got larger and larger"[20] following a playback of "I Am Woman." Aside from inspiring such spontaneous shows of unity, the track was also chosen as the official anthem of International Women's Year, as decreed by the United Nations in 1975. Reddy would encounter financial problems by the end of the decade that played a big part in her decision to perform the song at a Miss World contest in 1981, which unsurprisingly brought criticism from feminist groups. But this did little to stop "I Am Woman" from becoming one of the definitive vocalizations of female empowerment in music history—something that is attested to by countless feminist textbooks that use it as a prominent example of the movement in popular culture. The song is now so well known that in 2006, it was parodied in a Burger King commercial that featured hoards of men voicing a need to satisfy their exaggerated masculine appetites through an adapted set of lyrics. One shot even features a character throwing his underwear in a burning drum—an obvious tongue-in-cheek reference to the bra burning that became one of the enduring symbols of the second wave of feminism. Although the commercial prompted a minor outcry from those who felt it hijacked the movement for commercial or even misogynistic purposes, Reddy spotted the light-hearted spirit and gave it her blessing, helping to further dispel the myth that feminism goes hand-in-hand with humorlessness.

Artist: The Wailers

Song: "Get Up, Stand Up"

Songwriters: Bob Marley and Peter Tosh

Album: *Burnin'*

Label: Island Records

1973

Having formed in one of Jamaica's poorest areas, the Wailers had been making socially conscious statements from their earliest days, but by the start of the 1970s, the major lyrical theme running through the group's style of reggae was the bandmates' shared belief in Rastafarianism. In an attempt to defend it from domestic scepticism and communicate its core values across the world, numerous Wailers' songs made reference to the religion, but few did so as defiantly as "Get Up, Stand Up." Not only did it help take the ideals of Rastafarianism to a broader audience, the song now stands as a universal anthem of liberty for believers and nonbelievers alike.

The Wailers with Bob Marley (second left).
Courtesy of Photofest.

It was under the continuing British rule and economic dominance of white people that the new religion of Rastafarianism began to attract a small following among Jamaica's disenfranchised black population during the 1930s. The movement took a great deal of inspiration from the teachings of Marcus Garvey—an entrepreneur and activist who had spent much of the previous two decades attempting to galvanize displaced blacks around the world and was also said to have encouraged his fellow Jamaicans to look toward Africa for redemption through a divine leader.[21] When Haile Selassie was made emperor of Ethiopia in 1930, a section of Jamaica's black population regarded this as the fulfilment of Garvey's prophecy due to the fact that he was the only African ruler of one of the continent's independent states; as a result, the cult of Rastafarianism first began to emerge in the island's more rural areas. Taking its name from Selassie's given name of Ras Tafari Makonnen, the group regarded him as literally God incarnate or "Jah," and despite including elements of the Bible in their philosophy, followers also developed an Afrocentric way of living that included the ritual smoking of marijuana, the growing of hair into dreadlocks, a strictly natural dietary intake known as "ital" food, and the eschewing of alcohol, tobacco, meat, and even salt. This new religion enjoyed firm support among Jamaica's poor and desperate who now harbored the ultimate goal of leaving their current surroundings of hellish oppression ("Babylon") for a potential heaven on earth under Selassie in Ethiopia ("Zion"). But in among Jamaica's continued colonialism, the dominance of Protestantism, and the grim social legacy of the slave trade, Rastafarians were regarded by most as being outcasts—the lowest of the low.

Although not born into the religion, being an outcast was something that Bob Marley had become accustomed to from day one. Born as Nesta Robert Marley in 1945, he had been the product of a brief, interracial union between a white Marine officer in his 50s and a black, teenage Jamaican woman. Apart from enduring the taunting his mixed race brought him, Marley would also have to suffer the slums in the Trenchtown district of Kingston as he grew up. If nothing else, these testing conditions ensured that the boy swiftly learned how to take care of himself—so much so that his childhood friends would tellingly refer to him as "Tuff Gong." But the sounds circulating around Trenchtown had an even bigger effect on the youngster, and by the late 1950s and early 1960s, Marley had grown to appreciate R&B, soul, jazz, calypso, steel band music, and ska, which was a genre that was also associated with the island's ill-behaved youth, known colloquially to many as Rude Boys. While receiving a casual tutorial in music and marijuana usage from established local performer (and Rastafarian) Joe Higgs, Marley came across Bunny Livingstone and Peter McIntosh who appeared to harbor the same interest in performing as he did. Under Higgs's urging, Marley, McIntosh, and Livingstone formed the core trio of the Teenagers in 1961, but after going through a selection of different names and adding other members, they finally settled on calling themselves the Wailers. It was a name adopted to represent a cry from the ghetto of the downtrodden and destitute—a group of which Marley firmly considered himself to be a part.

The Wailers showed a penchant for reflecting their surroundings from the start, none more so than the early single "Simmer Down"—a call for Jamaica's Rude Boys to cool their hot-tempered behavior that impressed ska fans with its socially conscious sentiment and became a local hit in 1964. Over the next two years, the band drifted toward a rock-steady sound (a slower variation of ska) and consolidated its popularity until Marley left Jamaica in 1966 to be with his mother who was now living in the American state of Delaware. His experience of working the nightshift in a car factory was not a happy one, so Marley subsequently returned home in 1967; while he had been away, Selassie had paid an eagerly awaited visit to Jamaica, the effect of which was to noticeably raise the profile and militancy of Rastafarianism. With this newly heightened level of devotion visible across the land, Marley would also become a follower of the religion as he resumed duties alongside McIntosh and Livingstone (now calling themselves Peter Tosh and Bunny Wailer, respectively) and moved the Wailers into the realms of reggae—a new offshoot of rock steady. This spiritual and musical progression could be heard infiltrating their first full-length album *Soul Rebels* (1970) and other singles recorded at the time with the visionary and notoriously unpredictable producer Lee "Scratch" Perry (many of which would be compiled on 1973's *African Herbsman*). But while the Wailers remained popular at home, very few knew of the group abroad—this became patently obvious as the group embarked on a scantly attended U.K. tour in late 1971.

In an attempt to remedy that situation, the bandmates approached Chris Blackwell of the Island Records label, who had released some of the Wailers' earliest singles in the United Kingdom; he duly offered the group an advance to record an album for worldwide release. The result was 1973's *Catch a Fire*—an album that carried an acute awareness of sociopolitical issues in Jamaica, but at the same time managed to appeal to a rock audience thanks to Blackwell's deliberately slick production. It was a strategy that worked critically as the album received excellent reviews, but commercial success did not materialize despite the label's vigorous promotional campaign. Nevertheless, Blackwell wanted to capitalize on this industry interest, so the group returned later that same year with another album named *Burnin'*, which exhibited a devotion to Rastafarianism that seemed practically militant in comparison to its previous work. Over half the tracks contained a direct lyrical reference to the religion, but opening the album was the most powerful of them all—a stirring song called "Get Up, Stand Up" that communicated the fundamental beliefs of Rastafarians, while appealing to the still largely marginalized followers of Jah to resist repression.

A skittering drum roll fires off the song and after a short intro that establishes the slow, hiccupping reggae rhythm, the Wailers are immediately heard united in their delivery of the chorus that serves as a call to the listener to defend and to fight for his or her rights. But as Marley delivers the first verse, this nonspecific sentiment of resistance begins to give way to a more precise Rastafarian perspective that starts by rejecting Christian views that place too much importance on the afterlife and, as a result, undervalue life itself. The narrator critiques this school of thought as being incomplete and encourages those who have come to similar conclusions to preserve and protect their new beliefs. Another chorus is followed by a second verse that this time refutes the biblical prophecy that a benevolent God will return from the sky to redeem his most loyal and diligent followers. Instead, the song again offers the fundamental Rastafarian belief that deferring happiness equates to a lack of appreciation for life and claims that the Savior is, in fact, on earth already. As the verse ends, Marley can be heard exclaiming the name of Jah to emphasize the point. A more impassioned chorus is subsequently delivered with Marley adding several ad libs of solidarity, but it turns out to be Tosh who adds a final and particularly spirited verse that leaves no doubt over the song's message. He spells out an overall rejection of contradictory religious dogma and once again singles out the flawed idea of redemption after death for those who are prepared to suffer in life. As Marley did before him, Tosh stresses that "Almighty God is a living man" and adds that not everyone can continually be fooled into thinking otherwise. The pair combine with the rest of the group again for one last chorus that repeats until it almost reaches euphoric levels before "Get Up, Stand Up" finally fades out in a mantra of defiance.

The track did earn a single release in 1973 but made no impact, while *Burnin'* fared little better on the album charts. However, more critical acclaim greeted the Wailers in the press, and a number of established musicians were now being alerted to reggae's new and unusual sound. It was this high-profile fan base that proved to work in Marley's favor, especially when Eric Clapton covered the *Burnin'* track "I Shot the Sheriff" and released it as single that reached No. 1 in the United States and No. 9 in the United Kingdom in 1974. At this point, Marley was fronting the Wailers without Peter Tosh and Bunny Wailer, who left to pursue solo careers, but his reputation was rising rapidly; by the time 1974's *Natty Dread* and 1975's *Live!* emerged, reggae had arrived in the mainstream, and Marley was unquestionably the genre's most famous exponent. The message of Rastafarianism continued to be an intrinsic part of many of Marley songs, but "Get Up, Stand Up" remained his definitive expression of devotion, and the song would often provide a celebratory finale to Wailers' gigs, with the crowd being encouraged to participate in an extended segment of buoyant chanting. Even after severe doubts were inevitably raised over Selassie's divinity and indeed the entire religion after he died in 1975, Marley's Rastafarian beliefs were as ardent as ever and they were reiterated emphatically on the epochal *Exodus* (1977), which sold extremely well, establishing the singer as an international superstar. In particular, the epic title track of the album envisioned the people of Jah freeing themselves from their oppressed lives and making a glorious journey back to the fatherland—the ultimate Rastafarian goal. It was somewhat ironic to find that while Marley still stood by this look-to-Africa dictum, much of Africa was now looking toward *him* as a source of hope and redemption partly because of the immense success he cultivated from the humblest of beginnings, but also the huge political clout he now carried in Jamaica—something that *Time* magazine famously declared to be comparable to the government in 1976.

Although "Get Up, Stand Up" helped to create a broader awareness of the religion, it was not just dreadlocked Rastafarians attending Wailers' gigs, nor was it an exclusively black demographic buying their records around the world. The way in which Marley gave a voice to the maligned and marginalized was powerful enough to transcend race and religion, and nowhere was this more evident than in the nascent punk scene that became visible toward the end of the 1970s. This broader identification was especially prevalent in the United Kingdom where young, white punk rockers could be readily exposed to reggae through the numerous Jamaican communities that had been emigrating across the Atlantic Ocean since the 1950s. At that time, punks were looked upon by mainstream British society with a similar suspicion and distrust as Rastafarians had been in mainstream Jamaican society, so they felt a clear sense of affinity with the rebel spirit inherent in much of the genre—not least the work of Bob Marley and the Wailers. The Clash was a perfect example and could be heard experimenting with reggae as early as its first self-titled album in 1977, but in later years, reggae also provided a backbone to the socially conscious 2-Tone movement that was typified by the likes of the Specials, the English Beat, and Selector. It was a cross-pollination that also gave a prominent platform for the fight against Far Right groups that had been on the rise throughout the decade. Even in the United States, punk and reggae made excellent bedfellows, particularly through the Washington, D.C., outfit Bad Brains that impressed many underground music fans by fusing the ferocity of hardcore with the spirituality of Rastafarianism throughout the 1980s. By helping to reinstall music with a dissenting and righteous energy, reggae was arguably one of the missing links between the countercultural spirit of the 1960s and this new era of agitation emerging almost a decade later.

With this ability to communicate on a universal level, it was little wonder that Marley was treated as a "hero of mythic proportions"[22] and was frequently mobbed by people around the world during the last years of his life before finally succumbing to cancer in 1981. In a sad irony, Marley's unfaltering beliefs played a part in his death as the cancer started from a toe injury sustained from playing soccer; when it was suggested that the toe be amputated, he refused citing the reason that Rastafarians needed to be whole of body. Even so, Rastafarianism continues to attract more devotees thanks to his enduring legend and is almost inseparable from reggae music, but the legacy of "Get Up, Stand Up" has grown even further beyond its specific, religious inspiration. The chorus and title alone have now become all-purpose expressions of liberty and protests against oppression to the point of being used and adapted by the human rights organization Amnesty International during many of its public campaigns.

Artist: Neil Young
Song: "Southern Man"
Songwriter: Neil Young
Album: *After the Gold Rush*
Label: Reprise Records
1970

Artist: Lynyrd Skynyrd
Song: "Sweet Home Alabama"
Songwriters: Ed King, Gary Rossington, and Ronnie Van Zant
Album: *Second Helping*
Label: MCA Records
1974

While the political reforms of the civil rights era were much needed, few could argue that they had entirely ended racism in the South, and it was these remnants of prejudice that Neil Young lamented in "Southern Man" and, to a lesser extent, in "Alabama." However, these criticisms seemed a little too sweeping for southern rockers Lynyrd Skynyrd who responded to Young personally through the defiantly proud "Sweet Home Alabama" and briefly sparked rumors of a feud in the process. Although it turned out that both acts had a mutual respect for each other, it was definitely Lynyrd Skynyrd that ended up winning the battle of the protest songs.

It would be a deeply misguided music fan that refers to Neil Young's early work as protest music, but there is no denying that the Canadian played a significant part in

Neil Young.
Courtesy of Photofest.

providing America with at least two counterculture classics in quick succession during his more formative years. In 1967, the nation had first caught a glimpse of Young's lanky figure as he played a distinctive, chiming guitar line in Buffalo Springfield's first hit "For What It's Worth." Intended as a sedate reflection on clashes between long-hairs and police on LA's Sunset Strip, the track's success would see it being adopted as an all-purpose hippy anthem of resistance throughout the rest of the decade (see the entry on "For What It's Worth" in Chapter 3). Barely 18 months later, the group had already disbanded leaving Young to go solo, but he would also become part of Crosby, Stills, Nash & Young in 1969 alongside ex-Byrds' guitarist David Crosby, former Hollies member Graham Nash, and Young's old Buffalo Springfield bandmate Stephen Stills. As the crackdown on youthful rebellion continued across the United States, Young would this time play an even bigger role in documenting the turmoil by penning the band's hit single "Ohio" as an indignant response to the shooting of antiwar protestors at Kent State University in May 1970 (see the entry on "Ohio" in Chapter 4). With such antiestablishment credentials behind him, Young could certainly be guaranteed an attentive audience whenever he felt the need to voice an opinion on any pressing issue. So it was with typical reverence that fans greeted the swipe at regional racism woven into "Southern Man"—a track that emerged just months after the success of "Ohio" as part of Young's third solo album *After the Gold Rush*.

Although Young never publicly revealed his precise inspiration for the song, it was composed at a huge social turning point for the old Confederacy. The movement to bring racial equality to the United States had begun in the southern states during the 1950s and gained national publicity through various sit-ins, demonstrations, and boycotts all over the region. By the early 1960s, civil rights had become a national issue, and African Americans now had a number of political figures leading the movement with Martin Luther King Jr. (head of the Southern Christian Leadership Conference) being the most prominent. Finally, the 1964 Civil Rights Bill legally guaranteed equality for African Americans in housing, employment, and education across the country, but, nonetheless, "Southern Man" seemed to capture Young protesting at the institutional racism he felt was still evident in the birthplace of civil rights. There were certainly some prominent political defenders of segregation even in this new era—particularly George Wallace, whose openly racist policies earned him victories in five southern states during his American Independent Party candidacy in the presidential election of 1968 and later helped install him as Alabama governor for the second time in 1970. With such a significant proportion of the population still appearing to resist changes to the Dixieland way of life, the Civil Rights Act of 1964 certainly had not killed bigotry outright; in "Southern Man," it seemed as though Young remained very aware of this.

A swinging, yet sturdy rock beat starts the song off as the narrator directly addresses the southern man of the title, encouraging him to heed the Bible's word of solidarity and promising that the era of white terror tactics (particularly the practice of burning crosses) will soon be over. The second verse appears to liken the current racial disparity to the time of slavery, right down to the harrowing sound of black cotton plantation workers being whipped by their white masters before asking when atonement will be sought for the years of ill treatment. A change of tempo takes "Southern Man" into a more urgent sounding instrumental segment, punctuated by Young's spluttering guitar solo that matches the mood of simmering anger remarkably well. The slower, original rhythm eventually kicks back into place, and a repeat of the first verse is followed by lines sung through the perspective of the southern man himself, capturing the chilling rage in his promise to end an interracial relationship—seemingly by murderous means. The original narrator then returns to rhetorically ask how long these attitudes can continue before another extended solo dramatically concludes the song in a surge of frustration.

* * * *

"Southern Man" was not released as a single and the album *After the Gold Rush* received some less-than-positive reviews, but Neil Young's growing fan base ensured that the album eventually became the first of his solo works to hit the Top 10 in both the United States and the United Kingdom. Among the most avid of his devotees at the time were the members of Lynyrd Skynyrd, a proud group of self-confessed rednecks diligently developing their repertoire around some of the South's less glamorous venues. They had formed in the mid-1960s in Jacksonville, Florida, operating under a number of different names at first, but always centering around core members Ronnie Van Zant (vocals), Gary Rossington (guitar), Allen Collins (guitar), Larry Jungstrom (bass), and Bob Burns (drums). Initially taking musical inspiration from such British bands as the Rolling Stones, the Yardbirds, and Free, the group would later begin to model itself on a southern, blues-rock blueprint after some revelatory run-ins with early incarnations of the Allman Brothers Band. By the start of the 1970s, the group had settled on the name Lynyrd Skynyrd (an adapted reference to high school teacher Leonard Skinner with whom the band had a long-running feud) and had built an impressive local audience through tireless touring. However, the bandmates would remain unsigned until 1972 when Al Kooper stumbled upon them playing a show in Atlanta. Known for collaborations with Bob Dylan, the Rolling Stones, and the Who, as well as being a member of the Blues Project and Blood, Sweat & Tears, Kooper had become wise to the new crop of southern talent and felt Lynyrd Skynyrd would make a good addition to his MCA subsidiary label Sounds of the South. Aside from signing them, Kooper went on to produce their debut album *Pronounced 'Lĕh-'Nérd 'Skin-'Nérd* (1973), which struggled commercially but did contain the epic "Free Bird"—a song that had been Lynyrd Skynyrd's live showstopper for some time.

Their continuing love for Neil Young did not obscure the affront the Lynyrd Skynyrd bandmates had felt at the negative light "Southern Man" cast on their home and heritage back in 1970. This sense of irritation at his perceived generalization was inflamed again in 1972 when the Canadian offered similar sentiments through the song "Alabama" (featured on the album *Harvest*). This time, Young painted an unflattering picture of the South's decrepit condition and singled out Alabama for failing to progress socially in the same way as the rest of the country. Although not as damning or shocking as the violence of "Southern Man," it was clearly in the same vein—a fact duly noted by reviewers, many who seemed perplexed by this moment of self-imitation. But for Lynyrd Skynyrd, it was a step too far. Now boasting an augmented lineup featuring Ed King (guitar), Leon Wilkeson (replacing Jungstrom on bass), and Billy Powell (keyboards), the bandmates set about responding to Young and giving their fellow southerners a song to rally around. Despite hailing from Florida themselves, it was obviously the neighboring Yellowhammer State that needed the most defending, so the composition was given the name of "Sweet Home Alabama."

One of the most famous guitar intros in rock history opens the track, and as the rest of the band unite to create a slow but steady pace, it is easy to pick up on the celebratory mood. The first verse continues in this spirit and finds a gleeful narrator explaining that he is homeward bound, looking forward to seeing his family, and desperate to be reunited with his beloved native land. A small but spritely instrumental break is then followed by the infamous lines that acknowledge Neil Young's putdowns of

Alabama before stating that "a Southern man don't need him around anyhow." Van Zant's tone is not angry or spiteful, but instead beams with a sense of triumph and pride that grows even more pronounced as the subsequent chorus delivers its idyllic visions of a blue-skied Alabama. The second verse tackles the sensitive issue of the governor (who was still George Wallace at the time of writing and release); despite being addressed as a figure of admiration in the city of Birmingham, he is contrastingly saluted by a round of clearly audible booing from the Lynyrd Skynyrd backup singers. The narrator appears to offer regret that those opposing his policies were not able to have more of an effect, but then points at the Watergate scandal[23] seemingly as a way of illustrating that the North is far from free of its own political controversies. A repeat of the chorus is then followed by a buoyant and extended instrumental section that showcases Lynyrd Skynyrd's triple-guitar trade-off—a dynamic sound that would gradually become one of the group's hallmarks. As Van Zant returns to supply the final verse, he pays tribute to the Alabaman town of Muscle Shoals and its famous studio that had attracted a number of music stars hoping to capture its unique sound on their records throughout the 1960s and 1970s (Lynyrd Skynyrd would later record there, too). The Swampers mentioned in the same breath was a nickname given to the studio's house band whose inspirational musicianship is then cited as being another asset to the much-maligned state. The song's final choruses add further eulogies with Van Zant ad libbing some extra references to the governor and the state capital of Montgomery, while Powell's piano flourishes over the singer, providing the fade-out with an added exuberance.

The song had been played live while the band was touring to support *Pronounced...*, but this recorded version was captured during sessions for the follow-up *Second Helping* that emerged in spring 1974. "Sweet Home Alabama" was released as a single in the summer of the same year and quickly turned out to have a massive effect on Lynyrd Skynyrd's profile by earning widespread radio airplay, helping it to peak at No. 8 on the U.S. chart and ostensibly breaking the band into the mainstream as a result. The song's sense of southern pride would also be underlined when Lynyrd Skynyrd played live as the bandmates quickly took to an almost ritual unfurling of the Confederate flag onstage. But this new level of attention was not without its problems; the band's symbolic pledge of allegiance to Dixieland coupled with unfavorable interpretations of the song's more ambiguous lyrics left some querying whether Lynyrd Skynyrd bandmates were just simple rednecks or sinister racists. The final ad libs, in particular, came in for some close scrutiny given that Montgomery was the scene of some epochal civil rights marches that were brutally countered by local authorities in 1965. These flash points made Alabama's state capital an unfortunate symbol of resistance against integration in the years since, so Van Zant's cheerful references seemed questionable for those who remembered what happened. The mentions of the governor also raised eyebrows among liberals due to George Wallace's firm segregationist past and continually racist rhetoric. But the group made a point of criticizing Wallace's attitude in interviews, stressing that the boos heard in the song just after the first mention of the governor were reflective of their antiracist stance. Lynyrd Skynyrd's members would go on to demonstrate these progressive

The follically blessed Lynyrd Skynyrd in one of its many lineups featuring (front L–R)
Leon Wilkeson, Ronnie Van Zandt, Gary Rossington, Steve Gaines, and Billy Powell.
(Back L–R): Allen Collins and Artimus Pyle.
Courtesy of Photofest.

leanings by adding their vigorous support to the far more moderate Democrat Jimmy
Carter during his campaign for the presidential election in 1976.

A much more entertaining by-product of "Sweet Home Alabama" was the notion
that the naming of Neil Young represented the latest installment of a rock 'n' roll
feud. At first, the Lynyrd Skynyrd camp admitted that it had written the song by
way of protest and was unhappy at Young's sweeping statements on "Southern
Man." "We thought Neil was shooting all the ducks in order to kill one or two,"[24]
complained Van Zant, while Kooper even went so far to declare that the bandmates
"don't like Neil Young, and they were very insulted by the lyric to 'Southern Man.'
The first time they heard it they couldn't believe that anyone would play that on the
radio, so they got him back."[25] But whatever the extent of Lynyrd Skynyrd's initial
anger, it quickly became clear that Young enjoyed "Sweet Home Alabama" as much
as anyone and freely admitted to *Rolling Stone*'s Cameron Crowe in 1975 that he
would rather play that than "Southern Man" in concert. His appreciation for the
band in general even stretched to Young sending the Floridians demo versions of his
song "Powderfinger" in the hope that they might record it. Although Lynyrd Skynyrd never did follow through with Young's offer, it became clear this respect was still
being reciprocated despite the faux pas of "Southern Man." As the decade wore on,
Van Zant responded to repeated questions on the subject by declaring his continuing
adoration for Young and frequently wore one of his T-shirts on stage. This mutual
sense of respect would be underlined tragically toward the end of 1977 when Lynyrd
Skynyrd (now at the peak of success) released a fifth studio album *Street Survivors,*

which featured Van Zant again sporting his Neil Young T-shirt on the cover. Just days after the album emerged, the band's private plane crashed into a Mississippi swamp, killing the singer and two other members of the band's extended lineup. Young's response came shortly after the incident during a gig in Miami, where he would not only play a rare version of "Alabama" but incorporate lyrics from "Sweet Home Alabama" into the song by way of tribute. Rumors that Van Zant was buried in a Neil Young T-shirt persist to this day.

If there ever was a feud, Lynyrd Skynyrd has long since proven to be victorious. Whereas most look back on "Southern Man" and "Alabama" as weak links in the Young back catalog (even his biographer criticized the "finger-pointing"[26] of the former and the "overly simplistic"[27] nature of the latter), "Sweet Home Alabama" remains the aural definition of southern pride and, outside of "Free Bird," is the band's most celebrated track. However, its usage in wider culture is now so broad that it reaches across both sides of the Mason-Dixie line and, in some cases, even farther. Despite some fierce ongoing debate surrounding the possible racist connotations of Van Zant's lyrics, countless commercials have hijacked the song's feel-good vibe, including a high-profile TV campaign for Kentucky Fried Chicken. Just the song's title was a strong enough focal point for Alabama's tourist board that announced plans to market the state to potential visitors under the slogan Sweet Home Alabama in 2007. The instantly recognizable opening riff has also appeared on numerous film soundtracks, too, most notably the 2002 romantic comedy of the same name, which frequently portrays Alabama with as much affection as the song. Additionally, "Sweet Home Alabama" has been translated to represent cities as far afield as the Argentinean capital of Buenos Aires by singer Javier Calamaro on his 1998 album *Diez de Corazones*. What started out as Lynyrd Skynyrd's show of local pride has now practically become a folk song that gets debated and reinterpreted around the world—all of which is certainly a lot more than can be said for "Southern Man."

Notes

1. Quoted in "Protest Season on the Campus," *Time,* May 11, 1970.
2. Ibid.
3. Quoted in Robert Hilburn, "Joni Mitchell Looks at Both Sides Now: Her Hits— and Misses," *Los Angeles Times,* December 7, 1996.
4. Robb Webb, "Story of the Song: 'Big Yellow Taxi'—Joni Mitchell (1970)," *Independent* (London), October 29, 2004.
5. David Sinclair, "Conversation with a Wandering Dreamer," *Times* (London), February 11, 1991.
6. Alexis Petridis, "Joni Mitchell, Shine" *Guardian* (London), September 21, 2007.
7. Quoted in David Stubbs, "Ozzy Osbourne: His Satanic Majesty Repents," *Uncut,* December 1997.
8. Chris Smith, *The Greenwood Encyclopedia of Rock History: The Rise of Album Rock, 1967–1973* (Westport, CT: Greenwood, 2006), 33.
9. A version of this is available on *The Ozzman Cometh,* Sony, 1997. The track is still listed as "War Pigs," but features the original lyrics.

10. Barney Hoskyns, "Black Sabbath: Prole Metal to Ozzy and Beyond," *Creem*, April 1982.

11. Quoted in Vivien Goldman, "Marvin Gaye: Soul Searching," *Sounds*, October 9, 1976.

12. Quoted in Gavin Martin, "Marvin Gaye: Mr Midnight in the City of Angels," *NME*, December 11, 1982.

13. Quoted in James Maycock, "Gil Scott-Heron and Brian Jackson: Brothers in Arms," *Mojo*, December 2003.

14. David Dalton, "The Last Poets: The Progenitors of Rap," *Gadfly*, September 2000.

15. Figures from Cobbett Steinberg, *TV Facts* (New York: Facts on File, 1985), 86.

16. Gil Scott-Heron, *Small Talk at 125th and Lenox*, sleeve notes, Flying Dutchman Records, 1970.

17. Helen Reddy, *The Woman I Am* (New York: Jeremy P. Tarcher/Penguin, 2006), 17.

18. Ibid., 139.

19. Ibid., 154.

20. Betty Friedan, *It Changed My Life* (New York: Dell, 1976), 331.

21. Historians frequently refer to Garvey's promise of a divine leader (quoted in a number of different ways) as being the starting point of Rastafarianism, but there is still some scholarly dispute over whether he actually made such a statement.

22. Timothy White, *Catch a Fire* (New York: Henry Holt and Company, 1991), 22.

23. The Watergate Scandal revolved around the burglary of the Democratic National Committee in Washington, D.C, during 1972. The incident was later found to be part of a larger campaign of espionage carried out with the authorization of President Richard Nixon and led to his eventual resignation in 1974.

24. Quoted in Tom Dupree, "Lynyrd Skynyrd in Sweet Home Atlanta," *Rolling Stone*, October 24, 1974.

25. Quoted in John Tobler, "Al Kooper: Sweetheart of the South," *Melody Maker*, March 2, 1974.

26. Jimmy McDonough, *Shakey* (London: Vintage, 2003), 336.

27. Ibid., 373.

CHAPTER 6

RAGING AGAINST THE MACHINE (1977–1982)

No one could possibly argue that the spirit of political or social rebellion in music was completely dead during the mid-1970s, but compared to the same period in the previous decade, protest song pickings were certainly much slimmer. The baby-boom generation that caused such a stir in the 1960s had now grown up and its youthful agitation had inevitably been tempered, while some of the more popular modern acts erred more toward a sense of self-indulgence rather than continuing the philanthropic intentions of the folksingers and hippies before them. Such rock giants as Led Zeppelin and Pink Floyd seemed intent on making their work as verbose and extravagant as possible—a progression that was critically lauded, but also appeared to forsake consciousness in favor of creativity on many levels. Later in the decade, disco turned into a worldwide sensation, and while Chic, Donna Summer, and the Bee Gees may not have stretched the boundaries of music quite so hard, they too kept largely apolitical and concentrated instead on providing soundtracks for partygoers. As famously illustrated in John Badham's iconic film *Saturday Night Fever* (1977), the weekend thrills and fleeting glamor offered by nightclubs were an attractive alternative to the grim realities of a country slowly descending into a brutal recession that many Americans faced from Monday through Friday. The fact that these two genres were so commercially popular seemed to indicate that a desire for escapism and self-fulfillment had begun to dominate music culture, and fans and artists alike were looking for ways to forget their troubles rather than be reminded of them.

It took an entirely new generation to put any serious semblance of insurgency back into the mix, and it came in the form of punk rock, but rather than pick up where the counterculture of the 1960s left off, this was a rebellion made of a much different energy. Hope and unity were now succeeded by nihilism and misanthropy, and for their brief existence, the Sex Pistols summed up these attitudes better than most. As the United Kingdom experienced increased social disorder and high unemployment, the band issued a seething scream from the perspective of youths with no discernible future. But if they were doomed for the scrap heap, they planned on taking as much of the establishment as possible with them, and the British monarchy was a prime target for destruction as **"God Save the Queen"** (1977) so emphatically demonstrated. Their close contemporaries the Clash also riled against a stagnant wider society in their music but as it turned out, one of their most virulent early statements proved to be a more specific critique of the music industry as voiced through **"Complete Control"** (1977). There were more than a few American punk rockers adding their rancor to official figureheads and the hippy legacy, too, including the Dead Kennedys who warned against fascism in the disguise of pseudo-progressiveness in **"California Uber Alles"** (1979). But even their kind of antiestablishment clamor did not go far enough for the members of Minor Threat. Unsatisfied with the limitations of punk, the Washington, D.C., quartet made the genre sound harder and faster, and through the lyrics of **"Straight Edge"** (1981), singer Ian MacKaye declared his abstinence from the music world's staple vices of sex, drugs, and alcohol.

As mainly white kids screamed their irritation at the world and the people around them during this period, a parallel to punk was beginning to emerge in the black musical underground, too. The genre of hip-hop had been birthed at parties in the Bronx borough of New York during the early/mid-1970s, and initially, at least, this too was a source of escapism for those dealing with the area's alarming decline. Indeed, an apt crossover with disco at the end of the decade would provide the country beyond the Northeast with its first insight into this new musical phenomenon as the Sugar Hill Gang's dance-floor friendly **"Rapper's Delight"** (1979) became a hit across the United States. However, the increasing social and economic problems facing African Americans gradually injected the genre with a less frivolous flavor over the next few years, and hip-hop slowly seemed to become the black version of punk. The one single that marked the point of overlap clearer than any other was undoubtedly **"The Message"** (1982) by Grandmaster Flash & the Furious Five—a song that was so unyieldingly bleak in its portrayal of urban decay and destitution that even the group members themselves recoiled from its radically different feel at first. This new group of angry young men did not always offer society a better way of doing things, but a lack of alternative was not going to stop them from verbally lashing out at the way things were.

Artist: Sex Pistols

Song: "God Save the Queen"

Songwriters: John Lydon, Glen Matlock, Steve Jones, and Paul Cook

Album: *Never Mind the Bollocks, Here's the Sex Pistols*

Label: Virgin Records

1977

Despite the harsh social and economic conditions gripping the United Kingdom in 1977, many in the country still seemed happy to forget their troubles to celebrate the 25th anniversary of Queen Elizabeth II's reign as sovereign. For the Sex Pistols, however, the monarchy was merely a pointless and dehumanizing institution that actually contributed to the plight of so many British people. It was an injustice that they fiercely denounced through the punk rock roar of "God Save the Queen"; by releasing it as a single to coincide with these celebrations, the band succeeded in scandalizing the entire nation for good measure.

In retrospect, there is little doubt that the release of "God Save the Queen" in May 1977 denoted a new peak in the antagonistic potential of popular music, but the Sex Pistols did not become a target of national vilification in the United Kingdom overnight; it was something they had been working on for some time. John Lydon (nicknamed Johnny "Rotten," vocals), Glen Matlock (bass), Steve Jones (guitar), and Paul Cook (drums) played their first gig together at St Martins College of Art in London in November 1975, but were unceremoniously thrown off stage before finishing their set. It established an us-versus-them precedent for many of their earliest shows, a number of which led to physical confrontations between band and crowd. Although derided for their lack of musical ability, unkempt appearance, and open disdain for the very people for whom they were playing, the bandmates actually thrived off this negative energy, and it quickly encouraged them to be even more provocative. When compared to the grandiose and technically advanced music being created by Queen, Pink Floyd, Led Zeppelin, and many other of the United Kingdom's most popular acts, it was somewhat inevitable that the Sex Pistols' brand of deliberately amateurish punk rock would be dismissed. Gradually, the bandmates would find themselves in conflict not just with conservative music fans, but with the sizable conservative faction of British culture as a whole—and it was a contest that they all appeared to welcome with much enthusiasm.

Despite the lack of regard given to them by most orthodox concert promoters, the Sex Pistols continued to play a number of small gigs during 1976, some of which were set up by fans. One show in Manchester in June was famously organized by local band the Buzzcocks and was attended by audience members who would go on to form the Smiths, Joy Division, and even Simply Red. It was not an isolated incident either. Across the country, hundreds of bands were sprouting almost spontaneously following the realization that guitars were not solely instruments for the gifted and the stage was not just reserved for the beautiful. Spotting the buzz around the group and the small but visible punk fraternity that was developing, EMI Records offered the Sex Pistols a record contract and released the strikingly inflammatory debut single

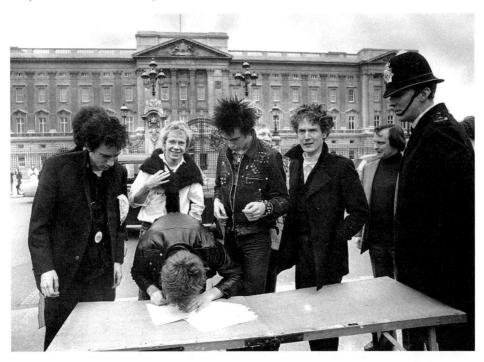

The Sex Pistols signing their short-lived second record contract with A&M Records in front of Buckingham Palace (the queen is not pictured). L–R: Johnny Rotten, Paul Cook (smiling), Steve Jones (checking the small print), and Sid Vicious. Standing next to Vicious is the band's manager, Malcolm McLaren.
Courtesy AP Images.

"Anarchy in the U.K." in November 1976. What they might have lacked in ability was now being more than made up in visceral energy and wry humor, but arguments over the band's musical credentials were quickly eclipsed by a scandal of far greater proportions following a TV appearance in December. After fortuitously finding themselves on the early evening *Today* program (original guest and EMI label mate Queen had pulled out at the last minute), Rotten, Cook, Jones, and Matlock were briefly interviewed by the show's drunken host Bill Grundy. His line of questioning quickly degenerated into an open invite for them to swear on the live broadcast, and Jones duly obliged with a short stream of expletives, much to the amusement of the band's entourage. This comical exchange resulted in an avalanche of complaints with one viewer apparently kicking his TV set in a blind rage at the band's disregard for common decency. A number of national newspapers subsequently carried the incident as a front-page story and the Sex Pistols (previously unknown outside the underground music scene) now had the hatred of the general public to enjoy.

In early 1977, the band replaced Matlock with Sid Vicious (aka John Ritchie)—a thuggish-looking fan with a well-established penchant for antisocial behavior and accordingly regarded as an ideal Sex Pistol. As incidents of disorder mounted and with continual bad publicity beginning to encircle the band, EMI opted to terminate their contract, but the Sex Pistols were subsequently picked up by A&M Records in March following a signing ceremony held outside Buckingham Palace. This publicity stunt was also organized to draw attention to the fact that the next single was scheduled to be a bitingly ironic rant called "God Save the Queen"—a song that shared its title with the British national anthem, but certainly did not contain the same pledge of allegiance. It had been a part of the Sex Pistols' repertoire for many months and was originally titled "No Future," but at the encouragement of manager Malcolm McLaren, the band renamed it in the knowledge that Silver Jubilee celebrations marking the 25th anniversary of Queen Elizabeth II's coronation were imminent. By coinciding the song's release, it was a perfect way for the Sex Pistols to gate-crash what was shaping up to be the most patriotic of parties. Additionally, it was a move guaranteed to cause yet more controversy in the media and ensure that traditionalists across the country would treat the band with even greater revilement. However, A&M also lost its nerve and terminated the band's contract within a week of the Buckingham Palace stunt after reports emerged of Rotten and Vicious instigating a violent skirmish with the powerful TV/radio presenter Bob Harris at a London club. Finally, a young Richard Branson stepped in and offered the group a third contract with his independent label Virgin Records, and "God Save the Queen" emerged at the end of May 1977, just over a week before the actual day of the Silver Jubilee.

Despite the general clamor to salute the queen, the mid-1970s had certainly not been the happiest time for her subjects. The United Kingdom had descended into a devastating recession that decimated industries, sent inflation spiraling, and enraged the workforce into carrying out regular strikes. As ever in times of economic decline, the rise of extremist factions was noticeable and even stretched to the realms of pop music (in 1975 alone, Eric Clapton and David Bowie had both made much publicized statements advocating Far Right thought in the United Kingdom). Additionally, the political troubles in Northern Ireland were spreading with the Provisional Irish Republican Army stepping up its bombing campaign in mainland Britain during the period. In among all this uncertainty, conflict, and discontent, the incongruous sight of people throwing lavish street parties as a royalist salute did not sit well with the Sex Pistols. In decades gone by, the British monarch was thought of as being God's representative on earth and the figurehead for the country's empire, but in the late 20th century, these ideas seemed ridiculously quaint for an iconoclastic punk band. Although virtually all of the country's political, social, and cultural institutions were fair game for the Sex Pistols, their opinion of the monarchy (and, more specifically, the queen) as hopelessly outdated symbolism was always voiced with particular vehemence. "Watching her on telly, as far as I'm concerned, she ain't no human being," snapped Rotten. "She's a piece of cardboard they drag around on a trolley."[1] It was precisely this sentiment that fueled the fury of "God Save the Queen."

The incendiary mood of the song is established instantly with the towering main guitar part Jones unleashes in the intro, and this sense of menace is quickly underlined by Rotten's vocal sneer. The first line alone is enough to cause consternation among conservative listeners as the narrator bluntly and brutally equates the supposedly just rule of the monarchy with a reign of outright fascism that has made its subjects docile. Before this almost treasonous notion has sunk in, the lyrical shock tactics continue with the declaration that the queen is simply inhuman and that England's dream-like devotion is creating a stagnant society. The next part signals a quicker, more urgent tempo to underpin the narrator's plea against subservience before Jones's main riff returns and Rotten delivers more tongue-in-cheek declarations of loyalty and love. The second verse hones in on the symbolic nature of the queen as a money-making attraction for the benefit of tourists rather than the benevolent figurehead she is purported to be. Additionally, a reference is made to injustices carried out in the name of the monarchy that was no doubt intended to incorporate both imperial crimes of old and the modern-day willingness to ignore the social plight of so many British people. At this point, the emphasis of "God Save the Queen" subtly shifts from being an expression of antiroyal rage to exhibiting a sense of nihilism and even bitterness. The idea of sinful behavior is rubbished as there is no worthwhile future for the narrator to preserve or protect—a philosophy that is driven home by images of the modern generation being nothing more than abandoned flowers at best or poison at worst. Following an aptly frustrated sounding solo from Jones, a final rebuke to nostalgia is issued before the bandmates unite for repeated howls of the phrase "no future" that are both vociferous and yet strangely dispirited. By the time "God Save the Queen" splutters to its end, the anger of the first lines has petered out to be replaced by a feeling of slightly impotent agitation.

The reaction to "God Save the Queen" could be little other than hostile, and the British music industry went to extreme lengths to ignore the song. Simply getting the single made was a trial in itself as staff members at Virgin's pressing plant initially refused to participate in its production. Branson used his diplomatic skills to persuade them to return to work so the release could still coincide with the Silver Jubilee, only to find that most major high street record shops refused to stock it not just because of the song itself, but the cover that featured a defaced image of the queen. Radio stations naturally gave it a wide berth with the BBC banning it from airplay because of the song's "gross bad taste,"[2] while national newspapers again clamored to splash the Sex Pistols over their front pages. However, all this publicity played straight into the hands of the band, and the single sold enough copies to reach No. 1 but was denied by the chart's ruling body, which underhandedly awarded the No. 1 spot to Rod Stewart's "I Don't Wanna Talk about It" in an attempt to stifle the controversy. In many cases, "God Save the Queen" did not even get to bask in the glory of being runner-up as some charts were printed with a blank entry at No. 2. However, the Sex Pistols would not go quietly and decided to mark the actual day of the queen's Silver Jubilee (June 7, 1977) by playing a celebratory gig in a boat on the River Thames, but after the vessel docked, chaos ensued with fights breaking out and several arrests being made. A few days later, the bandmates became personal targets of violence from members of the public who had taken offense at "God Save the Queen" with Rotten suffering tendon damage in his arm following a knife attack in London.

"God Save the Queen" truly was a high watermark in the Sex Pistols' notoriety, but through it all, they remained defiant in the face of the acrimony they received. While the song broke huge taboos at the time by hijacking the national anthem and lambasting the monarchy, its success in the face of such extreme censorship also demonstrated that the band was not alone in its standpoint. But as Rotten has since remarked, the song was not just another in a long line of measures to provoke anger, but rather it was a well-disguised vocalization of sympathy for the disenfranchised.

> You don't write "God Save the Queen" because you hate the English race. You write a song like that because you love them, and you're fed up with them being mistreated.[3]

This is an amusing irony given that so many of the English race responded to the supposedly philanthropic spirit of "God Save the Queen" with utter contempt and even violence, but it is partly for this ability to stir up such extreme emotions that the Sex Pistols are so completely adored today. The band would play its last gig in January 1978 (although it would reform in 1996 and play sporadically in subsequent years), but despite being together for such a short time, its musical influence across the world is immeasurable. "God Save the Queen" remains very much at the heart of the band's legend and is ever present in critics' lists of the greatest singles of all time. This sense of reverence reached a new height in 2007 (to mark the 30th anniversary of its original release), when British music magazine *NME* launched a campaign encouraging readers to buy the re-released[4] single again in the hope of sending it to No. 1 without fear of meddling from the chart's now more liberal ruling body. But three decades had evidently cushioned the song's sonic impact and lyrical shock value because "God Save the Queen" could reach only a paltry No. 42 this time around.

Artist: The Clash

Song: "Complete Control"

Songwriters: Mick Jones and Joe Strummer

Album: Nonalbum single in the United Kingdom/*The Clash* in the United States

Label: CBS Records (United Kingdom)/Epic Records (United States)

1977 (United Kingdom)/1979 (United States)

As the fury of punk rock took hold in the United Kingdom in 1977, the Clash was one of the band's that led the way thanks to an eye-opening image and an unmistakably brash sound. But as well as railing against the state of the nation, the bandmates were also inspired to take issue with the state of the music industry following a spat with their record company CBS over the unapproved release of new material. The protest took the form of "Complete Control" and added another target for the genre's early anger.

By early 1976, the Sex Pistols had played just a handful of gigs around London and released no music whatsoever, but their aggressive sound and confrontational demeanor were already proving to be a revelation for many who crossed paths with them—including the bands for which they opened. In April, one show saw them supporting the 101ers, who were beginning to enjoy minor critical acclaim and attracting a cult fan base around town for their energetic, R&B-tinged rock. As the Sex Pistols began their typically raucous set, it exhilarated the 101ers' singer Joe Strummer (born

The Clash (L–R): Nicky "Topper" Headon, Mick Jones, Joe Strummer, and Paul Simonon.
Courtesy of Photofest.

John Mellor) to the point that he immediately began to question the purpose of his own band. Indeed, just weeks after the gig, Strummer quit and began to forge a new group called the Clash, which followed in the footsteps of the Sex Pistols' fiery punk rock and actually made its live debut supporting them in July. After a few lineup alterations, the Clash established a core membership of Strummer (vocals, guitar), Mick Jones (guitar, vocals), and Paul Simonon (bass, vocals). Together, they rapidly became the Sex Pistols' most prominent contemporaries in the United Kingdom thanks to a striking image that made them look more like a gang than a band and a fierce sonic assault laced with an acute awareness of the country's social and political problems. But despite its lyrical rhetoric and musical ferocity, the group shied away from the more idealistic punk rock fans and bands and their determination to shake up the norms of society with Strummer for one reflecting "rock doesn't change anything. But having said that, I still want to try and change things."[5]

The Clash's debut single proved that commitment emphatically. Released in early 1977 on the high-profile CBS label, "White Riot" was a two-minute blitzkrieg of insurgent energy that sounded literally like the very act of social disorder it was named after. Inspired by the sight of rioting at London's annual Notting Hill Carnival by socially disenfranchised black people, the song lambasted the apathy of the white British population toward such problems and urged a similar reaction. Although some mistakenly interpreted the lyrics as having a white-supremacist lilt, there was no mistaking the overall conviction of the group, and if any band had a strong enough polemic to change anything, it was the Clash. With the Sex Pistols already creating a stir with their own incendiary debut single "Anarchy in the U.K.," there appeared to be a growing amount of evidence that punk was ushering in a new epoch within music at the very least. But as the Clash was about to find out, the old facets of the music *business* were keen to keep a firm control over this newfound sense of cultural liberation.

The band's decision to sign to CBS in the first place had been seen as a blow to the autonomy of punk by its more militant followers, many of whom thought the Clash would be better suited ideologically and practically to releasing its music independently. However, the allure of a £100,000 advance was too much to ignore for Strummer and his comrades, who also believed they had full artistic control despite leaving the negotiations to their manager, Bernie Rhodes. "We were completely in the dark," recalled the singer. "What did we know about record companies and contracts?"[6] That gap in their knowledge was illustrated almost immediately when CBS opted to release the track "Remote Control" as a second single against the Clash's wishes. The track had been lifted from the band's self-titled debut album (released shortly after "White Riot"), but was viewed by the bandmates as one of their weaker works—a viewpoint that was vindicated somewhat by its subsequent flop on the chart. The feeling of disillusion associated with this was being exacerbated by a growing sense of dissatisfaction with certain elements of the punk scene itself. The summer of 1977 saw this new genre extend rapidly beyond its underground origins and become a national phenomenon, but this growth had more than a few downsides. The suspicion that punk bands attracted for apparently encouraging public misbehavior resulted in some heavy-handed methods of suppression by authorities, which the Clash had experienced firsthand on many occasions. One particular incident around the time saw the band's van being searched by police, who uncovered nothing more than a towel, a pillowcase, and a room key that had been taken from a hotel. Even so, two members of the band were arrested; when the accused failed to show up in court, the rather extreme measure was taken to put them in jail. The indignant response to these familiar facets of oppression came in the shape of a brand new song (not included on the album) called "Complete Control." It was a phrase that the Clash's manager Bernie Rhodes was also fond of using during his early negotiations with the band over the level of power he could wield—which he initially insisted on being absolute.

The song was the first to be recorded with new drummer Nicky "Topper" Headon, who had come into the band as a permanent replacement for Terry Chimes, but the Clash's decision to enlist the famously unpredictable dub/reggae producer Lee "Scratch" Perry to work on the single grabbed far more attention. It appeared to be an outlandish move in theory, but if nothing else, it demonstrated the band's ambition to move beyond the simplistic realms of punk at a very early stage. That said, the track opens with a blaring guitar sequence that heralds the Clash reaching new levels of agitation as Strummer recounts the arguments between band and label over the release of "Remote Control," immediately establishing an adversarial atmosphere as a result. The next lines refer to a trip to Amsterdam to fulfil press commitments, which was clumsily placed in the middle of a U.K. tour, causing the band an unnecessary strain. Headon's drums stab through the wall of guitars for the first chorus as the song acerbically refers to the wisdom (or lack of) employed in these decisions and then rubbishes the idea of complete control of which the band had apparently been assured. The song then establishes a solid and steady rhythm going into the second verse as Strummer turns his attention to the unnecessary hostility endured by the group's members and their associates. First he rages against the sight of friends being run out of concerts before attacking the police for overzealously monitoring the band's movements and activities. A slightly different chorus then rhetorically asks if they have done something to deserve this harassment before issuing a demand for an all-encompassing band autonomy.

A searing, Mick Jones guitar solo sends "Complete Control" off into a gallop, and, at one point, Strummer can be heard saluting his bandmate's skill with much enthusiasm. The next verse redirects the song's anger squarely at the record label in all but name by slamming it for promising artistic freedom when the contract was signed and for having hidden financial motives in doing so—a sentiment that is concluded with yet another version of the chorus that succinctly demands "lemme see your other hand!" A moment of calm then materializes, but the band quickly begins to carry the song into its dense final section that starts with Strummer paraphrasing the media outcry toward punk as being an undesirable phenomenon destined to have only a short life span. He then immediately switches to the viewpoint of Joe Public and barks out a first-person admission of being mentally and physically controlled by society until his vocals become indecipherable in the mix. As "Complete Control" races to the end, its most prominent sound becomes that of Mick Jones, who spells out the first three letters of control that tellingly read as "C-O-N" and underline the band's ill feeling at being duped, but is also aimed at the listener as a warning against an all-round submissiveness. By the last few seconds, the song is virtually a blur of noise until Headon's juddering drum fills finally conclude the startling sound of the Clash biting the hand that feeds, but which also serves as a subtle critique of those who allow themselves to be controlled in any scenario.

The single emerged in September 1977 and took the Clash back onto the charts at No. 28 (still a highly respectable position for a punk band at the time), helping the quartet to achieve the upper hand in what was now a very public battle with its label. Press reaction was similarly positive, but some did criticize the band for its naive approach to the music business and the slightly petulant manner in which it chose to address the situation. Nevertheless, the release was accompanied by a verbose press statement issued by the band that clearly outlined the disparity between the intentions of the Clash and CBS.

"Complete Control" tells the story of conflict between two opposing camps. One side sees change as an opportunity to channel the enthusiasm of a raw and dangerous culture in a direction where energy is made safe and predictable. The other is dealing with change as a freedom to be experienced so as to understand one's true capabilities, allowing a creative social situation to emerge.[7]

Joe Strummer may have explained his belief that rock does not necessarily change anything early on, but true to his word, the Clash was still *trying* to change things as much as it could. And if the group could not do that, it was certainly making as much fuss as possible. The major label structure was never likely to suffer a hugely detrimental impact from the group's spirited protest, but there was no doubt that the anyone-can-do-this ideology of punk was gradually stretching to the business side of the music industry as well as the creative dimension. The surge of independent labels that cropped up in subsequent years in both the United Kingdom (Factory Records and Rough Trade Records) and the United States (SST Records and Dischord Records) demonstrated that complete control was not merely a myth, and genuine artistic autonomy was attainable for those who were willing to forgo the lump-sum advances that were normally associated with record deals. If nothing else, such a song as "Complete Control" was undoubtedly an enduring warning to any new band faced with the financial temptations of a major label.

CBS continued to act as the Clash's record label, but "Complete Control" did little to diffuse the tension between the two parties that remained firmly in place throughout the next few years. A major bone of contention was the label's initial refusal to release the debut album in the

SEX PISTOLS—"EMI"

The Clash was certainly not the only punk band to experience trouble with its record label during 1977. Fellow Londoners the Sex Pistols had signed with the huge EMI Records in late 1976 and subsequently released their debut single "Anarchy in the U.K." As part of the promotional campaign, the band appeared on a TV show called *Today*, where the bandmates were heard uttering a stream of four-letter words and caused a national outcry (see the entry on "God Save the Queen" for more information). The negative publicity and some similarly unfavorable feedback from EMI's top-level executives forced the label to rethink the band's contract. Although the Sex Pistols remained on EMI's roster in the short term, their fate was finally sealed in the first days of 1977 when stories about the group spitting and vomiting at Heathrow Airport broke in the press, further scandalizing EMI. Just days later, the label announced that the contract had been ended and cited the adverse publicity during the previous months.

The band's response was to compose and record "EMI," which captured singer John Lydon ostensibly ranting at the former label and its all-round mismanagement, its suspicious financial motives, and its inability to view the Sex Pistols as a serious proposition. Filled with a typical sneer and an understandable disgust, the song was chosen to be the final track on the group's debut album *Never Mind the Bollocks, Here's the Sex Pistols*, which was released toward the end of 1977. By that point, the lyrics also included a snipe at the A&M label at the very end of the track due to the fact that it, too, had signed the Sex Pistols in a wave of publicity following EMI's decision to back out, but dropped them with an even greater haste when it also became wary of the group's behavior.

United States, although a significantly amended version (which included "Complete Control") was eventually released in 1979. One of the major issues that both parties argued over continually was the retail price of releases, which the band constantly sought to keep down to affordable levels even though 1979's *London Calling* was a double album and the 1980 follow-up *Sandinista!* was a triple. While the bandmates were happy to let their personal finances suffer for the sake of their fans and the vision of their artistry, the business plan at CBS featured no such altruism. The constant challenge of balancing out the demands of the label and the strains of the music industry with its own integrity became a very familiar theme in the life span of the Clash, and "Complete Control" was a song and indeed a phrase that served as an anthem to this ongoing struggle. In one interview with British music magazine *NME* conducted during the spring of 1982—almost a full five years after the first major spat with CBS—the band and the manager were captured vehemently criticizing labels at length for their methods of keeping bands in financial debt so as to foster obedience (still a regular practice) and the frustrating inability of the Clash to gain access to strictly regimented radio playlists. It was a polemic that was dryly rounded off by Jones who deadpanned, "we've written a song about it. It's called 'Complete Control' and we hope to have it out by the summer."[8]

Artist: Dead Kennedys

Song: "California Uber Alles"

Songwriters: Jello Biafra and John Greenway

Album: Original version released as 7-inch single (later included on the 1987 *Give Me Convenience or Give Me Death* compilation); re-recorded version included on *Fresh Fruit for Rotting Vegetables*

Label: Alternative Tentacles Records/Optional Music

1979 (single version)/1980 (album version)

Having grown up despairing of the political apathy he felt was dangerously prevalent in America during the 1970s, Jello Biafra feared that California Governor Jerry Brown might take advantage of this situation to increase his own power to dictatorial levels. As a warning of this potential swing toward fascism, Biafra's band, the Dead Kennedys, released "California Uber Alles," which became one of American punk's defining singles. While Brown did not turn out to be the threat they feared, it is a song that continues to live on thanks to periodic lyrical rewrites that take aim at new figures of political suspicion.

With a name like Dead Kennedys, it always suspiciously seemed as if the band was trying to use bad taste to be provocative. But as they would continually stress during interviews, it was not the callus insult aimed at John F. Kennedy and Robert F. Kennedy that many thought it was. Instead, the name was intended to be a tombstone for the sense of political progressivism that the slain siblings embodied, as well as denoting what the band felt was a subsequent era of apathy and cynicism. It was something that the band's future singer Eric Boucher observed growing up in the midwestern mountain town of Boulder, Colorado. Born in 1958, Boucher had quickly developed a political awareness that was encouraged by his parents and distinguished him from other pupils at school. On one occasion, a U.S. Air Force pilot who had served in Vietnam was paraded during a sixth-grade class; in response, an unimpressed Boucher coldly questioned him about what it felt like to be responsible for bombing children in villages.

At that point, music had also become an interest following his first connections with the medium during the "British Invasion" of such bands as the Rolling Stones and the Beatles in the mid-1960s. However, during the following decade, the now teenage Boucher found that his hometown had not only become dominated by fans of album-oriented rock and soft-rock bands that he personally despised, but it was also attracting the hated bands themselves. "The Eagles lived in Aspen for a while, Elton John bought a place in Boulder, as did Stephen Stills, Joni Mitchell and Joe Walsh. In other words, it was total hell for me as a teenager . . . to this day Boulder is still a magnet for really snooty, high-brow yuppies and new age cults, and that had already started back then."[9] It was not just a case of musical snobbery on Boucher's part. Despairing at what he saw as a middle class that had done away with the radical ideas permeating through the 1960s in favor of personal fulfilment, the youngster mused on the greater problems such a mass mind-set might cause the country.

> This sort of apathy and putting your brain to sleep and becoming an obedient little poodle is a one way ticket to fascism. It's how people allow themselves to be taken advantage of by aspiring dictators.[10]

Like so many teenagers during the latter half of the 1970s, Boucher became attracted to the musical liberation offered by punk rock. Aside from being a follower of such homegrown acts as the Ramones, he also managed to experience the British explosion of 1977 firsthand during a summer visit to the United Kingdom. After returning to America, Boucher enrolled briefly at the University of California–Santa Cruz, but found the possibilities of studying acting and the history of Paraguay incomparable to the political edge of San Francisco's burgeoning punk scene. By early 1978, he had taken root in the city and immediately became a fixture at local gigs before inevitably forming his own group. After answering an advertisement for a singer posted by a guitar player calling himself East Bay Ray, the pair then recruited bassist Klaus Flouride, a second guitarist who operated under the mysterious moniker of "6025," and drummer Bruce Slesinger, who went under the slightly less unusual alter-ego of "Ted." By now, Boucher had himself adopted the name of Jello Biafra —cribbed partly from the wobbly dessert and partly from the short-lived African republic that broke away from Nigeria in 1967, but was incorporated back into the county in 1970 following a devastating famine.

This initial, five-strong incarnation of the Dead Kennedys played its first gig in July 1978, but soon trimmed itself to a quartet after 6025 left the band early the following year. One of the songs proving popular in the Dead Kennedys' early shows had stemmed from lyrics that Biafra had first written in Boulder with his childhood friend John Greenway, but upon moving to the West Coast, he had rewritten and presented them to the band as "California Uber Alles." The original inspiration had been the yuppie culture infiltrating his hometown, as well as what Biafra felt was a (post-Kennedys) generation devoid of ideals that was leaving itself open to political suggestion. But as Biafra settled into the Golden State, "California Uber Alles" was created after he saw not only the same kind of people from whom he had hoped to escape by moving away from Boulder, but more worryingly, he saw someone with an apparent will to manipulate these unmotivated masses for his own end—Governor Jerry Brown.

In 1975, Brown replaced Republican Ronald Reagan for what would be a dual term of eight years in total. During his tenure, the one-time Catholic priest in training and fervent objector to the Vietnam conflict gained a reputation for what seemed like an enlightened, Zen-like attitude to state politics. This included the embracing of environmental issues, welcoming more women and minorities to California's government, and curbing expenditure to the point where Brown himself refused to live in the lavish governor's mansion or be driven around in chauffeured limousines as was the norm. Famously, Brown instead opted to drive himself to work in a modest sedan and lived in an unremarkable apartment. On the surface at least, his was a governorship of Democratic ideals that were not just proposed but put into practice in a way in which the Kennedy brothers would arguably have approved.

However, Brown's critics saw something more sinister behind this new wave of progressive politics, and few were able to cast light on his hidden motivations better than his former aide J. D. Lorenz. Following a period as research assistant, Lorenz was then appointed as employment director as Brown began his first term in Sacramento. Although leaving Brown's staff shortly thereafter, it was the experience of witnessing him at work from such close quarters that provided Lorenz with the inspiration for his 1978 book *Jerry Brown: The Man on the White Horse*. Recounting numerous incidents, conversations, and flash points, the book painted an ultimately unflattering picture of Brown as a highly calculated politician with the ability to pay lip service to many, but commit himself to no one—all of which was shrouded by his apparently forward-thinking rhetoric. Additionally, Brown's private asides to Lorenz seemed to reveal a sinister undercurrent to the governor's personal ambition.

> Politics is a jungle and it's getting worse. People want a dictator these days, a man on a white horse. They're looking for a man on a white horse to ride in and tell them what to do. A politician can do anything he wants so long as he manipulates the right symbols.[11]

Biafra evidently had no doubt about Brown's motivations, and with the number of American counterculture movements now paltry in comparison to that of 10 years earlier, he feared the development of a new era of totalitarianism. Subsequently, Biafra and the Dead Kennedys spelled out these suspicions for the world to hear on "California Uber Alles." Released in June 1979 on the band's own Alternative Tentacles label, the track offered a protest against Brown's activities in office by virtue of vicious satire, while alerting the song's listeners to the issue at hand by envisioning a worryingly oppressive future. The title itself references the first line of Germany's former national anthem, which had been adopted after the First World War and used by the Third Reich to insinuate the superiority of its people. This nod to the most pernicious period of 20th century history informs the song's eerie feeling; from the opening thumps of Ted's drumming, the first rumbles of Flouride's bass, and the forbidding tones of Ray's guitar, the mood of the song is undoubtedly menacing. As Biafra begins the first verse, it becomes apparent that he is using his brief stint as an acting student to good use by singing it from the perspective of the governor and playing him as a figure of maniacal ambition. It is a state of mind strikingly channeled through Biafra's vocal delivery that simmers with tension as he laces his character with a darkly humorous sense of imbalance. At a time when most punk bands addressed their subjects in an unwaveringly direct and sometimes clubfooted manner, these were subtleties and skills that were already helping Biafra to stand apart from his peers.

Throughout the verses, the narrator outlines his vision for the state and country in frequently overt fascist language. First comes the promise that he will become not just president but Fuhrer before long and that one of his commands will be enforced meditation for children (Governor Brown was known as an advocate of the practice). The following verse continues to critique what Biafra had identified as a kind of neo-hippy form of liberalism carried out by "Zen fascists" with ultimately totalitarian intent. The image of the leader on a white horse (as mentioned in Lorenz's book) is referenced directly as the narrator explains how a coerced attitude of mellow contentment will cover the inevitable abuse of power. The final verse, however, is by far the most unsettling. Having been played at a speedy tempo, the song instantly slows down to a death march punctuated by Ted's militaristic drumming for the third and final segment of lyrics, which are set five years later in 1984 (an obvious nod to George Orwell's own vision of a dystopian future in his seminal novel *1984*). At this point in the narrative, dissenters—or people who are felt to be "uncool" by this administration's righteous terminology—are put down with measures that are lifted wholesale from Nazi Germany, but are still shrouded by the illusion of progressiveness. The song describes how people will be seized by secret police (dressed in easygoing casuals), told to take a concentration camp–style shower (but offered a flower to create a sense of security via solidarity), and finally gassed to death with organic poison (presumably to avoid damaging the environment). It is the retribution that is promised to anyone who dares to interfere with the future President Brown. With that, a final repetition of the chorus—which is simply the song's title repeated as a rallying statement of superiority—leads "California Uber Alles" to its juddering coda and closes the song's window into a nightmarish tomorrow.

Despite the underground popularity of the song, it did relatively little to dent the mainstream reputation of Governor Brown—he had already begun his second term by the time the single was released, having been reelected comfortably the year before. Even so, the band eventually re-recorded the track, and this faster, tighter version proved to be the highlight of its debut album *Fresh Fruit for Rotting Vegetables,* which emerged in 1980. (As an unfortunate side effect, the Dead Kennedys also began to notice that "California Uber Alles" was beginning to win them a number of neo-fascist punk fans who misinterpreted the song as a right-wing anthem.) Thankfully, Fuhrer Brown did not materialize after he failed to win the Democratic nomination for the 1980 presidential election, which was eventually won by his predecessor

JELLO FOR MAYOR!

In attempt to prove that his political mind produced more than hot air, Jello Biafra stood as a legal candidate for the position of mayor of San Francisco in 1979. Adopting "California Uber Alles" and borrowing the advertising slogan for Jello desserts ("There's always room for Jello") as a campaign song and a hook line, respectively, the singer was given the same amount of local media exposure as all of his opponents to air his policy. Initially, he was dared into running by Dead Kennedy drummer Ted, while on the way to a show by Ohio post-punk outfit Pere Ubu. As the band played that night, Biafra wrote his policies out on a napkin at a nearby table. They included such spoof measures as making businessmen wear clown suits and even rehiring laid-off civic workers as panhandlers to work in San Francisco's rich neighborhoods earning a 50-percent commission—a hilariously adroit criticism of recent job cuts that had affected city employees. However, the campaign was by no means a complete farce, and Biafra was at pains to underline the serious side of his manifesto that incorporated the idea of having police officers elected by the neighborhoods they patrol, banning cars to help curb pollution, and legalizing squats in empty, tax-delinquent buildings. Remarkably, Biafra received over 6,500 votes and came in fourth out of a field of 10. Stunned by the support this seemingly joke candidate had received, city officials passed a ruling shortly after the election decreeing that only people operating under their given name could run for the position of mayor.

in Sacramento—Ronald Reagan. Almost immediately, the new president began to draw fierce criticism for his conservative politics; realizing the threat of Jerry Brown was no longer pressing, Biafra rewrote "California Uber Alles" with an emphasis on the new premier and called it "We've Got a Bigger Problem Now." The song was issued as part of the 1981 EP *In God We Trust Inc.* (which also contained an emphatic rebuke to their unwanted Far Right "fans" titled "Nazi Punks Fuck Off") and splices some more relaxed, lounge-style interludes with furiously fast sections that are musically identical to "California Uber Alles" right down to the raucous chorus chants. Lyrically, the song also repeats Biafra's trick of singing from the subject's (Reagan's) perspective and makes references to the tense deadlock in the cold war, the administration's pandering to corporate needs via top-end tax cuts, and the dubious military interventions being carried out in Afghanistan and El Salvador, which were intended to quell left-wing uprisings.

The Dead Kennedys eventually broke up in 1986, but "California Uber Alles" continued to be a song that was referenced time and time again. Politically minded rap group the Disposable Heroes of Hiphoprisy offered another rewrite of the song in the 1992 album *Hypocrisy Is the Greatest Luxury.* They even sampled the original version, but this time aimed their anger at the vicious budget slashing carried out by then newly elected California governor Pete Wilson. As recently as 2005, the song was updated once again by Biafra himself via his collaboration with Washington state sludge-rock band the Melvins. On the 2005 album *Sieg Howdy!* (the second to be released under the name of Jello Biafra and the Melvins), a live track called "Kali-Fornia Uber Alles 21st Century" revised the original lyrics to critique yet another newly elected California governor—Arnold Schwarzenegger. Once again, Biafra plays the role of the former body builder and Hollywood star while touching on his much debated personal and political history. The song includes references to his use of steroids (albeit when they were still legal), alleged incidents of groping, sexist descriptions of Democratic opponents as "girlie men," and several lampoons of the catchphrases Schwarzenegger has used in his film roles. The additional factor of the governor's Austrian heritage helped make him an even more apt target for "California Uber Alles" with Biafra claiming that Schwarzenegger is "probably the closest to the original . . . desire for outright fascism"[12] encapsulated in the 1979 original. There appears to be no end in sight for the song's periodic rejuvenation as to this day, Biafra claims that he regularly receives rewritten lyrics that criticize a different politician with a similar hidden agenda.

Artist: Minor Threat

Song: "Straight Edge"

Songwriters: Ian MacKaye, Brian Baker, Lyle Preslar, and Jeff Nelson

Album: *Minor Threat* EP

Label: Dischord Records

1981

Punk rock's intentions to offer an alternative to the music establishment at the end of the 1970s did not go far enough for Minor Threat's Ian MacKaye, who prided himself on avoiding casual sex, drugs, and excessive alcohol use. It was a way of life that was vastly different to the kind lived by most bands, but he resolutely advocated it through the song "Straight Edge," which continues to stand as an anthem of abstinence for similarly minded hardcore punk rockers across the world.

As any punk rock historian, textbook, or foot soldier will proudly explain, one of the central motivations behind the musical shifts that occurred on both sides of the Atlantic during the late 1970s was the complete renouncement of rock's norms. The hugely popular acts that played their technically advanced music in cavernous, soulless stadiums were (in public at least) roundly despised by punk's first wave that felt such bands as Pink Floyd, Yes, and even Led Zeppelin were unnecessarily pretentious. In turn, the new generation of would-be rock stars sought to be closer to the audiences both literally, by playing in smaller, more intimate venues, and figuratively, by demonstrating that being in a band required only the most basic musical skill. But while the two factions were musically at odds, the culture of excess that had developed in tangent with the decade's biggest rock stars was not something that was so vociferously dismissed. Indeed, the principal vices of drugs, casual sex, and alcohol were retained by the likes of the Sex Pistols, the Ramones, and many of the other punk revolutionaries despite the supposed opposition of artistic ideology. The first band that invited people to take that extra step of abstinence was Washington, D.C.'s massively influential hardcore punk outfit Minor Threat. As well as being among the finest exponents of this ferociously precise and primarily American subset of punk, the band's lead singer, Ian MacKaye, proudly presented his clean-living lifestyle as a way for fans to further polarize themselves from the clichés of the music world. "A lot of the kids I knew in high school just started rebelling by getting high," he complained in 2001. "It was almost as if they looked it up in the local listings. How to rebel: GET HIGH! It seemed like the normal thing to do and I was not interested in being normal."[13]

That rejection of standard modes of rebellion was helped along partly by circumstance rather than by just outright defiance. In 1980, MacKaye's short-lived first band the Teen Idles had encountered many problems while attempting to play their fast and aggressive hardcore punk live simply because of their ages. Clubs and live venues took exception to the fact that the deliberately named Teen Idles were comprised of minors and often prohibited them from entering the premises to perform. By way of compromise, MacKaye suggested that the band and its underage fans should have "X"s drawn on their hands to provide a clear signal to venue staff that these people could not consume alcohol, but could at least watch the shows. As a child, MacKaye had experienced the detrimental effects of alcoholism through a family member and had been inspired by the strict antisubstance stance of the strikingly unpunk 1970s rock icon Ted Nugent. Privately, the young MacKaye made a vow to stay on the proverbial wagon throughout adult life, and the regulations regarding alcohol in live venues entwined perfectly with his personal mind-set—he could not drink, but he did not want to anyway. Subsequently, a dimension of punk, which quickly became known as "straight edge," had been established with the aforementioned "X" providing a neat emblem of this new, alternative existence. As the Teen Idles quickly sped toward their conclusion, MacKaye and drummer Jeff Nelson recruited bassist Brian Baker and guitarist Lyle Preslar to form Minor Threat. The new band played its first gig in December 1980—less than two months after the Teen Idles' final bow. By the summer of 1981, Minor Threat had released its self-titled debut EP, which contained what instantly became the anthem of sober punk rockers everywhere: "Straight Edge."

Musically, the song is a fearsome document of Minor Threat at its astounding best. The growling sound of Preslar's guitar during the introduction instantly grabs the listener's attention before Baker and Nelson unite the bass and drums into a typically primal and pulverizing rhythm. The exactness of the band is punctuated by MacKaye barking his lyrics in what seems like one continuous breath; in 45 seconds, the bludgeoning is over. Minor Threat recorded only 26 songs in its brief existence, but they all had something to say—none more so than "Straight Edge." The first verse begins with a noticeably understated but all-important establishment of personal parity with the audience—a dictum of equality that lay at the heart of all punk rock. MacKaye then spits out the vices being railed against from alcohol to cocaine to amphetamine before finally issuing a rallying cry of "I've got the straight edge" as the final, fist-clenching payoff line. The process is repeated again for the second and final verse, only this time the substances cited include marijuana and solvents.

Hardcore punk was by no means a genre that was unified by this way of thinking, and MacKaye would frequently be the subject of criticism from his own musical peers for his puritanical stance and an apparent inclination to be overly preachy. However, in this context it is clear that rather than commanding his followers into militancy, he is underlining the personal liberation associated with such a distinct choice of lifestyle. It is a standpoint that is clearly reflected in the penultimate lines of the song, which spell out a desire to stay in touch with reality and avoid using any kind of substance as a fleeting source of emotional support. MacKaye's biggest bone of contention was not simply *anyone* who chooses to drink or take drugs, but rather those who use them as counterproductive escapes or excuses for unacceptable behavior; it is this that "Straight Edge" makes a broader protest against.

During Minor Threat's existence, the front man was repeatedly asked to clarify the straight edge "manifesto," especially in light of the fact that the rest of the bandmates openly drank (although not to excess). In one interview during 1983—two years after the release of the *Minor Threat* EP—MacKaye explained the specific target of his rancor.

> There's nothing I hate more than hearing people use that shit [substance abuse] as an excuse. Too many times it's 'I'm sorry what happened last night, I was f—ed up.' . . . I don't like getting hit by some drunk [guy] just because he's drunk. I don't buy it. Can you imagine what drinking has done to people's conscience, just in what they've done under the influence and allowed themselves to do under the influence and when they sober up, realizing what they'd done? It's sad to me, it's sad.[14]

MacKaye further indicted excessive alcohol use as a way of killing independent thought, but also took pains to stress that his personal straight edge commitments were not intended to create an entire movement—it was merely an attempt to demonstrate the physical and mental benefits attainable through abstaining. "I'm not saying 'Don't go to bars.' I'm not saying, 'Don't drink alcohol.' I'm merely saying, 'Try to find a little more entertainment from your own resources.' As opposed to going out and buying it."[15]

Just a few months after Minor Threat's debut release came out, the four-track follow-up EP *In My Eyes* was released, which further blurred the line between Mac-Kaye merely making his own statement of defiance and sanctimoniously commanding everyone to follow suit. In particular, the track "Out of Step (With the World)" left many—including members of his own band—displeased with MacKaye seemingly telling people how they should live their lives. Although slightly longer than "Straight Edge," but boasting just as much musical power and velocity, the song addresses the same vices in an even more succinct manner with the lyrics reading quite simply as "Don't smoke, don't drink, don't f—." Although casual sex outside of meaningful relationships was not something referred to in "Straight Edge," it was also an activity blacklisted by MacKaye, feeling it to be similarly mindless and dangerously ignorant of the potentially negative physical side effects. It would only be a few years before the entire world would begin to think the same way with the onset of AIDS radically shaking up sexual attitudes in Western societies, so in that respect, at least, MacKaye was certainly ahead of his time.

Nevertheless, Nelson was uncomfortable at the apparent list of orders that dominate the song and attempted to persuade MacKaye to insert an "I" at the start of each line to help clarify that the lyrics were personally motivated rather than punk rock commandments. MacKaye initially refused and the two clashed before the singer relented and allowed an "I" to be added in brackets before the first line. Although united in a broader ideological sense with his bandmate, Nelson admitted that Mac-Kaye's dogmatic approach to straight edge living did not always match his own.

There was definitely a point in early Minor Threat where he was . . . preaching . . . It definitely was "holier than thou" sometimes. And how could it not be when you're presenting, so vehemently and so stridently, such an antiestablishment approach? My approach would have been more conciliatory [but] it would not have had quite the same impact, I don't think.[16]

The impact that MacKaye's conviction had was to spawn a handful of similarly inclined straight edge hardcore punk bands that took the lyrics of "Straight Edge" and, to a lesser extent, "Out of Step (With the World)" as a set of rules to which to adhere. Such bands as Boston's SS Decontrol and fellow D.C. outfit the Faith (featuring MacKaye's older brother Alec) took on the mantle with a zealousness that was at times ferociously militant. As the 1980s gradually wore on, the initial handful grew to a fully recognized genre of punk with MacKaye still at the forefront thanks to his pioneering post-Minor Threat project Fugazi. Even today, the lifestyle's popularity is clearly not waning, and this continued subscription to the straight edge ethos could easily be related to the modern day rejection of capitalism and consumerism, which grows evermore fierce itself. Alcohol, in particular, is inextricably linked to the music culture more than it has ever been; tours, venues, and festivals all frequently boast sponsorship deals with brands of whiskey, vodka, and, of course, beer. Pledging allegiance to the straight edge lifestyle can also be (and is often intended as) a simultaneous stand against the corporate co-opting of alternative culture. Furthermore, MacKaye's pledge to not sell band merchandise and keep gig ticket prices down to a universally affordable level (something retained in his post-Minor Threat musical projects Embrace, Fugazi, and the Evens) ties in with this rejection of the entertainment industry's ongoing mission to make money.

Whatever the modern applications of "Straight Edge," it is a song that documented one person's riling against the frivolity that music is so often associated with and illustrated the possibilities of another existence that was even more alternative than the perceived alternative scene of the time. Whether intentional or not, MacKaye's self-imposed code of conduct inspired following generations to do the same; for just one 45-second song, that ranks as a hugely impressive legacy.

Artist: Grandmaster Flash & the Furious Five

Song: "The Message"

Songwriters: Duke Bootee (Ed Fletcher), Melle Mel (Melvin Glover), Clifton Chase, and Sylvia Robinson

Album: *The Message*

Label: Sugar Hill Records

1982

After emerging from block parties in the Bronx and coming to commercial prominence on dance floors across the country, hip-hop was inextricably linked to having fun during the 1970s and early 1980s. However, "The Message" by Grandmaster Flash & the Furious Five gave the genre a grim (but much needed) injection of social realism by illustrating the existence of African Americans living in the most desperate circumstances and showed that hip-hop could be used to voice disaffection as well as soundtracking a good time.

Grandmaster Flash. Despite being the focal point of the group, he had very little to do with "The Message."
Courtesy of Photofest.

Hip-hop had been developing in and around the South Bronx district of New York since the early 1970s, but it was not until the end of the decade that a wider audience finally got an idea of what it actually sounded like. Built around the distinctive bass line featured in Chic's classic track "Good Times" and featuring three vocalists who took turns to talk rhythmically (or "rap" to the beat), the Sugar Hill Gang's "Rapper's Delight" gave commercial credence to this new form of music for the first time when it became a worldwide hit in 1979. But while its success opened up an almost literal wealth of possibilities for hip-hop, the glossy, disco-indebted sound and radio-friendly sheen to "Rapper's Delight" also left some artists feeling that they could do better than this comparatively lightweight representation of the genre. The fact that the members of the Sugar Hill Gang had been opportunistically assembled to record the song by Sugar Hill Records' owner Sylvia Robinson only added to the annoyance felt by those still paying their dues in the hip-hop underground. Bronx disc jockey (DJ) Joseph Saddler was one such example; given the immense amount of effort he had put into developing his reputation as part of Grandmaster Flash & the Furious Five, it was arguably an understandable feeling of irritation.

Born in Barbados in 1958, Saddler moved to New York as a child and spent his teenage years attending the earliest hip-hop parties where he would dance enthusiastically to such DJs as Kool Herc as they played the instrumental breaks in old funk, soul, jazz, and R&B records. It was a sight that inspired Saddler to try his own hand at DJing, and he did so with the intention of developing the techniques he saw being used at these gatherings. In particular, he used his enthusiasm for electronics to painstakingly build mixing equipment allowing him to ensure that the transition from record to record would be seamless—a slick contrast to the clumsy mixing performed by the likes of Herc. By the mid-1970s, Sadler's innovations and the dynamic sounding stage name of Grandmaster Flash were already helping him establish a firm reputation as one of the Bronx's finest DJs. Before long he added a collective of rappers (or MCs) who performed under the names of Cowboy, Kid Creole, Melle Mel, Mr. Ness, and Raheim; together they were billed as Grandmaster Flash & the Furious Five. The group's first single "Supperrappin' " emerged in 1979—the same year as the Sugar Hill Gang's "Rapper's Delight." But while the latter song enjoyed radio support and stormed dance floors across the world, Grandmaster Flash & the Furious Five were forced to watch enviously from afar as their offering failed to make any kind of mainstream impact.

The Sugar Hill Gang was the first to break the sound of hip-hop onto the chart, but the band would never repeat the success of its debut single. Its reputation would soon be overtaken by Flash and his crew who continued to impress music fans around New York before signing their own deal with Sugar Hill Records. Some of the DJ's most devout followers proved to be the members of the new-wave rock group Blondie who exhibited a clear hip-hop influence in their 1981 No. 1 hit "Rapture" not least by mentioning Flash by name and sending his profile skyrocketing in the process. The Clash also personally requested that Grandmaster Flash & the Furious Five open for it on one of the British punk band's numerous dates in New York. Meanwhile, Flash's dexterity behind the turntables would be demonstrated emphatically later that same year on the single "The Adventures of Grandmaster Flash on the Wheels of Steel"—a revolutionary track recorded in one take and spliced together entirely of snippets of other records. In the space of two years, Grandmaster Flash & the Furious Five had become the coolest name to drop in the world of hip-hop, and the Sugar Hill Gang now had to be content with relatively minor successes.

Hip-hop had come a long way from the block parties at which it was birthed back in the early 1970s, but the one theme still unifying this broadening genre was its upbeat mood. The vast majority of music made by hip-hop artists was still intended to make people dance and soundtrack a good time, but this was in stark contrast to the surroundings of the south Bronx. The area had been entrapped in a severe economic decline dating back to the 1950s when the building of the cross-Bronx expressway uprooted much of the area's affluent populace. After those families fled to the suburbs, the vacuum was filled with lower-income families attracted to cheaper housing; jobs in the area were dwindling and the Bronx spiraled into neglect during the late-1960s and early-1970s. Violent gang culture became rife, decimating the area even further and with the added effect of the worldwide recession biting hard during the mid-1970s, youth unemployment in the borough hit a staggering 60 percent.[17] By the dawn of the 1980s, it appeared that the most desperate areas such as these would be the last to feel any benefit from the new economic policies advocated by the incoming president Ronald Reagan. The staunch Republican's implementation of "trickle-down" economics meant top-level investment for businesses in the hope that subsequent growth would eventually mean more jobs and higher income being passed down to the workforce. For those living hand-to-mouth in the Bronx, the wait for any kind of improvement in their social situation had already been painfully long.

Grandmaster Flash & the Furious Five would be the first to explicitly reflect this situation via the medium of hip-hop, but initially many in the band took pains to avoid such a dramatic shift away from the carefree spirit for which they (and indeed the genre as a whole) were celebrated. They were first presented with "The Message" by Sylvia Robinson, which was a song that had been written by Sugar Hill Records' in-house songwriter Ed "Duke Bootee" Fletcher. The track dated back to a 1980 demo tape recorded by Bootee with a piano at his mother's house. It was much slower in tempo than what Grandmaster Flash & the Furious Five were used to, and they initially poked fun at the song's gritty vibe. Despite the group's reticence to record it in fear that the song would be poorly received by their hardcore fans, Robinson insisted and used Raheim and Melle Mel to record the vocals (Mel also wrote an extra verse of his own). After realizing Robinson's intent to release "The Message" as a single, Flash implored the rest of the Furious Five to participate in the recording, but it was too late. The track was finally released in 1982 and credited to Grandmaster Flash & the Furious Five despite the fact that only one member of the group (Melle Mel) had any role in composing the song and only two (Melle Mel and Raheim) actually rap on the recording itself.

The slow but strong beat that starts "The Message" is quickly colored by a distinctive synthesizer riff that echoes across the song and instantly becomes its main musical hook. The first words are delivered by Melle Mel as he tensely remarks that his hectic surroundings are like a jungle and are threatening to consume him—a striking introductory statement that underlines the unsavory mood. Suddenly, the sound of glass breaking pierces the tension and the narrator unleashes a stream of images that document a deeply unpleasant environment of foul smells, incessant noise, infestations, and violent drug addicts. The most depressing thought, however, proves to be a sobering realization that there are no financial or practical means by which to escape this hellish existence. Understandably, a sense of simmering anger is audible as the song goes into its famous chorus refrain (repeated throughout the song) that flatly protests "don't push me, cause I'm close to the edge" for there is only a limited amount of ill-treatment, dehumanization, and destitution that the narrator can take. The second verse adds to the bleakness through its story of a homeless woman who had come to the city looking for opportunity, but found only a slow decline into the sleazy world of sexual entertainment and eventually prostitution.

At this point, the voice of Raheim takes over, but the narrative does not lighten up in the slightest. His part of the song begins with the narrator observing that his mother uses television as a way of pointless, detrimental escapism and then adds that his own financial woes are leading to an existence of fear for his loved ones. The problems are seemingly endless for this character; saddled by poor education, strangled by awful economic conditions, irritated by ineffective infrastructure, and blighted by ill-health, his frustrations are almost at the point of outward violence. Of course, these are sentiments that could tell the tale of any number of people living in the worst parts of the Bronx—and indeed America as a whole—during the early 1980s. An instrumental break then brings a moment of respite for the listener, but Raheim soon returns to illustrate hopelessness from a child's perspective. The youngster in question complains to his father of alienation and drug abuse at school before expressing his desire to forsake any ambition or hope in favor of an easy, manual labor job. A grim depiction of gang activity then follows and includes a girl being pushed in front of a train, a man being stabbed, and the all-around threat of violence that heightens at night.

Melle Mel returns for the extended last verse and in an especially unforgiving set of lyrics, he paints a horrific picture of life in a ghetto—from an insalubrious birth to a shocking death. An innocent child begins life with nothing and becomes bitter at his situation while aspiring to the apparently opulent life of gangsters and criminals. The boy then drops out of school and begins to try his hand at petty crime only to be put in prison where an existence of violence and sexual abuse leads to suicide. This image of a lifeless body hanging inside a jail cell is certainly hard to forget, but "The Message" still has one more unpleasant facet of Bronx life to communicate in the final section, which is the only contribution the rest of the band make to "The Message." In the song's last seconds, the Furious Five are heard innocently chatting on the street and bemoaning the news of a friend's mother getting robbed when a police car rolls up and arrests them for no apparent reason. This highlighting of police victimization —a commonly held grievance among black people during the era—is just about the only disturbing part of big city life not mentioned in the song's lyrics. But through this alarming skit, "The Message" manages to tick every ghastly box. If the song itself did not do enough to force the point home to a listener, then the accompanying video surely would. Filled with footage of New York City's most disenfranchised (including some especially stark shots of horribly dilapidated Bronx housing projects), it left no uncertainty about the content of this particular message.

Despite the unflinchingly depressing content and the significantly slower beat, "The Message" was a clear success. Relatively, the No. 62 position hardly made it a sensation, but it was still one of the few hip-hop singles to even register on the chart at this early stage of the genre's mainstream development. The song, however, did crack the Top 10 in the United Kingdom and went on to sell over a million copies. More importantly, it ushered in a new era of social conscience for hip-hop—something that would become one of the genre's most prominent characteristics and ensure that it would become so much more than the fad that many people were convinced it was. This also helped to ensure that it was a critical success with *Rolling Stone,* for one, enthusing at this radical departure from the rap norm and heralding the song as a "detailed and devastating report from underclass America."[18] While the Sugar Hill Gang could claim to have started the first epoch of hip-hop with "Rapper's Delight," Grandmaster Flash & the Furious Five carved out a new era with "The Message," but at a fairly great personal cost. Flash's initial reluctance to record the song and Robinson's use of Melle Mel to record the vocals caused a shift of balance within the group, while the debate over the song's composer credits caused a rift between the band and its label. The band's first album *The Message* finally was released at the end of 1982, but by the following year, Melle Mel and Flash had gone their separate ways and became embroiled in a legal battle over the right to use the group's name.

With hip-hop now outselling all other genres of music, there is little doubt that a significant proportion of this success is built on "The Message." The song's chorus, in particular, is now an instantly recognizable expression of anxiety that has been revisited and referenced frequently in everything from public information films to tracks by extreme metal bands. This has helped the song transcend hip-hop into wider pop-culture phraseology, so while most people may not be familiar with Grandmaster Flash & the Furious Five, they will probably know those lyrics. It is partly due to this that "The Message" is continually regarded as not just a hip-hop classic, but one of the most important songs ever. Among many other accolades, it was voted No. 51 in *Rolling Stone*'s list of the 500 Greatest Songs of All Time in 2004. Despite the internal problems that fractured the band soon after "The Message" was released, Grandmaster Flash & the Furious Five also occupy legendary status as was proven in 2007 when they became the first hip-hop act to be inducted into the Rock and Roll Hall of Fame. "The Message" may not have done much to directly change or even offer a solution to the situation in the poorest parts of the Bronx, but it certainly inspired other rap artists to document their environment in their music so that others might feel the same sense of injustice. Were it not for songs like this, today's music fans might have ended up listening back to hip-hop's first releases and mistakenly assume that life in the Bronx during the early 1980s was a constant party.

Notes

1. Quoted in "The *Rolling Stone* 500 Greatest Songs of All Time; 173. 'God Save the Queen,' Sex Pistols," *Rolling Stone*, December 9, 2004.

2. Ibid.

3. Quoted in *The Filth and the Fury*, Julien Temple, director, 2000.

4. This was actually the second re-release. The song was also issued in 2002 to mark the queen's Golden Jubilee and reached No. 15 in the United Kingdom.

5. Quoted in Ira Robbins, *The Big Takeover*, retrievable at www.rocksbackpages.com

6. Quoted in Jon Savage, *England's Dreaming* (New York: St Martin's Press, 1993), 304.

7. Quoted in Robbins, *The Big Takeover*.

8. Quoted in Charles Shaar Murray, "The Clash: Up the Hill Backwards," *NME*, May 29, 1982.

9. Quoted in Ben Myers, *American Heretics: Rebel Voices in Music* (Hove, England: Codex, 2002), 116.

10. *The California Report*, KQED radio broadcast, July 14, 2006 (streamed online at www.californiareport.org/domains/californiareport/archive/R607141630/e)

11. Quoted in J. D. Lorenz, *The Man on the White Horse* (Boston: Houghton Mifflin, 1978), 142.

12. The California Report, KQED radio broadcast.

13. Quoted in *True 'til Death—The Story of Straight Edge*, BBC Radio 1 documentary, 2001.

14. Quoted in Michael Azzerad, *Our Band Could Be Your Life* (New York: Back Bay, 2002), 136.

15. Ibid., 137.

16. Ibid., 135.

17. Figure quoted in Jeff Chang, *Can't Stop, Won't Stop* (New York: St Martin's Press, 2005), 13.

18. Kurt Loder, "Grandmaster Flash, 'The Message,'" *Rolling Stone,* September 16, 1982.

CHAPTER 7

SIGNS O' THE TIMES
(1982–1985)

Ronald Reagan and Margaret Thatcher first met in 1975 when he was the governor of California in the United States while she was leader of the opposition Conservative Party in the United Kingdom. Aside from being charmed by his personal warmth, Thatcher also recalled years later in her autobiography how even at this first meeting, she felt an almost instant sense of political commonalty with Reagan. Indeed, it was a meeting that seeded almost an entire decade of close political alliance following Thatcher's rise to the role of prime minister in 1979 and Reagan's victory in the presidential election of 1980. Together, they subsequently combined to spearhead a move toward Western conservatism that also helped to strengthen the bond between the United Kingdom and the United States in a way not seen since the Second World War. Although they were by no means united on all issues, both Reagan and Thatcher increased military spending, reignited the cold war with a firmly anticommunist rhetoric, took a probusiness stance on the economy, and were always forthright about their beliefs in traditional social values. With their continuing personal bond, it was little wonder that both the press (and the premiers themselves) frequently referred to this allegiance as a "special relationship."

However, while both Reagan and Thatcher appeared to be working in parallel, musical opposition to their regimes also appeared to be emerging in parallel, too. Across both sides of the Atlantic Ocean, a great deal of rock's modern consciousness was undoubtedly rooted in the sometimes harsh and socially questionable effects of neoconservatism. In the United Kingdom, barely a year had passed since Thatcher became prime minister before the ska group the English Beat issued its self-explanatory "**Stand Down Margaret**" in 1980, but there was a lot more to come. The Falklands War of 1982 was initiated in defense of a small set of islands in the South Atlantic belonging to the United Kingdom, but which had been invaded by Argentina. Despite this encroachment onto British soil, it was a conflict that aroused significant ill feeling, and easily the most famous and most affecting song released in relation to this event was Robert Wyatt's sullen ballad "**Shipbuilding**" (1982). U2's "**Sunday Bloody Sunday**" (1983) made no overt criticisms of the government, but the song's frustration at ongoing troubles in Northern Ireland certainly seemed to resonate particularly loudly during this time as Thatcher's stern policy over the British-ruled land produced a peak of terrorist activity—including an attempt on her life in 1984. The prime minister's refusal to outwardly criticize the apartheid regime in South Africa and support the campaign to release the country's political prisoner Nelson Mandela also provided a subtext for the Special AKA's single "**Nelson Mandela**" (1984). The Smiths meanwhile were a band who could be the most damning of all when it came to Thatcher; in one interview, their charismatic front man, Morrissey, even went so far as to declare that her entire political history was made up of "violence and oppression and horror,"[1] before adding a wish that she be assassinated. Despite that, the group's most effective protest song turned out to be "**Meat Is Murder**" (1985)—a plea for animal rights, which was a subject that Morrissey treated with an equal amount of militancy.

Meanwhile, the artistic backlash at Reagan's administration was just as noticeable. By the start of the 1980s, Bruce Springsteen was practically a poster boy for the American values of hard work and perseverance as they were two qualities that had helped him become a star. However, that did not stop him from recording the 1982 album *Nebraska* as an elegy for those who had reaped no such economic rewards. Although not released until two years later in 1984, out of the *Nebraska* album sessions came "**Born in the U.S.A.**" (1984), which documented a Vietnam War veteran's cry for recognition. The government's military mobilizations in a number of Central American countries also proved to be a hot topic in the liberal realms of the rock world. Among many others to critique this, post-punk trio the Minutemen took a particularly fierce and politically sophisticated stand in a number of tracks, especially "**Untitled Song for Latin America**" (1984). Arguably the most controversial aspect of Reagan's tenure was the growth of an arms race that heightened the sense of dread over a potential nuclear war to an intensity exceeded only during the Cuban Missile Crisis of 1962. Despite the myriad of understandably forbidding songs that touched on this, it was Nena's "**99 Luftballons**" (a strangely chirpy tune sung in German) that managed to have the most commercial success in addressing this threat. It was all part of the tide of indignation that for the most part was interconnected if not aimed at exactly the same target. Furthermore, for all the fury that punk had offered in the years before, a general lack of widespread popularity had limited the impact of the genre's complaints. In contrast, the spirit of protest had now been taken up by some big name acts, and, as a result, a new sociopolitical awareness was truly beginning to reemerge in the mainstream.

Artist: Robert Wyatt

Song: "Shipbuilding"

Songwriters: Elvis Costello and Clive Langer

Album: N/A

Label: Rough Trade Records (United Kingdom only)

1982

As Great Britain went to war with Argentina in 1982 over the tiny Falkland Islands in the South Atlantic Ocean, the predictably patriotic reaction did not encompass singer Elvis Costello, who wrote "Shipbuilding" as his despairing response. The composition was first recorded by Robert Wyatt, who used his distinctive voice to give Costello's lyrics a powerful and arresting effect. It was a combination of creativity that produced one of the more unusually sedate protest songs in music history.

Such were the domestic problems being suffered by Great Britain and Argentina in early 1982 that both governments would have gladly welcomed a foreign diversion. Following the Conservative Party's 1979 election victory, Margaret Thatcher's first years as British prime minister were beset with difficulties. The recession that had forced out the previous administration showed no signs of abating, over 3½ million people were out of work, civil unrest was rife, and questions about her leadership credentials were numerous. Subsequently, the possibility of her reelection for a second term was very much in doubt. Meanwhile in Argentina, the radical right-wing administration known in Spanish as the Proceso de Reorganización Nacional (or more simply the Military Junta) was also running into similar problems. Propelled on by Argentina's own dire economic straits, members of the Junta had seized power as part of a military coup in 1976 and quickly instigated a brutal campaign—often referred to as the "Dirty War"—to rid the country of left-wing factions and minimize verbal or physical dissenters. But with the pre-Junta financial strife still evident nationwide, their popularity diminished swiftly and in March 1982, President Leopoldo Fortunato Galtieri (who had been installed as head of state only four months before) faced an increasingly vigorous wave of agitation calling for the return of democracy.

Looking for a quick way to reunite the country and knowing the effect that foreign conflict can have in achieving this from his substantial military service, Galtieri decided to initiate what he felt would be a short campaign to reclaim the nearby Falkland Islands in April 1982. This small set of islands in the Atlantic Ocean had been ceded to the British in 1833 and now represented one of the last remnants of the old British Empire, but Argentina had always disputed its status as British territory. Galtieri felt that the island's weak defenses coupled with the huge distance from the British mainland would help to make annexation attempts relatively easy. In the short term at least, he succeeded in the aim of uniting the country under a blanket of patriotism. Mirroring the largely symbolic nature of the Argentine invasion, the British launched a similarly symbolic operation to reclaim the Falklands almost immediately. Despite a large proportion of the public being previously unaware of the territory's British sovereignty, the nation's attentions and allegiances were galvanized by this distant battle.

With the aforementioned specter of unemployment looming so ominously over the country, the war also helped to provide a prospective reprieve for the shipbuilding industry that had been centered in the north of England for centuries. The historic power of the British Empire had been fortified by its dominant Royal Navy—a necessary strength for any island country to have. But the postwar years had seen an overall reduction in productivity that began to erode this once thriving industry. However, the threat of a drawn-out conflict that was almost entirely based at sea heralded a potential upturn in fortunes for those still trying to scratch out a living in the neglected shipyards.

Support for the war in Britain was by no means comprehensive. Many felt the measures being undertaken by the government in retaking a small and largely useless set of islands (notable mainly for a very high population of sheep) were futile. Despite the general swing in support of Thatcher, there were those who had their initial annoyance at the prime minister's policies engrained even further by the Falklands crisis. The London-born artist Elvis Costello certainly fell into the latter category. He had begun his recording career during the British punk explosion during the late-1970s and, for a time at least, was clumsily tied into the scene by the music press. Costello had subsequently developed into a rock mainstay in both his homeland and in the United States thanks to the combination of his intelligent songwriting skills and multigenre style of his backing group the Attractions. Regarded as an archetypal angry young man of the period and always keen to address political issues both in song and in print, he rarely kept his distaste for Thatcher hidden and paid close attention to her policy in the Falklands. Around the same time, Costello was played a piece of music that established producer Clive Langer had written, but for which he needed lyrics. Costello added the final piece to the puzzle with a set of lyrics that he regarded at the time as the best he had ever written. However, Langer felt the lead vocals would be ideally suited not to Costello but to the liltingly emotive tones of British singer Robert Wyatt.

By the early 1980s, Robert Wyatt had earned a distinguished status as a solo artist as much by chance as by his own talent. After experiencing limited success in the 1960s with the Daevid Allen Trio and Wilde Flowers, Wyatt became the drummer for Soft Machine, which became one of Britain's most celebrated progressive rock bands toward the end of the decade. In 1971, he left to form Matching Mole, subsequently giving himself a greater musical input than he had previously been afforded in Soft Machine. But in 1973, Wyatt suffered a horrific tragedy when during a drunken party in London, he fell from a third floor window leaving himself paralyzed from the waist down and confining him to a wheelchair. Although forced to give up drumming, he nevertheless continued to sing and built a solo career around a much admired voice. As the years went by, Wyatt developed a firmly politicized lyrical slant and even became a member of the Communist Party of Great Britain.

The lyrics that Costello presented him with for the song—known as "Shipbuilding"—were not quite of the same radical disposition, but Wyatt took to them immediately and recorded the single, which was first released in August 1982. By that time, the Falklands conflict was already over. Just 74 days after the first Argentine invasion of the islands, Britain declared an end to hostilities on June 20, losing 225 men in the interim period compared to 750 on the opposing side.[2] The battle had not been without its difficulties for the British (who also lost six ships), but the speed and effectiveness of the operation to reclaim the land had been undeniable. Galtieri's hasty decision and lack of preparation was crucial, and even though the might of the British Empire was fading, it still had enough prowess to deal with the Argentine threat with relative ease. The Junta's final throw of the dice resulted in failure; Galtieri was removed just days after the end of the war, and democracy returned to the country during the following year. Meanwhile, Thatcher received many accolades for her firm handling of the entire affair and was rejuvenated politically by a new bout of public approval—a factor that then led directly to her winning a second term during the general election of 1983.

"Shipbuilding" may have arrived a little late, but the sentiment contained within still resonated deeply among those not swept up in the sudden patriotic fervor. The angry young man of old had clearly disappeared as Costello confirmed his attributes as a matured and thoughtful songwriter with a set of lyrics encapsulating the contradictions of war through the experiences of a small, English shipbuilding community. Echoing those who failed to see the point of the Falklands conflict, the opening line asks the universal question of whether the entire effort is justified, but then he applies it to the prospect of a family enjoying some brief prosperity through the recommencing of war. Wyatt's plaintive and resigned tone underlines the bittersweet mood of the song, for the material positives that the shipbuilders gain are offset by personal hardships. As the community's finely crafted ships are sent off to war, their lovingly conceived sons would invariably follow close behind, initially under the impression that they would return before Christmas—which in this rare case,

THE CRASS CRUSADE

One of the most virulent musical attacks on the entire Falklands War came courtesy of the anarchist Essex punk band Crass. Formed in 1977, the group had always been noted in punk circles for its firmly left-wing stance, iconoclastic viewpoints, confrontational music, and provocative band imagery. As the Falklands conflict developed, the members of Crass acted on their rage dramatically by releasing the single "How Does it Feel (To Be the Mother of 1000 Dead)?" in October 1982. Like "Shipbuilding," it emerged well after the conflict itself was over, but the song's criticism of Prime Minister Margaret Thatcher and her role in the war showed that not all ill feeling had abated. Alarmed at the song's content, the Conservative Member of Parliament Tim Eggar even called for the band to be prosecuted under the Obscene Publications Act. Undeterred, the band continued its personal assault on Thatcher, even going to the extreme lengths of creating an elaborate political hoax in 1983 in the hope of discrediting her. Known as the "Thatchergate Tapes," the band created a fake telephone conversation between the prime minister and U.S. President Ronald Reagan by splicing together parts of speeches the two heads of state had made. In the dialogue, Thatcher appeared to insinuate that she allowed the British ship HMS *Sheffield* to be destroyed in May 1982 to justify an escalation of the war, while Reagan alludes to using Europe as a nuclear buffer zone in the event of a war with the Soviet Union. The tape was circulated among the press anonymously; for a time, it was thought that the tape was a piece of propaganda circulated by the KGB (the Soviet Union's secret police and intelligence agency). Finally, in January 1984, the *Observer* (London) newspaper exposed the hoax and traced the tapes back to the Crass bandmates, who by then were on the verge of splitting up.

many of them thankfully did. But hidden underneath that weak assurance given by one of the song's protagonists is the knowledge that the return home may not be anything as swift—if at all. Indeed, it is duly noted that once the positive outlook that so often greets the beginning of a war has subsided, the shipyards will be reopened and families will inevitably have to be informed of the deaths of their sons. An added complication is the division within the community at large where the narrator hints at violent clashes resulting from local debates over the war's justification and effects. The track's starkest moment comes in the frequently quoted lines "Diving for dear life, when we could be diving for pearls," which summates the sense of waste involved in such an operation and could accordingly be applied to just about any conflict.

The cruel ironies are deftly highlighted and married perfectly to Wyatt's emotive delivery to create a song that avoids crude political sloganeering in favor of illustrating the futilities of war in a more personalized and arguably more effective manner. It was this artistic subtlety that made "Shipbuilding" such a huge critical hit. The influential British music publication *NME* made the single No. 3 in its end-of-year list, while the listeners of John Peel's BBC Radio Show (the main platform for alternative music in the country) voted it as the second best song of 1982. Despite such support, it was far too morose to gain exposure of mainstream media, and the single failed to chart when it first emerged, although a re-release in 1983 saw it sneak to No. 35. That same year, Costello re-recorded "Shipbuilding" for his own 1983 album *Punch the Clock* and managed to communicate its continuingly valid sentiment to a slightly broader audience. Played at virtually an identical pace and executed with the same weary tone, Costello's vocal is not quite as hauntingly fragile as Wyatt's, but this slightly elongated version boasts an elegant trumpet solo played by jazz legend Chet Baker, whom Costello invited to contribute to the track after seeing him play a show in London during the album's recording. The two marginally differing interpretations of the song also mirrored the artists' slight difference in opinion over the song's spirit; Wyatt referred to "Shipbuilding" as "punk on valium, punk without the energy,"[3] while Costello felt it to be "less of a protest song than a warning sign."[4] But its articulate indictment of the Falklands War was never in doubt, and "Shipbuilding" remains the subject of admiration in the United Kingdom to this day as a perfect timepiece of the era, but also as a sad reflection of the seldom seen by-products of any war.

Artist: U2
Song: "Sunday Bloody Sunday"
Songwriters: Bono and The Edge
Album: *War*
Label: Island Records
1983

The deaths of 13 Catholic protestors in Northern Ireland in 1972 was dubbed Bloody Sunday by the press and ignited years of religious conflict that even spilled across the rest of the United Kingdom. Having formed at the height of these troubles, U2 made its neutral, nonsectarian protest against the violence in 1983's "Sunday Bloody Sunday," which continued to be a musical beacon of hope and peaceful resolution for years after.

U2 (L–R): Adam Clayton, Larry Mullen Jr., The Edge, and Bono.
Courtesy of Photofest.

The massacre of protestors that occurred in the Northern Irish city of Londonderry on Sunday, January 30, 1972, amounted to more than just an incident—it provided one of the largest social and political turning points in the history of the British Isles. The roots of this cataclysmic flash point stemmed from the official partitioning of Ireland in 1921, which had created two states. The larger, southern republic was populated by a majority of Catholics who were in favor of independence from the United Kingdom, while the much smaller northern area was dominated by loyalist Protestants. Aggrieved not only by having their country divided up, but also for being treated as inferior minorities in this newly created satellite of the United Kingdom, Catholics in Northern Ireland spent the next several decades striving to be treated with civil rights and were supported wholeheartedly by their southern compatriots. However, as the 1960s drew to a close, these protests were now attracting violence with Catholics being attacked, and the police repeatedly found themselves fielding accusations of failing to intervene or, worse still, actually aiding Protestants in their hostility.

By the end of 1969, the government of Northern Ireland requested that British troops be sent in to patrol the province and help contain or possibly prevent further outbreaks of violence. Initially, Catholics in the area welcomed the move, feeling that it would help to ensure their safety, and they famously greeted the first arrivals with friendly gestures of tea and sandwiches. But as the clashes continued, the army's presence served only to further divide the population due to the troops' heavy-handed attempts at policing the area. In July 1970, an operation to suppress a burgeoning terrorist group calling itself the Provisional Irish Republican Army (IRA) (a breakaway faction of the mainstream and then comparatively peaceful IRA) ended in a gunfight and four civilian deaths. The following year, government implementation of internment without trial caused huge amounts of controversy with Catholics again feeling that they were being persecuted by this policy. Measures like this served only to exacerbate the already escalating violence and deepening division across Northern Ireland, but it was the arrival of Sunday, January 30, 1972—or "Bloody Sunday" as it would become known—that saw the doors to nearly three decades of widespread conflict swing open.

On the day in question, several thousand Catholics protesting internment without trial took to the streets of Londonderry, but were faced with barricades put up by the army. A relatively minor face-off ensued with marchers throwing projectiles, but troops reacted strongly by opening fire on the largely unarmed crowd. Many were shot in the back while attempting to run away; of the 13 fatalities reported that day, more than half were in their teens or early twenties. A government report into the incident released a few weeks later in April 1972 controversially exonerated the army from blame, reasoning that the soldiers were reacting to the threat of gunmen (possibly snipers) and protestors carrying nail bombs. But regardless of this much-disputed investigation, the political and social damage had already been done. Incensed by what appeared to be an unprovoked massacre, young Catholics all over the country were driven into the increasingly partisan and violent campaign to unite Ireland. The effect of this polarization was immediate. Just days after Bloody Sunday, protestors in Dublin marched on the British Embassy carrying 13 replica coffins before burning the building down, by the end of the year the Provisional IRA had intensified its bombing campaign to unprecedented levels, and by 1974, attacks on mainland Britain were becoming alarmingly regular. Furthermore, the threat of Catholic terrorism was countered by the increasing number of Protestant paramilitary groups, inevitably creating a scenario in which one side systematically retaliated against the other's actions.

For anyone growing up in Ireland during the 1970s, these troubles were an inescapable part of everyday life, and the fledgling U2 bandmates were no exception. The members had originally met in Dublin when Paul "Bono" Hewson (vocals), David "The Edge" Evans (guitar), and Adam Clayton (bass) were among the respondents to an advertisement put on a school notice board by Larry Mullen Jr. (drums) in 1976 calling for people to start a band. Originally playing as a five-piece band called the Hype (with Evans's brother Dik on guitar), the band was trimmed and rechristened U2 in time for a talent show being held in the city of Limerick on

St. Patrick's Day, 1978. After winning first prize and securing the services of respected manager Paul McGuinness a few months later, the quartet released its first album *Boy* in 1980. The songs won notice for their strikingly original sound that combined the energy of punk with The Edge's bright-sounding guitar work, Bono's distinctive vocals, and the furious rhythmic power of Mullen and Clayton, who helped to anchor the band.

A sizable cult audience immediately formed around the band and solidified when the follow-up *October* was released in 1981. As U2 made its first strides toward mainstream popularity, the complicated issues of the quartet's homeland were even further away from being resolved than ever. While working on material for what would be the group's third album, The Edge etched out a seismic, two-bar guitar riff and wrote a set of politically charged lyrics inspired by the continuing problems, even criticizing paramilitary groups (both Catholic and Protestant) operating in Northern Ireland by name. Upon presenting the song to Bono, the singer spotted the potential for it not only as a great piece of work, but also as being something that could compromise the bandmates' own safety given the extremist tactics now being employed across the whole of the United Kingdom. After Bono edited the song's lyrics to excise any explicit sectarian references, this track was given the momentous name of "Sunday Bloody Sunday" and was chosen to be the bombastic first song on the band's next album, which was tellingly entitled *War* and was released in early 1983.

The mood is set instantly thanks to Mullen putting his marching band experience to good use in the song's strict, militaristic drum introduction that deliberately creates an atmosphere of confrontation. Then comes The Edge's riff that chimes out with a huge amount of gravitas over Mullen's beats and so begins a song that clearly wants, if not demands, to be heard. The passion of Bono's voice is evident from the first lines that express disbelief at the constant stream of images and reports from incidents of sectarian violence that by now were the norm. The narrator then continues the second verse by describing the harrowing scenes of carnage, suffering, and emotional pain being endured by children, brothers, sisters, and parents alike, but to which many have become immune due to the constant media exposure and the comfort zone offered by television (a viewpoint expressed explicitly in the final verse). Also alluded to are the many casualties claimed during the previous 15 years, but who have not led the warring factions to any kind of resolution or even victory for any side.

In the song's most rousing and optimistic segment, a vision of unity, hope, and reparation is offered as Bono's vocals are drenched with an echoing effect to help his words resonate with an extra emotional impact while the music (now featuring a striking violin part) swells to an intense peak. Interestingly, the events of Bloody Sunday are not referenced specifically, but rather the resurrection of Jesus Christ (which also took place on a Sunday) is referred to in some of the last lines as being a battle that he won. Although not the most predictable of lyrics in this context, it was not unknown for the U2 bandmates to express parts of their firm Christian beliefs in song and in print at the time. With each of the verses being divided by the song's anthemic chorus, "Sunday Bloody Sunday" was as much of a musical achievement as a lyrical one, denoting the band's intention to be as popular as possible while retaining its sense of substance.

The song was released as a single in the Netherlands only, but from the very first live performances, "Sunday Bloody Sunday" was always one of the pinnacles in any U2 set. The group debuted the song on a small tour in late 1982 before *War* had been released and was naturally extremely apprehensive about playing it on a date in the Northern Irish capital of Belfast. Using the gig as a trial and vowing not to play it again should it prove unpopular, the group was overwhelmed by the positive reaction the track received, but was dismayed when assumptions were made about "Sunday Bloody Sunday" being pro-Catholic—despite the line "But I won't heed the battle call" clearly expressing a nonsectarian, nonviolent pledge. Once the band returned on tour after the album's release, Bono took great pains to ensure that the song was not misconstrued as such and introduced it virtually every night by explaining "this song is not a rebel song."[5] During the middle section he would often unfurl a gigantic white flag to further underline its peaceful intentions and lead the crowd into chants of "No More!" When put together, these factors clearly illustrated the fact that "Sunday Bloody Sunday" was above all a "scream for compassion."[6] During interviews, Bono carefully explained the band's reasoning with the song and frequently pointed out that all of U2's members hailed from varying religious backgrounds. Bono himself had a mother who was Protestant and a father who was Catholic, the combination of which was still scorned in many parts of Ireland. Knowing firsthand the painful complexities that the country and its people were having to endure, he argued that "some things are black and white—but the troubles in Northern Ireland are not . . . "Sunday Bloody Sunday" [was meant] to take the image of Northern Ireland out of the black and white and into the gray, where it truly belongs."[7]

The ongoing clashes in Northern Ireland throughout the rest of the decade ensured that "Sunday Bloody Sunday" would be revered by anyone with a knowledge or sympathy toward the land. Accordingly, the importance of the song in U2's live appearances rarely waned for the entirety of the 1980s. If anything, there were certain junctures where the song's power and emotional resonance enjoyed rejuvenation. The rendition performed at London's Wembley Stadium for the Live Aid benefit concert in July 1985 proved to be a highlight of the day's events with the mid-song shouts of "No More!" taking on a whole new significance in light of the concert's attempt to alleviate African famine. But on Sunday, November 8, 1987, U2 was touring the United States following the release of its epochal *Joshua Tree* album when news filtered through about an attack by the Provisional IRA on the annual Remembrance Day memorials (held to mark the end of World War I) in the town of Enniskillen, Northern Ireland. Eleven people perished that day while one other victim spent 13 years in a coma before dying in 2000; the incident is still regarded as one of the most brutal of the entire era of hostilities. Performing a slightly altered but near-monumental version of "Sunday Bloody Sunday" in Denver, Colorado, that very same night, Bono embarked on a mid-song rant that remains synonymous with the track today.

I've had enough of Irish-Americans who haven't been back to their country in twenty or thirty years come up to me and talk about the resistance, the revolution back home. And the glory of the revolution. And the glory of dying for the revolution. F—the revolution! They don't talk about the glory of killing for the revolution. What's the glory in taking a man from his bed and gunning him down in front of his wife and his children? Where's the glory in that? Where's the glory in bombing a Remembrance Day parade of old age pensioners, their medals taken out and polished up for the day. Where's the glory in that? To leave them dying or crippled for life or dead under the rubble of the revolution, that the majority of the people in my country don't want. No more![8]

Toward the end of the 1990s as the area inched itself closer toward a peaceful resolution and sectarian violence slowly decreased in frequency, "Sunday Bloody Sunday" still made regular appearances in U2 sets. It would often be rededicated according to current events and the city in which the band would play, from war-ravaged Sarajevo in 1998 to New York City after the attacks of 9/11. For a song named after a specific event and associated with a certain time, it is remarkable to see how well "Sunday Bloody Sunday" has aged. At its heart lies a protest for empathy and by avoiding any overtly political rhetoric, Bono's editing of the original lyric undoubtedly gave the song an added human dimension that still ensures its poignancy. "That's what we want from our music—freedom, I suppose. And a little bit of humanity,"[9] explained the singer in 1984. The achievement of these goals—especially with "Sunday Bloody Sunday"—undoubtedly helped U2 become the global success it still is.

EX-BEATLES FOR A UNITED IRELAND

Following the Beatles' breakup in 1970, both primary songwriters John Lennon and Paul McCartney embarked on further musical projects—Lennon as a soloist (augmented frequently by his partner Yoko Ono) and McCartney is his new band Wings. Partly due to their Irish heritages, Lennon and McCartney were both greatly infuriated by the killings in Londonderry. Lennon's 1972 album *Some Time in New York City* contained two songs dealing with the problems—one of which was actually called "Sunday Bloody Sunday," but apart from the subject matter was not related to the U2 song. In the song Lennon argues for a reunited Ireland while positing the idea that loyalist Protestants should be repatriated back to the mainland of the United Kingdom. Also on the album was a melancholic rumination ironically entitled "The Luck of the Irish," which bemoaned the treatment that Irish Catholics had received not only in recent times but the centuries of repression suffered at the hands of the British beforehand. McCartney meanwhile composed the song "Give Ireland Back to the Irish" in a rage after hearing about the massacre and released the track as a single barely a month after the incident. However, the potentially inflammatory content of the song led to it being banned from radio airplay in the United Kingdom; despite that, it still managed to reach No. 16 on the charts. As it happened, "Give Ireland Back to the Irish" did cause trouble as shortly after its release, the brother of Wings' Northern Irish guitarist Henry McCullough was attacked by loyalists angered by the song's plea for a united Ireland.

Artist: Nena

Song: "99 Luftballons"/"99 Red Balloons"

Songwriters: Carlo Karges, Uwe Fahrenkrog-Peterson, and Kevin McAlea

Album: *99 Luftballons*

Label: Epic Records

1984

With the United States and the Union of Soviet Socialist Republics (USSR) embroiled in a dangerous political face-off at the start of the 1980s, the threat of a possible nuclear conflict began to draw a number of protests from popular culture. One of the most successful incorporations of such themes in music came courtesy of Nena, who released "99 Luftballons" with huge success in the United States despite the fact that it was sung in German. Today, it is widely remembered almost as a novelty hit, but behind the language barrier and dated, synth-pop sound lies an enduring document of cold war dread.

Ever since the 1962 Cuban Missile Crisis had brought the United States and the Soviet Union to the brink of nuclear war, the two superpowers had sought to avoid such a near miss by working toward a détente. This state of relaxed tension built up gradually during the remainder of the 1960s and lasted through most of the 1970s, but in 1979, relations speedily deteriorated again due to a number of particularly dramatic events. The fall of the American-installed Shah in Iran robbed the United States of a Middle Eastern ally, while the socialist revolution in Nicaragua meant that the Soviet Union now had another sympathizer perilously close to American soil. Most crucial, however, was the USSR's decision to aid the government of Afghanistan in its fight against U.S.–funded, anti-Soviet insurgents. With defense expenditure subsequently ballooning on both sides of the Iron Curtain, the political situation seemed to descend to a new state of fragility in 1983. During a speech in March, President Ronald Reagan infamously referred to the USSR as the "evil empire."[10] Just days later, he outlined a proposal for an antiballistic system that would be permanently on standby in space to intercept missiles mid-flight should an enemy ever attempt to launch them. Because of its fanciful nature, critics dubbed the program "Star Wars"; while it was fantastically ambitious, it also seemed to denote how real the threat of a nuclear war had become again.

Meanwhile, a terrifying indication of the USSR's readiness for such a conflict came in September 1983 when a Korean passenger plane flying from the United States accidentally ended up over Soviet airspace en route to Seoul, resulting in the craft being shot down and everyone on board being killed. With tensions at a new high, a highly realistic military operation called Able Archer 83 was initiated by NATO (North Atlantic Treaty Organization) across Europe in November—a risky maneuver given that Soviet intelligence agents were especially worried about training exercises being used as a disguise for a genuine nuclear strike. The sense of public paranoia was palatable and spread across a demographic that included "more bishops than Berrigans, doctors and lawyers with impeccable Establishment credentials, archconservatives as well as diehard liberals."[11] It was also a factor that was spilling out into many facets of popular culture. In cinematic terms alone, 1983 saw a number of films dealing with the sense of nuclear nerves, doomsday dread, and an apocalyptic holocaust. The motion picture *WarGames* played on the fear of accidental obliteration due in this case to an overenthusiastic computer hacker playing havoc with defense systems. Additionally, the TV movies *The Day After* and the desperately bleak U.K. production *Threads* attempted to depict a world adapting to life immediately after the bomb drops.

Oddly, one of the most commercially popular musical addresses on the subject would emerge in the United States from a virtually unknown West German five-piece group called Nena. The band was comprised of singer Gabriele Susanne Kerner with her then boyfriend Rolf Brendel on drums, keyboard player Uwe Fahrenkrog-Petereson, guitarist Carlo Karges, and bassist Jürgen Dehmel. Brendel and Kerner had previously been in a band called the Stripes, but her dislike for singing in English resulted in them disbanding and the couple subsequently formed Nena in West Berlin during 1981. Taking its moniker from Kerner's childhood nickname, the band demonstrated a clear musical appreciation for new-wave pop (Blondie was a common comparison) and released its debut single "Nur geträumt" in the bandmates' native land in 1982 with huge success. The following year, the single was succeeded by the nagging but catchy "99 Luftballons." This track's lyrics had been inspired by Karges witnessing the release of a plethora of balloons at the finale of a Rolling Stones concert—a sight that left the guitarist pondering "what might happen if they floated over the [Berlin] wall to the Russian side."[12] This train of thought gave rise to "99 Luftballons" and its dark tale about a military misunderstanding that leads to catastrophe. With diplomatic relations in a decidedly precarious shape, not to mention that fact that the dividing line between East and West (signified then by the cold sight of the Berlin Wall) ran straight through the band's hometown, such an occurrence seemed uncomfortably plausible.

Despite beginning with a slow, reflective tone, the vast majority of "99 Luftballons" boasts a jaunty melody and an instantly memorable synthesizer hook that disguises the doomed narrative. The literal translation from German to English at first reveals the narrator wistfully imagining the eponymous number of balloons drifting toward the horizon. It is a harmless enough image, but as the song changes gear into a more danceable tempo, a concurrent panic sets in to the lyrics as the balloons begin to resemble some kind of craft in their formation. The already jittery defense personnel bolt into action, apparently misreading the objects for some kind of offensive move and proceed to dispatch 99 planes to counter the "threat" as 99 ministers scream their support for conflict. Naturally, the ensuing war lasts 99 years to complete the song's artistic symmetry, and the song's final verse (sung like the first verse in the style of a ballad) reflects that there are no victors to speak of as the narrator picks up a solitary balloon among the ruins of the world before somberly letting it go. Throughout the song, it is interesting to note that there are no references made to the United States, the USSR, or any other countries involved in the complex set of military allegiances that had developed at the time. Despite Karges's initial pondering over what would happen if the balloons at the Rolling Stones concert had shown up on Soviet radar, he had obviously realized—like so many others—that the potential for misinterpretation was a worldwide worry.

Looking to build on its success in West Germany by breaking the band abroad, Nena made several attempts to rewrite "99 Luftballons" in English with the help of friends and even a university professor, but in trying to retain the original's imagery, the song would lose its melodic appeal. Finally, Nena's manager asked Kevin McAlea—then a touring musician with Barclay James Harvest—to make an attempt. Rather than being overly concerned with recreating the exact narrative of "99 Luftballons" as had been the previous intention, he instead sought to produce a set of lyrics that would have the same aural flow, even if the original meaning was partially compromised in the process. After dashing off his lyrics on the back of an envelope, McAlea presented them to the Nena bandmates who were impressed enough to re-record it with Kerner now more willing to sing in English than she was during her time with the Stripes.

The new version—entitled "99 Red Balloons" for the simple reason that the addition of "red" provided a useful extra syllable—seemed to revolve around two children who actually buy 99 balloons during the first verse and release them into the sky, triggering an alert. The language becomes a lot more direct and features pointed militaristic references as the song goes into the buoyant middle section with the narrator describing how "the war machine springs to life" during this state of alert. The next verse is when the ministers meet, exclaiming to troops that this is the real thing, and, in contrast to the nonspecific political nature of the original, there is even a reference to the president being contacted. The final descriptions of panic involve the dispatch of jet fighters to deal with the perceived problem, and while communicating the high level of technology being used in this airborne scenario, McAlea charmingly manages to retain the original mention of Captain Kirk. As "99 Red Balloons" winds down with the same sense of postwar melancholy, the narrator again laments the ruins in which she stands and, as in the original, releases a solitary balloon, but then recalls the lost friend from the start of the song. Although extremely similar to the original in terms of arrangement and structure (the vocal melody and synthesizer hook certainly remain the most prominent features), the lyrical cadence of the song audibly loses a little smoothness in translation despite McAlea's best rewriting efforts.

Through both "99 Luftballons" and "99 Red Balloons," Nena scored No. 1 hits in no less than 15 countries around the world. Bizarrely, it would also manage to reach No. 2 in the United States in March 1984—but with the German version rather than the English one. Although there were many more tracks dealing with the same issues and fears circulating at the time, none had anything like the level of worldwide success. Nena fans in their homeland (if nowhere else) could no doubt feel an extra poignancy in the song especially given their understanding of the original lyrical imagery. Additionally, its apt reflection of the era's political situation would be reinforced at almost exactly the same time as the song's peak of popularity thanks to strategic American deployment of the highly controversial Pershing II defense missiles in West Germany, which sparked huge protests during early 1984. But its success in America seemed based more on surface-level public enjoyment of the track's sound rather than its sentiment. It was a good song to dance to in a nightclub or to whistle to when it played on the radio, but few seemed sufficiently moved by the lyrics of the song (even when explained or translated) to adopt a staunch antinuclear stance. The strange irony was that just as "99 Luftballons" revolved around an accidental war, it would become an accidentally successful protest song. Instead of adopting its concerns or taking action to prevent the potential disaster it described, most American listeners merely chose to enjoy "99 Luftballons" as an infectious pop song that had the extra novelty of being sung in German.

In breaking the band outside of West Germany, "99 Luftballons" also became something of an albatross for Nena. Critical success, for example, was almost nonexistent; the group's debut U.S. album of the same name received one star and an unceremonious trashing in *Rolling Stone* in April 1984. Even in the United Kingdom where the song had hit the top slot, the typically unkind press paid more attention to Kerner's unshaven armpit hair than any of the band's music. One-hit wonder status was quickly ascribed, and although the band did enjoy more success in West Germany, it would eventually wane there too, resulting in the group's breakup in 1987. The ensuing years have clearly been unkind to the song, and it is now regarded as a novelty or at least a timepiece both in sound and, of course, in lyrical concern—particularly as the cold war would soon experience a thaw after Mikhail Gorbachev became head of state of the Soviet Union in 1985. Apart from steering the USSR away from the guerrilla war in Afghanistan and moving funding away from defense, Gorbachev also began a series of negotiations with Reagan, helping to curb the arms race that had cast a shadow over world peace during the first half of the 1980s. Even with its outdated fears and quaint sonic sheen, there are some that still have a certain sentimental fondness for "99 Luftballons," most notably the donor who in 2006 pledged a reported $35,000 to the Hurricane Katrina relief fund in return for VH1 playing the video to the song repeatedly for one whole hour.

Artist: The Special AKA

Song: "Nelson Mandela"

Songwriter: Jerry Dammers

Album: *In the Studio*

Label: 2-Tone Records (United Kingdom)/Chrysalis Records (United States)

1984

The Specials/Special AKA was a group with a long history of speaking out over social and political issues affecting the United Kingdom, but by the mid-1980s, keyboardist Jerry Dammers felt the need to point listeners in the direction of events farther afield. Especially important was the racially divisive apartheid regime in South Africa and the continued incarceration of Nelson Mandela for his actions in trying to force change across the country during the 1960s. In the hope of raising awareness over his plight, Dammers wrote the song "Nelson Mandela," which helped to provide a major building block for a subsequent campaign to free the political prisoner.

In the few years the group was together, the Special AKA (and all its related incarnations) had many different lineups, a number of name changes, and a varying degree of success. But the one constant throughout all of this was the group's awareness of its sociopolitical surroundings and an ability to reflect them in its music. Initially inspired by the sound and sneer of British punk, the group made its earliest live performances as the Automatics around its hometown of Coventry, England, in 1977. Gradually, the group would show a more dominant ska/reggae influence while changing its name first to the Coventry Automatics, then the Special AKA, the Coventry Automatics, and then finally just the Special AKA for the sake of brevity. After landing a tour-support slot with the Clash in 1978 (as well as benefiting from a brief spell under the same management), the Special AKA finally settled into a solidified lineup featuring Terry Hall (vocals), Neville Staples (vocals, percussion), Lynval Golding (guitar, vocals), Jerry Dammers (keyboards), Roddy Radiation (guitar), Sir Horace Gentleman (bass), and John Bradbury (drums). This combination of both black and white members was an unusual sight in British music at the time, but just through the choice of personnel, the Special AKA was a far more accurate representation of the country's increasingly multiracial populace than any quartet of Mohawk-haired punk rockers doing the rounds.

The group released its debut single "Gangsters" on its own 2-Tone label in 1979 and found itself with a Top 10 hit thanks to the song's upbeat energy (handy for radio airplay) and the group's ability to combine multicultural musical influences (useful for positive press). Yet another name change would see the group becoming known as the Specials in time for the release of the self-titled debut album that emerged later that same year with huge success. A clear sense of social conscience flowed through the bulk of the material, manifesting itself in references to the problems of racial tension, youthful delinquency, urban decay, and even the need for wider usage of birth control. A heightened political emphasis followed in 1980's *More Specials,* but for most fans and critics, the Specials hit an all-around creative peak in 1981 with the release of the single "Ghost Town." Filled with an eerie, haunted ambience and played at a wake-like pace, the song documented the effect of violence and abandonment not only in the groups' hometown of Coventry, but in so many parts of the United Kingdom. For anyone coming of age in the early 1980s, it was a time of limited optimism due to rising unemployment, a vicious recession, and an omnipresent ill feeling due to the economic policies of Prime Minister Margaret Thatcher. It was something that the members of the Specials had seen firsthand while on tour since their gigs (initially celebrated for an uproarious party atmosphere) were now becoming outlets for simmering anger and frequently resulting in mass brawls. Although essentially a coincidence, there was a horrible aptness to the single hitting No. 1 on the U.K. chart during the summer of 1981 just as widespread inner-city rioting erupted, literally reducing numerous areas in the country to ghost towns.

Aside from marking a doomy nadir in the fortunes of their homeland, "Ghost Town" also did something similar for the bandmates' relationships with each other. Tension within the group led to a mass exodus, leaving just Dammers and Bradbury as the only steady members in a constantly fluctuating lineup; they marked the radical change by reverting back to the name of the Special AKA. As they set about recording their third album, Dammers emerged as the group's primary songwriter, and the keyboardist began to expand his lyrical concerns to incorporate worldwide issues, as well as those still plaguing the United Kingdom. The 1982 single "War Crimes," for example, addressed the escalating violence in the Middle East, but another concern that started to preoccupy Dammers was that of the black political prisoner Nelson Mandela. His story stemmed as far back as 1948 when the National Party (NP) took control of Mandela's native South Africa. Part of the party's reform measures was the legal segregation of black South Africans (who were numerically superior) from white South Africans descended from European settlers—a policy more commonly known as apartheid. However, this resulted in an inevitable discrepancy in the way that the two groups were treated; services, employment opportunities, and general freedoms were openly restricted for black people in the region, and as resentment against the regime grew, so did the NP's violent enforcement. Through his membership in the African National Congress (ANC), Mandela was initially committed to a nonviolent struggle against the NP's policies, but the killing of 69 protestors in the town of Sharpeville on March 21, 1960, added a more militant dimension to the antiapartheid movement.

As a direct result of this massacre, Mandela quickly became the leader of the ANC's armed faction and advocated a campaign of sabotage against the government, but he was captured and given a five-year jail sentence in 1962 initially for the charge of leaving the country illegally. In a subsequent trial of ANC leaders in 1964, Mandela admitted his part in conspiring to sabotage and was handed a life term. Unsurprisingly, the conditions he endured in jail were brutal despite being a low-classification prisoner. As a black South African, he was given fewer provisions, allowed less contact with the outside world, and was subjected to noticeably harsher treatment from guards in general. Despite that, Mandela steadfastly maintained his antiapartheid standpoint and even managed to study for a law degree via correspondence with the University of London. It was this sense of courage in the face of constant personal and political harassment that inspired Dammers to address Mandela's plight. As recording sessions for the Special AKA's new album dragged on at great cost through 1982 and 1983, the track "Nelson Mandela" proved to be comparatively simple as it was recorded in a matter of days with Elvis Costello, reggae star Ranking Roger, and ex-Special Lynval Golding all adding guest vocals.

The first thing that becomes apparent in "Nelson Mandela" is its sense of vibrancy that not only contrasts with the years of oppression endured by the song's subject, but also with the vast majority of protest songs overall. Clearly, the intention is not to dwell on Mandela's personal suffering, but to celebrate his spirit of resistance; this comes across both in the a cappella chorus that begins the song as well as the spritely intro that shows an obvious influence of traditional African music. The main lyrics—delivered by Stan Campbell, the Special AKA's vocalist at the time—begin with an acknowledgment of Mandela's 21 years of incarceration and a brief reference to the inhumane way he has been treated. But a salute to the continued strength of Mandela's mind (no doubt inspired partly by his scholarly pursuit) swiftly restores the song's feeling of hope before Campbell asks for the listener directly to recognize his struggle. A repeat of the chorus pleads for his release and continues the buoyant spirit as Campbell returns to highlight Mandela's loyalty to the ANC. But again, the track does not let political language dominate and concentrates on addressing the audience directly in its plea for awareness. An extended instrumental section occupies the middle part of "Nelson Mandela" in which the celebratory tone is highlighted thanks to an exuberant trumpet riff, a lively saxophone solo, and even a flourish of flute. Campbell's

ARTISTS UNITED AGAINST APARTHEID

One of the most prominent U.S. pop-culture movements to object to apartheid in South Africa was orchestrated via the Artists United Against Apartheid. This group was set up by Steve Van Zandt in 1985 just after the guitarist had left Bruce Springsteen and the E Street Band at the height of their success. Van Zandt had traveled to South Africa following his departure and had become aware of Sun City—a lavish gambling and entertainment resort incongruously located in the heart of a repressed black region of the country. The area had played host to many of the world's top musical acts, but Van Zandt gathered an impressive number of stars (including Bono, Bruce Springsteen, Bob Dylan, Ringo Starr, jazz legend Miles Davis, and countless others) who responded to this symbol of oppression by recording the protest single "Sun City" in 1985. Aside from making a defiant pledge to never play there themselves, the vast array of artists offered a clear lyrical indictment of the entire apartheid regime that brutally segregated blacks and whites in South Africa while also criticizing U.S. President Ronald Reagan and his comparatively timid policy of "constructive engagement" with the country. Although the lyrics did not address the plight of Nelson Mandela as directly as the Special AKA did in "Nelson Mandela," the black activist was nevertheless depicted in the video, which ended with footage of a mass rally calling for his release. Both the "Sun City" single and subsequent album of the same name (also released in 1985) met with moderate commercial success, but in assembling such an array of respected talent, Van Zandt helped to bring an unprecedented amount of public attention across the United States to the antiapartheid cause. He would later make an appearance at the Wembley Stadium concert in 1988 (partly organized by the Special AKA's Jerry Dammers), which marked Mandela's 70th birthday.

last verse merely repeats the period that Mandela has spent in prison and uses a final set of rhetorical questions in the hope that the song's listeners will stop ignoring the issue. The music then drops out briefly to be replaced by a heartbeat pulse that emphasizes the call for Mandela's release before the instrumentation returns and the chorus is repeated until the track fades out.

While the Special AKA was incredibly simple and direct in its protest, the group wisely stopped short of administering any kind of condensed lecture on Nelson Mandela's long and complicated history. That was clearly being left to listeners to research for themselves, but what "Nelson Mandela" did do was to offer an uplifting wake-up call. It was a theme that continued in the song's video, which featured nothing more than the group giving a chirpy performance (Dammers's toothless smile is especially amusing) while onlookers dance enthusiastically. The only image of Mandela comes via a black and white picture of him in his younger days—the very same one used as the cover of the single when it was released in March 1984. Although critical reviews were mixed, the audience-friendly approach paid dividends as "Nelson Mandela" reached No. 9 in the United Kingdom and secured the band what would essentially be its last chart success. The subsequent album *In the Studio* fared less well in comparison and the Special AKA would effectively disband within the year. However, the single had a clear effect in making Nelson Mandela a recognizable name across the United Kingdom with Bradbury, in particular, remembering that "a lot of people had never heard of the guy before that."[13]

Although the Special AKA was no more, Dammers became even more determined to finish what he had helped to start with "Nelson Mandela." As a number of high-profile artists across the world began to pledge support for the jailed South African and voice objection at the NP's regime, it gradually became the most prominent issue in rock's collective conscience outside of famine relief in the poorer parts of the African continent (see the sidebar). For his part, Dammers worked to harness this growing awareness by involving himself heavily in the burgeoning Artists Against Apartheid movement, and he had a hand in organizing a notable benefit concert in Clapham Common, London, in 1986. However, this would be easily eclipsed by the event staged at Wembley Stadium two years later to mark Mandela's 70th birthday. The high-profile gig brought together the likes of Stevie Wonder, Bryan Adams, Simple Minds, and Steve Van Zandt and was broadcast around the world. Dammers again played a pivotal role in the concert's organization, which attracted plentiful coverage in the mainstream media. By the end of the 1980s, the slogan "Free Nelson Mandela!" had become almost omnipresent and was being parroted by everyone from prominent governments around the world to teenage pop music fans making their first tentative forays into political righteousness.

Shortly after the arrival of the NP's Frederik Willem de Klerk as South African president in 1989, it was announced that Nelson Mandela would finally be freed and the ban on the ANC Party would be reversed. Mandela's release in February 1990 was another worldwide TV event, and it signaled the most significant step yet taken toward the end of apartheid—a factor that also led to de Klerk and Mandela being jointly awarded the Nobel Peace Prize in 1993. The following year saw the first fully democratic elections take place in South Africa, and it would be Mandela (now head of the ANC) who emerged victorious, installing de Klerk as his deputy in the process. In the space of four years, Mandela had gone from prisoner to president, and there was no one who could doubt the role that Jerry Dammers had in laying the groundwork for this progression. Not only did he bring an initial spate of attention to a subject that few in the United Kingdom had any knowledge of through the song "Nelson Mandela," Dammers also helped to make the campaign to free him *the* bandwagon to mount—even for those in the very highest political echelons. "Before those gigs, Margaret Thatcher was saying Mandela was a terrorist," argued the keyboardist in 2007. "Afterwards, she was saying it was her that set him free."[14]

Artist: Minutemen

Song: "Untitled Song for Latin America"

Songwriter: D. Boon

Album: *Double Nickels on the Dime*

Label: SST Records

1984

Fueled by the huge political intellects of guitarist D. Boon and bassist Mike Watt, post-punk trio the Minutemen addressed the issues of the Reagan era with far more depth and sophistication than virtually any of their contemporaries. A particular source of rancor for the group was the growing number of military interventions in Central America, which the bandmates began to criticize before many in the United States even knew about them. However, they saved their most stinging and influential attack for "Untitled Song for Latin America"—a song that left listeners with little doubt over how serious the government's actions in these countries were.

For the Minutemen, just being in a band was a political statement. It was an assertion of power, autonomy, and self-sufficiency that stood separately from the everyday sub-jugation of the working class—something the band's two main members knew plenty about. Both bassist Mike Watt and guitarist Dennes "D" Boon met in 1972, in San Pedro, California, while still in their early teenage years. Despite being technically part of the greater Los Angeles (LA) area, the blue-collar harbor town was a world away from the city's glamorous reputation. Boon's father was an ex-navy man who now worked servicing car radios, and the family lived in a less-than-salubrious housing project converted from old World War II barracks, while Watt's father was still in the navy and had been stationed in the town since 1967. Feeling that the area was not the safest place for her young son to be roaming after school, Boon's mother had already encouraged him to play guitar and then coerced Watt to play bass, thereby giving them the basis of a band, which would help keep them occupied.

After gradually learning the sonic difference between the two instruments and the significance of tuning the strings (they famously thought that having them tight or loose was entirely a personal preference), Watt and Boon entertained themselves by playing covers of rock staples. They also augmented their substantial political and his-torical intelligence with the similarly minded lyrics of Creedence Clearwater Revival, Blue Öyster Cult, and Bob Dylan. But as they graduated from high school in 1976, it was their exposure to the earliest stirrings of punk rock through the pages of such American music magazines as *Creem* that propelled the pair forward. Watt and Boon felt inspired by the idea that members of such bands as the Ramones and the Clash were regular, everyday people like them, and they were creating the kind of music that did not seem too far away from the noises the two were making. Through this revelation, Watt and Boon realized that there were new possibilities for a couple of nondescript young men in an unremarkable town—but fame and money were not on their minds. It was the idea of being in control of something rather than something being in control of them that excited the duo the most; in a place like San Pedro where the majority of people were ruled by their jobs, it seemed like a form of liberation worth having. "When you talk about the people who are disenfranchised, and then you look at the guys who can't get in bands ... it's kind of close," explained Watt. "The thing about having a say in your workplace, having a say in your economics, is the same idea as having a say in your music."[15]

Watt and Boon soon met another San Pedro local called George Hurley, who was also of firm working class standing (his father was a machinist), and along with singer Martin Tamburovich, they formed the Reactionaries in 1978. But the quartet lasted just a few months with Boon and Watt forming the Minutemen shortly afterward, ini-tially with a different drummer, but Hurley was soon reenlisted to complete the trio. Continually (and wrongly) associated with the band's propensity for extremely short songs, the name was chosen for its allusion to the Minutemen militia, famed for its contribution to the Revolutionary War. Furthermore, Watt also claimed that the name inferred to the band being minute (small) as opposed to the huge, world-famous rock stars that they had listened to growing up. In musical terms, they had progressed from their first loves and had begun to look to some of the more angular post-punk bands from the United Kingdom, such as the Pop Group and Wire, for inspiration while also learning from the wildly inventive rhythms employed by Captain Beefheart & His Magic Band—a cult blues-rock outfit from the 1960s. The unusual combination of influences gave the Minutemen an intense but strangely spastic sound from the very beginning. Their first EP *Paranoid Time* emerged in 1980 on SST Records—a label set up by the trailblazing LA hardcore band Black Flag. Given the disparity between Black Flag and the Minutemen in musical terms, it was a release that seemed unlikely. But while the Minutemen did not always have the same ferocious power as Black Flag, they certainly had a similar antiestablishment mind-set, as well as the all-important independent spirit that united all factions in America's blossoming underground music scene.

At the forefront of the band's remarkably short bursts of music sat an acutely left-wing lyrical consciousness that became apparent just by such song titles as "Joe McCarthy's Ghost," "Fascist," and "Paranoid Chant." Even the instrumental track was entitled "Sickles and Hammers"—a reference to the flag of the Soviet Union. Furthermore, the Minutemen's very existence was based on a sense of prudence that was almost regimental and completely deliberate. Having always avoided extravagance in their youth (if only because they simply could not afford it), Watt, Boon, and Hurley employed the same ethic in the Minutemen by recording cheaply, writing prolifically, keeping tour expenses to a minimum, and holding down jobs when not working in the band. The Minutemen's lack of mainstream success over the years meant these measures were arguably a financial necessity. But for the bandmates themselves, this necessity doubled as a political statement in a dawning era of materialism, which again underlined a sense of autonomy and kept them on a level to which average working-class people could relate. The band summated this standpoint by adopting the simple band motto that declared "We Jam Econo."

From the outset, the Minutemen laced many of their songs with themes of racism, inequality, and working-class frustration, which they had all experienced firsthand in San Pedro; as the first term of Ronald Reagan's presidency wore on, the band was given much more to rile against. With the United States still entrenched in the ongoing cold war as he took office in 1981, Reagan immediately turned a great deal of attention to the socialist revolutions occurring in Central America, fearing that the countries involved either were or would become allied with the Soviet Union and could eventually present a close geographical threat to the U.S. mainland. One of the president's first controversial measures involved the funding of a right-wing government in El Salvador in the hope of mounting a counterinsurgency campaign against the Marxist Farabundo Martí National Liberation Front. With the two sides locked in an increasingly violent civil war (which began in 1980 and would not end until 1992), critics of Reagan's allegiance protested at the idea of U.S. dollars being used in the murder and torture of many thousands of El Salvador's civilians as the government attempted to suppress the country's left-wing factions.

It was not by any means an isolated incident. That same year saw the United States begin funding a guerrilla group called the Contras, who opposed the popular left-wing revolution in Nicaragua that had installed the Sandinista National Liberation Front into power in 1979. However, the Contras' activities were discovered to be extremely unruly —particularly the deployment of underwater mines in one of the country's main ports (illegal by international law), and it was also subsequently discovered that they were accountable for many atrocities and human rights violations. After these revelations were made public and federal funding was stopped in 1983, the United States persisted in covert funding by the equally illegal means of selling arms to Iran and using the proceeds in the Contras' continued campaign. Known as the Iran-Contra affair, it developed into one of the biggest scandals to blight Reagan's two terms in the White House and ended in 1986 with the World Court ruling that the United States had to pay reparations for the damage caused to Nicaragua. Despite the verdict, the United States refused to pay the fine. Although the interventions in El Salvador and Nicaragua were the central controversies, there was also a strong U.S. presence in Honduras, a continuing political influence in Guatemala, and skirmishes in Grenada, which was subjected to an American invasion in 1983 and where another U.S.-friendly government was financially aided in the country's subsequent election of 1984.

Within the Minutemen camp, Boon, in particular, was highly active in voicing disapproval of this foreign policy early on and followed developments closely long before they became big stories in the mainstream press. In 1981 he had written the song "Song for El Salvador," which appeared on the band's first full album *The Punch Line,* and had subsequently joined as a member of the self-explanatory activist group United States Out of Central America and the Committee in Solidarity with the People of El Salvador—an organization dedicated to finding an alternative to the right-wing government established and supported by the United States. Boon would continue to refer to the cause both on record and in public, but his most direct and powerful indictment of this continued meddling did not come until the Minutemen released their third and most celebrated album *Double Nickels on the Dime* in 1984. It undoubtedly represented a peak in the band's creativity: 46 songs[16] conceptually spread over four sides of vinyl. Three of the four sides represented a member of the band, while the remaining side was called "Chaff," at the start of which was "Untitled Song for Latin America."

From the very first note, there is a tense, urgent energy running through the track that emanates from Watt's insistent bass riff, Boon's jagged guitar stabs, and Hurley's manic drumming. The three distinct styles of musicianship had gelled together to give the Minutemen a unique and immensely powerful sound, and it was on songs like this that it became clearly evident. Boon's vocals seem caught halfway between singing and remonstrating as he voices an obvious disgust at the seemingly neoimperialist intentions of the United States—but without ever directly mentioning the country by name. He does not have to because references to the creation of Contras and the mining of harbors make the subject of his anger clear enough. The narrator then goes on to declare that these acts are comparable to those carried out by irresponsible children and touches on the parallels between current foreign policy and the colonial theft of old. A blistering guitar solo then fills in a short, lyricless interlude before Boon returns to deliver the final denunciation with a brutal directness.

I would call it genocide, any other word would be a lie.

In the Minutemen's typically quick manner, the song starts, gets to the heart of a complex political matter, finds time for a highly entertaining solo, and then blows itself out after barely two minutes. If nothing else, "Untitled Song for Latin America" brings home the beauty of jamming "econo" perfectly.

Boon's commitment to the cause did not end there. Despite the slight objections of Watt, who felt it was reducing an intricate problem to the realm of soapbox sloganeering, Boon would often place a sign saying "U.S. Out of Central America" on stage next to him as he played and frequently handed out flyers and stickers with the same sentiments written on them. On one occasion in 1985, some members of the audience at a show in New Orleans took exception to the trio's political viewpoints, but the Minutemen refused to back down or even mediate and a fight duly ensued. Boon was also beginning to write more songs directly attacking American intervention, most notably "The Big Stick," which took its title from the policy of Big Stick Diplomacy adopted by President Theodore Roosevelt who had used the term to describe the protection of U.S. economic interests in Latin America way back in the early 1900s. Yet again, this demonstrated Boon's huge knowledge of past U.S. relations with the rest of the continent and underlined an acute interest in history that Watt remembers was already firmly in place when the two had met as children. If Boon was soapbox sloganeering, he certainly had a huge and sturdy platform on which to stand. In any case, "The Big Stick" would appear on the Minutemen's fourth album *3 Way Tie (For Last)*, but by then, the band had already come to an untimely halt. Shortly after finishing a tour in support of R.E.M., Boon tragically died just a few days before Christmas, 1985, after a van driven by his girlfriend crashed, killing them both instantly.

Although Watt admits that his band was unlikely to have radically altered many people's political viewpoints at the time (if only because of their very limited exposure), the bandmates certainly raised awareness of the government's policy in Latin America among their peers. Indeed, one of the most prominent bands to take up the subject after Boon's death was the Minutemen's old touring companion R.E.M., which not only made public criticisms of these interventions, but also incorporated references to the plight of Latin Americans in "The Flowers of Guatemala" (from 1986's *Lifes Rich Pageant*) and "Welcome to the Occupation" (from 1987's *Document*). At the very least, "Untitled Song for Latin America" was one of the most emphatic songs to address this aspect of government policy, and it came from a band that wielded a small but concentrated influence in the music world. While so many artists of the era were preoccupied with the buildup of nuclear arms, the stringent anticommunist spirit, or the harsh economic measures, it was through songs like this that the Minutemen showed their superior political intelligence by pointing out the effects of the Reagan government in other corners of the world, too. Although modern concerns are not so directly channeled toward Central America, the debate and criticism over U.S. intervention in distant lands remains vociferous, particularly in the case of the full-scale invasion of Iraq in 2003. If D. Boon had been alive to see those events unfold, it seems likely that he would have been prepared to get into as many fights as were necessary to fully communicate his sense of disapproval.

Artist: Bruce Springsteen
Song: "Born in the U.S.A."
Songwriter: Bruce Springsteen
Album: *Born in the U.S.A.*
Label: Columbia Records
1984

Although Bruce Springsteen avoided being sent to Vietnam himself, he could not avoid coming face-to-face with veterans of the conflict as he toured the United States with the E Street Band years later. After gaining this unpleasant insight into the lives of America's forgotten soldiers, the singer composed "Born in the U.S.A." in a bid to communicate the frustration of being ignored by your own country. Its success helped make Springsteen into an icon of popular culture, but a significant number of his fans mistook this anguished tale of marginalization as a patriotic clarion call—much to the singer's continuing disappointment.

Bruce Springsteen playing in his native New Jersey in 1984.
Courtesy AP Images.

Were it not for him failing a medical and giving a set of erratic answers on the army questionnaire, Bruce Springsteen may well have served in the Vietnam War. Born as he was in 1949 in Freehold, New Jersey, Springsteen's mature teenage years coincided perfectly with American escalation of the conflict. Indeed, the prospect of military service seemed to delight his father who had always been unenthusiastic about his son's interest in music and felt that a stretch in the army would help the youngster become a man. But while Springsteen avoided the draft, Bart Haynes—the drummer in his first band the Castiles—was not so lucky and barely six months after departing for Vietnam in May 1967, the news filtered back to his bandmates that he would not return. Despite that early setback, Springsteen carried on with the Castiles and a number of other outfits before forming the E Street Band out of a selection of musicians he had come across in and around the Jersey beach town of Asbury Park. Their blend of R&B, soul, rock 'n' roll, and a charmingly romantic lyrical streak initially struggled in terms of sales. The first two albums (both released in the United States in 1973) enjoyed patronage in the media, while Springsteen himself was frequently touted with a hyperbolic "new Dylan" tag by his label Columbia, but commercial success was not forthcoming. With the threat of having his recording contract terminated, Springsteen reemerged with the all-time classic that was *Born to Run* in 1975, and a steady ascent to superstardom began. Over the next five years, the E Street Band would become a regular feature in the world's arenas, communicating its invigorating blue-collar rock songs and everyday themes through an infamously epic and energetic live show. Once 1980's double album *The River* secured the No. 1 spot on the Billboard chart (as well as a first Top 10 single in the shape of "Hungry Heart"), Springsteen began to boast the status of being a chart heavyweight, too.

The touring schedule following *The River* allowed Springsteen to get an extensive view of the American heartland, and, in many cases, it was a sobering sight. The election of President Ronald Reagan in 1980 had led to the implementation of a string of stern measures designed to pull the country out of the worst recession since the 1930s. The idea of trickle-down economics was central to government policy and revolved around top-level tax cuts that would encourage industry growth, thereby creating more jobs and passing down the financial benefits to the workforce. In reality, it was a slow process and to make things even more untenable, those most in need found that the already strained welfare system had been subjected to severe cutbacks. Even while the number of unemployed peaked at almost 10 million, Reagan seemed strangely unsympathetic and complained of his irritation at hearing that "some fellow in South Succotash had just been laid off."[17] The harshness of the era inspired Springsteen to turn inward both artistically and personally and on January 3, 1982—just days short of the first anniversary of Reagan taking office—he recorded the songs that would comprise *Nebraska* on a simple 4-track recorder in a rented house in New Jersey. Released later that same year, it was an album filled with isolation and despair as told from the perspective of those forgotten people in every South Succotash across the land. Springsteen's spare use of mainly guitar and harmonica suited these desolate tales perfectly, and while the bleak tone damaged his commercial clout (the album was scantly promoted and sold a fraction of what *The River* had sold), critical praise of the album was rapturous.

One of the songs recorded during that day bore the title of "Born in the U.S.A." and revolved around a bitter Vietnam veteran who, after serving his county abroad, comes home to find his country is now treating him with a cold indifference. The inspiration for the song (which had originally been called "Vietnam" before Springsteen lifted the final title from a film script he had been sent by director Paul Schrader) stemmed from a few years previously when Springsteen had happened across a copy of *Born on the Fourth of July*. The book contained the harrowing memoirs of Ron Kovic, who sustained injuries on the front line that left him paralyzed. Following his return to the United States, Kovic became an ardent antiwar activist, making numerous protests but also found—like many other veterans—that he was virtually shunned by the nation that had asked him to fight in the first place. The idea that he would come back as a war hero proved to be a lie. Instead, the incapacitated Kovic served as an embarrassing reminder of the war that the United States could not win, and his huge personal sacrifice escaped recognition as a result (Kovic's story was turned into the Oliver Stone film of the same name starring Tom Cruise in 1989).

Following a chance meeting between the two, Kovic convinced Springsteen to perform a Vietnam veterans benefit in 1981, all of which propelled the singer on to write his own depiction of a disenfranchised ex-soldier—but one who would simultaneously represent the story of many more, too. However, Springsteen's manager John Landau felt "Born in the U.S.A." did not fit in with the rest of the material on *Nebraska*, so the song was left off the final album release.[18] The shelving of "Born in the U.S.A." was only temporary, however, and before *Nebraska* had even been released, Springsteen presented the song to the E Street Band to see if the bandmates could flesh it out. The lonely sounding acoustic guitar on the original 4-track version was done away with, as was the quietly agitated vocal melody. They were both replaced with a prominent synthesizer riff courtesy of keyboard player Roy Bittan, an explosive drum beat pounded out by Max Weinberg, and Springsteen's startling holler. Together, they bring home the protagonist's struggle via the song's bombastic cries of distress, exemplified best by a chorus that literally screams the title in a frustrated anguish rather than patriotic pride.

The intertwined story begins with the narrator recalling his humble beginnings in an unforgiving and already decimated town. With few prospects to start with, he has an altercation with local authorities and ends up joining the army (a continual route of escape for many with no discernible future career). Upon his return from Vietnam, he discovers the realities of recession and the experience of being all but abandoned by his country of birth—socially, professionally, and personally. After ruing the loss of a brother during a battle at Khe Sanh and remembering the relationship he struck up with a local woman, the narrator rages at the worthlessness of this ultimate sacrifice. He may have escaped the conflict with his own life, but recognizes that he is doomed to live it as an outcast with no compassion, no hope, "nowhere to run . . . nowhere to go." The constant protests that he was born in the U.S.A. appear to be irrelevant because the U.S.A. is not listening, and as the song launches into the instrumental coda, an extended howl of raw fury is heard being expelled into the heart of the mix. After a brief breakdown, the instrumental section briefly reprises before being faded out in the commercially released version—thus curtailing an extended jam that continued in the studio for several more minutes. Showing the virtually telepathic level of communication they had established through years of touring and recording, Springsteen and the E Street Band nailed this definitive version after just two takes. Landau (who was also acting as co-producer for these sessions) remarked that it was simply "the most exciting thing that ever happened in a recording studio."[19]

"Born in the U.S.A." first hit record stores in June 1984 as both the title and lead track of Springsteen's seventh album. It quickly stormed to the top of the charts and practically welded him to radio playlists and magazine covers worldwide. Although not released as a single until later in the year (at which point it hit the Top 10 as did all the other six singles to be lifted from the album), "Born in the U.S.A." was monolithic enough to be picked up as an album track. It also began most shows that the E Street Band would perform during the mammoth stadium tour that would last well into 1985. But it soon became apparent that part of Springsteen's wild success was being built on the back of a chronic misappropriation by fans who interpreted "Born in the U.S.A." as a fist-clenching anthem of national honor rather than a plea for reciprocated loyalty. For those not closely acquainted with his back catalog (particularly the grim portrayal of American life presented in *Nebraska*), it was perhaps an understandable mistake given the imagery Springsteen was surrounding himself with at the time. The album, for example, featured a clear image of the stars and stripes, which was intended to represent the Woody Guthrie-esque idea that America exists for the benefit and preservation of everyone. This was hardly an *anti*-American suggestion, but as history had already shown, this subtle spin on patriotism was susceptible to being misconstrued by casual observers (see Chapter 2 on Woody Guthrie for another example). The song itself meanwhile was epitomized by the domineering sound of the E Street Band, not to mention the towering chorus that, removed from the everyday struggle described in the verses, sounded like a pledge of allegiance. The video also did little to clarify the original spirit of "Born in the U.S.A." as it combined footage of the band playing with snapshots of blue-collar life in a way that ambiguously straddled the line between saddening and celebratory.

This inaccurate public assessment filtered through into the political sphere as the 1984 presidential campaign went into high gear. In September, conservative media pundit George Will attended a Springsteen concert and honing in on the combination of flags coupled with the energy of the performance, wrote it up as being an affirmation of the American existence. That ill-informed evaluation was followed by the somewhat insulting notion that the country might not be facing such hard times if the workforce put as much effort into making American products as Springsteen and the E Street Band applied when making their music. The Republican camp picked up on this train of thought, and just days later, Reagan looked to boost his chances of a second term by name-dropping Springsteen during a rally in New Jersey, explaining that his songs embodied the hopes and dreams of the American people that as president, he would help realize. After being prompted by sceptical journalists, Reagan's backroom staff explained that he genuinely did have a personal appreciation of the singer and even went so far to claim that his favorite song was "Born to Run."

Springsteen himself responded on stage a few days later by saying that he did not think President Reagan's fandom stretched to *Nebraska* before beginning "Johnny 99," one of the album's darkest moments. The song centers around a laid-off car-plant worker in Mahwah, New Jersey (as opposed to "South Succotash") who commits murder in a state of desperation and instead of settling for a 99-year jail sentence, actually asks for the electric chair under the rationale that he would better off dead. The political chain reaction did not stop there either. After hearing of Reagan's attempt to appropriate "Born in the U.S.A." and Springsteen's subsequent rebuttal, Democratic candidate Walter Mondale then tried to publicly claim that the singer endorsed his campaign, but was forced into a correction when Landau issued a statement denying any such support had been offered. The song even attracted commercial interest with Chrysler offering a reported $12 million for its use in a TV spot, which Springsteen flatly refused.

The euphoric manner in which "Born in the U.S.A." was delivered musically clearly overwhelmed the bitter emotions that informed its lyrics and that has no doubt contributed to Springsteen's gradual habit of performing the song acoustically in the vein of its original version. Although played in its full version during the 1980s and the early 1990s (well after Springsteen had split from the E Street Band), he first returned to the stripped down version during the solo tour to support *The Ghost of Tom Joad,* which was released in 1995—an album considered to be a natural successor to *Nebraska* thanks to its similarly minimal folk leanings. Even when the E Street Band reconvened toward the end of the 1990s, the stark acoustic version of "Born in the U.S.A." was retained with the famous chorus usually only being sung once or twice. These live efforts and repeated print clarifications have helped to reiterate the original intentions of protest, but the song remains dogged by a persistent association with the traditional facets of patriotism. It is a factor that Springsteen grudgingly acknowledges with hindsight as unavoidable.

> In order to understand the song's intent, you need to invest a certain amount of time and effort to absorb both the music and the words. But that's not the way a lot of people use pop music . . . for years after the release of the album, at Halloween, I had little kids at my door with their trick or treat bags singing "I was born in the U.S.A." They were not particularly well versed in the "Had a brother at Khe San [h] lyric . . . ". But they all had plenty of lung power when the chorus rolled around. I guess the same fate awaited Woody Guthrie's "This Land is Your Land" around the campfire. But that's never made me feel any better.[20]

Artist: The Smiths

Song: "Meat Is Murder"

Songwriter: Steven Morrissey and Johnny Marr

Album: *Meat Is Murder*

Label: Sire Records

1985

As the magnetic front man of the Smiths during the 1980s, Steven Morrissey attracted an unprecedented level of devotion from fans who analyzed and, in some cases, lived by his every word. Knowing the kind of power he wielded among the band's following, Morrissey used it to give a platform to the cause of animal rights through the hard-hitting track "Meat Is Murder." It is a theme that is ongoing through his solo career, and the singer has even won official recognition from animal rights groups for his work in raising awareness.

Before the first Smiths album had even seen the light of day, it was clear to everyone in and around the band that there was an unprecedented emotional connection between the bandmates and their fans. Originally, they had formed in Manchester in 1982 when a young, enthusiastic, and hugely ambitious guitarist named Johnny Marr arrived at the doorstep of local recluse Steven Morrissey. The two were only vague acquaintances, having met once previously at a Patti Smith gig in the city, but while Marr had pursued his interest in music by forming bands and playing shows, Morrissey had managed only a few unsuccessful auditions before trying his hand at music journalism instead. Marr was actively seeking a partner to sing lyrics to the music he

The Smiths (L–R): Andy Rourke, Morrissey, Johnny Marr, and Mike Joyce.
Courtesy of Photofest.

had been working on and was propelled into making this unannounced visit after learning that the legendary song-writing team of Jerry Lieber and Mike Stoller (responsible for such American rock 'n' roll classics as "Hound Dog," "Yakety Yak," and "Jailhouse Rock") had formed in much the same way. The deeply literate and remarkably articulate Morrissey had, in fact, been furiously writing lyrics during his self-enforced isolation. The duo's mutual love of classic pop as well as modern punk also helped cement a bond that was virtually instant.

With the realization that each was the other's muse, they moved rapidly in adding Marr's old school friend Andy Rourke on bass and Mike Joyce on drums, who had impressed them at his audition for having the audacity to turn up while under the influence of hallucinogenic drugs. By the end of 1983, the Smiths had released only two singles, but the devotion they were receiving even at this point bordered on the unnerving. Marr's immense skill on the guitar and suave good looks earned him much admiration, but it was Morrissey who proved to be the band's unlikely magnetic force from the beginning. Working as a photographer for *NME* at the time, Kevin Cummins was frequently employed to document the band's rise for the British music publication and witnessed the extreme reactions they elicited from fans at close quarters.

> I'd never seen that connection with an artist and an audience before . . . even with punk, the singer wouldn't throw himself into the audience or allow the audience onto the stage to hug him, which became de rigueur. Once the first kid came on stage, that was it for all time.[21]

Indeed, the floodgates had already been opened so wide that the band's label was forced to hire a car especially so Morrissey could be ferried from place to place without being mobbed in public.

The Smiths finally released their hotly anticipated, self-titled debut album in February 1984, and it served only to further entrench the bandmates' appeal among their fans. Alongside the truly unique charisma he exhibited on stage, Morrissey boasted an ability to write about alienation, tragic romanticism, and latent desire with a wit, charm, and empathetic accuracy that was simply uncanny. In an era of high unemployment, widespread social upheaval, and few immediate prospects for young people, Morrissey's beautifully sung vignettes of apprehension and awkwardness were being identified with on a mass scale. When asked about the reason for their devotion, Smiths fans would (and still do) simply reply that it sounded like Morrissey was singing about their lives specifically. Accordingly, such strong allegiances translated onto the U.K. charts very well with *The Smiths* reaching No. 2 shortly after release and the single "Heaven Knows I'm Miserable Now" (not included on the album) taking the band into the Top 10 for the first time during the summer. With a resolute and rabid fan base in tow, the Smiths quickly set about recording a full second album completely aware of the power they wielded over their fans. The ever outspoken Morrissey made no apologies for wanting to influence his fans' way of thinking, arguing that "popular music should be used in order to make serious statements because so many groups sell masses and masses of records and don't raise people's level of consciousness in any direction. We find that quite sinful."[22] The statement being made by the

Smiths on this occasion was on the subject of animal welfare, and they did so by bluntly naming the new album *Meat Is Murder*.

Once again, the recording created much discussion before it even arrived in stores with the music press, in particular, seizing on the opportunity to quiz Morrissey about his beliefs on the subject of animal rights. By far the most revealing and entertaining of interviews conducted at the time was by the famously irreverent publication *Smash Hits*. In the article, he explained that he once had a "moderate bacon fetish"[23] as a child until realizing the suffering that animals went through and accused many meat eaters of failing to make the connection between meat and real animals. Upon being asked what he might say to Kentucky Fried Chicken founder Colonel Sanders should they meet in heaven, Morrissey dryly replied that words were redundant and that he would simply "resort to the old physical knee in the groin."[24] Somewhat more controversially, he also professed support for the radical Animal Liberation Front (ALF), which had been in the news during the previous year after claiming that members of the group had poisoned thousands of chocolate bars in retaliation to a British confectionary manufacturer conducting animal-based experiments into the effects of teeth rotting. The contamination was revealed to be a hoax, but thousands of chocolate bars were withdrawn, causing a huge loss of revenue for the parent company—which also withdrew from animal testing soon after. Despite the apparent willingness of the ALF to cause widespread panic and endanger the health of the general public, Morrissey applauded the tactics reasoning that

> polite demonstration is pointless. You have to get angry, you have to be violent otherwise what's the point? There's no point in demonstrating if you don't get any national press, TV or radio, or nobody listens to you or you get beaten up by the police. So I do believe in these animal groups but I think they should be more forceful and I think what they need now is a national figure, a national face ... I think they need some very forthright figure head.[25]

It seemed from this speech of sorts that Morrissey was putting himself forward for that very role with the album's title track "Meat Is Murder" essentially providing him with a manifesto.

Following the abundant prerelease debate, *Meat Is Murder* emerged in February 1985 sporting a Warhol-esque front image lifted from Emile de Antonio's 1968 documentary about the Vietnam conflict entitled *In the Year of the Pig*. The inscription on the soldier's helmet originally read "Make war, not love," but was doctored to bear the album title for its appearance as a Smiths cover. The track of the same name was saved until the end and understandably so, considering the emotional impact contained within. It becomes patently clear that shock is the band's goal from the opening 45 seconds during which there is barely a note of actual music to be heard. Instead, the listener is greeted with a horrifying collage of cows in pain (lifted from Morrissey's sound effects album), buzzing blades (embellished with a ghostly reverb effect by engineer Stephen Street), and a forbidding machine-like tone that fades in and out (actually the sound of a piano added backwards with extra echo). The cumulative effect of this studio trickery is intended to mimic the ambience of a slaughterhouse, and the mood it creates is desperately stark. Fading into the aural melodrama comes the intro of the song itself, and the pace is deathly slow. Joyce's drums sound akin to a funeral march, Rourke provides a bass line that broods in the background as though it were a mourner, and Marr's siren-like guitar part seems as if it is leading the entire wake. Death hangs heavy on the song, and that is before the first line of lyrics has even been uttered.

When the first words do materialize, they send "Meat Is Murder" into even more impassioned realms. A suitably subdued and mournful sounding Morrissey begins by suggesting that the bovine cries of pain are equivalent to those of humans before lamenting the horror of beautiful creatures being killed for the sake of food and rhetorically asking whether the listener knows how animals meet with their death. As the song progresses, the narrator creates almost idyllic images of mealtime domesticity—the turkey being served at Christmas or the associated smells of home cooking—before destroying them with the claim that these products of human consumption are essentially created through brutal slayings. It is a viewpoint that is summed up (deliberately) through the main hook and the song's catchiest lyrics:

It's death for no reason, and death for no reason is murder.

Once the lyrics are dispatched in their entirety, the distant sound of cows returns to color the end section, and "Meat Is Murder" fades out with the same array of excruciating sound effects with which it began.

Having such a massive youth icon as Morrissey endorsing animal rights through these harsh and unforgiving sentiments was enough to create many new converts to the cause. Some even felt the song to have so much swaying power that "thousands turned vegetarian on the spot."[26] A nearly impossible suggestion to verify though it may be, the persuasive power of "Meat Is Murder" coupled with Morrissey's virtual deification among Smiths fans meant that such a pledge of allegiance was entirely plausible. It had taken only a year for the singer to spawn a small army of followers who all adopted his hairstyle, bookish glasses, and effeminate posturing by way of tribute, so shunning meat certainly required less visible effort in comparison. Morrissey definitely did manage to convince his fellow bandmates that the cause was a worthy one. Marr and Joyce converted, although a compromise over fish was reached with Morrissey as both the guitarist and the drummer were extremely partial to tuna sandwiches. Rourke also added his support, but later admitted that after a period of abstaining, he began to supplement his diet with sneaky portions of meat away from Morrissey's surveillance.

The fact that *Meat Is Murder* reached No. 1 in the album chart (the only album the band ever released to make it all the way to the top) clearly showed that just by sales and exposure alone, the Smiths were helping to put the issue into a broader spectrum. However, this would soon become a mixed blessing for Morrissey. Immediately after the album's release, the band embarked on a nationwide tour lasting almost until the end of March, and it was during this selection of dates that one fan's newly created commitment to vegetarianism became known to Morrissey in the most unusual way. "Meat Is Murder" had become the emotional peak of the set throughout this tour, and the band would save it until close to the end every night; during one performance, a string of sausages with the words "Meat Is Murder" inscribed on them was thrown toward the singer. Not only did they hit him squarely in the face, one even entered his mouth just as he opened it to sing a line from the song, causing him to partially bite one of the offending delicacies. Clearly shocked and upset, Morrissey left the stage for a few moments before returning under duress to perform the remainder of the show.

The Smiths would eventually split in 1987, but until then "Meat Is Murder" was a song, a phrase, and an ideology that went hand-in-hand with the group. While the members of the quartet presented themselves as a united front on the subject, it was Morrissey who obviously felt strongest on the issue and made the most amount of effort in promoting the cause. This was underlined as he embarked on his solo career in 1988, and although the references to animal rights were never made as explicitly in a song as they were in "Meat Is Murder," Morrissey never shied away from the issue. The video for his second solo single "Everyday Is Like Sunday" (1988), for example, features a fleeting shot in which the sullen main character (who wears an antimeat T-shirt throughout) runs away in disgust at the sight of a butcher's shop. She is also seen writing the phrase "Meat Is Murder" on a postcard and during one scene set in a café even goes so far as writing "Cruelty Without Beauty" on a note and placing it on a table occupied by two of her fellow diners before petulantly throwing a fur coat owned by one of them onto the floor. A later video for the song "Interesting Drug" (1989) also features numerous moments of proanimal rights imagery and depicts Morrissey himself handing out literature on the subject to a group of school boys. The boys then proceed to raid an animal experiment laboratory to free the captive rabbits held within.

Morrissey's commitment to exposing cruelty has not waned in the slightest, and this constant promotion of animal rights led the organization known as People for the Ethical Treatment of Animals (PETA) to honor him with a special award in 2005. Even as recently as 2006, he refused to tour Canada in response to the country's government-approved seal-culling campaign (much to the dismay of the many vegetarian Canadians looking forward to seeing him that year). It is difficult to argue that Morrissey has the same level of adulation and sphere of influence during these latter years as he did while operating as part of the Smiths, but his position as a bastion of the cause has been firmly established. In the shape of "Meat Is Murder," Morrissey can claim to have recorded the most pertinent and effective protest against inhumane animal treatment yet.

Notes

1. Quoted in James Henke, "Oscar! Oscar! Great Britain Goes Wilde for the 'Fourth-Gender' Smiths," *Rolling Stone,* June 7, 1984.

2. Figures according to British Broadcasting Corporation.

3. Quoted in Robert Sandall, "The Triumph of a Late Bloomer," *Daily Telegraph* (London), October 2, 2003.

4. *Punch the Clock,* liner notes, Edsel Records, 2003.

5. Quoted in *Under a Blood Red Sky* (album), Island Records, 1983.

6. Adrian Thrills, "War and Peace," *NME,* February 26, 1983.

7. Quoted in Jim Miller, "Stop in the Name of Love," *Newsweek,* December 31, 1984.

8. Quoted in *Rattle and Hum* (film), Phil Joanou, director, Paramount, 1988.

9. Quoted in Miller, "Stop in the Name of Love."

10. Ronald Reagan, address to the National Association of Evangelicals, retrievable at www.presidentreagan.info/speeches/empire.cfm

11. James Kelly, "Thinking about the Unthinkable," *Time,* March 29, 1982.

12. Quoted in Kurt Loder, "Nena's '99 Luftballons' Soars Up the US Charts," *Rolling Stone,* March 15, 1984.

13. Quoted in Alexis Petridis, "Please Look After This Band," *Mojo,* January 2002.

14. Quoted in Nick Hasted, "Jerry Dammers: A Ghost From the Past," *Independent* (London), April 20, 2007.

15. Quoted in Michael Azerrad, *Our Band Could Be Your Life* (New York: Back Bay, 2002), 80.

16. There were 46 tracks on the original vinyl release. The 1987 CD reissue featured 44 tracks, and the 1989 version featured 43. Both were edited to fit the limited running time of the format.

17. Quoted in William E. Smith, "Stumping in South Succotash," *Time,* March 29, 1982.

18. This original recording was eventually issued as part of the 4-disc box set *Tracks* in 1998 and was also included on the condensed, single disc version *18 Tracks* released the following year.

19. Quoted in Eric Alterman, *The Promise of Bruce Springsteen* (New York: Back Bay, 2001), 158.

20. Bruce Springsteen, *Songs* (New York: Avon, 1998), 163.

21. Quoted in Toby Manning, "A Rush and a Push and the Land Is Ours," *Q Special Edition: The Inside Story of the Smiths and Morrissey,* May 2004.

22. Quoted in *The Old Grey Whistle Test,* BBC Television, aired February 12, 1985.

23. Quoted in Tom Hibbert, "Morrissey Interviewed," *Smash Hits,* January 31, 1985.

24. Ibid.

25. Ibid.

26. Andrew Collins, "The Flesh Is Willing," *Q Special Edition: The Inside Story of the Smiths and Morrissey,* May 2004.

CHAPTER 8

REBELS WITHOUT A PAUSE (1986–1993)

The mid-1980s are often remembered as being a period of growing consumer culture, financial greed, and social self-interest; in contrast, the music world became gripped by an omnipresent sense of humanitarianism during the same period. For rock's biggest names, there was no shortage of good causes to champion and an equally plentiful number of public platforms on which to do it. Most famously, the intercontinental Live Aid concert of 1985 and the affiliated charity singles by Band Aid and USA (United Support of Artists) for Africa mobilized just about the entire industry into raising awareness about the famine in Africa, and to this day, it remains a defining example of how music can mix with philanthropy. The Farm Aid spin-off of the same year sought to raise money for the benefit of America's struggling farmers again attracted an array of middle of the road stars. Elsewhere, the campaign to end apartheid in South Africa gathered steam, environmental concern was growing rapidly, the nuclear arms race was admonished, cold war politics came into question, and, of course, the economic difficulties of life under President Ronald Reagan in the United States and Prime Minister Margaret Thatcher in the United Kingdom still inspired musical indignation. It was somewhat ironic to find that during this extremely fertile period of social and political anger, protest music also seemed to reach a new peak of petulance, too. Australian singer and alternative icon Nick Cave, for example, saved the bulk of his rage for the journalists who dared to give him a bad review; in the song "**Scum**" (1986), he unleashed a torrent of anger that, in a certain respect, revealed just as much about his own ego as it did the unfairness of the British music press. Perhaps the height of triviality was reached by the Beastie Boys who sneered about nothing more important than being deprived of pornography and cigarettes in "**(You Gotta) Fight for Your Right (to Party!)**" (1987), but tapped into the frustrations of a generation of spoiled teenagers in the process.

Although Cave and the Beastie Boys acted as welcome antidotes to the seriousness of many of their contemporaries, they were isolated cases, and by the end of the 1980s/start of the 1990s, a markedly radical streak had begun to emerge. After struggling to shake off its early image as a frivolous fad, hip-hop undoubtedly moved to the forefront of politically charged music, and the band most directly responsible was Public Enemy. The Long Islanders had already startled the world with the adventurous sound and emphatically pro-black ideals of the 1988 album *It Takes a Nation of Millions to Hold Us Back*. But the following year, they upped the ante on both fronts with "**Fight the Power**" (1989), which issued a stinging rejection of African American apathy and warned that there was much work to do if black people were to be completely free of social and political oppression. Their attempts to raise consciousness were hugely influential across genres and across races, and the spirit of Public Enemy's rousing rhetoric could clearly be heard in the work of rock outfit Rage Against the Machine, which seemed intent on making *every* song a protest song. As it turned out, none would have as much impact as the band's very first single "**Killing in the Name**" (1993)—an inflammatory call to rebellion that could apply to practically anyone.

But it was in the racially divided city of Los Angeles that protest music took a turn into the most extreme realms. Years of economic decline had left the primarily African American areas in the South Central district verging on destitution and rife with gang-related crime. Police measures to combat this grew steadily hasher in conjunction, but many in the area resented their overzealousness, arguing that it frequently crossed over into outright racism and, in some cases, physical brutalization of the black community. A summation of this viewpoint could not have been put in more blunt terms than those expressed by rappers N.W.A. (Niggaz With Attitude), who showed their disgust by putting the local authorities on trial in the narrative of "**Fuck tha Police**" (1988) and ended up as targets of the Federal Bureau of Investigation (FBI) as a result. The song also contained grim warnings of the violence that may erupt if the Los Angeles Police Department (LAPD) continued to implement the law without restraint; it was a vision that materialized in 1992 when rioting claimed 55 lives after the acquittal of officers accused of beating black motorist Rodney King. The fragile peace that followed this event was something that the government sought to preserve, even if it meant trying to ban obscure thrash metal tracks like Body Count's "**Cop Killer**" (1992), which was a retribution fantasy written by rapper Ice-T as a response to the King incident. The issue of how, and to what extent, the constitutionally guaranteed right of free speech applies to music had surfaced before, but these two songs seemed to test the strength of the First Amendment more than any others in history.

Artist: Nick Cave and the Bad Seeds

Song: "Scum"

Songwriters: Nick Cave and Mick Harvey

Album: Issued free on flexi-discs, but later released on the CD format of *Your Funeral . . . My Trial*

Label: Homestead Records (United States)/Mute Records (United Kingdom)

1986

As a young music fan, the words of the British music press helped inspire Nick Cave to form a band and eventually move from Australia to London in 1980. However, the subsequent experience of swinging in and out of favor with the very same publications as a singer for the Birthday Party and the Bad Seeds irritated him greatly. Finally, Cave's unforgiving temperament drove him to kick back through "Scum"—a foul-mouthed, comically violent, and viciously funny protest song directed squarely at his two journalistic nemeses.

The British music press has long been regarded as one of the world's most ruthless institutions. Positioned on rock music's cutting edge, many of these weeklies and monthlies are used by fans as the central barometer that gages the very latest trends and the most original sounds in the United Kingdom. Entire careers have been built on (or at least kick-started by) championing from these much read and much respected column inches, but conversely, there has long been a trend of such writers and

Nick Cave.
Courtesy of Photofest.

publications apparently seeking to knock down what they built up. Even today, fickleness is a common accusation leveled by artists who have been subjected to this erratic treatment. It is because of this vicious swing from adoration to abomination that the term "backlash" is so readily associated with such fabled music magazines (past and present) as *NME, Melody Maker, Sounds, Smash Hits, Q,* and many more. However, it was only a matter of time before that backlash suffered its own backlash.

One avid reader of the music press was Nick Cave. Born into an Anglican family in Warracknabeal, Australia, in 1957, Cave grew up with a love of literature provided by his mother and father (a librarian and an English teacher, respectively). He also had a passion for music, which led him to forming his first band in the late 1970s called the Boys Next Door. Its innocent-sounding name hid a band that clearly held the wild sounds and dangerous possibilities of punk close to its heart, and each member referred to the imported press closely for inspiration. Despite an initial indifference to the burgeoning genre, British magazines began to closely chronicle the initial explosion of punk bands, such as the Clash, the Sex Pistols, and the Damned, as well as the subgenres it quickly spawned, particularly the post-punk offshoot that was characterized during the same period by the likes of Magazine, the Fall, and Joy Division. Living virtually as far away from the U.K. music scene as was humanly possible and with practically no chance of ever hearing much of punk's smaller (and quite probably more interesting) bands, the words of *NME* and *Melody Maker* writers were just about the only source of information that the Boys Next Door had to go on.

The aforementioned tendency of the country's foremost rock scribes to exaggerate in their articles seduced Cave and his bandmates into believing that the United Kingdom was the place to be. Punk's impact in Australia had been minimal, so, in the hope of finding some recognition for their own music as well as finally getting to hear the rabidly celebrated bands they had read about, the four bandmates decided to relocate to London in 1980 and changed their name to the Birthday Party (after the 1957 Harold Pinter play). Not only were they broke within days of arriving in London, they were also disappointed to find that the energy and vitality of punk's first waves had dissipated and the somewhat lighter bands now being lauded by the music press, such as the Teardrop Explodes and Echo & the Bunnymen, were, by Cave's own assessment, nowhere near as good as they had been led to believe.

The feeling of being duped about the possibilities of London were at least numbed a little by the positive effects that moving had on the Birthday Party's own standing in the music scene. The band's visceral, cacophonic blasts of feral punk coupled with the waif-like Cave delivering mesmerizing and markedly confrontational performances meant that it stood out from the crowd dramatically. Instantly, the press had something genuinely new to write about; 1981's album *Prayers on Fire* and the following year's *Junkyard* earned high praise with one reviewer summating the live experience particularly well by explaining "watching them is a bit like standing too close to a firework—dangerous but compulsive."[1] Furthermore, the added attraction of the violence that occasionally occurred between band and crowd during its gigs meant that the Birthday Party reviews, features, and news pieces all had an extra element of tabloid-like sensationalism woven into them. Although Cave was lauded as a Goth icon, the singer treated virtually all journalists with contempt and suspicion due to the displeasure he felt at the kind of publicity both he and his band were receiving. As a result, an archetypal love/hate relationship began to develop between the two factions. Even at this relatively early point, the simmering tensions made for some highly entertaining interviews, but by 1983, many commentators viewed the Birthday Party bandmates as being past their best and argued that they had failed to progress past their intense initial impact. The about-turn in critical reception was far from helpful for the band's progress, but it proved to be the tension between its members that actually prompted the Birthday Party's demise. With Cave and guitarist Rowland S. Howard no longer seeing eye to eye in any sense and their most musically pivotal member Mick Harvey citing a lack of artistic advancement or direction, the band split up at the end of the year. However, it was only a matter of months before Cave and Harvey began sowing the Bad Seeds.

Despite not even having a solvent lineup in their earliest months, Nick Cave and the Bad Seeds (to give the band its full name) managed to muster a rough and ragged collection of "songs" that eventually earned a release in the summer of 1984 under the title of *From Her to Eternity*. Given the patchy material on show and the lack of favor Cave had enjoyed with the press in the last days of the Birthday Party, the bandmates were somewhat shocked to find that their debut garnered an overwhelmingly euphoric critical reaction. Made up of a selection of fractured tracks that sounded more like rough sketches than fully developed tracks, the album made for a challenging and occasionally impenetrable listen, but it was this that seemed to attract so much acclaim.

In particular, *NME*'s Mat Snow (with whom Cave also lived for a period) wrote an extended review of unprecedented enthusiasm, beginning and ending his article with the direct declaration that *From Her to Eternity* ranked as "one of the greatest rock albums ever made."[2] Despite the incessant ego massaging that he received, Cave's revulsion at the antics of the press seemed only to grow, and it finally began to get the better of him the following year when the band's second album *The Firstborn Is Dead* emerged.

Hindsight sees this album established as superior to the first by most Bad Seeds followers, but at the time, the press reaction was mixed. Cave subsequently became incensed at what he saw as the whimsical trashing of an album not because of any lack in musical power, but because the band (or rather he) was old news and no longer had any editorial clout. Indeed, it was *NME*'s Snow who was one of the first to criticize Cave just months after he had written the celebratory review of *From Her to Eternity*. Well before *The Firstborn Is Dead* had been released in June 1985, Snow took a swipe at it via a small review of "Yu-Gung" by the German industrial outfit Einstürzende Neubauten (whose central member Blixa Bargeld doubled as the Bad Seeds guitarist) by saying that the single had a "psychological edge disappointingly absent from the forthcoming Nick Cave LP."[3] In the grand scheme of things, it seemed like a fairly benign comment, but for Cave it was the straw that broke the camel's back.

As the Bad Seeds worked on producing their third "proper" album, Cave decided to release a stopgap album of covers in the summer of 1986, which was issued partly to pay tribute to his favorite artists (such as Johnny Cash, the Velvet Underground, the Sensational Alex Harvey Band, and others), but also as a calculated move designed to goad his critics and invite them to bemoan his willful indulgence—which they duly did. Tellingly, it was given the amusing title of *Kicking against the Pricks,* and there was precious little effort made by any member of the band to disguise who the eponymous targets were, but a more direct indictment of the music press was lurking beyond the album. To coincide with the release of *Kicking against the Pricks,* Snow was dispatched to interview Cave for *NME,* and a famously frosty encounter ensued. Snow had become aware of a nonalbum track called "Scum" that had apparently been written about the press, in general, but Cave tersely corrected Snow and informed him that he "wrote it about you,"[4] before insulting Snow personally. Cave continued by explaining his feelings toward the press while simultaneously revealing his own outrageous sense of self-importance.

> If someone says something good about me, they're doing their job; I have no complaints. They get no medal, they get their wage. That's all. But if they say something bad, then that really gets [me] ... everything that's said against me offends me, whether it's true or not. I can't fathom these people who flunked their arts courses and became rock journalists ... yet it is these people whose opinions are lauded as being gospel.[5]

As the Bad Seeds embarked on another tour in support of the album, the track in question was sold in the briefly used flexi-disc format (essentially a paper-thin piece of vinyl) at every gig. It was through this method that the public assassination of Snow—and to a lesser extent, another female journalist named Antonella Black[6]—got its first airing. Essentially an unashamed rant, "Scum" is set to a deliberately repetitive and turgid rhythm punctuated only by Bargeld's shrill guitar motif that sounds like an accident repeated over and over. Clearly, the band is trying hard to make sure attention is not diverted away from Cave's venom, but manages to create a suitably dissonant backing, too. As if to herald the bile about to be expelled, the track opens with the disgusting sound of Cave summoning an impressive amount of phlegm from the back of his throat and so begins his unforgiving but darkly humorous protest against the British music press with Snow providing a prominent focal point. The lyrics come thick and fast with Cave spitting them out in a crazed stream of consciousness, almost immediately aiming more abuse at Snow and slamming his apparent hospitality toward him during their days of cohabiting as merely a rouse to gain a professional advantage for himself. After briefly touching on the unscrupulous professional parallels with Black (who gets off lightly in comparison), Cave homes in on the offending article and menacingly warns that he remains grudgeful before the drum beats drop out and he launches into the song's profanity-laden apex of anger. Proceedings come to an end with a comic-book-style fantasy of Snow being murdered, as the scorned perpetrator envisions the blood springing from six gunshot wounds and the sense of peace and relief that would follow. And with that, the act of retribution is done, and "Scum" collapses to its conclusion with no more elegance than with which it began.

An eye for an eye may have been his motivation, but in this instance, Cave clearly took a little more in return, but he did so in a style that was all his own: unreasonable, ungraceful, unrepentant but entertaining for all concerned, including his target and ex-friend. As reflected in its limited circulation on flexi-disc, "Scum" was a largely frivolous moment for the Bad Seeds. It allowed Cave to vent his spleen but little else, and initially many fans knew nothing of the song other than what they might have read in the press. It did, however, graphically illustrate Cave's fiery temperament and disregard for journalists or any potential critic or interviewer. This certainly did not mean that the Bad Seeds were guaranteed a good review at every juncture, but for a while at least, those who dared to criticize him knew that somewhere, Nick Cave was reading their informed opinions . . . and quite probably getting very upset about them. Today, the song is thought of as little more than an amusing footnote in the continuing career of the Bad Seeds, but it has taken on a cult status among fans and music journalists nevertheless. If anything, "Scum" has served Snow's reputation better in the long run as few music journalists can boast that an article they wrote prompted an established artist to record and release an entire song in response. For his part, Cave allows himself a wry smile when questioned on his vengeful young self, but time may not have healed all of his old wounds. In a 2006 interview with the British newspaper *Guardian* (London), Cave recounted the incident with good humor, but confessed to still being able to remember the sentence in Snow's Einstürzende Neubauten review that tipped him over the edge—almost word for word. Over 20 years after the confrontation, forgiving and forgetting is evidently not something he is completely prepared to do.

Artist: Beastie Boys

Song: "(You Gotta) Fight for Your Right (to Party!)"

Songwriters: Mike Diamond, Adam Yauch, Adam Horovitz, and Rick Rubin

Album: *Licensed to Ill*

Label: Def Jam Records

1986

As a group of punk rockers with a penchant for infantile behavior, the Beastie Boys rarely let the social and political ills of the early 1980s influence their work, but that did not mean they had nothing to complain about. As the group began to dabble in the relatively new genre of hip-hop, one of its biggest hits turned out to be "(You Gotta) Fight for Your Right (to Party!)"—a song that both echoed and satirized the boredom of a generation growing up under the conservative glare of Ronald Reagan. Although it brought the trio huge success, it would also create a loutish typecast that would follow the group members for years to come.

From the very start, the Beastie Boys were nothing if not funny, but their japes and jokes were not always welcome among the more righteous factions of hardcore punk as it developed into a distinct genre across the East Coast during the early 1980s. The first incarnation of the band materialized in 1981 as Adam Yauch, Mike Diamond, Kate Schellenbach, and John Berry began harboring hopes of creating a New York equivalent of the Washington, D.C.–based groups they so admired—particularly Bad Brains that earned much respect for their pioneering mix of reggae, punk, and Rastafarian spirituality. Although Bad Brains were not necessarily exponents of the same dictum, many hardcore punk outfits of the time adhered to the sometimes overly pious idea of being "straight edge" by resolutely refusing to drink or take drugs and even showing an open contempt for those who did (see the entry in Chapter 6 on "Straight Edge" by Minor Threat). But while the Beastie Boys enjoyed the ferocity of the music associated with this drug-free standpoint, the fun-loving

The Beastie Boys getting the party started in 1987. (L–R): MCA, Mike D, and Ad-Rock.
Courtesy of Paul Natkin Archive/Getty Images

bandmates certainly did not practice abstinence and injected their deliberately uncomplicated lyrics with adolescent humor and tales of comically antisocial behavior. The band's debut EP *Polly Wog Stew* encapsulated these simplistic themes perfectly upon its release in late 1982. The opening track "Beastie Boys," for example, simply spelled out the band's name repeatedly, while "Egg Raid on Mojo" (one of the more complicated lyrical narratives) merely involved the story of pelting eggs at a bouncer who would not let them into a nightclub. Inevitably, their avoidance of serious issues and generally amateurish attitude left the more sanctimonious exponents and fans of hardcore punk unimpressed, with some going so far as to write the band hate mail.

The band's rudimentary style—both musical and lyrical—still earned the first formation of the Beastie Boys a spot supporting Bad Brains in New York in 1982. Even so, the appeal of hardcore punk was already waning with Diamond and Yauch especially having their attention distracted by the sound of a new musical form called hip-hop that had been birthed in the Bronx, but was now beginning to filter into their regular stomping grounds of Brooklyn and downtown Manhattan. The band began to adapt around these new interests, with Berry leaving to be replaced by another ex-hardcore punk named Adam Horovitz, after which the Beastie Boys made their first inroads into hip-hop but did not to forget to take their collective sense of humor with them. The *Cooky Puss* EP (released in 1983) marked their first journey into the realms beyond hardcore with the title track consisting of a basic beat married to a prank phone call made to ice cream parlor. Although perilously close to novelty, the track did at least herald a change in tack for the band. Shortly afterward, they attracted the advances of a burgeoning local record label called Def Jam, which was headed by a white New York University (NYU) student named Rick Rubin and a black entrepreneur in the making called Russell Simmons (whose brother Joseph was a member of the increasingly successful Queens-based rappers Run-DMC). Under Rubin's guidance, the band quickly styled itself as a triple-vocal hip-hop crew rather than an instrument playing band and further refined its image by shedding Schellenbach to leave an unholy trinity of bratty young men with attitude to spare. Keeping in the spirit of the inherently egotistical nature of hip-hop's leading showmen, the remaining trio now began operating under the monikers of The King Ad-Rock (Horovitz), MCA (Yauch), and Mike D (Diamond). It would quickly became clear that the Beastie Boys now seemed intent on causing irritation to a different set of music fans.

As the group continued to hone its rap skills, Rubin used his position as producer to add elements of the hard rock and metal bands he had loved as a teenager. The combination of musical styles added to the Beastie Boys' well-established sneer and a comical penchant for mischief created a signature sound that provided a common link between the string of singles released on Def Jam throughout 1985 and 1986. It was largely impossible to take these frat-boy caricatures and their sex/drinking/partying-based concerns particularly seriously but even less so when the debut album finally earned a release at the end of 1986, if only because it was called *Licensed to Ill* ("Ill" being a street-slang term for joke). Released as a single shortly afterward, one of the album's most prominent songs "(You Gotta) Fight for Your Right (to Party!)" went a long way in summing up the Beastie Boys as a whole—silly, funny, obnoxious even, but very self-aware and adroitly satirical. The first verse finds the protagonist (voiced in turn by all three Beastie Boys) attempting to escape going to school, but is swiftly told he must by his mother and then finds himself resenting the authoritarian teacher once he arrives. The second verse is even more banal in its disaffection, with the protests now being aimed at his parents for prohibiting smoking and preventing the consumption of pornography. Finally, the ill feeling in the last verse is derived merely from being told to get a haircut, to dress properly, and to turn down the loud music that is no doubt emanating from the narrator's bedroom. It is the very fabric of adolescent angst to the point of being a cliché, but it is addressed in a manner that could not be less subtle and, in the same way, could not be more humorous.

The song's simple sound was masterminded by Rubin whose intention was to lampoon hugely popular bands of the era, such as Motley Crue and Twisted Sister. Subsequently, he opted to deliberately lace it with bombastic drums, over-the-top rock guitars playing just three chords for nearly the entirety of the song, and a faux-heavy metal solo that is clearly intended to be daftly comical rather than dazzlingly complicated. The video for the track was similarly unserious; placed on high rotation at the time of release and now remembered as a staple of MTV's playlist throughout the second half of the 1980s, it featured the group members and their rowdy friends causing havoc at a party, partaking in a huge custard pie fight, and one hysterical shot right at the start of the clip (before the music has started) even contains MCA hitting himself on the head with a gigantic dildo.

A sense of affluent rebellion dominates "(You Gotta) Fight for Your Right (to Party!)" from start to finish, and although the bandmates' sneers and shouts are certainly raucous, a purposeful insurgency is clearly something they have no inclination to organize. Despite the spirited spleen venting, it seems obvious that the song's narrators have nothing to truly complain about, and they are merely taking pleasure in "blowing trivial problems up to a level their more serious-minded musical peers would use to talk about *real* issues."[7] Ultimately, it proves to be conservative reaction to a conservative set of circumstances set in an era characterized by the conservative social and political attitudes employed by President Ronald Reagan and his Republican administration—a triple-pronged irony that Charles M. Young of *Playboy* encapsulated perfectly in an article about the band in 1987:

> What most adults don't understand about most teenagers is that most teenagers are extremely conservative most of the time, even as they are engaging in obnoxious behaviour designed to differentiate themselves from most adults. Most teenagers enjoy a heavily structured life, are threatened by deviations from the conforming norm and will ridicule those enamoured of deviating from the norm. In this way, most teenagers are exactly like most adults, the only difference being that teenagers piss their lives away in high school while adults piss their lives away in corporations. Most teenagers do, after all, grow up to be most adults.[8]

Both "(You Gotta) Fight for Your Right (to Party!)" and *Licensed to Ill* fed off each other's popularity and became unparalleled in their success during the early part of 1987. The single hit No. 7 on the U.S. charts and No. 11 in the United Kingdom, both of which propelled the album on to become the biggest selling hip-hop album of the decade. The anthemic chorus and its rambunctious call to arms became a familiar sound at virtually every student party and rock disco on both sides of the Atlantic Ocean for the rest of the year, but such widespread popularity seemed to suggest that not everyone was tuned in to the song's sideways look at loutishness. As the Beastie Boys became more popular, they found that the very people they were satirizing in "(You Gotta) Fight for Your Right (to Party!)" were now making up increasingly significant sections of their audience. Worse still, the bandmates found themselves being drawn into a self-fulfilling prophecy with their own conduct spiraling into an actual embodiment of the very thing they intended to ridicule. "On the *Licensed to Ill* tour we really homed in on being jackasses," recalled MCA glumly in 2004. "We were taking the piss out of frat guys and then suddenly they were our whole audience and they were going, Yaaaaaaaaaaaaaah!"[9]

As the success of *Licensed to Ill* continued on the back of succeeding singles, such as "No Sleep Till Brooklyn" and "She's on It," the Beastie Boys' reputation as lairy, sexist, Neanderthal figures continued to grow in the press particularly in light of their stage show that toured the world throughout the year. Performing with beers in hand, a caged, topless go-go dancer on one side, and a giant, hydraulic penis behind, the trio was now indulging its sense of humor in ways that made it harder to separate the art from the artist. In the United Kingdom especially, the infamously brutal tabloid newspapers seized on the scent of scandal and portrayed the trio as being disgusting, depraved, and almost seditious. Embellished if not completely fabricated stories of swearing at disabled children and attempting to overturn parked cars during some European dates circulated in the press; such was the extent of sensationalist journalism that preceded their first tour of Britain in May 1987 that a member of British Parliament even raised the question of whether Ad-Rock, Mike D, and MCA should be allowed in the country at all.

By the time the U.K. leg of the tour began, there were many who decided to attend their shows not for the music and certainly not the irony, but instead for the spectacle of (and the chance to mirror) three supposedly uncontrollable young men in the throes of destruction. That, too, was an image that briefly became reality during a gig in Liverpool during which the trio was pelted with bottles only for Ad-Rock to begin hitting some back with a baseball bat. The following day, Ad-Rock was arrested and spent a weekend in police custody after a female fan claimed she was hit by a returning projectile struck by the belligerent Beastie. It may not have been a monster that "(You Gotta) Fight for Your Right (to Party!)" had spawned, but its huge success definitely aided an unpleasant growth of some kind. The joke within the song was getting old and to make matters worse, those fans who did not understand the Beastie Boys' humor were now starting to severely damage the band's reputation with their incomprehension. The incident in Liverpool alone sparked another media furor, and it would be five years before the band felt confident enough to return to the United Kingdom without fear of demonization.

Even with the Beastie Boys' subsequent career establishing the trio as true pioneers in hip-hop, "(You Gotta) Fight for Your Right (to Party!)" still haunts them. Although Ad-Rock, MCA, and Mike D do begrudgingly recognize its undeniable place in the group's colorful history (not least in the liner notes of 1999's *Sounds of Science* anthology), a sense of embarrassment over the whole period remains. Hindsight has long restored the sense of dumbed-down satire to the track, and confusing the band with the narrator is not something that is easily done some 20 years later— especially as the Beastie Boys are now elder statesmen within their genre and have not played the track since the year of release. But despite this timepiece nature, the trivial concerns of teenagers all over the world still exist in sufficient numbers to make "(You Gotta) Fight for Your Right (to Party!)" worthy of a hearty shake of the fist— albeit with a knowing smile.

Artist: N.W.A.

Song: "Fuck tha Police"

Songwriters: Ice Cube (O'Shea Jackson) and MC Ren (Lorenzo Patterson)

Album: *Straight Outta Compton*

Label: Priority Records

1988

Having struggled to earn credibility from their East Coast counterparts during the late 1980s, West Coast hip-hop acts finally emerged as forces to be reckoned with thanks partly to N.W.A.'s ferocious sound and brutally honest portrayal of life in the more deprived areas of Los Angeles. With anger growing in the city's African Americans communities over extreme and possibly racist policing measures, the group recorded a seething and aggressive response in the form of "Fuck tha Police"— a song that typified the new subgenre called "gangsta rap," but also met with a wave of stern criticism that extended as far as the FBI.

As President Ronald Reagan campaigned for what would turn out to be a successful reelection in 1984, he played heavily on the beginnings of an economic upturn by claiming that it was morning in America once again. But while economic fortunes across the country as a whole had begun to improve particularly during the latter half of Reagan's first term, there remained a number of areas caught in what seemed like an unchanging and immovable dusk. One of the most contentious Republican policies of the time was the administration of so-called "trickle-down economics." It was an idea that placed an emphasis on creating financial growth and investment through offering tax relief to the highest-bracket earners and businesses. Supporters of the plan argued that this top-level regeneration would then in theory descend downward to help regenerate the nation's most impoverished areas and relieve a workforce still reeling from the vicious depression that peaked at the start of the decade. In practice, however, the trickling down proved to be a desperately slow process, and those who happened to be at the very bottom of the economic ladder spent much of Reagan's tenure and beyond looking upward with empty expectancy.

The mainly African American inhabitants of the South Central district of Los Angeles certainly seemed like the kind of people who needed help the most, but had to wait the longest to get it. The racial makeup of the area shifted dramatically from predominately white to predominately black during the 1960s and 1970s, but with the subsequent decline of many manufacturing industries (particularly in the motoring sector), employment dwindled and poverty flourished. The disintegration of the community would accelerate further during the 1980s with the development of gang violence and the influx of crack cocaine, but the government response to these grave problems was largely unsympathetic. The press-friendly "War on Drugs" campaign encouraged the youth of America to distance themselves from the drug culture and was endorsed by none other than First Lady Nancy Reagan, who famously advised that those tempted should "just say no." Meanwhile, her husband strongly advocated prison sentences for drug offenders, but chose to cut funding for addiction programs, thereby creating what seemed to be a hugely unrealistic circle of measures that appeared ineffective in keeping the problem under control.

Toward the close of the decade as the gang epidemic continued to grow, the LAPD initiated Operation Hammer in 1987—a measure designed to curb this urban blight by arresting large numbers of black and Hispanic youths with only minimal evidence to connect them to gang activity. Thousands of men were arrested particularly during Operation Hammer's peak in 1988, but the number of charges filed was significantly fewer. During one extremely heavy-handed raid in August of that year, two South Central apartment buildings were raided and virtually ransacked by police in what was supposed to be a major drug bust. Unfortunately, echoing the very gangs they were attempting to combat, officers destroyed furniture, appliances, and walls needlessly while even going so far as to spray-paint various pro-police slogans—effectively rendering several families homeless in the process. The result, however, was merely "trace amounts of crack and less than six ounces of marijuana."[10]

Inevitably, accusations of intimidation, brutality, and overt racism were leveled at the LAPD for its actions not just during the August debacle, but the general manner of policing during the era. Meanwhile, the palpable tension among the various ethnic groups of South Central LA was serving only to heighten problems plaguing the district. However, it was around the same time that this pressure-cooker environment gave birth to a new subgenre of music. Up until the late 1980s, hip-hop had been almost exclusively the preserve of East Coast artists—particularly those hailing from New York City. West Coast artists had long been dismissed as inferior imitators who lacked the talent or credibility to compete, but one group that single-handedly bucked that trend was a five-piece crew from Compton called N.W.A. (Niggaz With Attitude).

The key member and linchpin for the group's formation was Eric "Eazy-E" Wright, who had spent most of the mid-1980s adapting to the entrepreneurial spirit of the time—albeit in a manner of which Ron and Nancy would not have approved. Known in South Central for making a reasonable income as a drug dealer, Eazy-E also had ambitions to build himself a music business empire incorporating act management and a record label called Ruthless, which was shored up partly through his ill-gotten gains. The diminutive but still intimidating young man knew Andre "Dr. Dre" Young, O'Shea "Ice Cube" Jackson, and Antoine "DJ Yella" Carraby from their involvement in fledgling hip-hop crews and had come across Mik Lezan through his solo work. The five men talked about the possibility of forming some kind of local supergroup that Eazy-E then christened with its less than commercial moniker. Lezan would quickly leave the group, but with the enlistment of Eazy-E's neighborhood friend Lorenzo "MC Ren" Patterson keeping them as a quintet, the definitive lineup of N.W.A. set about recording its first official album.

The resulting *Straight Outta Compton* (first released in August 1988) made an impact that was beyond seismic and was certainly not localized to just the hip-hop community either. Dominated by images of gang violence, drug culture, sexual aggression, misogyny, homophobia, and unfathomable amounts of bad language, the shock value alone was enough to ensure N.W.A. huge amounts of exposure. Almost always pictured scowling at the camera and occasionally touting guns, too, there seemed to be a threat associated with the group's very presence. Criticism naturally came thick and fast from all sides, but contrary to the accusations leveled at the bandmates, glorification of these themes was not necessarily the intention. As the band's most prominent members, Eazy-E, Dr. Dre, and Ice Cube argued that they were merely products of their environment and, as such, were acting as journalists documenting a way of life that society would rather ignore. But it was impossible to ignore the songs on *Straight Outta Compton*—particularly when one of them bore the title "Fuck tha Police." Musically, the track (and indeed the entire album) reflected how N.W.A. had created a sea change in West Coast hip-hop. Known previously for being banal and lightweight in comparison to their grittier East Coast cousins, Dr. Dre and DJ Yella had conspired to prove that Los Angeles was now preparing a serious challenge to New York's hegemony within the genre. Gangsta rap (as it would be termed by the press) was the newest innovation and nowhere was this clearer than in "Fuck tha Police" thanks to an audacious mesh of ultra-funky beats, swaggering horn samples, suave guitar riffs, and slick scratches. But as an articulation of rage at the treatment received by young black men in the ravaged streets of Compton and the social Armageddon simmering as a result, the song served as a stark wake-up call.

The premise of "Fuck tha Police" is cleverly based on a courtroom scene in which Dre plays the judge while Ice Cube, Ren, and Eazy-E stand as prosecutors taking it in turn to deliver accusations of brutality and oppression against the police department. The language is not pretty, but neither are the accusations. First up, Ice Cube is invited to take the stand and unleashes a sustained lambaste in which he riles against police singling out blacks who exhibit material wealth and associate the sight with illegal activity—drug dealing in particular. In addition to brief allusions to latent homosexuality in the LAPD, Ice Cube adds an indignant view on black police officers using excessive force on black youths just to avoid accusations of racial favoritism from their white colleagues. By way of a grim finale, he spits out a warning that a form of violent and bloody retribution will be the inevitable outcome unless practices are changed.

Ice Cube is replaced by Ren for the next segment that begins with the rapper being needlessly pulled over. There is no letup in the onslaught of abrasive lyrics as Ren also begins to paint another ugly and ultimately nihilistic picture of police persecution. On this occasion, the visions of revenge are hammered home with a savage power as Ren explains his fantasies of executing a police officer and even goes so far as to demonstrate the sound of his weapon (complete with a chilling gunfire sample). Finally, Eazy-E takes the lead vocal for the last verse, which is preceded by the sound of his home being raided. Once again, the theme of retaliation dominates, and, in concluding, the prosecutor suggests that stripped of weaponry and badges, the police are simply sitting ducks "waitin' to get shot." A damning "verdict" is then delivered by Judge Dre who slams the LAPD representative with a stream of slurs before the officer is dragged away screaming racial obscenities. It is a barely believable, five-minute sonic onslaught with a shocking outcome, but when it comes to making a point, "Fuck tha Police" leaves no trace of ambiguity.

The mainstream reaction to "Fuck tha Police" was never going to be anything other than outrage even though it was not released as a single and was completely removed from the clean version of *Straight Outta Compton* that was made available. Conservative media regarded N.W.A. as a threat to the country's youth by virtue of the perceived idea that the track actively advocated and encouraged killing officers (which it does not at any point), while local police departments showed their disgust at the group by refusing to patrol its live shows during a few dates on its 1989 tour. The backlash came to a head when FBI Assistant Director Milt Ahlerich wrote to N.W.A.'s record label Priority in August and issued what essentially amounted to a cease and desist order. Referring to the content of "Fuck tha Police," the letter argued that

> advocating violence and assault is wrong, and we in the law enforcement community take exception to such action . . . Law enforcement officers dedicate their lives to the protection of our citizens, and recordings such as the one from NWA are both discouraging and degrading to these brave, dedicated officers.[11]

News of the letter broke in a *Village Voice* cover story two months after the letter was written, but the FBI quieted its protestations after sympathetic California Congressman Don Edwards rapped it for attempting to censor the group. As if all this was not enough, the members of N.W.A. also found themselves being shunned from certain corners of the hip-hop community with many feeling that their depictions of violence would be damaging for the ongoing effort to establish the genre in a wider popular culture.

On the surface, "Fuck tha Police" seemed unforgivable in terms of sentiment, but cursory listens rarely revealed what lay at the heart of the song. Although the brutal visions of revenge killings were prominent, they were essentially fantasies cultivated from extreme duress and secondary in terms of importance to the song's main objective of illustrating and protesting against the oppressive environment in South Central LA during the era. Furthermore, the notion that the bandmates were journalists was given an added credibility in the knowledge that a huge proportion of their fan base consisted of white youths living in affluent suburbs who knew nothing of the deprived and desperate lives being lived by people in areas like Compton. As many in the profession might well argue, having the opportunity to offer a hugely engrossing insight into an unknown world is tantamount to a journalistic scoop. N.W.A. was nothing if not engrossing, and the world of police harassment was for most an unknown or ignored problem. In those respects (as well as many others) "Fuck tha Police" was front-page news. But even more pertinently, the bloodbath predicted by Ice Cube during the track's first segment would become a virtual reality in the years following. As the issue of overzealous policing continued to grind with the inhabitants of Los Angeles, the beating of Rodney King in 1991 (see the entry on Body Count's "Cop Killer" later in this chapter) marked a high-profile nadir in the LAPD's reputation. The subsequent trial and acquittal of the officers involved led to huge race riots breaking out across the city in late April and early May 1992 and 55 people losing their lives in the week-long period of violence—enough deaths to be classed as a bloodbath by anyone's standards. With hindsight, it is tempting to conclude that the members of N.W.A. were not just journalists, but soothsayers to boot.

Artist: Public Enemy

Song: "Fight the Power"

Songwriters: Chuck D, Eric "Vietnam" Sadler, Hank Shocklee, and Keith Shocklee

Album: *Do the Right Thing* soundtrack; later issued on the Public Enemy album *Fear of a Black Planet*

Label: Motown Records (soundtrack version), Def Jam Recordings/Columbia (album version)

1989 (soundtrack version), 1990 (album version).

Public Enemy's arrival on the music scene in the late-1980s was nothing short of revelatory. Aside from giving hip-hop a new sonic power that attracted attention from many other genres, the group members also made it explicitly clear that their music was intended to politicize and empower black Americans everywhere. Of the many Public Enemy tracks that attempted to do this, none were as vibrant or as virulent as "Fight the Power," which instantly established itself as one of music history's ultimate voices of protest upon release.

Public Enemy featuring Professor Griff (back left), Terminator X (center with raised arm), Flavor Flav (front left), and Chuck D (front right) all flanked by the SW1s.
Courtesy of Photofest.

Compared to most young black Americans growing up in the 1970s, Carlton Riden-hour had reasonably little to complain about. Born in 1960, his parents had moved to Roosevelt, Long Island, when he was still in elementary school, and the teenager grew up in a well-to-do area of the suburbs that gradually became inhabited with an increasing number of middle-class African Americans. His mother helmed a commu-nity theater group, his father owned his own business, and eventually Ridenhour enrolled at Adelphi University to develop his graphic design talents. A life of inner-city inopportunity this definitely was not. While at the college, he fell in with Hank Shocklee, a mobile DJ operating under the name of Spectrum City, who spotted Ridenhour's talent in other areas when he unleashed a dominant, booming voice during an open-mic rapping contest one night in 1979. With Ridenhour added to Spectrum City as a vocalist, the two were then invited to be a part of a campus radio show hosted by another hip-hop enthusiast (and Spectrum City fan) Bill Stephney. Spectrum City's popularity on both the Adelphi University station and later on the Long Island rock station WLIR-FM grew at great speed. Through this notoriety, they attracted the friendship of more like-minded souls. Harry Allen was not only a classmate of Ridenhour, but he visited Spectrum City during its broadcasts regularly, while Richard Griffin was employed to handle the crew's security during public performances. The most unlikely allegiance, however, was with the clownish, idiosyncratic yet extremely talented musician William Drayton, who called himself MC DJ Flavor (later to become Flavor Flav) and became another vocalist for the group. Inspired by the hard-edged beats and slice-of-lifestyle lyrics of such groups as Run DMC, the Spectrum City collective eventually released its own single in 1984, but to little acclaim and even fewer sales.

That first deflating experience of recording left Ridenhour—or Chuck D as he was now calling himself—with little intention of becoming a full-time rapper. However, there were still many who admired his prowess on the mic, including music entrepreneur Rick Rubin who had just formed Def Jam Recordings. After relentlessly pursuing him to sign to the label, Chuck finally relented in 1986 (with a little persuasion from old friend Bill Stephney, who was now a Def Jam employee), but he insisted on bringing his old Spectrum City crew members with him, and they renamed themselves Public Enemy. Alongside Flav and Griffin, Chuck enlisted Norman Rogers to become DJ under the pseudonym of Terminator X. Shocklee also became the chief producer by heading up the so-called "Bomb Squad"—an offshoot of the band responsible for creating beats for them to rap over. By this time, seven years had passed since Chuck and Shocklee had first crossed paths, and the former was already thought of in some circles as being too old to be a force in hip-hop. However, time had allowed all members to become more politically and culturally astute—a factor that would seed one of Public Enemy's greatest assets.

Like Chuck, the rest of the group's members had grown up in upwardly mobile surroundings, but as the decade wore on, they began to rile against the politically complacent attitudes they felt were becoming prevalent among similarly privileged African Americans. From the front man's perspective, the civil rights era had bred opportunity for only a small proportion of his race, yet these crumbs of prosperity were proving to be enough to nullify radicalism—"they're going for Mercedes, Audis and B.M.W.s ... this is what all these boot-lickin', handkerchief-head, materialistic niggers want!"[12] While the comfortable aspired for even more comfort, the poverty-stricken black underclass merely aspired for just the merest taste of fortune. In between the two strata, Public Enemy observed a vacuum of leadership. Although such figures as Al Sharpton and Jesse Jackson acted as African American spokesmen during the 1980s (the latter even running for Democratic presidential candidate in the 1984 and 1988 elections), they could not offer anything like the unifying rhetoric that Malcolm X or Martin Luther King Jr. had given during the 1960s. Aside from singular exceptions, such as Grandmaster Flash and the Furious Five's "The Message" (1982) (see Chapter 6) and Run DMC's "It's Like That" (1983), rap music was still primarily concerned with frivolity and also offered black Americans little in the way of sociopolitical unity.

Lamenting these major shortcomings in black culture, Public Enemy injected an overt radicalism into its image and sound. Stephney encouraged the bandmates to make every track political, with "statements, manifestos, the whole nine,"[13] while Griffin (a longtime Nation of Islam devotee) was appointed the band's Minister of Information—the same title given to Eldrige Cleaver during his time with the radical Black Panthers organization in the 1960s. The association did not stop there as Griffin—or Professor Griff as he was now known—was also placed in charge of the S1Ws (Security of the First World). This subsect of group members dressed in black-power berets, army regalia, and brandished fake Uzis to symbolize their status of being armed with knowledge. But references to bygone eras of radicalism were not enough, so in conjunction with its political slant, Public Enemy also carved out a standpoint that involved attacking and debunking conservative institutions of popular culture, as well as taking mass media to task for its white bias. This part of the group was addressed with Allen's affiliation as publicist—or "Media Assassin"—helping to ensure that the band received fair representation in the press. It was through this combination of information, awareness, and access that Chuck famously envisioned hip-hop as being the black CNN—a source of freely available sound and vision that had the power to galvanize a fragmented race of people. As the band released its first album *Yo! Bum Rush the Show* in April 1987, he spelled out Public Enemy's aims with clarity and distinction.

> We're out for one thing only, and that's to bring back the resurgence of black power. We're out for the preservation and the building of the young black mind; trying to make people aware, making 'em educate themselves. We represent the young black male in America.[14]

Despite the militant standpoints being projected, Public Enemy was not able to execute it anything like as convincingly at first. Though not without its moments of righteous anger, *Yo! Bum Rush the Show* sounded sonically underdeveloped and occasionally featured an apolitical braggadocio that seemed out of place. Critical reaction was mixed, and sales were again disappointing; a year later, however, the group's incendiary second album *It Takes a Nation of Millions to Hold Us Back* (1988) saw the bandmates making a quantum leap thanks to its firestorm of atonal samples conjured up by the Bomb Squad, Chuck and Flavor Flav's newly authoritative vocal skills, and a refined sense of cultural rage. Not only was the album instantly recognized in critical circles as a major watershed in hip-hop, public reaction was ecstatic and the bandmates finally had not just the respect but the *idolization* of their peers both within the genre and beyond. Put simply, there was nothing else like them, and as rap moved from being thought of as a fad to becoming a cornerstone of black culture, no one was speaking with more verve, definition, and authority as Public Enemy. Not only were young black Americans listening, but they were getting ready to follow. Chuck was a reluctant figurehead, having initially intended to be a catalyst of insurgence rather than one of its leaders. But with this new streak of black empowerment blooming, he took up the mantle of spokesperson nonetheless.

It was not long before Public Enemy was moving on again; in June 1989 (barely a year after *It Takes a Nation of Millions to Hold Us Back*), the group returned with its most startling moment. Used as a central motif in Spike Lee's 1989 film *Do the Right Thing*—a fictional representation of some very nonfictional racial tensions in New York at the time—the single "Fight the Power" was the ultimate rallying cry. The track begins with a jingle from the radio station featured in the film and then kicks in with one of the Bomb Squad's finest sonic concoctions—a funky yet forbidding beat that underpins the onslaught of expression throughout the song. Chuck begins the first verse by mentioning "The Funky Drummer" (James Brown's seminal 1970 track sampled in this and many other Public Enemy tracks), as well as paying homage to the motivational power of music itself. His towering voice gives a huge sense of gravitas to "Fight the Power" and from the first few lines alone, an undeniable feeling of agitation is established. Chuck then asserts the importance of freedom of speech before launching into the track's monumental chorus for the first time. The second verse closes in on the central message, first by advocating the internalization of knowledge (offered partly through the group's lyrics) as a way of fostering political advancement and cultivating social resilience. The idea of racial equality is then swiftly debunked as a façade as Chuck goes on to insist that progression toward this goal requires a greater level of mental strength.

Another chorus follows before an instrumental interlude featuring some stylish scratching from Terminator X brings the song to fever pitch levels. It is at this point that Chuck unleashes his most provocative lyrics to date. The third verse begins with a visceral denunciation of Elvis Presley—an idol for most of America—but to Public Enemy, a racist and a thief of black musical culture that he then used to become hugely successful. A similar condemnation of the all-American hero John Wayne follows with Chuck stating his sense of black pride via a reference to James Brown's "Say it Loud—I'm Black and I'm Proud" (see Chapter 4). He also protests that "most of my heroes don't appear on no stamps" in anger at the perceived manner in which African American icons are denied positions of importance in history. As if committing something close to cultural treason by accusing Elvis of outright racism was not enough, Chuck then takes a verbal flamethrower to the "rednecks" who are viewed to be the United States' most important historical figures. A final call to black people warns against the dangers of complacency, specifically by name-calling the track "Don't Worry, Be Happy" by Bobby McFerrin—a No. 1 single in 1988 but utterly despised by Public Enemy for its happy-go-lucky attitude. The last segment repeats the central clarion call, and the track concludes with an extended instrumental colored with an array of jazzy saxophone tones.

If the song alone did not drill the message of empowerment and insubordination home to the listener, then the video surely did. Directed by Spike Lee and shot in the same area of Brooklyn as *Do the Right Thing,* it visualized the intentions of "Fight the Power" to the point of intimidation. The full seven-minute version begins with archive footage of the March on Washington in 1963, reminding the viewer of how hundreds of thousands of protestors made their case for civil rights in an extremely ordered and strangely solemn way. An abrupt cut takes the video back to the video's location with Chuck barking his rejection of those outdated methods through a meg-aphone. "We ain't rollin' like that no more. Matter of fact, the young black America, we rollin' up with seminars, press conferences and straight-up rallies . . . we ain't going out like that '63 nonsense."[15] Passivity and politeness are outdated on Public Ene-my's terms and as the playback starts, a huge mobilization of people is revealed. They are filmed carrying placards representing some of America's major cities, numerous images of black cultural figures, and depictions of the by-now infamously provocative Public Enemy logo featuring a beret-clad comrade in a rifle sight. Interspersed with footage of the crowd of thousands purposefully striding through Brooklyn cheering and giving numerous Black Power salutes, there are also scenes of the band perform-ing the song in front of a huge backdrop featuring both the band logo and a giant image of Malcolm X. Anyone who witnessed the video's making would have no doubt found the experience inspiring, but Lee's handling of the final cut is more than a little rousing itself. It was occurrences such as this that led to the FBI to create a study of rap music and its possible effects on national security in which Public Enemy was ref-erenced by name.

Critical response to "Fight the Power" was euphoric, and although the single failed to chart in the United States, it reached a highly respectable No. 29 in the United Kingdom. However, it was just then that things began to unravel slightly for Public Enemy, particularly after the anti-Semitic content of an interview given by Pro-fessor Griff to the *Washington Times* in May 1989 began to circulate around the world. In the following months, pressure from liberal media, as well as turmoil inside the group, led to Chuck first standing by Griff, then firing him, then reinstating him, and then Griff leaving the group of his own accord just before the third album *Fear of a Black Planet* emerged in April 1990. The album was received with even more adula-tion than its predecessor due to the Bomb Squad's continued inventiveness and a political standpoint that had moved with the times. It also featured "Fight the Power" as its closing track in a slightly shorter, remixed form that began with an excerpt from a Martin Luther King Jr. speech and concluded with a vocal reprise not featured on the original soundtrack version. But even though he was no longer in the band, Griff's controversy had arguably sullied its broader appeal. Although few would argue that Public Enemy was still the biggest and most important hip-hop band in the world at the time (Top 10 placing for the album in both the United King-dom and the United States demonstrated this further), it was during the emergence of "Fight the Power" in 1989 that the bandmates were at the height of their powers to motivate a nation of millions.

In the time since, just the song's title has become an all-purpose phrase of protest and rebellion, and it has also transcended the barriers of hip-hop, too. The 1991 block-buster *Terminator 2: Judgment Day*, for example, featured a youth named John Con-nor as its main character. As well as already having a rebellious nature, it is revealed that Connor's destiny is to lead the human race in a battle against self-aware machines—to fight the power if you will—and for the entirety of the film is shown wearing a Public Enemy T-shirt. Meanwhile, the proudly political band Manic Street Preachers emerged in the United Kingdom amid a storm of sloganeering in 1992 with their album *Generation Terrorists*. Despite being born and raised in the isolated valleys of south Wales and specializing exclusively in guitar-based rock music, the quartet frequently heralded Public Enemy as one of its greatest influences—even going so far as to steal lyrics. Chuck and a slightly modified version of the crew are still going today, and while it is generally conceded that they are not the force they once were, "Fight the Power" still represents a vision of Public Enemy at its best—inflammatory, iconoclastic, and sonically untouchable. Moreover, as Adam Yauch of the Beastie Boys notes, "Public Enemy made hip-hop that was more than entertainment. They inspired a lot of people who believed that you can effect change through music."[16] It is because of that inspirational feel that "Fight the Power" continues to be one of the first points of reference for anyone with an interest in protest music of any kind.

Artist: Body Count

Song: "Cop Killer"

Songwriters: Ice-T (Tracy Marrow) and Ernie-C (Ernie Cunnigan)

Album: *Body Count*

Label: Sire Records

1992

Ice-T's reputation for portraying the criminal aspects of Los Angeles life in gritty detail was already well established through his hip-hop career and had long been the target of censorship attempts. Initially, the violent, revenge fantasy narrative of "Cop Killer"—released with his metal project Body Count and written as a protest to the police beating of Rodney King—seemed in keeping with his back catalog. However, as the city descended into rioting following the trial of officers accused of beating King, a heightened sense of tension resulted in the song becoming the center of a storm of controversy that again left Ice-T wondering if his right to free speech existed at all.

If the wider world did not quite understand N.W.A.'s aural complaints about brutality and racial persecution in its song "Fuck tha Police," then the events that occurred by Hansen Dam Park, Los Angeles, during the late hours of Sunday, March 3, 1991, appeared to provide an explicit visual accompaniment. It was there that a group of LAPD officers finally caught up with motorist Rodney King after he had led them on a car chase through the Lake View Terrace suburb of the city. King had spent much of the day drinking with friends; his high-speed driving initiated a pursuit, but King failed to stop immediately, fearing that his previous conviction for a bungled robbery would result in him being sent back to prison. The noise and commotion of the eventual police seizure woke a nearby resident named George Holliday, who proceeded to film the disturbance and subsequently captured a sequence of footage in which King lies rolling on the ground while the apprehending officers rein several kicks and many more baton blows to his head and body. The footage was broadcast on a local TV network the very next day, and before the middle of the week, the incident had become a national scandal. The outcry was immediate; in a city still descending into deeper racial divisions, the soon to be ubiquitous footage heightened a sense of injustice and alienation that had been a part of life in the black community in Los Angeles for many years already. An unforgiving response from the area and its inhabitants was inevitable.

Already an established name in the West Coast rap scene, Ice-T (real name Tracy Marrow) had come to prominence through a willingness to document his firsthand experience of gangs in the deprived areas of the city. Born in 1958, the young Marrow lost his parents early in life and by his teenage years found himself living with an aunt in the increasingly notorious South Central LA, where he quickly became embroiled in gang life and the burgeoning culture of hip-hop. Initially operating as a thief and even a pimp, Ice-T eventually began to concentrate on music as being a more secure way of earning a living—a factor which no doubt had a part to play in the decision to name his 1987 debut album *Rhyme Pays*. Subsequent albums, such as *Power* (1988) and *The Iceberg/Freedom of Speech . . . Just Watch What You Say* (1989), marked an evolution in Ice-T's work, expanding beyond the purely hedonistic realm to incorporate social commentary and political criticism. His knack for storytelling would also produce frequently brutal narratives of young protagonists leading lives of crime, violence, and desperation. Accusations that he was glorifying these antisocial acts were often aimed at many of his songs—and were not always denied by Ice-T himself. However, he remained bullish in his assertion that this was the life that he had once known and the life that many young black men continue to lead in a city where gang culture boasted an increasingly firm foothold. Like many in the new gangsta-rap subgenre, the sights, sounds, and scenes of Los Angeles were a primary influence in the music Ice-T created.

In the first half of 1991, Ice-T was beginning to branch out into new terrain and proving himself to be an artist of multiple talents. While preparing to release his fourth solo album—the future hip-hop classic *OG: Original Gangster*—Ice T was also winning praise for his first major film role playing (as preemptive irony would have it) a police officer in the Mario Van Peebles film *New Jack City*. Meanwhile, his musical growth continued with the unleashing of a new, thrash-metal side project called Body Count. The quintet of Ice-T, Ernie C (lead guitar), D-Roc (guitar), Mooseman (bass), and Beatmaster V (drums) made its recorded debut on a self-titled track included on Ice-T's solo album *OG: Original Gangster*. But shortly after, the band began to operate as a separate entity and appeared on the inaugural bill of the Lollapalooza Festival that toured across the United States during the summer of 1991. Already an integral part of the set by this time was a song entitled "Cop Killer"—an angry and abrasive revenge fantasy written in the wake of the Rodney King incident that was subsequently included as the last track on the band's debut album *Body Count*. Eventually released in March 1992, *Body Count* turned out to be a typically harsh listen. Aside from the relentless speed and crunching grind of the music, Ice-T's lyrics encompassed the kind of gritty themes that he had long been associated with, but even in this provocative context, "Cop Killer" still stood out as being an especially contentious point.

Immediately before it begins, the preceding track on the album, "Out in the Parking Lot," sets the scene with a quietly enraged Ice-T giving a direct, spoken-word dedication to the LAPD and declaring his desire for violent retribution against the more belligerent members of the force. It is a sternly delivered and deeply unsettling preamble, but the searing guitar introduction that denotes the beginning of "Cop Killer" instantly converts this brooding mood of injustice into a sonic fury. The character that Ice-T creates in the song is clearly an isolated vigilante who describes his assassin-like attire and crude killing equipment in the first verse and gives an insight to his homicidal mind in the second. Ice-T spits out each line with a deliberately unhinged force, and the pounding beat seems to reflect the narrator's excitement at his impending actions. The chorus is almost worryingly euphoric in both its emphatic rebuttal of police brutality as well as the cold-blooded refusal to consider the victim's family. Although the two tracks go about their business in contrasting ways, "Cop Killer" certainly does echo the thematic concerns of N.W.A.'s "Fuck tha Police," and that similarity is driven home through the extended middle section in which the bandmates are heard shouting "Fuck the police" in unison. Meanwhile, Ice-T adds further dedications—specifically to then chief of the LAPD Darryl Gates, who had long been the subject of criticism for such heavy-handed gang-control policies as Operation Hammer (see the entry on "Fuck tha Police" by N.W.A. in this chapter). But the most pertinent acknowledgment is given to the main source of inspiration for the song—Rodney King himself.

As incendiary as the song's content seemed to be, the reactions first registered toward "Cop Killer" amounted to little more than a murmur, especially during 1991 when the band was playing it live. Ice-T's profile revolved around his rap career and with Body Count being regarded as little more than an opportunity to indulge in his love of heavy metal, the track received only fleeting coverage in the media. Those journalists who did attempt to take him to task were met with Ice-T's typically articulate and calmly considered retorts of justification.

> One thing about me that might bother people is that I have a morbid fascination with violent actions. It doesn't mean I want to do it . . . If you've got both your feet on the ground, you should be able to swallow this . . . I like *The Terminator,* I seen it a hundred times, but I don't want to go and shoot up no restaurant.[17]

For the short term, these arguments were sufficient in placating potential critics, but a new era of political sensitivity was about to be ushered in through a wave of destruction and disorder.

Just four weeks after the *Body Count* album first arrived in record stores, the long awaited verdict of the Rodney King trail was delivered in Simi Valley on April 29, 1992. Three of the four policemen accused of beating King were acquitted, while the 12-strong jury (none of whom were African American) failed to agree on the remaining officer. The verdict had been influenced greatly by the opening segment of Holliday's video edited out by most TV stations in which King is seen charging the officers. The quartet also claimed that King (who did not testify) had strenuously resisted arrest and suspected he was under the influence of narcotics. However, the delicate balance of the trial escaped much of the onlooking world and with the seemingly damning film footage still being broadcast in its edited form on a daily basis, the verdict appeared to be unfathomable. Just minutes after the acquittal was announced, a number of disturbances in Los Angeles were reported and by early evening, a truck driver was filmed by a helicopter TV crew being attacked and killed by a mob of black youths. Before the day was over, Mayor Tom Bradley had declared a state of emergency, and the National Guard had been deployed. The Los Angeles riots would continue over the next five days; by the time calm was finally restored, 55 people had died and approximately $1 billion worth of damage had been done to the city.

Following the riots, "Cop Killer" had an inevitably greater potential for creating civil disobedience, but oddly, the first official noises of disquiet at the song came not from California but in Texas where police authorities campaigned to have the album withdrawn. The Fraternal Order of Police (a nationwide union for law enforcement officers) soon followed suit, declaring Body Count's music to be unquestionably dangerous. Before long, the storm of negative publicity had reached corporate and governmental levels with President George H. W. Bush voicing fleeting—albeit firm—criticism of the song. Meanwhile, Vice President Dan Quayle blasted the Time Warner company for apparently placing profit over decency (sales were indeed on the increase and the record company had packaged a number of units in a rather tasteless body bag as a promotional gimmick).

"Cop Killer" finally passed into a state of immortality in July when a shareholders meeting at Time Warner that had already been picketed by the song's opponents was livened up further by the appearance of Charlton Heston. The legendary actor (and prominent member of the National Rifle Association) began the fiercest critique yet, even going so far as to dramatically recite actual lyrics. Bemused by the delayed uproar at a song that was over a year old, Ice-T attempted to stand firm by repeating his previous responses to accusations of encouraging violence, but the unsilent majority of Middle America could not be placated in the same way as music journalists. With both Ice-T and Time Warner executives now receiving death threats over the song, the rapper announced that he would withdraw the track during a press conference on July 28, less than two weeks after Heston had added his opinion to the debate. In his statement, Ice-T lamented that the spirit of the song had been grossly misconstrued and that it was "not a call to murder police."[18]

Ice-T had been no stranger to censorship before this point; *Rhyme Pays* was one of the first albums to be plastered with an "advisory" sticker warning parents about the possibility of unsuitable content. However, this latest outcry enraged him so much that Ice-T made the decision to re-release *Body Count* toward the end of 1992, with a new version of "Freedom of Speech" (originally from *The Iceberg/Freedom of Speech . . . Just Watch What You Say* album) replacing "Cop Killer." This substitute song featured Jello Biafra—a similarly minded libertarian and singer of San Francisco punk legends the Dead Kennedys—but despite this differentiation from the original, "Freedom of Speech" remained startlingly provocative in its defense of the first amendment. At one point, Ice-T even aims a personal slur at Tipper Gore who had spearheaded a movement to place sales and airplay restrictions on music deemed unsuitable for family consumption through her work as the head of the Parents Music Resource Center (PMRC). Since its inception in 1985, the organization had sustained criticisms from many artists concerned that their right to expression was being curtailed. Following the controversy over "Cop Killer," it was not difficult to see why Ice-T felt the need to reiterate his own fury on the matter. In a final, disillusioning twist, Time Warner made the decision to drop him from its label altogether shortly after the album had been released in its edited form.

What had started as an angry statement of protest against overzealous policing had ended up becoming Ice-T's personal battle against censorship, but the entire story is perhaps best summed up by a remark the rapper made to a journalist an entire year before "Cop Killer" made him a social and political pariah.

> Freedom of Speech is a great concept, it sounds good, but it has never applied and will never apply.[19]

The entire chain of events marked a clear peak in Ice-T's success, but as the uproar died away, his profile also experienced a downturn. Body Count continued in its coarse hybridizing of metal and rap periodically and continues to perform and release music today despite three members of the original lineup passing away since its formation. Ice-T's solo career has also continued with much less controversy, but in more recent times, his acting exploits have brought more attention his way than the musical ones. Perhaps the best known of these performances is the ongoing role in the popular U.S. series *Law & Order: Special Victims Unit*. Ironically, his character, Odafin Tutuola, is a police detective.

Artist: Rage Against the Machine

Song: "Killing in the Name"

Songwriters: Zach de la Rocha, Tom Morello, Tim Commerford, and Brad Wilk

Album: *Rage Against the Machine*

Label: Epic Records

1993

Just the name should have been enough to suggest that Rage Against the Machine was not a group likely to write songs about the pleasures of conformity. But it was a mind-set that was underlined from the band's very first single "Killing in the Name." Aside from achieving a new level of vigor in protest music thanks to its ferocious rap-metal hybrid, the song also contained an infamously profane phrase that has gone on to become the literal definition of social rebellion in the years since.

As the 1990s dawned in the United States, a recession fueled by the 1987 stock market crash held firm over the country, unemployment was back in the ascendancy, and the Republican administration led by George H. W. Bush had sent troops into another foreign war—this time as part of a coalition to battle Iraqi forces that had invaded the small but oil-rich land of Kuwait. Defended by the government as a firm stand against the megalomania and aggression of Iraq's president Saddam Hussein, there were still many who felt it to be a measure of continued American arrogance abroad. Despite this and many other contentious issues in foreign and domestic spheres, aural discontent was not hugely prevalent. As Bush campaigned for a second term in 1992, the most famous rock band of the day was Nirvana, which (along with many of its perceived contemporaries in the so-called "grunge" movement) concentrated on introverted reflections and feelings of resignation in its music. In the process, Nirvana connected with millions of young music fans and subsequently highlighted the new strain of rebellion—one that simply opted out into its own subculture of apathy rather than attempting to change or even take issue with a mainstream culture. In hip-hop circles, too, political rage and social frustration had

Rage Against the Machine (L–R): Brad Wilk, Zack de la Rocha, Tim Commerford, and Tom Morello. The "EZLN" on de la Rocha's shirt refers to the Zapatista Army of Mexico, which the band supported in its revolutionary efforts.
Courtesy of Photofest.

begun to dissipate as the genre slowly found its way into more commercial areas. Just three years earlier, N.W.A. had been yelling "Fuck tha Police" and Public Enemy was instructing its followers to "Fight the Power," but the subsequent success of more chart-friendly acts, such as C & C Music Factory and MC Hammer, marked a new era in which hip-hop began its extremely lucrative development into a lifestyle associated more with excessive living rather than eruptive indignation.

There may not have been a shortage of things to shout about, but there certainly seemed to be a shortage of people willing to do the shouting. Rage Against the Machine, however, was a band with disestablishmentarianism running through its veins. Gravitating together as a quartet in Los Angeles during the summer of 1991, the two most prominent members also happened to have a family heritage that was steeped in social activism and political agitation. Guitarist Tom Morello's father fought in Kenya's revolutionary war against British colonial rule during the 1950s, and it was Morello's uncle Jomo Kenyatta who would eventually become the first democratically elected head of state for the African nation in 1963. His mother, Mary Morello, spearheaded an initiative titled Parents for Rock and Rap, which served as an attempt to counter movements for censorship in music—particularly the Parents Music Resource Center (see the sidebar). Morello himself studied political science at the prestigious Harvard University; after graduating in 1986, he worked for a time as an adviser to Democratic Senator Alan Cranston while still practicing religiously on his guitar in a bid to emulate such axe heroes as Led Zeppelin's Jimmy Page.

Meanwhile, singer Zach de la Rocha's early years were influenced by his father Roberto's role in the art collective Los Four, which laced its work with images of Chicano political history. During his adolescent years, de la Rocha had his political fire stoked further by the straight edge polemic of such hardcore bands as Minor Threat and by the discontent of hip-hop's most compelling voices, Public Enemy being one of the most significant.

Morello and future drummer Brad Wilk first met de la Rocha at an LA club where the latter was showing his prowess as a rapper. De la Rocha then enlisted his childhood friend Tim Commerford to play bass, and the quartet immediately set about working on a righteous and raging rock/rap fusion that quickly made it stand apart from its peers. And yet, for all the bandmates' radicalism, there were few groups that represented their hometown as well as Rage Against the Machine represented Los Angeles. The racially diverse makeup of the group (one white member, one black, and two Chicano) exemplified the city's multicultural contrasts in a sadly uncommon manner. In musical terms, the palatable sense of tension and fury in their songs reflected a Los Angeles on the brink of implosion, particularly after the riots of April 1992 that followed the "not-guilty" verdict of four police officers accused of beating black motorist Rodney King.

PMRC

The Parents Music Resource Center was set up in 1985 and spearheaded by Tipper Gore—wife of then Senator Al Gore who would later become vice president during the Clinton administrations. Concerned that the sexual and/or violent lyrical content of modern music may be negatively influencing America's youth, the organization sought to establish a rating system that would help warn parents that the CDs, records, and cassettes their children were listening to may be unsuitable. This move toward censorship outraged many artists and even though the PMRC's influence had waned by the time Rage Against the Machine had formed, the band still took the opportunity to express its disgust at the organization's legacy. Touring as part of the Lollapalooza Festival in July 1993, the bandmates appeared on stage during the Philadelphia date completely naked with only duct tape fixed to their mouths and a letter scrawled on each of their chests. Commerford had "P," de la Rocha had "M," Wilk sported an "R," and Morello wore the "C." The only sound being made (apart from the crowd's boos) came from the band's guitars, which emitted only feedback for the entire 15 minute "set."

From the very start, there was an incendiary element to Rage Against the Machine, quite literally. The first music the band issued took the form of a self-released cassette with a picture of the stock market on the front and a single match fixed to the inside of the sleeve. The music only confirmed the serious intent held by the band to issue a wake-up call to the masses and propel them into a rebellion against their own lives. For Rage, the instrument of oppression was Western capitalism in its entirety as enforced by governments (both Republican and Democratic), police, consumerism, mass media, and even art. With this in mind, the bandmates' decision to sign with Epic Records (after being offered a deal on the strength of that cassette) led to accusations of hypocrisy that would dog them for the rest of their career. But by aligning themselves with one of the world's largest labels, the members of Rage Against the Machine afforded themselves a strong platform from which to communicate their message. The

FURTHER TARGETS OF RAGE: THE CASE OF MUMIA ABU-JAMAL

Having been a former Black Panther as well as a prominent radio journalist with a penchant for reporting cases of police misconduct, Mumia Abu-Jamal had already been the subject of FBI surveillance for many years prior to his 1982 conviction for killing a police officer in Philadelphia. Rage Against the Machine frequently contested the verdict, claiming that the trial was constitutionally flawed, the testimonies of several witnesses were unreliable, and the accounts of police officers attending the incident were biased. The band's continued support of Abu-Jamal culminated in two benefit concerts that the bandmates organized and headlined. The first took place in August 1995 in Washington, D.C., but a much more ambitious event was held in New Jersey in January 1999 with the Beastie Boys and Bad Religion also featured on the bill. Proceeds of $80,000 from the latter show were donated to the International Concerned Family and Friends of Mumia Abu-Jamal organization, and de la Rocha even went so far as to address the United Nations about the case a few months later. In 2001, the death sentence given to Abu-Jamal was overturned, but he remains imprisoned.

most notable offspring from this ideologically polarized marriage emerged in February 1993 with the band's first single "Killing in the Name." Once again, the provocative cover image alone was enough to gain a clear indication of Rage Against the Machine's mind-set. The horrific photograph taken in Saigon during 1963 (which had also been used for its self-titled debut album released in November 1992) depicted a Buddhist monk setting himself on fire as a protest at the oppression of his religion by the Vietnamese government of the time. As if the cover was not startling enough, the music certainly matched it in terms of shock value at the very least.

The foreboding opening chord of "Killing in the Name" is repeated four times—each one rings out like an ill-tempered siren—and the sense of something disharmonious materializing is immediate. The drums then kick-start a furious introduction featuring Morello riffing with a fearsome dexterity that then slows down to a moodier pace after de la Rocha's first shout of the song's title, slowly revealing the front man's simmering anger in the process. The main bone of contention is clearly authority figures and institutions that hide prejudiced leanings but continue to use their position of social supremacy to avoid criticism and to even exonerate themselves from wrongdoing in certain circumstances. At one point, de la Rocha even goes so far as to mention those who wear "the badge," naturally implicating the police as the main target of Rage. But the power of "Killing in the Name" lies not in its attempts to denounce anything as specific as the police, but more through the way it embodies rebellion of virtually any kind through the utterance of one simple and ultimately timeless expression.

Disrupting the track's progression are sections filled with Wilk's stabbing drum fills during which de la Rocha sneers at the listeners with increasing venom for allowing themselves to be controlled. But it is the final, expletive-ridden crescendo that hammers home the point of the song with a force that is bludgeoning yet hugely inspiring. Leading by example, de la Rocha sets out what could well have been a summation of Rage Against the Machine's entire existence and a possible ideal for its followers to live by: "F— you, I won't do what you tell me." The coda starts initially as a discordant mess of noise with de la Rocha almost whispering the words, but the bandmates unite suddenly for the final seconds as the singer uses a characteristically venomous vocal tone to shout over his musical comrades. It is a simple expression of protest, but one that absolutely everyone could relate to, and as Morello concedes, it was a benchmark that the band would be constantly compared to over the eight years it would be together. "I don't think there's a Rage song that really resonates in the way this does. The core of all rebellion is the denying of repressive authority and I think that is summed up very succinctly in 'F— you, I won't do what you tell me.' "[20]

It was never likely that such an open-ended statement of defiance would end up failing to connect with a mass audience. Heavy radio exposure helped in this respect, and although the airplay edit was naturally excised of all profanity, the extended version was hardly a secret given that it had already been available for three months via the band's album. It was even less of a secret in the United Kingdom after a hapless BBC Radio 1 DJ accidentally played the uncut album version during the station's weekly Sunday afternoon Top 40 rundown. While a nation of teenagers sniggered at this verbal desecration of the Sabbath, their parents registered an avalanche of complaints with the broadcaster's governing body. The video clip was given plentiful rotation, too. MTV aired the uncensored version during the late night, with the band playing what appears to be a riotous set in an intimate venue, as well as capturing de la Rocha intervening when a member of security becomes overzealous trying to control a fan. The singer and the bouncer exchange glares, and the whole sequence is set to the first repetitions of the song's infamous main phrase, hinting that even everyday oppression should be resisted if not fought. Strangely, despite the media support, "Killing in the Name" was possibly a little too confrontational for some tastes as it made only a middling No. 25 in the United Kingdom and did not chart at all in the United States. But the single played a clear part in the subsequent ascendancy of Rage Against the Machine into the limelight. By August 1994, its first album had sold a million copies in six different countries around the world, and there could be little doubt that many of those record buyers were attracted by the band's excitingly loud embodiment of disobedience.

Thanks to that extensive fan base, Rage Against the Machine was able to politicize massive amounts of people, alerting them to many cases of injustice, corruption, and

FURTHER TARGETS OF RAGE: THE CASE OF LEONARD PELTIER

The concluding track (and final single from) Rage Against the Machine's debut album was "Freedom." The video for this song profiled the case of Leonard Peltier —a Native American activist who in 1977 was given twin life sentences for the murders of two FBI agents during a gun battle that had taken place two years earlier at the Pine Ridge Indian Reservation in South Dakota. A campaign protesting Peltier's incarceration as a political prisoner had been running long before Rage Against the Machine had even formed, arguing that among other things, the FBI had coerced testimonies from several witnesses and thus his conviction was unsafe. Capitalizing on the boost in profile Peltier had received thanks to the highly played video, the band organized a benefit concert called For the Freedom of Leonard Peltier in April 1994 at California State University alongside Cypress Hill and the Beastie Boys. The event raised over $75,000, which was then donated to his defense costs.

containment all over the world that the band felt were being ignored (see the sidebars). The jolt that Commerford, Wilk, Morello, and de la Rocha provided was unparalleled by any of their contemporaries in both hip-hop and rock music during their entire existence. But "Killing in the Name" was the song that endured beyond their eventual breakup in 2000 and even through their re-formation in 2007. The song's defiant central refrain is still inextricably linked to the spirit of the band and continues to encapsulate a sense of rebellion applicable to underdogs everywhere. From ethnic minorities suffering racially motivated brutality by white police right through to the moody teenager being told to do his homework by a scolding mother, there is virtually no one who has not identified with the sentiment of "Killing in the Name" at some point in his or her life. As a modern anthem of nonconformity, it has no equivalents.

Notes

1. Neil Norman, "The Birthday Party, Africa Centre, London" (live review), *NME,* September 12, 1981.

2. Mat Snow, "Nick Cave: From Her to Eternity" (album review), *NME,* May 19, 1984.

3. Quoted in Mat Snow, "Nick Cave: Prick Me Do I Not Bleed?" *NME,* August 23, 1986.

4. Ibid.

5. Ibid.

6. Black's 1985 article in another publication named *ZigZag* captured Cave in a heroin-induced stupor before again getting verbally abusive, this time at her personal line of questioning.

7. Angus Batey, *Rhyming and Stealing: A History of the Beastie Boys* (London: Independent Music Press, 1998), 18.

8. Quoted in Charles M. Young, "Smart Talk with the Beastie Boys," *Playboy,* July 1987.

9. Quoted in Phil Sutcliffe, "The Beasties and Their Boroughs," *Los Angeles Times,* May 9, 2004.

10. Jeff Chang, *Can't Stop, Won't Stop* (New York: St Martin's Press, 2005), 323.

11. Letter reprinted in Dave Marsh and Phyllis Pollack, "Wanted for Attitude," *Village Voice,* October 10, 1989, 33.

12. Quoted in Harry Allen, "Public Enemy: Leading a Radio Rebellion," *BRE,* February 1988.

13. Quoted in Chang, *Can't Stop, Won't Stop,* 247.

14. Reprinted in Ian Fortnam, "Public Enemy's Back Pages," *Vox,* February 1996.

15. "Fight the Power" music video, Spike Lee, director, Def Jam Records, 1989.

16. Quoted in Adam Yauch, "The Immortals—The Greatest Artists of All Time: 44) Public Enemy," *Rolling Stone,* April 15, 2004.

17. Quoted in Andy Gill, "Ice-T," *Q,* September, 1991.

18. Quoted in Chang, *Can't Stop, Won't Stop,* 398.

19. Quoted in Gill, "Ice-T."

20. Quoted in Ben Myers, "Rage Against The Machine," *Kerrang!,* September 3, 2005.

CHAPTER 9

MODERN LIFE IS RUBBISH (1994–1998)

Mainstream music had enjoyed a sustained level of sociopolitical consciousness throughout the entirety of the 1980s, but the cyclical nature of pop culture meant that a lull was inevitable. In the United Kingdom, years of Conservative Party rule and the consistent protests it raised gave way to a penchant for hedonism that provided a sub-text to the rave scene of the early 1990s and the Britpop explosion that followed. Pop's political engagement was not as prevalent as it had been a few years before, although one of the notable exceptions was "**Their Law**" (1994) by dance group Prodigy. But even that was inspired simply by the threat of government measures affecting the recreational rights of young music fans rather than any of the country's broader ills. Other voices of protest in the United Kingdom were also sporadic and against the norm. Pulp's "**Common People**" (1995) might have lampooned and lambasted the curious trend of class tourism, but the band's rage went largely unnoticed to many in the upbeat atmosphere of the time. And while there could be no mistaking Asian Dub Foundation's intentions in "**Free Satpal Ram**" (1998), it was a song that had its roots in a miscarriage of justice dating back over 10 years before.

Meanwhile in the United States, the cold war was over, there was no conflict directly involving American troops (save for the brief war with Iraq in 1991), the economy was experiencing an upturn, and Democratic President Bill Clinton enjoyed a reasonable amount of popularity. It was an atmosphere that again inspired much less rancor from the pop world than Clinton's Republican predecessors George H. W. Bush and Ronald Reagan had to endure. However, there was one minor theme of irritation that seemed to run through the country's more conscientious acts, and it revolved around the growing influence of the media. As the technological age dawned, an explosion of television channels saturated the land, radio remained extremely important, and tabloid journalism was more popular than ever. Numerous songs touched this cultural trend with a less than positive attitude; "Radio Song" (1991) by R.E.M. satirized the banality and repetition of DJs, "Television, the Drug of the Nation" (1992) by the Disposable Heroes of Hiphoprisy made unflattering observations of a country being dumbed down, "MTV Makes Me Want to Smoke Crack" (1993) illustrated Beck's hyperbolic desperation with the unrealistic images used by the network, while Bruce Springsteen's "57 Channels (and Nothin' On)" (1992) just expressed simple boredom of choice. However, judging by their modest chart positions (at best), none of these songs really struck a huge chord with the nation; while Michael and Janet Jackson's "**Scream**" (1995) used some painful personal experiences to attest to this growing problem, its commercial success undoubtedly stemmed more from the pair's star profiles, which of course had been built up *by* the media.

Artist: The Prodigy

Song: "Their Law"

Songwriters: Liam Howlett and Pop Will Eat Itself

Album: *Music for the Jilted Generation*

Label: XL Recordings (United Kingdom)/Mute Records (United States) 1994

In an era of economic strain and reduced prospects for young people in the United Kingdom, the outdoor rave scene acted as a social outlet for many music fans across the country during the early 1990s and gave rise to such successful acts as the Prodigy. But drug usage and a perceived lack of social order at these gatherings prompted the government to attempt a crackdown with some hastily proposed legislation. Angered at such a heavy-handed suppression of youth culture, the group recorded "Their Law" as a direct and stinging response.

By the end of the 1980s, a massive youth culture movement—the likes of which had not been seen since the emergence of punk rock music a decade earlier—was beginning to develop across Great Britain. The phenomenon was dubbed acid house and stemmed both from a wider availability of the drug called ecstasy (a street name for the psychedelic stimulant MDMA), as well as the import to the United Kingdom and the growing audience for electronically created music with a hypnotic ambience and dance-floor friendly tempo. For many people, consuming the former heightened the enjoyment of the latter, and that, in turn, gave rise to a myriad of clubs where the two could meet to create an unprecedented environment of revelry. The euphoric effects of the drug coupled with the scene's adoption of a smiley face as an unofficial logo emphasized the positive communal energy of acid house and appeared to be situated opposite the harsh political climate of the time. Under the leadership of Margaret Thatcher (who had been prime minister since 1979), the Conservative government advocated attitudes of free enterprise, entrepreneurialism, and self-interest with Thatcher herself famously declaring that there was "no such thing as society."[1]

By the beginning of the 1990s, the culture of acid house had expanded outward both sonically and geographically. The evolution of dance music had now produced

Singers of British rock band Prodigy, Keith Flint and guitarist Liam Howlett (right), in 2006.
Courtesy of ATTILA KISBENEDEK/AFP/Getty Images.

a subgenre characterized by a more powerful and incessant stream of beats that was given the apt moniker of hardcore. Its growing popularity was reflected in the rise of "raves"—huge outdoor gatherings attended by thousands and often located in remote parts of the countryside. Nightclubs could remain open only for a certain number of hours on any given evening, but in contrast, the larger raves had the potential to last entire weekends with an array of DJs and musical acts being lined up to perform around the clock while various frenzied light effects could also be employed to enhance the experience. With ecstasy still providing audience members with an unnatural level of stamina, such lengthy durations became the norm rather than the exception. One landmark event, in particular, occurred in May 1992 when around 40,000 people conglomerated at Castlemorton Common in Hereford for a marathon rave. Initially, police had prevented a similar gathering in Bristol, but the organizers merely moved into the similarly remote area among the Malvern Hills, spreading the word discretely among disappointed attendees. The duration of this impromptu event was prolonged to a week in total due to a second surge of revelers who traveled to the site after watching the first reports on national news bulletins.

One of the acts that became quickly popular in the rave scene was an outfit from Braintree, Essex, named the Prodigy. Unlike the DJs who would remain rooted to their turntables for their sets, the Prodigy boasted a lineup that resembled a genuine band. As the group's central creative force, Liam Howlett would orchestrate their sounds, MC Maxim Reality would add vocals, while Keith Flint and Leeroy Thornhill added energized dance routines to rouse the crowd. It became a winning live combination, but Howlett's ability to add a subtly tuneful element to the group's pulsating and powerful music helped it gain an audience outside of the hardcore ravers who would probably dance to a car alarm if they were given enough ecstasy. A limited release of their first recording "What Evil Lurks" resulted in a deal with burgeoning dance label XL Recordings. The subsequent singles "Charly" and "Everybody in the Place" hit No. 3 and No. 2 on the U.K. charts, respectively, catapulting the group onto a mainstream platform almost immediately. Although the debut album *Experience* just missed the Top 10, the Prodigy was still the most prominent example of how this initially underground culture had evolved to resemble a clearly definable mobilization of musically minded youth.

Gradually, the rave scene and its many exponents began to suffer from overexposure and media coverage that swung from a tone of suspicion to the outright demonizing of the whole culture. A moral panic swept the nation's tabloid newspapers and was propelled on by the slowly increasing (but still relatively rare) number of deaths associated with ecstasy usage. By 1993, the Conservative government—now under the leadership of John Major—was beginning to draw up proposals for legislation entitled the Criminal Justice and Public Order Act. Although encompassing measures to deal with a range of perceived threats to public order (including the extremely controversial alteration of the law allowing arrestees the right of silence), one of the most contentious sections was designed specifically to counteract the organization of outdoor raves and to prosecute those who tried to flout it. Denounced as draconian by civil liberties groups, it was nevertheless seen as being directly related to the events that transpired at Castlemorton Common in 1992 and was an ominous sign that the spontaneity of the era was being curbed.

The idea of not being able to play in such environments did not seem like a threat in itself to the aspirations of the Prodigy. Following its early success, the quartet quickly began to encounter a degree of creative limitation in catering to people in altered states, and Howlett, in particular, picked up on a new streak of inspiration provided by the rockier bent of such bands as Rage Against the Machine, Nirvana, and the Red Hot Chili Peppers. It was something that was clearly audible in the Prodigy's second album *Music for the Jilted Generation* that eventually earned a release in July 1994. Although the album retained the group's electronic roots, much of the collection boasted a rock dynamic and a rebellious, confrontational edge that made for an exhilarating listen and simultaneously set it aside from the increasingly generic rave sound. However, the principle of control and oppression as embodied so clearly in the proposed Criminal Justice and Public Order Act riled the band into action; as the band's main member, Howlett, in particular, was very outspoken in his criticism.

The government are trying to make out the whole scene is bad, and they want to stop everyone going out and having a good time . . . Basically, there aren't going to be big outdoors raves anymore. They're not giving them licenses in the first place now 'cos of the alleged disturbance and noise pollution, and all the drugs. And 'cos of that, the punters have lost faith a bit . . . Events happen up until the last minute and then they get cancelled, and so people stop bothering . . . it does annoy me, the government telling young kids what they can do.[2]

The title of the album was also intended to be an acknowledgment to the generation of British youth who had struggled among the government-endorsed attitude of self-preservation during the 1980s and had grown up listening to rave music as a communal outlet of chemically aided joy—only to find that it too was now being seized. The Prodigy's politics were certainly not integral to the music it made, but *Music for the Jilted Generation* contained one succinct statement of defiance that neatly summed up the increasingly aggrieved feelings harbored by Britain's youngsters.

Although it never earned a single release, the track "Their Law" clocked in at almost seven minutes long and earned a considerable amount of attention not only for the fact that it featured the popular British dance-rock band Pop Will Eat Itself (PWEI), but also for its obvious reference to the impending Criminal Justice and Public Order Act. The song begins with a vocal sample of a man decrying a general lack of respect for the law, which echoes the common sound-bite given by local authorities and Conservative politicians in the wake of larger raves. Providing a major indication of the Prodigy's broadening musical palette, a menacing guitar crunch then initiates a tense intro that builds until a pounding hip-hop beat ignites the simmering mood of insurgency. Just before the two-minute mark, the instrumentation drops out entirely for PWEI's front man Clint Mansell to deliver what are virtually the song's only lyrics in a snarling and deliberately direct manner—"F— 'em, and their law." Pointed, unforgiving, and extremely simple, the lyrics exemplified a frustrated rage that needed to be conveyed at the time while remaining a safe distance away from any overly righteous rhetoric that would have been ill-fitting for such a band as the Prodigy—especially given the fact that the band was celebrated for communicating energies rather than edicts. After this first vocalization of defiance, "Their Law" continues to build as the central riff drops out as Howlett adds some siren-like synthesizer effects and a sinister keyboard motif, while Mansell can again be heard intermittently exclaiming "crackdown at sundown"—another reference to police tactics and media headlines. The two sections continue to alternate (although another searing guitar overdub is added in the final minute) and after a string of repetitions, Mansell adds one final cry of the main expletive-saddled lyric to finish the track.

The intention of "Their Law" was not to offer a sound argument against this threatened new legislation or critique it as being a crude example of an outdated, out-of-touch government in need of replacement as some opponents did. Those were issues and viewpoints to be debated elsewhere. The Prodigy bandmates merely wanted to issue a shout of resistance against the establishment from a generation of disaffected British youth, and in doing so, they helped draw further parallels with the punk movement before them. That proverbial middle finger was illustrated quite literally inside the album sleeve of *Music for the Jilted Generation,* which featured a large drawing of a ravine. On one side is an army of aggressive-looking police officers with a grim, gloomy metropolis depicted in the background. On the other side is a green, idyllic landscape crawling with people attending an open air gathering (the large speaker system certainly hints at a rave) while one scraggy-looking rebel is depicted in the act of cutting a rope bridge that connects the two areas just as police are starting to cross over to him. The single-digit gesture he aims toward the riot-gear-clad officers speaks volumes and underlines the sleeve's allegorical realization of "Their Law," not to mention the Prodigy's own rebellious attitude toward this form of social persecution.

Despite being a standout track on an album that would reach No. 1 in the United Kingdom, as well as being an exhilarating point in the Prodigy's live show for years to come, "Their Law" was not the start of any concerted protest movement. Those against the bill did gather to voice their grievances in two notable demonstrations held in London during 1994—one in July and one in October, which resulted in a riot centering around Hyde Park. This incident again made national news and the front pages of some ever unsympathetic tabloids, so it came as little surprise to find that the Criminal Justice and Public Order Act came into force during November 1994. Part V of the Act contained four points listed under the explicit subheading of "Powers in relation to raves" and among the actions outlawed were open air gatherings of more than 100 people who are intending to play loud music "characterized by the emission of a succession of repetitive beats."[3] The police were also given power to seize sound equipment that may appear to be destined for usage in such environments. Despite this, the evolution of dance music would suffer few discernible effects from the Criminal Justice and Public Order Act, and the Prodigy, in particular, would go on to scale new heights, particularly with the 1997 album *The Fat of the Land,* which established the band worldwide. The environments in which dance music was enjoyed, however, were subject to much stricter regulation following the implementation of the Act, and a uniquely improvised period in British music was brought to an end.

While alternative culture was seen as being the target of the Conservative government, a subtle irony would develop just three years later in the run-up to the 1997 general election. In what is now thought of as one of the masterstrokes of the election campaign, opposition leader Tony Blair shrewdly aligned himself and his Labour Party with the youth culture—especially music—in the hope of wooing younger voters. Despite being a very different, guitar-dominated entity by then, many of the music scene's biggest names, such as Oasis, came of age in the late 1980s and early 1990s when rave culture was still ascendant. Evidently, many still harbored ill feelings at the attack on youth liberties carried out by Thatcher and Major during those years and so provided ringing endorsements of Blair's apparently refreshing attitude. It was due partly to this encouragement that other members of the jilted generation took to the ballot box in 1997 and responded to years of Conservative Party members' oppression in the most potent way possible by ousting them from government. As a result, the Labour Party swept the elections via a landslide victory, and Tony Blair would remain prime minister for the next 10 years.

Artist: Michael Jackson and Janet Jackson

Song: "Scream"

Songwriters: Michael Jackson, Janet Jackson, James Harris III (aka Jimmy Jam), and Terry Lewis

Album: *HIStory: Past, Present and Future, Book I*

Label: Epic Records

1995

By the start of the 1990s, decades of near constant publicity had made Michael Jackson the most famous person in the world, but when the media glare spiraled out of control following child abuse allegations in 1993, the singer was left reeling. After the case was resolved, he set about repairing the damage done to his career, starting with a comeback single recorded with his sister Janet called "Scream," which raged against unfair press treatment during the molestation scandal. Although it reestablished him in the charts, Michael's extravagant behavior after the single's release would result in the media regarding him with ridicule instead of suspicion.

While most pop stars learn to deal with the often intense glare of the media as part of their adult careers, it was merely a fact of life for Michael Jackson from an extremely early age. Born in the town of Gary, Indiana, in 1958, the boy's immense musical talent led him to join the Jackson 5 (a soul/R&B outfit comprised of his brothers and managed with an iron fist by their father, Joe) when he was six years old. Michael was the youngest member of the group, and when most children his age would have been attending elementary school, he was spending time touring the network of American clubs and bars used by fledgling black musicians to hone their acts (known as the "chitlin' circuit"). By 1969, the Jackson 5 were signed to Motown Records, having their first hit single "I Want You Back" and enjoying their first taste of national stardom. As their lead vocalist, Michael was naturally the center of attention for press and public alike, but as the 1970s dawned, this intensified further with the launch of a solo career. Initially at least, this turned out to be just as successful as the Jackson 5, and by 1975, Michael had amassed enough material to warrant the release of a *Best Of* collection—traditionally something reserved for artists in the twilight of their careers. Before he had even become eligible to vote, Michael had become an instantly recognizable figure in America, but it was still nothing compared to the kind of profile he would develop in years to come.

The 1979 album *Off the Wall* (Michael's first for Epic) clearly marked the point at which a child star became an adult icon. A slick collection of R&B songs inflected with some obvious references to the disco phenomenon that was still popular around the world at the time, the album spawned no less than four Top 10 hits in the United States (two of which were No. 1s). It also proved to be a slap in the face to those critics who felt the memory of Michael as an angelic little boy would continue to define him. But this success would be dwarfed by the release of *Thriller* in 1982. Now recognized as the best-selling album of all time, its ability to straddle numerous genres yet still exhibit an instant accessibility created a cross-racial appeal, and it spent an entire year in the Top 10 of the U.S. album chart as a result. Michael's innovative use of promotional videos (particularly the epic production for the ''Thriller'' single) added an extra clout to the sales campaign, while his astonishing talent as a performer seemed to peak at the same time, too. Especially indicative of this was his appearance at Motown's 25th Anniversary (broadcast in May 1983) during which he unveiled his now trademark ''moonwalk'' to rapturous applause. Everything came together at once for the singer who was turning only 25, but was undoubtedly the most famous man on the planet.

As *Thriller* continued to sell an unprecedented number of copies, Michael's immense public profile would be mirrored—and indeed exacerbated—by the rumors surrounding his personal life. Through stories circulated in the more sensational areas of the world's press, an unusual picture of the singer's offstage existence began to reveal itself. Over the course of the decade, it was reported (among many, many other things) that he slept in an oxygen-enriched chamber to prolong his life, that he had offered to pay $1,000,000 for the bones of the ''elephant man'' Joseph Carey Merrick, and that he had countless cosmetic surgery procedures performed in an attempt to maintain a boyish appearance. These purported eccentricities heightened the alluring myth around Michael, and while he frequently denied such stories, many of the journalists who reported them claimed that they were actually concocted by the singer himself in a bid to maintain the public's interest. ''Much of that was orchestrated by Michael Jackson for the purposes of publicity because Michael told his attorneys that he wanted to be the greatest show on earth,'' explained his biographer J. Randy Taraborrelli. ''In fact, he gave his attorney John Branker and his manager Frank Dileo a copy of [P. T.] Barnum's[4] biography and told them, this is what I want my life to be like.''[5]

It was an absurd yet amusing media circus that encircled Michael Jackson past the release of *Bad* (1987) and *Dangerous* (1991), but if the fanciful tales of chambers and fossils were self-created, the story that broke in August 1993 certainly was not. Just months after establishing the Heal the World Foundation designed to raise awareness of the suffering of children across the globe, Michael was accused of molesting 13-year-old Jordan Chandler—a friend and frequent visitor to his Neverland Valley Ranch in California. An instant tabloid sensation erupted, and the attention Michael was now receiving was of a far more unsavory kind. Graphic descriptions of the alleged sexual acts were made public, and many other aspects of the singer's personal life were also revealed by everyone from security personnel right through to Michael's sister LaToya who attested to the fact he regularly held sleepovers at home with young boys. The embarrassment was complete when the police investigation warranted a close examination of Michael's genitalia to see if the description Chandler had given was accurate. The details of this intensely humiliating process were again pored over worldwide. Throughout the entire affair, Michael was also fighting a painkiller addiction, and although it was something he claimed to have developed after cosmetic surgery, tabloid speculation allowed for many other possible causes. His success over three decades meant that a cross-generational audience was now translating to a cross-generational scrutiny—all of which forced the clearly beleaguered and emotional singer to appear on television in December 1993 and rile against the treatment he had recently received by the media.

> I am particularly upset by the handling of this . . . matter by the incredible, terrible mass media. At every opportunity, the media has dissected and manipulated these allegations to reach their own conclusions. I ask all of you to wait and hear the truth before you label or condemn me. Don't treat me like a criminal, because I am innocent.[6]

Chandler refused to testify and a multimillion dollar settlement was reached out of court in 1994, but the damage to Michael's life and career had already been huge. Having played a crucial role in establishing him as a megastar (with Michael apparently participating gamely), the media had now helped to transform the singer into something closer to a pariah. Many in the music world wondered if the self-proclaimed King of Pop had been dethroned permanently, but with questions still lingering over the case, the Jackson camp set about plotting a recovery, and there was no argument that Michael's music would be his strongest weapon in this campaign. As a result, it was decided that his next album would be a double disc of both new material and a collection of his most popular singles—an elaborate package with the similarly grandiose title of *HIStory—Past, Present and Future, Book I*. The first single "Scream" (released in May 1995) was also a big event as it turned out to be the first ever musical collaboration with his younger sister Janet, who had been enjoying solo success on her own terms since the mid-1980s. On the surface, it was a fitting (and press-friendly) show of sibling solidarity in the wake of the turmoil that the entire Jackson family had endured over the previous two years. But a closer examination of the song's lyrical content revealed that it was more specifically Michael who was channeling an uncommon rage over his personal ordeal.

The track itself begins with an ominous buzzing and a disembodied scream before the main beat kicks in, establishing a purposeful tempo to this hard-edged pop song. There is an unmistakable anger audible from Michael's very first words as he voices his sense of frustration at being the victim of injustices, conspiracies, and lies, but he follows it up with a determined declaration that he will overcome them all. Janet then continues this mood of irritation with some more opaque lines that appear to refer to unjustified moral criticisms and the act of selling souls—a common way of paraphrasing the unscrupulousness of some journalists. Echoing her brother's sentiment, she too promises to rise above these tribulations and continue the fight against persecution. The two then join forces to voice their confusion and confess to being at a breaking point as the song goes into its distinctive chorus in which they simply issue a plea for their unnamed nemesis to stop this constant pressurizing.

At this point, it is not hard to calculate what both Jacksons are taking issue with, especially for those listeners with a reasonable amount of knowledge about Michael's recent tabloid history. But the second verse brings their target into a much clearer focus, especially in the first lines in which Michael tellingly explains he's "tired of you tellin' the story your way" and bemoans the way in which this misleads people. Janet subsequently weighs in with more exasperated references to a game in which the rules are being unfairly changed and the damaging mental effects being suffered as a result. It is yet another obvious allusion to ill-treatment at the hands of the media and one that seems particularly pertinent considering that Michael was apparently an enthusiastic player of the publicity game at one time. Janet then insinuates that those responsible for these lies find some kind of sick pleasure in what they do before the duo goes into the second chorus, which is an especially notable moment as it contains a extremely rare moment of profanity from Michael. It was something that shocked both fans and critics at the time, but again underlined the strong feelings running through "Scream." A brief breakdown sees Janet giving a segment of a cappella singing that describes her feelings of disgust toward the TV, and that is followed by a screaming guitar solo. The last minute of the track is filled with repetitions of the chorus that build up to a dramatic finale that is punctuated again by an actual scream.

"Scream" met with a passable reaction from the critics, but the commercial success it enjoyed (No. 5 in the United States and No. 3 in the United Kingdom) proved that Michael's fan base was still gargantuan. Despite the song's impassioned protest, it was never likely to change the operations of the media, but for a time at least, reportage of Michael's life and career had moved away from the realm of frenzied speculation seen during the molestation scandal. This was partly down to the sense of pomp woven into his comeback, which was clearly designed to reestablish Michael Jackson as an icon and to show the world that he had returned from his troubles as an even more dynamic pop star. The video for "Scream" was especially representative of this, and despite Michael's reputation for extravagance in this area, the Mark Romanek–directed clip eclipsed every production both before and after with its total cost of approximately $7,000,000. But the grand scale of this return began to seem a little excessive as *HIStory—Past, Present and Future, Book I* was released in June 1995. The double album came packaged with an extended section of sleeve notes featuring hearty endorsements from a number of Michael's famous friends, including Steven Spielberg, Elizabeth Taylor, and even Jacqueline Kennedy Onassis. This hint of self-importance was emphatically expanded on when a 60-foot statue of Michael (similar to the one on the cover of the album) was floated along the River Thames in London during release week and then exhibited across Europe as part of the ongoing promotional campaign. It may have been understandable that the singer would want to project the image of being unflappable in the face of scrutiny, but for many, this was merely going into the realm of tasteless self-deification.

Any sympathy that "Scream" may have evoked was quickly turning to ridicule; this was demonstrated most memorably (not to mention bizarrely) during an incident at the Brit Awards in 1996. Michael had accepted the invitation to play at the high-profile music industry ceremony in London (which was broadcast on British television) and on the night, proceeded to mime "Earth Song"—a track on the *HIStory* album that had recently hit the No. 1 spot in the United Kingdom. The typically elaborate and almost theatrical performance featured dozens of actors playing impoverished characters who heralded Michael melodramatically as though he were a messiah. Halfway through the song, Jarvis Cocker—lead singer of the British band Pulp—showed his contempt for the spectacle by invading the stage and, at one point, bending over to give the audience a close-up view of his bottom. Another media storm commenced instantly, and, although drunk at the time, Cocker stood by what he did, explaining that his "actions were a form of protest at the way Michael Jackson sees himself as some kind of Christ-like figure";[7] he certainly was not short of support in this viewpoint with music publication *Melody Maker* even declaring that he should be given a knighthood by the queen. While Michael could not claim quite so vehemently that the media were representing him in the skewed way that "Scream" had suggested, he was now merely a figure of fun—an improvement in relative terms perhaps, but certainly not the kind for which he would have hoped. In the time since, the legacy of the track itself in Michael's extensive back catalog has long dissipated to the point that it has been left off almost every one of the subsequent collections, anthologies, and overviews released since 1995. Predictably, there were precious few responses to the song's pleas for fair representation in the press when rumors again began to circulate at an extraordinary rate following a second round of molestation charges brought against Michael in 2003—of which he was eventually found not guilty.

Artist: Pulp

Song: "Common People"

Songwriters: Jarvis Cocker, Nick Banks, Steve Mackey, Russell Senior, and Candida Doyle

Album: *Different Class*

Label: Island Records (United Kingdom)/Polygram Records (United States)

1995

Years on the very outer reaches of the music scene almost spelled the end of Pulp, but a brief conversation with a girl at college inspired Jarvis Cocker to write "Common People"—a song that lambasted the idea of class tourism and faking destitution just as it was becoming fashionable in the United Kingdom. Although not everyone realized exactly how angry a statement it really was, it helped make Pulp one of the most successful British bands of the decade. Moreover, it has turned out to be an enduring document of an unusual trend in the country's history and an overall reminder of how many people hate the sight of someone trying to be something that he or she is not.

By the time Jarvis Cocker enrolled at London's St Martins College of Art to study film in 1988, his band Pulp was all but finished. Cocker had formed the group (originally called Arabacus Pulp) while still at school in his hometown of Sheffield during 1978, but the group rarely enjoyed anything more than fringe recognition for its ramshackle indie and amusing 1970s style fetish. As lead singer, Cocker was the only constant member; after years of toil and countless lineup changes, he decided to put Pulp in the back of his mind and embarked on a belated attempt at further education instead. Shortly after arriving in London, he made a brief acquaintance that eventually altered the fortunes of the band and changed Cocker's life radically. During a socializing session after lectures, a Greek girl studying a similar course caught the Pulp front man's eye, and, during a conversation, it transpired that she hailed from a well-to-do background. According to Cocker's recollection, the girl confessed that despite her parents' wealth, she had a desire to live in the poorer parts of London, feeling that it would be an exotic and interesting way of understanding how common people

Uncommon people: The members of Pulp (L–R): Jarvis Cocker, Nick Banks, Candida Doyle, Steve Mackey, Mark Webber, and Russell Senior.
Courtesy of Photofest.

without money and privilege exist. Having grown up in a working-class area of one of England's most industrial cities, Cocker had experienced the banal realities of this kind of environment for a long time and struggled to see the appeal in social slumming. Although the two failed to establish any kind of lasting friendship, the conversation stuck with Cocker, and he would eventually return to it for musical inspiration.

Toward the end of his studies, a new lineup of Pulp began to take shape featuring Steve Mackey (bass), Russell Senior (guitar, violin), Candida Doyle (keyboards), and Nick Banks (drums); together, the quintet made another concerted effort at success. A string of low-key releases throughout the early 1990s earned the bandmates a deal with the prestigious Island Records; in 1994, their first album for the label, *His 'n' Hers,* crept into the Top 10 of the U.K. album chart. But even with the critics now lauding Pulp for its increasingly slick sound, wry lyrical observations, and a humorous penchant for the seedier side of life, a real hit single still proved elusive. In the summer of the same year, Cocker presented his bandmates with a song called "Common People," which was based on his brief conversation with the Greek girl at college and composed on a small, unsophisticated keyboard. Apart from Doyle, who seemed instantly taken, the rest of the Pulp bandmates did not rate the track as being particularly good, let alone a potential hit, but a full band version was slowly created as they worked on potential material for a follow-up to *His 'n' Hers.*

Oddly, as the band attempted to breathe life into Cocker's observation of this mysterious Greek girl's downward social aspirations, the idea of class tourism was also starting to permeate through many areas of British life simultaneously. There was nothing essentially new in this concept of authenticity through an association with the everyday, but to see it in so many areas of popular culture at once made it into a phenomenon of sorts. In music, the prime example of working-class grit came from the members of the Manchester outfit Oasis, who proudly wore their unprivileged roots like badges of honor and whose songs seemed like ideal soundtracks to frivolous, weekend hedonism. Although their actual background was not quite as financially strained as they sometimes made it out to be, it struck a huge chord with the nation nonetheless and narrowed the gap between the glamor of rock stardom and the menial-labor life of the man on the street. Their main musical rival at this point was Blur, whose members were positively bohemian compared to Oasis, and yet, as they released their third album *Parklife* in 1994, they too appeared to be adopting a lowbrow image as an attempt to tap into the spirit of the time. In one interview, singer Damon Albarn even went so far as to say "I started out reading Nabokov, and now I'm into football [soccer], dog-racing and Essex[8] girls."[9] It was one of many statements that would lead to him being lampooned for his faux-working-class rhetoric for years to come.

It was not just the titans of Britpop that were fighting for the attention of the masses. In other realms of culture, too, this attitude was extremely prevalent. In 1994, the men's magazine *Loaded* launched and covered its pages with stories about soccer, women, drinking, drugs, and music under the understanding that these were the main pastimes of the working class. In terms of turnover, it was a theory that could not be argued with as sales skyrocketed rapidly, inspiring a number of copycat publications in the process. So dominant was this swing toward the common people through the era that it was even satirized on prime-time television. In one episode (first broadcast in 1997) of the popular BBC sketch comedy *Harry Enfield and Chums,* two of the show's reoccurring teenage characters Kevin and Perry are seen trying to shed their suburban middle-class upbringing by instantly adopting coarse language, uncouth mannerisms, and, in the case of Perry, drawing a beard on his face with a pen in the hope of emulating Oasis singer Liam Gallagher. This was, of course, a greatly exaggerated observation of what was happening, but there were plenty who felt genuinely patronized by this sudden, and in some cases inaccurate, depiction of working-class life. Although Cocker had written "Common People" originally from a personal experience, the song also tied into his own strong distaste for the cultural hijacking that was becoming the norm.

> It seemed to be in the air, that kind of patronising [sic] social voyeurism, slumming it, the idea that there's a glamour about low-rent, low-life. I felt that of *Parklife* ... there is that noble savage notion. But if you walk round a council estate,[10] there's plenty of savagery and not much nobility going on.[11]

It was into this ongoing atmosphere of class co-option that Pulp finally released "Common People" as a single in May 1995.

Beginning with a bubbling synthesizer line punctuated by a siren-like guitar riff, the song's intro sets a steady pace, and Cocker quickly begins a narrative that recalls the encounter at St Martins. But rather than stay true to the original circumstance, he uses an artistic license to state that the Greek girl was studying sculpture and that she had a sexual interest in him (Cocker admitted in later years that she was not a sculpture student and it was actually he who was interested in her). Nevertheless, the girl's intentions to break away from her rich background to live, socialize, and even sleep with common people are explained through the first verse and chorus. The song gathers a little pace, and, initially, the narrator plays along by showing her around a typical supermarket, instructing her to pretend she is poor to fit in with the other shoppers. But it is a concept the girl mistakenly believes to be a joke, and for the narrator, this lack of comprehension underlines the foolishness of what she is trying to do.

With that, "Common People" bursts into a gallop, and Cocker dispenses with the storytelling in favor of a direct and sneering rebuke at those who feign low social status by renting meager apartments, getting average jobs, wasting time in bars, and disowning their education. The critique gets even more pointed as the narrator argues that these facades of destitution can be ended with a simple phone call to daddy before the following chorus flatly states that no matter how much someone of privilege might try to empathize, he or she will never truly get to know what it feels like to have no prospects beyond a life of pointless hedonism. A guitar solo dominates the instrumental section, which ends with a juddering succession of drum fills, and the final chorus adds one further sentiment of indignation by claiming that although the common people might seem welcoming to anyone trying to emulate them, they are, in fact, laughing at the stupidity of those who feel that to be poor is to somehow be cool. As the song goes into the last section, it simmers down slightly with Doyle's synth riff leading the song again, but the final seconds see an explosion of fury that is propelled by Banks's powerful drum rolls and Cocker's shouts of annoyance. After the track powers to an end, it feels like someone has just left the room in an almighty huff.

The effort that Pulp made in transforming "Common People" from a keyboard-based ditty to a towering pop song was more than worthwhile. The single was at once funny, angry, and extremely catchy, and that combination saw it reach No. 2 on the U.K. chart—a position where it stayed for four weeks. National radio play was ubiquitous, while the video also gained heavy rotation on MTV, quickly becoming one of the most enduring images of the Britpop era thanks partly to an appearance by film actress Sadie Frost, who played the Greek girl. In one particularly memorable shot that seemed to symbolize the social and financial gap between the two characters, she is seen pushing a shopping cart around the supermarket with a miniature Jarvis Cocker inside as if she were literally about to purchase him. It was the ideal visual accompaniment; in a time that saw British music dominated by lyrical themes of fun, hopefulness, and apolitical hedonism, "Common People" stood out clearly as being a rare song that "brimmed with a splenetic sense of rage."[12]

At the end of June 1995—just weeks after the single's release—Pulp played a prestigious headline slot at the three-day Glastonbury Festival in southwest England.

The band had been asked to be the headliner only after the Stone Roses pulled out at the last moment, but the band's recent chart success made its appearance monumental, and it became clear that Pulp was now a big-league name. "Common People" provided the night's uproarious finale,[13] and the constant airplay ensured that the tens of thousands of fans sang every word with gusto—except for a largely unfamiliar section toward the end of the song, during which much of the crowd fell silent. The reason was because the version they had been hearing for weeks on the radio had been edited for brevity and was just over four minutes long. However, the original recording (clocking in at just under six minutes) that the bandmates were now performing live contained an extra set of lyrics. Although retail copies of the single carried "Common People" in its entirety, much of the public would not come across it until it appeared on the album *Different Class,* which emerged toward the end of 1995. It was only then that the full extent of the song's rage really became apparent.

The added part starts immediately after the lines that criticize the idea of poor being cool (around 3.25 on the track) and suddenly reestablishes the steady pace of the intro. The narrator then issues a vaguely intimidating warning that common people have the potential to be savage (just as Cocker remarked publicly) while acerbically adding that the reason for this ill temper is simply because "everybody hates a tourist" who can distance himself or herself from this unpleasant reality in an instant while everyone else is stuck with it. The song then leaps back into a faster pace and again issues a seething dismissal of those pretending that they have no future before finally repeating the previous lyrics about posing in paltry accommodation again and going into the same final section as the single edit. Cutting this part of the song away may have been a necessary thing to do to ensure success, but it also took away the most damning element of "Common People" and meant the precise sentiment of protest that Pulp was conveying missed the listeners who happily sang along with it on the radio.

Different Class went on to hit No. 1 on the U.K. album chart and spawned four more Top 10 singles, while reviews were unanimously positive. Even in the United States, where the band's very British themes understandably made no commercial impact, critics still celebrated Pulp for its idiosyncrasies and newly found pop prowess. "Common People" was undoubtedly the catalyst for this attention and praise, but not only did the song turn out to be a watershed for Pulp's career, it gradually became a reflection of an entire period in British cultural history. The taste for working-class life that so many non-working-class people acquired during the mid-1990s has meant that "Common People" is no longer just a pop song, but a sociological study—so much so that the BBC commissioned a documentary entirely devoted to the origins, impact, and legacy of the track in 2005. Researchers working on the program even attempted to trace the Greek girl who inspired Cocker to initially write the song but, sadly, to no avail. Despite the cultural significance the song has accrued over the years, it is still the abridged version that gets played on the radio and on MTV, and, to this day, the real fury of "Common People" remains hidden from the masses for which it speaks.

Artist: Asian Dub Foundation

Song: "Free Satpal Ram"

Songwriters: Aniruddha Das (Dr. Das), John Pandit (Pandit G.), Steven Savale (Chandrasonic), Sanjay Tailor (Sun-J), and Deedar Zaman (Master D)

Album: *Rafi's Revenge*

Label: London Records (United Kingdom)/Polygram Records (United States)

1998

After a catalog of high-profile miscarriages of justice were brought to light during the 1980s and 1990s, the British legal system was under fire. Although the conviction of Satpal Ram for murder had been identified as potentially unsafe in 1992, his case did not receive widespread media attention until the end of the decade when London group Asian Dub Foundation released the single "Free Satpal Ram." Marrying the story of his case to an extremely modern fusion of musical genres, it took a verbal flamethrower to standards of prosecution and raised unprecedented awareness of Ram's alleged ill-treatment. The song's immense power and a continuing political campaign both played pivotal parts in the prisoner's eventual release in 2002—15 years after he was first sent to jail.

N.W.A. had released "Fuck tha Police" as a scathing indictment of victimization by the Los Angeles Police Department in 1989, but the bandmates were not the only people in the Western world to harbor ill feelings against those maintaining law and order at the time. During the late 1980s and 1990s, the British legal system was also being subjected to some intense and occasionally embarrassing scrutiny across the country as a string of high-profile convictions went under reexamination. The most notable cases included that of the "Guilford Four" who were imprisoned in 1975 for the bombing of a pub in London as part of the Irish Republican Army's terror campaign in mainland Britain. The three men and one woman were sentenced to life imprisonment, but were released in 1989 after it was revealed that police had almost certainly edited their original statements (this struggle was later turned into the film *In the Name of the Father*). The "Birmingham Six" were accused of a similarly motivated attack of a pub in Birmingham and were also jailed in 1975, but after years of campaigning, they too had their convictions quashed in 1991 following the revelations that evidence had been suppressed. Around the same time, the movement to free the "Bridgewater Four" was gaining momentum. This group of men had been jailed for the 1978 murder of newspaper boy Carl Bridgewater after he disturbed a burglary, but they would eventually be cleared in 1997—although one of the defendants had already died in prison. These were just three examples of how the scales of justice were seemingly being tampered with, and public confidence in the police naturally slumped to a new low.

Although it was given comparatively little media coverage during the early 1990s, the case of Satpal Ram was yet another that was hotly contested. He had been jailed for life following an incident at an Indian restaurant in Birmingham in 1986. At the time of his sentencing, it was reported that an argument over the volume of music being played in the establishment led to Ram becoming verbally abusive to a party of diners. This led to a confrontation in which Ram apparently stabbed and killed a man named Clarke Pearce before eventually fleeing. The prosecution also claimed Ram was so drunk that doctors could not treat him for the wounds he had received in the fracas. Ram, however, claimed that it was he who had been racially abused, that Pearce had attacked him first with a broken glass, and that he had used the knife (a tool he had because of his job as a warehouse worker) in self-defense. He also insisted that his trial was severely flawed partly because his provided lawyer had misread the pathologist's report on Pearce's death and had subsequently advised him to change his plea from self-defense to manslaughter. Furthermore, Ram added that translators were not provided in the court to take testimonies from waiters who could verify his account as they had witnessed the attack. Meanwhile, supporters of the defendant maintained that Pearce had died only because he refused to be treated by a woman in the hospital and later discharged himself. Ram continually protested his innocence while pushing for an appeal; in 1992, the Free Satpal Ram campaign was boosted when the case was first identified as being another possible miscarriage of justice in the national press.

Over the next few years, the campaign to free Ram would grow and begin to receive some enthusiastic support by the members of Asian Dub Foundation (ADF). The group had formed in London in 1993 as a collective based around a community program designed to teach local children about music technology. Two of the teachers, John Pandit (turntables, programming) and Aniruddha Das (bass), enlisted the vocal skills of a 15-year-old student named Deedar Zaman before adding guitarist Steven Savale and DJ Sanjay Tailor to complete the lineup. Their first album *Facts and Fictions* emerged in 1995 and boasted a multicultural mix of hip-hop beats, ragga rhythms, rock guitars, and a whole lot more besides. Their eclectic energy and acutely conscious lyrics contrasted vastly with the more straightforward, apolitical guitar rock being released by such outfits as Oasis and Blur, which dominated the U.K. music scene at the time—and it was a completely intentional departure. While these groups appeared to encourage nostalgia for British culture of the 1960s and 1970s, ADF specifically sought to forge new paths for music that would reflect the country's multiracial makeup and repeatedly slammed its more popular counterparts for what it felt was a reactionary attitude.

Although ADF's debut was roundly ignored by fans and critics in the United Kingdom, things began to change as the group released the single "Naxalite" in 1997—the first material from what would be ADF's second album and proof that the bandmates had elevated their sound to an even more dynamic level. With the additional praise for an exhilarating live show helping to increase its profile, ADF used its growing platform in the press to raise awareness about the political and social issues the band members felt needed to be addressed. The case of Satpal Ram was at the forefront of this agenda, particularly as it appeared that his plight was worsening. Still incarcerated and with two dismissed appeals behind him, Ram was now being subjected to constant relocations across the British prison system and also complained of frequent mistreatment by wardens as well as unfairly long stints in isolation. Asian Dub Foundation had long been a supporter of his cause and originally had written "Free Satpal Ram" for its French-only album *R.A.F.I.* in 1997. The song featured a brooding monologue chronicling Ram's case over a fairly straightforward techno beat, but the group re-recorded the song and released it as a single in early 1998. It would turn out to be huge benefit to both Asian Dub Foundation's musical reputation and Satpal Ram's attempts to clear his name.

The tone of urgency is set instantly in "Free Satpal Ram" thanks to some furious string samples and Zaman's raucous exclamation of "self defence is no offence." A pounding beat unleashes the intro's simmering energy and tension, at which point it becomes clear that Asian Dub Foundation is demanding attention and doing everything it can to motivate the listener. Zaman's lightning-fast rapping is almost too quick to understand, but an attentive listen reveals accusations of the legal system being grossly unfair and that those responsible for administering universal justice are actually little more than a biased secret society. The idea of knowing your rights is also dismissed as an ineffective way of protecting against victimization, but these general references to the inadequacies of the law are then replaced by the first specific views on Ram's case. The last part of the first verse acknowledges his period of 10 years in prison as being completely without foundation and points out that this is not an isolated case. After a pregnant pause, the song then blasts into a chorus that vehemently calls for Ram's release via repetitions of the title and also features insistent shouts of his innocence as Savale's buzz-saw-like guitar riffs add to the furious storm of sound.

The second verse retorts the defendant's version of events on the night in question through Zaman's rapping, reiterating that it was the group of diners who racially abused Ram first before attacking him physically. The point is again made that self-defense was his only intention and Ram's fear for his own life forced him into acting, after which "Free Satpal Ram" launches into another chorus with similar verve. A rousing wall of noise (punctuated by some prominent scratching an almost unhinged guitar solo from Savale) provides the instrumental middle section, after which Zaman returns to deliver lines that bear closer resemblance to a speech rather than lyrics to a song. In this section, he address the "Birmingham Six," the "Guilford Four," the "Bridgewater Four," and the additional cases of Winston Silcott[14] and the "King's Cross Two"[15] as miscarriages of justice in the United Kingdom. It is a damning list, but Zaman asks how many more will end up being added and then declares that ADF is taking a stand in an attempt to redress the balance. With a final warning that it could happen to anyone, he throws out an open invite for everyone to join in the fight against injustice before a final chorus rounds off "Free Satpal Ram" with an unrelenting ferocity.

Despite having had no chart success or mainstream radio airplay prior to this single, "Free Satpal Ram" still managed to hit No. 56 in the United Kingdom thanks to growing support in the underground music scene. The subsequent release of *Rafi's Revenge* also in 1998 (which included this re-recorded version of "Free Satpal Ram") was met with an overwhelmingly positive critical response and would also earn a nomination for the extremely prestigious Mercury Music Prize for album of the year. Meanwhile, the band was heartened by a wider consciousness being raised among the public as a result of the track. "It's not just about him [Ram] defending himself in a racial attack and getting done for murder," explained Das. "It's also about prison conditions, how people are treated in prison, the whole procedure of the penal system. Now it's coming out in the media."[16] However, the effect was understandably most visible in the Free Satpal Ram campaign, which gained huge momentum as Asian Dub Foundation continued to speak tirelessly about the case to fans, press, and even other bands. After initially giving the band support for its musical talent, Primal Scream also became prominently involved with the campaign and played a benefit gig for Ram shortly after the single was released. Members of the Scottish group would later show further solidarity to the cause by chaining themselves to the gates outside the Home Office[17] during 1999 in protest of Ram's continued mistreatment.

In the two years after the release of "Free Satpal Ram," regular press reports were made on the case, and the continuing publicity culminated in a petition of over 50,000 signatures (featuring some high-profile names, such as members of the British band Massive Attack and famous author Irvine Welsh) being handed to Prime Minister Tony Blair in 2000. The following year, Home Secretary Jack Straw made the unusual step of personally intervening to reject the parole board recommendation that Ram be released. But in 2002, a European Court ruling decreed that Straw had no right to overrule the recommendation; at long last, Ram was finally released and was met outside by Pandit among others. By the time he emerged back into the public, Ram had served almost exactly 15 years and had been moved to over 70 different prisons. Although expressing an obvious delight at being released, Ram and his supporters expressed fury at Straw's decision, which cost the defendant another 18 months of freedom. Ram also maintained that he was still not free of the initial allegation of murder and vowed to clear his name in relation to Clarke Pearce's death. But whether guilty, innocent, or otherwise, Ram's newly granted liberty could be directly linked to "Free Satpal Ram," and it was a fact that was acknowledged both in the press and by the man himself. In what had been a distinctly apathetic era, Asian Dub Foundation had galvanized thousands of music fans into supporting a specific cause, and now the result of their efforts was clear for all to see.

Notes

1. Quoted in Douglas Keay, "AIDS, Education and the Year 2000," *Woman's Own*, October 31, 1987.

2. Quoted in Simon Reynolds, "The Prodigy: Touched by the Hand of Prod," *Melody Maker*, July 16, 1994.

3. Criminal Justice and Public Order Act, Part V, Section 63, 1994, http://www.opsi.gov.uk/acts/acts1994/Ukpga_19940033_en_1.htm.

4. P. T. Barnum was a 19th century showman known for his elaborate hoaxes and flagrant self-promotion. He also set up what would eventually become known as the Barnum & Bailey Circus.

5. Quoted in Danny Kelly, "Michael Jackson: What? Me? Worry?" *Q*, August 1995.

6. Michael Jackson, statement first aired on *CNN*, December 22, 1993.

7. Quoted in Barney Hoskyns, "Michael Jackson at 40," *Independent* (London), August 29, 1998.

8. An Essex girl is a term given to the horribly sexist British stereotype of all women from said area being blonde, promiscuous, and unintelligent.

9. Quoted in Jon Wilde, "Bleurgh!" *Loaded*, September 1994.

10. Council estates are equivalent to housing projects—areas of accommodations subsidized by local authorities for people on low income.

11. Quoted in Phil Sutcliffe, "Common as Muck" *Q*, March 1996.

12. John Harris, *The Last Party* (London: 4th Estate, 2003), 219.

13. A recording of this live version is available on the deluxe two CD edition of *Different Class* (Island Records, 2006).

14. Winston Silcott was one of the "Tottenham Three" who were jailed in 1987 for the murder of a policeman in London. Following tests that indicated evidence had been tampered with, all three convictions were quashed in 1991.

15. The "King's Cross Two" refers to Badrul Miah and Showkat Akbar who were tried in relation to the murder of a youth in London in 1994. Akbar was given three years for violent disorder but after blood from the victim was found on Miah's clothes, he was given a life sentence even though the actual assailant was never definitively determined as the attack was carried out by a larger mob. The judge in the case admitted that the pair was shouldering the blame for the incident.

16. Quoted in David Stubbs, "Asian Dub Foundation," *Uncut*, August 1998.

17. The Home Office is the government body responsible for security issues in the United Kingdom.

EPILOGUE

The 20th century may have ended on a reasonably content note, but a sea change on both sides of the Atlantic occurred after the cataclysmic terrorist attacks of 9/11, which plunged the West into a new age of political uncertainty. A second war with Iraq resulted in 2003, and it was this event, in particular, that sparked a renewed sense of anger in music and added another turn to the cycle of pop culture. With the protracted conflict appearing to lack justification and sparking the most vociferous anti-government sentiment since Vietnam, a number of classic antiwar songs from the 1960s and 1970s were revisited, but the artists of the new generation offered their own unique critiques—the most effective of which took issue not just with the foreign policy of U.S. President George W. Bush, but also the skewed representation of the war in the press. Mass media—television especially—was even more influential than it had been in the 1990s with 24-hour news cycles now providing constant coverage of the U.S.–led "War on Terror," but not always with the neutrality that it warranted. Punk rock trio Green Day took this source of misinformation to task and denounced the Americans that accepted it without query in "**American Idiot**" (2004) while with "**B.Y.O.B.**" (2005), System of a Down offered a maniacal rant at recruitment advertisements on television selling army life as some kind of party. These were just two songs from an era of protest music that has produced enough material to fill an entire book in itself. But with Bush holding on to the presidency and continuing to implement the occupation of Iraq despite such huge disapproval from the American people, another shift toward apathy has been noticeable as the cycle of pop culture begins to take another predictable turn.

Artist: Green Day

Song: "American Idiot"

Songwriters: Billie Joe Armstrong, Mike Dirnt, and Tre Cool

Album: *American Idiot*

Label: WEA International Inc.

2004

The atmosphere across the United States following 9/11 was understandably tense, but for Green Day, things were not helped by the media whose portrayal of the government's subsequent "War on Terror" leaned a little too close to outright scaremongering for the California punk trio. The seriousness of the situation led Green Day to ditch the goofiness that had made the bandmates famous in the 1990s, and they returned from the musical wilderness with "American Idiot"—a song that raged at the manipulative effects of biased reporting. It not only skyrocketed them back to fame, but also offered one of the most damning musical critiques of the Republican administration heard during the entire era.

Pop music in the 1990s certainly was not ablaze with righteousness, but even in this era of apathy, Green Day's attitude was more apolitical than most. The trio of Tre Cool (drums), Mike Dirnt (bass, vocals), and Billie Joe Armstrong (vocals, guitar) had first emerged with the albums *39/Smooth* (1990) and *Kerplunk!* (1991) and

The members of Green Day take a break from riling against American idiocy in 2004. (L–R): Billie Joe Armstrong, Tre Cool, and Mike Dirnt.
Courtesy AP Images/CP Adrian Wyld.

diligently earned a place at the top of the American underground punk scene through relentless touring. The group's grassroots popularity attracted Reprise Records (a subsidiary of the giant WEA company), which subsequently signed it—an almost unheard of occurrence at the time, especially as the majority of major labels were still preoccupied with finding alternative rock bands that would replicate the success of such acts as Nirvana and Pearl Jam. Though some of the group's more militant punk rock peers were resentful at seeing the band supposedly "selling out," the 1994 album *Dookie* was an unprecedented success. Helped in no small way by the smash-hit single "Basket Case," Green Day's third album sold millions of copies worldwide, elevated the band to superstardom, and transformed its previously unrecognized brand of catchy and entertainingly silly punk rock into a mainstream idiom. It was a genre the bandmates would continue to define throughout the decade through such albums as 1995's *Insomniac* and 1997's *Nimrod;* as the trio continued through to the end of the decade, it was clear that Green Day was a central inspiration for a new generation of bands, such as Blink 182, Sum 41, and Good Charlotte. However, after 2000's subdued *Warning* was quietly received both in terms of sales and critical acclaim, Green Day seemed to be a fading star while the groups that had been so clearly weaned on the group's style of punk began to overtake it in both areas. As coincidence would have it, the hugely controversial presidential election—held just weeks after *Warning* was released—provided the spark that would turn the band's fortunes around in the long term.

The primary candidates in the race for the White House that year were Al Gore (Democrat and vice president under the outgoing Bill Clinton) and George W. Bush (Republican and son of former President George W. H. Bush). Opinion polls before the election had been too close to call, and in a contest as close as this, every vote seemed doubly crucial. As the results came in, the nationwide popular vote and the electoral vote had gone narrowly in favor of Gore, but the state of Florida (governed by Bush's brother "Jeb") emerged as the tie breaker for the entire campaign. The two candidates boasted an almost identical number of total votes within the state that recounts could not clarify. After almost a month of confusion, the U.S. Supreme Court voted to halt the recounts and awarded the state and therefore the presidency to Bush, who still had over half a million less of the popular vote than Gore. In the extended postmortem that followed, one of the many arguments offered by Gore's supporters was that if the Green Party candidate Ralph Nader had not been an option for swing voters, the Democrats would have been successful in their campaign. It was an argument that could easily be applied to Armstrong, who had gone to the voting booth with the intention of voting for Gore if only because it meant not voting Republican. At the last moment, his desire to see a viable third option in American politics led the front man to support Nader. "It was about conscience... I thought that if 5 percent of the population could vote for this guy [Nader], there would be another party. Can you imagine America with *three* parties?"[1]

The controversy surrounding the entire affair was immense and became further engrained as President Bush's first period at the White House unfolded during 2001. The Islamic terrorist organization Al-Qaeda admitted involvement in the attacks on the World Trade Center and the Pentagon on September 11, and this prompted Bush to launch his self-styled "War on Terrorism" which manifested itself in the invasion and eventual overthrow of the Taliban regime in Afghanistan. The regime was seen to be closely connected to Al-Qaeda, as well as being the likely hiding place of the organization's leader, Osama bin Laden, although attempts to find him continually failed. Furthermore, a U.S.–led coalition embarked on a much criticized (and under UN law, technically illegal) invasion of Iraq in 2003, during which the country's dictator, Saddam Hussein, was deposed due to the hotly disputed intelligence that he had access to weapons of mass destruction. Opponents of the Bush administration accused it of harboring numerous ulterior motives in this operation —particularly that of establishing control of the Middle East's wealth of oil. Coverage of all these events naturally saturated the media, and in the wake of the biggest terrorist atrocity to be committed on U.S. soil, tension and paranoia began to be common emotions. The psyche of Islamic fundamentalism became a crucial area of knowledge for virtually everyone in the Western world, and TV reports, debates, and documentaries on the subject were therefore guaranteed ratings winners. The idea that people with the same convictions as those who perpetrated the atrocities in New York City and Arlington, Virginia, were part of the American population at large continued to be drilled home by the omnipotent media for years after 9/11, and the inevitable by-product was a continually reinforced feeling of fear.

It was an observation that the members of Green Day were also making as they labored on writing and recording a seventh album during the latter half of Bush's first term in office, but their belief in the need to wage foreign wars to heighten domestic safety was not as certain as the president's. Aside from feeling perturbed over the War on Terrorism and dubious about the reasoning behind it, Armstrong also noted that the skewed, progovernment reporting of these tumultuous events simply amounted to scaremongering and was making things only worse. "We have a media—especially television—that doesn't tell us the truth . . . A lot of it is just right-wing entertainment, and so the story isn't told. And these people are getting away with it."[2] It was because of these grievances that Green Day made the decision to document the situation in a hugely ambitious concept album that would see the bandmates exceed both the expectations of themselves as a band and the conventions of punk rock as a genre. Referred to as a punk rock opera by critics and Armstrong himself, the album *American Idiot* (released in September 2004) was based around a fictional young man attempting to find his own way through life with the confused fabric of modern America providing the backdrop. The album's opening track, title song, and first single serves as this one man's refusal to be like the paranoid and unquestioning masses around him. "The song "American Idiot," that's the political climate he's set in," pointed out Dirnt shortly after the album's release. "That's what is the catalyst for getting out of town, getting his own beliefs and heading out on his own journey."[3]

Compared to some of the album's more inventive moments, "American Idiot" is an instantly recognizable Green Day track in musical terms. Played at breakneck speed, powered by Cool's manic drumming, boasting just four guitar chords in the entire song, and featuring Armstrong barking out his dissent, its simplistic nature and fist-clenching spirit is the very essence of classic punk rock. But in this context, these well-established expressions of rage are used to vocalize a much newer ill—that of media manipulation. The character in the song begins by rejecting hysteria cultivated by the press and criticizing the wider population for allowing themselves to be subliminally controlled through it. He also acknowledges his own potential persecution at the hands of those who might feel him to be unpatriotic, but still, it is a small price to pay for having a broader perspective on the problems affecting the country. The song also plays on a central irony that while the constant availability of news and information should be giving people a broader worldview, it actually appears to be fostering a strange docility. It is a critique that is spelled out in the song's most cutting moment, which Armstrong encouraged the band's audience to sing with brio every night of the mammoth world tour that followed the album's release:

Information age of hysteria, calling out to idiot America.

The line leads the song into a final chorus that implores the listener, if not the entire country, to not go blindly into this new age of tension and uncertainty. A furious instrumental section closes the song and in less than three minutes, "American Idiot" has slammed home a seething rebuttal of the information age through a fantastically catchy pop song.

While "American Idiot" railed forcefully against the effect of modern media, the irony was that they absolutely loved it. Within weeks of the single being released, Green Day was again receiving radio, press, and TV coverage all over the world thanks to the single's ascent to No. 3 on the U.K. chart, as well as becoming the first of the band's songs to appear on the U.S. Hot 100. As a result, the band's popularity levels easily surpassed those experienced during the mid-1990s and an entirely new generation became exposed to the power of punk rock. Those who had followed the trio's entire career noted the radical change of tack in Armstrong's lyricism, which had been anything but serious up to "American Idiot" but was now brimming with all kinds of anger, frustration, and disaffection. This radical about-face in Green Day's artistic motivations seemed to reflect how serious the sociopolitical strains on American life had become, but even so, there were some who found it hard to give Green Day's new sense of consciousness the kind of credence that it deserved. After all, the group's members had established a reputation as an eternally adolescent bunch of pranksters who wrote songs about masturbating, called their albums slang words for excrement, and had even named themselves after a term used to describe an entire day spent smoking weed. The charge of cynical political bandwagon jumping was something that Armstrong responded to by adamantly insisting, "I've always written about what's around me, whether it's about being a kid and masturbating in front of the television, or now, being scared to death in front of the television."[4]

Even though the song or the album never referred to political players directly by name, "American Idiot" was identified by fans and critics as being one of the era's most prominent musical indictments of the Bush administration. For Green Day, the government was essentially the root of the current climate of fear, and the band was never shy of publicly admitting a desire to see Bush removed from office. Green

VOTE FOR CHANGE TOUR

Whereas Rock against Bush was a campaign initiated by punk artists mainly in the hope of politicizing fans of the genre, the Vote for Change tour had a much broader scope. It was orchestrated by the MoveOn Political Action Committee, an organization established in 1998 with the intention of gathering financial support for progressive candidates and government policies. In late September and October of 2004, MoveOn brought together 17 of the biggest names in American music (of which Green Day was not one) that performed on a two-week tour of simultaneous shows in the country's "swing" (evenly balanced) states —Pennsylvania, Michigan, North Carolina, Missouri, Ohio, Wisconsin, Iowa, and, of course Florida, all in the hope of raising revenue and swaying voters to the Democratic cause. In terms of attracting high-profile names to lend their support, MoveOn would have struggled to do much better. The three main acts Pearl Jam, R.E.M., and Bruce Springsteen and The E Street Band were established legends, while the smaller acts, such as Death Cab for Cutie, Jurassic 5, and Bright Eyes, all invited support from their younger fan bases. During a date in Cleveland, Springsteen was even joined on stage by John Kerry, but this still failed to have the desired effect. Of the eight "swing" states that the tour visited, only three were won by Kerry—Wisconsin, Michigan, and Pennsylvania. Despite failing in its primary objective of removing Bush as head of state, the scale of the Vote for Change tour proved to be a watershed in musical activism with many of the artists admitting that pledging explicit support to one specific candidate was nothing short of an emergency measure. MoveOn continues to have an active and high-profile role in promoting progressive politics. After the 2006 midterm election, the organization was cited in many areas of the media as being a key force in helping the Democrat Party to regain majority control of Congress thanks to its tireless fund-raising efforts.

Day was not the only one in the genre of punk to feel that way. After suffering from insomnia following the 2000 election as well as being disenchanted by the low turnout among young voters, "Fat" Mike Burkett—the singer of the legendary San Francisco punk band (and Green Day's close musical contemporaries) NOFX—set up the PunkVoter.com Web site, declaring "our goal is to educate, register and mobilize over 500,000 of today's youth as one voice."[5] In the lead-up to the 2004 election, the site published critiques of the Bush administration by the punk community's most revered names, posted potentially discrediting articles relating to Bush's commercial interests that were usually withheld by the mainstream press, and brought together similarly minded bands to contribute politically inspired songs to the two volumes of the *Rock against Bush* compilation that featured, among others, Foo Fighters, Blink 182, Bad Religion, and, of course, Green Day. NOFX also headed a Rock against Bush tour that sought to further reinforce the message in tangent with the president's own campaign for reelection in the months immediately before polling day.

Despite PunkVoter.com receiving more attention courtesy of Green Day's patronage, the hope that mobilizing young voters would be enough to remove Bush from office proved to be forlorn. The election again looked to be a close-run affair with Democratic candidate John Kerry providing the main opposition; although the youth turnout surged sharply with over 4½ million more 18- to 29-year-olds casting votes than the 2000 election, Bush still won a clear majority of both the popular vote and the electoral vote. There was no debate this time around—the president had won a second term by a margin that was beyond doubt, and the sense of disappointment and anticlimax among his opponents was palpable. For its part, Green Day accepted another four years of Republicanism, but took heart in the prospect of a potentially more enlightened and less apathetic future electorate. "I don't think any of the effort [to defeat Bush] was wasted," offered Dirnt. "The youth vote was up and if anything [the result] got people's awareness up of knowing we can't be passive in the next election."[6] Continuing on from that point, the real-life cartoon character that is Tre Cool added his own typically comedic take on the positives that he envisioned emerging in future years, arguing that the older Bush voters would simply die off and that "the younger, cooler generation will vote accordingly."[7] Whether this turns out to be the case or not, "American Idiot" did capture the mood of a significant part of the nation upon its release. Given the outcome of the 2004 election, the continued campaign against terrorism, and the ever-increasing exposure Americans have to all forms of media, it is a song that has continued to remain relevant for much longer than Green Day would have probably liked.

Artist: System of a Down

Song: "B.Y.O.B."

Songwriters: Daron Malakian and Serj Tankian

Album: *Mezmerize*

Label: American Recordings/ Columbia Records

2005

System of a Down had a well-established reputation as one of America's most politically outspoken groups from its earliest days in the mid-1990s. So when the music world was jolted into action following 9/11 and the subsequent war with Iraq in 2003, it was no surprise to see the Los Angeles firebrands protesting against the U.S. government louder than most. However, as this wave of political action in rock died down around it, System of a Down remained as angry as ever, and for "B.Y.O.B.," in particular, the bandmates redirected their aim toward some misleadingly lighthearted commercial campaigns for army recruitment.

Although originally of Armenian heritage, Serj Tankian was actually born in the city of Beirut, Lebanon, in 1967, and it was the country's civil war that would provide some harrowing early memories for the future System of a Down singer. Despite enjoying a degree of postwar stability, growing tensions over the religious demographic in Beirut led to widespread conflict breaking out in 1975 when Tankian was eight years old. Having already fled political instability in Armenia and now surrounded by more upheaval in Lebanon, Tankian's parents were forced to relocate again; this time they looked to the Hollywood district of Los Angeles in a bid to find a more stable environment. It was there that Tankian would finally settle, finding solace in the sizable Armenian community, as well as exposing himself to Western popular culture. But his experience in Beirut would also stay firmly lodged in his mind right through to adulthood—"one thing I can say is that if you've ever heard bombs fall in a city, you will have a different sensitivity to dropping bombs on a city."[8]

System of a Down (L–R): Daron Malakian, John Dolmayan, Serj Tankian, and Shavo Odadjian.
Courtesy AP Images/Jim Cooper.

By 1993, Tankian had met guitarist Daron Malakian, and the pair combined first to form Soil; feeling a gradual sense of frustration at the lack of exposure and artistic progression, however, they dissolved the band two years later. Almost immediately, they put together System of a Down and by 1997 had eventually settled on a final lineup that coincidentally included fellow Armenian Americans Shavo Odadjian (bass) and John Dolmayan (drums). The band's demo tapes showed a shared appreciation for such heavy rock and metal legends as Faith No More, Slayer, and Metallica, but the group's unpredictable and idiosyncratic musical style helped it stand apart from other bands in the genre—a fact that led American Recordings boss Rick Rubin to offer the band a deal. The self-titled debut released in 1998 attested to the quartet's originality, but also demonstrated the extent of the bandmates' political mind-set, especially in relation to the group's shared heritage. The album was dedicated to the unrecognized genocide of Armenians in 1915 at the hands of the neighboring Turkish Ottoman Empire—an incident mentioned in speeches later made by Adolf Hitler and evidently an inspiration in his policy of Jewish genocide during World War II. A number of songs on *System of a Down* also made reference to this grim episode of early 20th century history, and the group's determination to push through political acceptance continued outside of music. Tankian, in particular, had been vocal on the subject ever since his teenage years after learning that his grandparents were some of the lucky ones to survive, and he wholeheartedly supported a resolution proposed in 2000 that would officially mean U.S. recognition of the event. The resolution, however, was vetoed at the last moment by outgoing President Bill Clinton, leaving a bitterly disappointed Tankian to blame the decision on the government's unwillingness to lose Turkey as a strategic ally in the Middle East.

In a relatively apathetic era of pop music, System of a Down's members had already distinguished themselves for an outspoken attitude on such issues as this, but as they returned with new material, that broader apolitical trend was reversed virtually overnight. In the same week the group celebrated a mainstream breakthrough by hitting No. 1 in the United States with its second album *Toxicity,* commercial airplanes were hijacked and used to attack the Twin Towers in New York and the Pentagon in Washington, D.C., on September 11, 2001. In total, almost 3,000 civilians perished, and the atrocities were quickly traced back to the Muslim fundamentalist organization Al-Qaeda, headed up by wealthy Saudi Arabian Osama bin Laden. In the midst of worldwide confusion and an inevitable sense of fear, System of a Down's attempt to explain the incident was typically swift and came through a Tankian-penned essay called *Understanding Oil,* which was posted on the band's Web site on September 13. In it, the singer appeared to go against the patriotic fervor sweeping the country by criticizing decades of U.S. foreign policy in the Middle East, arguing that it had been geared to secure access to the region's wealth of oil and to foster conflict for the benefit of the arms industry—all of which had led to the events of 9/11. While echoing the rest of Western world by calling for the perpetrators of these terrorist attacks to be brought to justice, Tankian also pleaded for the United States to gear its policy in the Middle East toward a lasting peace and to make a concerted effort in finding renewable energy sources. In the climate of pro-American feeling, the post received much criticism and even earned the band death threats. As a result, the singer's informed thoughts on achieving peace were promptly removed by the band's label and replaced instead by a simpler statement in which Tankian gave thanks for the American orphanages that raised his grandfather during the Armenian genocide.

During the next 18 months, the United States embarked on what President George W. Bush would infamously declare to be the "War on Terror" that not only incorporated the destruction of bin Laden and the Al-Qaeda cell, but any other associated groups deemed to be a threat. Gradually, the focus of attention would shift to Iraq with the American government arguing that the country's dictator, Saddam Hussein, had weapons of mass destruction capable of reaching U.S. soil that could be ready for use within 45 minutes of his command. Bush was given permission to use troops in Iraq by the U.S. Senate toward the end of 2002, and knowledge of the imminent invasion sparked a wave of global public protest—most notably the marches coordinated to take place around the world on the same weekend in February 2003. Naturally, System of a Down took an active part in this opposition not just by turning up, but by using filmmaker Michael Moore to record the demonstrations for the video to its song "Boom!" (from the band's 2002 album *Steal This Album!*—a collection of material hastily released to counter an Internet leak of unfinished tracks). Despite the attempts of the band and the millions that turned out in a last ditch attempt to avert the conflict, the United States led a coalition of forces into Iraq the following month, declaring that the intention was to liberate the land from its oppressive regime.

By the end of 2003, Saddam Hussein had been overthrown and captured, but Iraq erupted into a subsequent civil war that required a prolonged American troop presence in the country. Additionally, the reelection of Bush in 2004 all but ended the hope that American forces would quickly withdraw, and to add insult to injury for many antiwar factions, the weapons of mass destruction cited as being a threat to the United States were never found. It was to this backdrop of ongoing foreign warfare and its continually reducing justification that System of a Down set about recording its fourth album. Having shown a keen political awareness from such an early stage, there was little chance that the group would not find some streak of inspiration in the turmoil; Malakian especially had cause to keep an eye on the situation given that he had family members still living in Iraq. But as he worked on musical ideas in the studio, he happened to see a television advertisement for army recruitment and picked up on a disconcerting subtext in the way the commercial called upon America's youth to serve their country.

> Well I'm watching the army ad and it's saying, "Come and make a career and meet new friends and go new places . . ." Everybody's going to the party, have a real good time![9]

Rather than communicate the dangers or even just the realities of conflict, Malakian was horrified to see the idea of national service being sold as a carefree experience akin to that of an open-invite party. With the additional input of Tankian, the guitarist channeled his disgust into a song that became an indictment of the devious way Americans were encouraged to fight the country's latest battle. In keeping with the idea of war being a party, the song was named "B.Y.O.B.," but instead of standing for the often used invite to Bring Your Own Beer/Bottle/Booze, System of a Down changed it to mean Bring Your Own Bomb.

Beginning with a manically fast guitar riff, the menacingly heavy intro to "B.Y.O.B." is played at a ferocious speed until Malakian is heard squealing "why do they always send the poor?" in a practically demonic voice. It is a sentiment that critiques the recruitment of people with relatively few career opportunities and is very similar to that of many anti-Vietnam songs (see the entry on Black Sabbath's "War Pigs" for one example). But as Tankian begins his lead vocals, the track speedily surveys many other unpleasant elements of conflict—many of which seem specifically related to the Iraq War. Delivering the first verses at a barely comprehensible pace, the singer expels a stream of images that appear to relate to the uses of religion, technological mind control, and political lies in creating loyalty. At this point, Malakian, Odadjian, and Dolmayan relent in their pounding rhythm to go into a catchy and almost danceable chorus that is deliberately juxtaposed to the chaos of the verse. During this segment, Tankian reflects this new, buoyant mood by promising a metaphorical party (like the one Malakian saw being sold in the recruitment commercial) where people will dance in the desert and bomb the sunshine—a clear nod to the terrain and climate of the Middle East.

Another instantaneous tempo change launches "B.Y.O.B." back into a second furious verse where more fleeting references to oil, the pursuit of freedom, and the way in which war leaves some participants effectively obsolete all hurtle past in a frenzied stream. The upbeat chorus once again returns to the song before a deranged, expletive-laden middle segment finds Malakian forcefully screaming a declaration that the party has started and the revelers are choosing to ignore the knowledge that they are doing the bidding of a fascist regime by attending. The band continues to pummel out a brutal rhythm as both Malakian and Tankian embark on a pulverizing vocal exchange that expands on the opening question of why poor people are always asked to fight by also querying why presidents are always excused. Without pausing for breath, a repetition of the second verse and another chorus leads the song into a final sequence in which "B.Y.O.B." hammers home its central theme about the uneven recruitment process with a new level of intensity. By the time the song comes to an end, it has not just made a point; it has violently bludgeoned it into the listener's head. Anything more mannerly or sedate would simply not have been in keeping with System of a Down's style.

"B.Y.O.B." was released in May 2005 and quickly became System of a Down's biggest hit, reaching the Top 30 in both the United States and the United Kingdom and eventually earning the band a coveted Grammy Award for Best Hard Rock Performance in 2006. Meanwhile, System of a Down's ambitious decision to release the albums *Mezmerize* (on which "B.Y.O.B." was included) and *Hypnotize* within months of each other in 2005 also proved to be successful with both earning positive reactions in the world of metal and scoring the quartet two No. 1s on the U.S. album chart. But perhaps more than anything, it proved the System of a Down bandmates' ongoing willingness to voice protest in their work when so many other artists had let this fury fall by the wayside. Before the events of 9/11, they had been a rarity among high-profile bands for tackling such

AXIS OF JUSTICE

In an effort to continue his activism outside of recorded music, System of a Down singer Serj Tankian formed the nonprofit Axis of Justice organization in 2002 with guitarist Tom Morello—formerly of the similarly minded political rockers Rage Against the Machine, but then playing with a new group called Audioslave. The idea first came about when the pair witnessed audience members at the touring festival Ozzfest using racist symbols and imagery during 2002. In response, the pair colluded to have antiracist literature passed out at subsequent shows, but quickly decided to expand the scope of the subject matter to develop a network of activism resources and charity groups that could all be connected through the Axis of Justice. One of the first issues the organization took measures to address was the passing of a law in Santa Monica, California, restricting food from being given out to homeless people. In a high-profile protest, both Tankian and Morello knowingly flouted the legislation in 2003 and literally handed out food as a way of drawing attention to what they felt was an absurd ban on feeding the hungry. The organization is now affiliated with hundreds of grassroots and global organizations that promote human rights, environmentalism, political awareness, and social justice. Its own Web site is now the group's main tool, but Axis of Justice booths are still seen at concerts by artists allied to the cause. Meanwhile both Tankian and Morello continue to contribute to a regular broadcast on Los Angeles radio station KPFK during which a selection of so-called "rebel music" is played between guest interviews and discussions on current issues.

political issues as the Armenian genocide. In the immediate aftermath of the attacks on New York and Washington, D.C., they again made a point of speaking out against U.S. policy in a way for which few initially gave them credit. At the peak of antiwar feeling in 2003, the quartet suddenly boasted millions of people around the world who shared a desire to show their distrust of the government. But in the time since then, a noticeable feeling of apathy had begun to creep back into mainstream music, leaving System of a Down as one of the reduced number of bands keeping the spirit of dissent alive. As folksinger Devendra Banhart glumly observed in 2006, the failure of the U.S. government to take notice of huge worldwide opposition coupled with the subsequent reelection of President Bush in 2004 had left the antiwar faction with the "feeling of being reduced to a tick—a tick that's being flicked off by what we feel is this gargantuan beast that we stand no chance against."[10] Although voicing a similarly dispirited mood in some interviews, the members of System of a Down emphatically proved that they were refusing to completely give up expressing their political convictions through music as evidenced by the sonic power of "B.Y.O.B." and indeed a significant number of other songs on both *Hypnotize* and *Mezmerize* .

Despite the group members announcing that they would go on a period of hiatus in 2006, System of a Down's political energy lives on mainly through Tankian's efforts as part of the Axis of Justice organization (see the sidebar), as well as his own solo work. The singer's debut solo album *Elect the Dead* emerged in 2007 and featured many tracks that lamented flaws in Western democracy, as well as railing against the continued American occupancy of Iraq. Especially indicative of this was the lead single "Empty Walls," which came complete with a darkly satirical video featuring elementary school children using toys to act out major events in the War on Terror, including the 9/11 attacks, the toppling of Saddam Hussein, and even the horrific abuse of Iraqi prisoners carried out by U.S. soldiers during the occupation. Furthermore, the quest to have the Armenian genocide of 1915 officially recognized is still ongoing, but much to Tankian's dismay, his determination to continue addressing weighty issues is not necessarily shared in the way it once was by his contemporaries or those in the wider music media. "You tell industry people about the end of the world, and they're like, 'Great!' "[11]

Notes

1. Quoted in Alex Pappademas, "Power to the People (With Funny Haircuts)," *Spin,* November 2004.

2. Quoted in Ian Winwood, "Nobody's Fools," *Kerrang!,* July 10, 2004.

3. Quoted in Dan Martin, "Bush! The Fightback Starts Here," *NME,* November 20, 2004.

4. Quoted in Tom Lanham, "A Night at the Opera," *Alternative Press,* October 2004.

5. www.punkvoter.com/about/about.php

6. Quoted in Victoria Durham, "Know Your Rights," *Rock Sound,* March 2005.

7. Ibid.

8. Quoted in Ben Myers, *System of a Down: Right Here in Hollywood* (Shropshire, England: Independent Music Press, 2006), 13.

9. Quoted in "BYOB: System Of a Down," *Kerrang!,* December 17, 2005.

10. Quoted in Andrew Purcell, "Don't Mention the War—Unless You're Over 50," *Guardian* (London), June 23, 2006.

11. Quoted in Austin Scaggs, "Serj Tankian's Down Side," *Rolling Stone,* November 1, 2007.

APPENDIX

Songs Listed Chronologically

"We Shall Overcome"

"The Preacher and the Slave"
Joe Hill (songwriter)
1911

"Strange Fruit"
Billie Holiday
1939

"If I Had a Hammer"
The Weavers
1949

"This Land Is Your Land"
Woody Guthrie
American Work Songs—Songs to Grow On, Vol. 3
1951

"Masters of War"
Bob Dylan
The Freewheelin' Bob Dylan
1963

"Mississippi Goddam"
Nina Simone
Nina Simone in Concert
1964

"A Change Is Gonna Come"
Sam Cooke
Ain't That Good News
1964

"I Ain't Marching Anymore"
Phil Ochs
I Ain't Marching Anymore
1965

"Eve of Destruction"
Barry McGuire
Eve of Destruction
1965

"For What It's Worth"
Buffalo Springfield
Buffalo Springfield
1967

"Alice's Restaurant Massacree"
Arlo Guthrie
Alice's Restaurant
1967

"The Unknown Soldier"
The Doors
Waiting for the Sun
1968

"Revolution"/"Revolution 1"
The Beatles
 "Hey Jude" single B-side ("Revolution")/*The Beatles* (aka *The White Album*)
("Revolution 1")
1968

"Say It Loud—I'm Black and I'm Proud"
James Brown
Say It Loud—I'm Black and I'm Proud
1968

"Don't Call Me Nigger, Whitey"
Sly & the Family Stone
Stand!
1969

"1969"
The Stooges
The Stooges
1969

"Fortunate Son"
Creedence Clearwater Revival
Willy and the Poor Boys
1969

"War"
Edwin Starr
War & Peace
1970

"Ohio"
Crosby, Stills, Nash & Young
Single only, but later included on Neil Young's compilation *Decade* (1977)
1970

"Big Yellow Taxi"
Joni Mitchell
Ladies of the Canyon
1970

"Southern Man"
Neil Young
After the Gold Rush
1970

"War Pigs"
Black Sabbath
Paranoid
1970/1971

"What's Going On"
Marvin Gaye
What's Going On
1971

"The Revolution Will Not Be Televised"
Gil Scott-Heron
Small Talk at 125th and Lenox (first version)/*Pieces of a Man* (main version)
1970/1971

"I Am Woman"
Helen Reddy
I Am Woman
1972

"Get Up, Stand Up"
The Wailers
Burnin'
1973

"Sweet Home Alabama"
Lynyrd Skynyrd
Second Helping
1974

"God Save the Queen"
Sex Pistols
Never Mind the Bollocks, Here's the Sex Pistols
1977

"Complete Control"
The Clash
Nonalbum single in the United Kingdom/*The Clash* in the United States
1977 (United Kingdom)/1979 (United States)

"California Uber Alles"
Dead Kennedys
Original version released as 7-inch single (later included on the 1987 *Give Me Convenience or Give Me Death* compilation); re-recorded version included on *Fresh Fruit for Rotting Vegetables*
1979 (single version)/1980 (album version)

"Straight Edge"
Minor Threat
Minor Threat EP
1981

"The Message"
Grandmaster Flash & the Furious Five
The Message
1982

"Shipbuilding"
Robert Wyatt
1982

"Sunday Bloody Sunday"
U2
War
1983

"99 Luftballons"/"99 Red Balloons"
Nena
99 Luftballons
1984

"Nelson Mandela"
The Special AKA
In the Studio
1984

"Untitled Song for Latin America"
Minutemen
Double Nickels on the Dime
1984

"Born in the U.S.A."
Bruce Springsteen
Born in the U.S.A.
1984

"Meat Is Murder"
The Smiths
Meat Is Murder
1985

"Scum"
Nick Cave and the Bad Seeds
Issued free on flexi-discs, but later released on the CD format of *Your Funeral . . . My Trial*
1986

"(You Gotta) Fight for Your Right (to Party!)"
Beastie Boys
Licensed to Ill
1986

"Fuck tha Police"
N.W.A.
Straight Outta Compton
1988

"Fight the Power"
Public Enemy
Do the Right Thing soundtrack; later issued on the Public Enemy album *Fear of a Black Planet*
1989 (soundtrack version), 1990 (album version)

"Cop Killer"
Body Count
Body Count
1992

"Killing in the Name"
Rage Against the Machine
Rage Against the Machine
1993

"Their Law"
The Prodigy
Music for the Jilted Generation
1994

"Scream"
Michael Jackson and Janet Jackson
HIStory—Past, Present and Future, Book I
1995

"Common People"
Pulp
Different Class
1995

"Free Satpal Ram"
Asian Dub Foundation
Rafi's Revenge
1998

"American Idiot"
Green Day
American Idiot
2004

"B.Y.O.B."
System of a Down
Mezmerize
2005

Songs Listed Alphabetically

"Alice's Restaurant Massacree"
Arlo Guthrie
Alice's Restaurant
1967

"American Idiot"
Green Day
American Idiot
2004

"Big Yellow Taxi"
Joni Mitchell
Ladies of the Canyon
1970

"Born in the U.S.A."
Bruce Springsteen
Born in the U.S.A.
1984

"B.Y.O.B."
System of a Down
Mezmerize
2005

"California Uber Alles"
Dead Kennedys
Original version released as 7-inch single (later included on the 1987 *Give Me Convenience or Give Me Death* compilation); re-recorded version included on *Fresh Fruit for Rotting Vegetables*
1979 (single version)/1980 (album version)

"A Change Is Gonna Come"
Sam Cooke
Ain't That Good News
1964

"Common People"
Pulp
Different Class
1995

"Complete Control"
The Clash
Nonalbum single in the United Kingdom/*The Clash* in the United States
1977 (United Kingdom)/1979 (United States)

"Cop Killer"
Body Count
Body Count
1992

"Don't Call Me Nigger, Whitey"
Sly & the Family Stone
Stand!
1969

"Eve of Destruction"
Barry McGuire
Eve of Destruction
1965

"Fight the Power"
Public Enemy
Do the Right Thing soundtrack; later issued on the Public Enemy album *Fear of a Black Planet*
1989 (soundtrack version), 1990 (album version)

"Fortunate Son"
Creedence Clearwater Revival
Willy and the Poor Boys
1969

"For What It's Worth"
Buffalo Springfield
Buffalo Springfield
1967

"Free Satpal Ram"
Asian Dub Foundation
Rafi's Revenge
1998

"Fuck tha Police"
N.W.A.
Straight Outta Compton
1988

"Get Up, Stand Up"
The Wailers
Burnin'
1973

"God Save the Queen"
Sex Pistols
Never Mind the Bollocks, Here's the Sex Pistols
1977

"I Ain't Marching Anymore"
Phil Ochs
I Ain't Marching Anymore
1965

"I Am Woman"
Helen Reddy
I Am Woman
1972

"If I Had a Hammer"
The Weavers
1949

"Killing in the Name"
Rage Against the Machine
Rage Against the Machine
1993

"Masters of War"
Bob Dylan
The Freewheelin' Bob Dylan
1963

"Meat Is Murder"
The Smiths
Meat Is Murder
1985

"The Message"
Grandmaster Flash & the Furious Five
The Message
1982

"Mississippi Goddam"
Nina Simone
Nina Simone in Concert
1964

"Nelson Mandela"
The Special AKA
In the Studio
1984

"1969"
The Stooges
The Stooges
1969

"99 Luftballons"/"99 Red Balloons"
Nena
99 Luftballons
1984

"Ohio"
Crosby, Stills, Nash & Young
Single only, but later included on Neil Young's compilation *Decade* (1977)
1970

"The Preacher and the Slave"
Joe Hill (songwriter)
1911

"Revolution"/"Revolution 1"
The Beatles
"Hey Jude" single B-side ("Revolution")/*The Beatles* (aka *The White Album*) ("Revolution 1")
1968

"The Revolution Will Not Be Televised"
Gil Scott-Heron
Small Talk at 125th and Lenox (first version)/*Pieces of a Man* (main version)
1970/1971

"Say It Loud—I'm Black and I'm Proud"
James Brown
Say It Loud—I'm Black and I'm Proud
1968

"Scream"
Michael Jackson and Janet Jackson
HIStory—Past, Present and Future, Book I
1995

"Scum"
Nick Cave and the Bad Seeds
Issued free on flexi-discs, but later released on the CD format of *Your Funeral . . . My Trial*
1986

"Shipbuilding"
Robert Wyatt
1982

"Southern Man"
Neil Young
After the Gold Rush
1970

"Straight Edge"
Minor Threat
Minor Threat EP
1981

"Strange Fruit"
Billie Holiday
1939

"Sunday Bloody Sunday"
U2
War
1983

"Sweet Home Alabama"
Lynyrd Skynyrd
Second Helping
1974

"Their Law"
The Prodigy
Music for the Jilted Generation
1994

"This Land Is Your Land"
Woody Guthrie

American Work Songs—Songs to Grow On, Vol. 3
1951

"The Unknown Soldier"
The Doors
Waiting for the Sun
1968

"Untitled Song for Latin America"
Minutemen
Double Nickels on the Dime
1984

"War"
Edwin Starr
War & Peace
1970

"War Pigs"
Black Sabbath
Paranoid
1970/1971

"We Shall Overcome"

"What's Going On"
Marvin Gaye
What's Going On
1971

"(You Gotta) Fight for Your Right (to Party!)"
Beastie Boys
Licensed to Ill
1986

BIBLIOGRAPHY

Print

Alterman, Eric. *The Promise of Bruce Springsteen*. New York: Back Bay, 2001.

Azerrad, Michael. *Our Band Could Be Your Life*. New York: Back Bay, 2002.

Badger, Anthony, J. *The New Deal—The Depression Years, 1933–1940*. London: Macmillan, 1989.

Batey, Angus. *Rhyming and Stealing: A History of the Beastie Boys*. London: Independent Music Press, 1998.

Bonior, David E., Steven M. Champlin, and Timothy S. Kolly. *The Vietnam Veteran: A History of Neglect*. New York: Praeger, 1984.

Carson, Clayborne, ed. *The Autobiography of Martin Luther King Jr*. New York: Warner Books, 1998.

Chang, Jeff. *Can't Stop, Won't Stop: A History of the Hip-Hop Generation*. New York: St Martin's Press, 2005.

Collin, Matthew. *Altered State: The Story of Ecstasy Culture and Acid House*. With contributions from John Godfrey. London: Serpent's Tail, 1998.

Crisafulli, Chuck. *The Doors: When the Music's Over*. New York: Thunder's Mouth Press, 2000.

Dunaway, David. *How Can I Keep From Singing: Pete Seeger*. Cambridge, MA: Da Capo Press, 1990.

Fong-Torres, Ben. *The Doors by the Doors*. New York: Hyperion, 2006.

Friedan, Betty. *It Changed My Life*. New York: Dell, 1976.

Goddard, Simon. *The Smiths: Songs That Saved Your Life*. Surrey, England: Reynolds and Hearn, 2002.

Gulla, Bob. *The Greenwood Encyclopedia of Rock History: The Grunge and Post-Grunge Years, 1991–2005*. Westport, CT: Greenwood, 2006.

Guralnick, Peter. *Dream Boogie: The Triumph of Sam Cooke*. New York: Back Bay, 2005.

Guterman, Jimmy, and Owen O'Donnell. *The Worst Rock 'n' Roll Records of All Time*. New York, Citadel, 1991.

Harris, John. *The Last Party*. London: 4th Estate, 2003.

Janosik, Maryann. *The Greenwood Encyclopedia of Rock History: The Video Generation, 1981–1990*. Westport, CT: Greenwood, 2006.

Klein, Joe. *Woody Guthrie: A Life*. London: Faber and Faber, 1981.

Lorenz, J. D. *Jerry Brown: The Man on the White Horse*. Boston: Houghton Mifflin, 1978.

MacDonald, Ian. *Revolution in the Head*. London: Pimlico, 2005.

Marcus, Greil. *Invisible Republic*, London, Picador, 1998.

———. *Mystery Train*. London: Faber and Faber, 2000.

Margolick, David. *Strange Fruit*. New York: Ecco Press/Harper Collins, 2001.

Markowitz, Rhonda. *The Greenwood Encyclopedia of Rock History: Folk, Pop, Mods, and Rockers, 1960–1966*. Westport, CT: Greenwood, 2006.

McDonough, Jimmy. *Shakey*. London: Vintage, 2003.

Myers, Ben. *American Heretics*. Hove, England: Codex, 2002.

———. *Green Day: American Idiots and the New Punk Explosion*. Independent Music Press, Shropshire, England: Independent Music Press, 2005.

———. *System of a Down: Right Here in Hollywood*. Shropshire, England: Independent Music Publishing, 2006.

Reddy, Helen. *The Woman I Am*. New York: Jeremy P. Tarcher/Penguin, 2006.

Rogan, Johnny, *The Complete Guide to the Music of the Smiths & Morrissey/Marr*. London: Omnibus, 1995.

Savage, John. *England's Dreaming*. New York: St Martin's Press, 1993.

Scrivani-Tidd, Lisa. *The Greenwood Encyclopedia of Rock History: The Early Years, 1951–1959*. Westport, CT: Greenwood, 2006.

Smith, Chris. *The Greenwood Encyclopedia of Rock History: The Rise of Album Rock, 1967–1973*. Westport, CT: Greenwood, 2006.

———. *The Greenwood Encyclopedia of Rock History: From Arenas to the Underground, 1974–1980*. Westport, CT: Greenwood, 2006.

———. *100 Albums That Changed Popular Music*. Westport, CT: Greenwood, 2007.

Smith, Gibbs M. *Joe Hill*. Salt Lake City, UT: Peregrine, 1984.

Springsteen, Bruce. *Songs*. New York: Avon, 1998.

Steinberg, Cobbett. *T.V. Facts*. New York: Facts on File, 1985.

Strong, M. C. *The Great Rock Discography* (6th ed.). Edinburgh, United Kingdom: Canongate, 2002.

———. *The Great Indie Discography* (2nd ed.). Edinburgh, United Kingdom: Canongate, 2003.

Werner, Craig. *Up Around the Bend: The Oral History of Creedence Clearwater Revival*. New York: Spike, 1998.

———. *A Change Is Gonna Come: Music, Race & the Soul of America*. Ann Arbor: University of Michigan Press, 2006.

White, Timothy. *Catch a Fire*. New York: Henry Holt and Company, 1991.

Wilkinson, Paul. *Rat Salad*. New York: St Martin's Press, 2007.

Williams, Paul. *Bob Dylan, Performing Artist. 1960–1973, The Early Years*. London: Omnibus, 1994.

Wolff, Daniel. *You Send Me: The Life & Times of Sam Cooke*. With S. R. Crain, Clifton White, and G. David Tenenbaum. New York: Quill, 1995.

Electronic

Allmusic, www.allmusic.com
Christgau, Robert, www.robertchristgau.com
National Public Radio, www.npr.com
Rock's Back Pages, www.rocksbackpages.com
Rolling Stone, www.rollingstone.com

INDEX

About the Author

HARDEEP PHULL is a music journalist who writes for such publications as *NME, Rock Sound, Independent* (London), *Metro, Record Collector,* and *Dazed & Confused.*